THE SEPOY AND

STUDIES IN MILITARY AND STRATEGIC HISTORY
General Editor: Michael Dockrill, Reader in War Studies,
King's College, London

Published titles include:

Nigel John Ashton
EISENHOWER, MACMILLAN AND THE PROBLEM OF NASSER:
Anglo-American Relations and Arab Nationalism, 1955–59

Peter Bell
CHAMBERLAIN, GERMANY AND JAPAN, 1933–34

G. H. Bennett
BRITISH FOREIGN POLICY DURING THE CURZON PERIOD,
1919–24

David Clayton
IMPERIALISM REVISITED: Political and Economic Relations
between Britain and China, 1950–54

John P. S. Gearson
HAROLD MACMILLAN AND THE BERLIN WALL CRISIS,
1958–62

Kendrick Oliver
KENNEDY, MACMILLAN AND THE NUCLEAR TEST-BAN
DEBATE, 1961–63

Simon Trew
BRITAIN, MIHAILOVIC AND THE CHETNIKS, 1941–42

Steven Weiss
ALLIES IN CONFLICT: Anglo-American Strategic Negotiations,
1938–44

Studies in Military and Strategic History
Series Standing Order ISBN 0–333–71046–0
(*outside North America only*)

You can receive future titles in this series as they are published by placing a standing order.
Please contact your bookseller or, in case of difficulty, write to us at the address below with
your name and address, the title of the series and the ISBN quoted above.

Customer Services Department, Macmillan Distribution Ltd
Houndmills, Basingstoke, Hampshire RG21 6XS, England

The Sepoy and the Raj

The Indian Army, 1860–1940

David Omissi

Department of History and
Centre for Indian Studies
University of Hull

in association with
KING'S COLLEGE, LONDON

Published by
MACMILLAN PRESS LTD
Houndmills, Basingstoke, Hampshire RG21 6XS
and London
Companies and representatives
throughout the world

First edition 1994
Reprinted 1998

ISBN 0–333–55049–8 hardcover
ISBN 0–333–72976–5 paperback

A catalogue record for this book is available
from the British Library.

This book is printed on paper suitable for recycling and
made from fully managed and sustained forest sources.

10 9 8 7 6 5 4 3 2 1
07 06 05 04 03 02 01 00 99 98

Printed and bound in Great Britain by
Antony Rowe Ltd, Chippenham, Wiltshire

In Memory
of
My Parents

Truly, though our element is time,
We are not suited to the long perspectives
Open at each instant of our lives.
They link us to our losses: worse,
They show us what we have as it once was,
Blindingly undiminished, just as though
By acting differently, we could have kept it so.

Philip Larkin

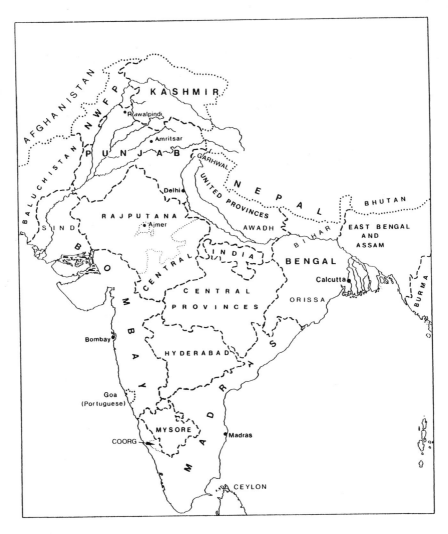

States and Provinces of the Indian Empire, 1909

Contents

List of Tables

List of Abbreviations

AD   Army Department
ADC   Aide-de-Camp
AG(I)   Adjutant-General (India)
ANZAC Australian and New Zealand Army Corps
BEF   British Expeditionary Force
CAB   Cabinet Office and Records, Public Record Office
CIGS   Chief of the Imperial General Staff
CGSI   Chief of the General Staff, India
CID   Committee of Imperial Defence
CIH   Central India Horse
C-in-C Commander-in-Chief
Cmd.   Parliamentary Command Paper
CNS   Chief of the Naval Staff (First Sea Lord)
CO   Commanding Officer
DAAG   Deputy Assistant Adjutant-General
DAG   Deputy Adjutant-General
DCIGS Deputy Chief of the Imperial General Staff
DCNS   Deputy Chief of the Naval Staff
DMOI   Director of Military Operations and Intelligence
FO   Foreign Office and Records, Public Record Office
FPD   Foreign and Political Department, Government of India
GI   Government of India
GOC   General Officer Commanding
GS   General Staff
HD   Home Department, Government of India
ICO   Indian Commissioned Officer
ICS   Indian Civil Service
IDC   Imperial Defence College
IMA   Indian Military Academy
IMR   Indian Military Requirements Committee and Papers
IO   India Office and Records
KCO   King's Commissioned Officer
KGO   King George's Own
L/MIL Military Department and Records, India Office
L/P&J Political and Judicial Department and Records, India Office

MD	Military Department
NCO	Non-Commissioned Officer
NWFP	North West Frontier Province
OC	Officer Commanding
OTC	Officer Training Corps
PRO	Public Record Office
QMG	Quarter-Master General
RA	Royal Artillery
RAF	Royal Air Force
SSI	Secretary of State for India
UP	United Provinces (now Uttar Pradesh)
USS	Under-Secretary of State
UTC	University Training Corps
VCIGS	Vice-Chief of the Imperial General Staff
VCO	Viceroy's Commissioned Officer
WO	War Office and Records, Public Record Office

Glossary of Indian and Military Terms

akali Originally a staunch follower of the Sikh Guru Gobind Singh; in the twentieth century, initially a volunteer to take over Sikh temples, later a member of the Shiromi Akali Dal.

Aryan One belonging, to, or descended from, the ancient people who spoke the parent Aryan language (sometimes called Indo-European) from which Sanskrit, Greek, Latin, Teutonic, Persian, Celtic and Slavonic (and their modern representatives) are derived; the language spoken by them, and its derivatives; one of those who invaded and conquered India around 1500 BC. From Sanskrit *arya*, 'of noble birth'.

Arya Samaj Society of the Aryan People'. A movement for Hindu reform, established in 1875 by Dayandanda Saraswati.

Assami A payment made, or debt incurred, by a *silladar* trooper upon receiving his uniform, weapons and horse from his regiment.

babu A Hindu title of respect, equivalent to Mr or Esq; an Indian clerk or official who writes in English; often used slightingly by British of Hindus, especially Bengalis, with an superficial education in English.

bania A Hindu moneylender or merchant, especially of grain.

batta A field allowance for soldiers.

battalion A body of infantry, normally several hundred strong, composed of companies and forming part of a regiment.

bhadralok 'Respectable people'. The higher literate castes of Bengal.

bhalwa A pigmented substance used by dhobis to mark and identify their washing.

Brahmin A member of the first *varna*, traditionally priests and scholars. From Sanskrit *brahman*, 'prayer' or 'praise'.

caste Ascribed ritual status in the Indian, especially Hindu, social hierarchy. From Portuguese *casta*, 'race', and Latin *castus*, 'pure' or 'chaste'.

company A body of infantry, usually of between one or two hundred men, normally led by a captain, lieutenant or subedar, and forming part of a battalion.

Coorg A mountainous province of Southern India; a high-caste inhabitant of that province.

dharma Personal duty or conduct appropriate to one's status; moral obligation; law. From Sanskrit 'decree' or 'custom'.

dhobi An Indian washerman.

doab A tongue of alluvium between two converging rivers. From Persian *do*, 'two', and *ab*, 'water'.

Dogra An Anglo-Indian military term used to denote a high-caste inhabitant of Kangra (a Himalayan province).

Dravidian Pertaining to the non-Aryan people of India, or to their languages.

durbar The court, public audience or levée of a ruler.

Dusserah An annual Hindu festival, lasting nine nights or ten days in the month of Jaistha (September–October).

fatwa A decree in accordance with Muslim law.

furlough A permit or licence given to a soldier to be absent from duty for a stated time. Cf. German *Urlaub*.

ghadr Revolt or revolution; whence Ghadrite.

got An exogamous subcaste or clan, especially of the Punjab.

Gujar A cultivator of Northern India.

gurdwara 'The door of the Guru'. A Sikh temple, generally also the centre of Sikh social activity.

Guru Preceptor; religious teacher; an epithet applied to the founder of Sikhism, to each of his nine successors, and to the Sikh scriptures.

Granth Sahib The collected writings of the Sikh gurus.

hartal A stoppage of work as a sign of mourning or protest; from Hindi *hat*, 'shop' or 'market', and *tala*, 'bolt for the door'.

havildar An Indian NCO, equivalent in rank to a sergeant.

Hindi The major Aryan vernacular of Northern India, spoken (with many dialects) from the frontiers of Bengal to those of the Punjab and Sind.

Hindustan 'The country of the Hindus'; originally the region of the river Indus; in the colonial period, normally used to denote Upper India (the plain of the Ganges, except Bihar and Bengal); sometimes all of India.

Id The Muslim festival which marks the end of Ramazan.

izzat Honour, prestige, reputation or standing.

jagir An assignment of government revenue from a district, originally in return for public (especially military) service.

jagirdar The holder of a *jagir*.

Jat A member of the principal cultivating caste of the Punjab and Rajputana, of proverbial stupidity.

jati 'Genesis', 'origin' or 'birth'. Used to denote any living group or species, especially local caste or lineage.

Jemadar An Indian company officer, immediately junior to a subedar, and corresponding to a lieutenant.

jihad A religious war of Muslims against unbelievers in Islam.

kacchhera Underclothes worn by Sikhs as a mark of their religion.

kanga A bracelet worn by Sikhs as a mark of their religion.

khaki Dust-coloured; dull brownish yellow; a fabric of this colour used in British and Indian Army field uniforms. From Urdu and Persian *khaki*, 'dusty'.

kirpan A sword or dagger worn by Sikhs as a mark of their religion.

Khalifa 'Deputy of god'. The spiritual head of Islam; until the early twentieth century, the Sultan of Turkey.

Khalsa A political and military brotherhood within Sikhism, founded in the seventeenth century by Guru Gobind Singh; a member thereof.

Kshatriya A member of the second, or warrior, *varna*.

lathi A stout stick or stave, often ringed or ferruled.

lakh One hundred thousand.

Lingayat A member of the South Indian sect who worship the *lingam*, or phallus, as a symbol of the god Shiva.

mahant A religious superior or guardian of a shrine or temple.

Mappila A Muslim fisherman or cultivator of Malabar, of low status and usually landless; also Moplah.

naik An Indian NCO, corresponding in rank to a corporal.

Pathan The name of a Pashto-speaking Muslim people inhabiting south-east Afghanistan and the North West Frontier.

pir A Muslim spiritual leader.

purdah Seclusion or isolation, especially of Muslim women. From Urdu and Persian *pardah*, 'veil' or 'curtain'.

Raj Kingdom or principality; rule; often used loosely to denote British rule of India.

Raja An Indian prince or ruler; a title of nobility.

Rajputana 'The land of the Rajputs'. A North Indian province, now Rajasthan.

Rajput A Kshatriya of the most prominent military and landholding caste-cluster of Northern India, distinguished by its martial spirit and aversion to handling the plough.

Ramazan The ninth month of the Muslim year, observed as a thirty-day fast during the hours of daylight; also *Ramadan*.

regiment A body of soldiers, composed of one or more infantry battalions or several cavalry squadrons, and usually led by a colonel.

risaldar An Indian cavalry officer.

satyagraha 'Soul-force' or 'truth-force'. Non-violent resistance to oppression as advocated by M. K. Gandhi.

sehajdari A Sikh who is not baptized as a Khalsa, and who does not observe the Khalsa code of discipline.

sepoy An Indian soldier employed under European, especially British, discipline; an Indian infantry private. From Persian and Urdu *sipahi*, 'soldier' or 'horseman'.

shikar Hunting.

shudra A member of the fourth *varna*, of cultivators or labourers.

Sikh A member of the religious sect founded in the Punjab as a branch of Hinduism in the fifteenth century.

silladar An irregular cavalryman who provides, or pays for, his own weapons, horse and accoutrements. From Urdu, *silahdar*, 'armour-bearer' or 'squire'.

sirdar A military chief or leader; the Commander-in-Chief of the Army in India; from Persian *sar*, 'head' and *dar*, 'possessor'.

sirkar The state or government; also sircar.

sowar An Indian cavalry trooper. From Urdu sawar, 'horseman'.

squadron A body of cavalry, usually of between one and two hundred men, composed of several troops and forming part of a regiment.

subedar The senior Indian officer of an infantry company.

subedar-major The senior Indian officer of an infantry battalion.

subaltern A British junior military officer.

Swadeshi An Indian nationalist movement, originating in Bengal, which advocated the support of indigenous industries using home-produced materials (especially cotton). From Sanskrit *sva*, 'one's own' and *desa*, 'country'.

talwar An Indian sword or sabre.

Tamil The leading Dravidian language of South India; a speaker of that language.

Urdu The royal camp'. The language of the Muslim conquerors of Hindustan, derived from Hindi, but written in the Arabic script, and with a large admixture of Persian and Arabic loanwords. From *zaban-i-urdu*, 'the language of the camp'. Also called Hindustani.

varna One of the four castes – Brahmins, Kshatriyas, Vaishyas and Shudras – into which all Indian society is ideally divided. From Sanskrit 'colour' or 'class'.

Acknowledgements

When I started this book, I feared it was too ambitious a project for a young historian with no background in South Asian studies; having completed it, I can see that my fears were justified. Without the help of many people, it would not have come even to this imperfect fruition. Its defects are all my own.

My first acknowledgement goes to Michael Dockrill, the general editor of the series in which this book appears – it is thanks to his goodwill and support that it has eventually seen the light of day. Peter Marshall and John MacKenzie offered timely advice at the outset of my project, and made constructive comments as it ran its course. David Arnold suggested many fruitful questions, encouraged me when I feared I would never find the answers, and offered perceptive criticism when I thought I had. I learned a great deal from exchanging ideas with Jan-Georg Deutsch, Douglas Peers and Heike Schmidt, and I was happy to borrow many of their insights. I might have missed some useful sources had not Sandra Gregory, Lawrence James, David Killingray, Mahesh Rangarajan, Charlie Smith and Megan Vaughan drawn my attention to them.

Apurba Kundu and Katherine Turner read the entire typescript and pointed out countless ways in which it could be improved. Marcus Ackroyd, Judith Brown, Bob Currie, David Edgerton, Barbara English, Joshua Getzler, Ramchandra Guha, Tony Henderson, Theo Hoppen, Tony Kirk-Green, Dirk Kolff, Dominic Omissi, Nicholas Owen, Douglas Reid, Pritam Singh, Andrew Thompson and Brian Wilkinson each read one or more chapters and between them suggested many changes for the better.

My undergraduate students at Oxford and Hull made many robust comments on my work. I am particularly grateful to Reena Dhanda and Richard Hesp for reading the earlier chapters, and to Fiona Thomson for providing what she described – unforgettably – as 'the view from the pond'.

I learned much when I presented my work for discussion at seminars, workshops and conferences. This forced me to clarify my ideas, to defend them in hot debate, and to modify them upon cooler reflection. For this I am grateful to the Commonwealth and South Asian History Seminars at the University of Oxford; the

Imperial and Military History Seminars at the Institute of Historical Research, University of London; the History and South Asian Studies Seminars at the University of Hull; the `Guardians of Empire' Conference and the South Asian History Seminar at the School of Oriental and African Studies, University of London; the War Discussion Group at the Royal Military Academy, Sandhurst; the British Association of South Asian Scholars; and the Punjab Research Group. For the chance to present my work I am thankful to Brian Bond, John Darwin, Clive Dewey, David French, Freda Harcourt, Tony Heathcote, Sean McKnight, Subrata Mitra, Andrew Porter, Brian Holden Reid, Ian Talbot and B. R. Tomlinson.

My trip to India in 1991 would have been much less useful and enjoyable had it not been for the diverting company of Karen Thornley and the hospitality of the Kumars, the Mansinghs, the Mehras and the Sahnis.

The staff at the India Office, the Public Record Office, the Indian Institute Library, the Liddell Hart Centre for Military Archives, and the National Army Museum were always friendly and helpful.

My colleagues at the University of Hull sheltered me from much undergraduate teaching while I worked on the closing chapters. Without their forbearance, the typescript would have been delivered even further behind schedule than it finally was. Belinda Holdsworth and John Smith at Macmillan Press waited patiently for me to abandon further work on it.

My two deepest debts remain to be acknowledged. The second of these is to the Warden, Fellows, Students and Staff of Nuffield College, Oxford. It was my honour and pleasure to hold a Prize Research Fellowship at Nuffield from 1989 until 1992. It was during those years that this project was conceived, researched and mainly written.

My most profound debt is to my parents. Sadly, neither of them lived to see this book completed. It is dedicated to their memory.

Preface

This book is a social and political history of the Indian army during the apogee of colonial rule.

The Indian Army is of especial interest to historians of empire because of its central yet deeply ambiguous place within the colonial order. With the army absorbing up to half of all central government revenue, military policy expressed, with especial clarity, the priorities and concerns of the colonial state. Armed force was always a mainstay of imperial rule. British domination in India was largely the product of military conquest, a process to which armies were clearly central. Colonial rule retained much of its military and coercive character even after annexation had given way to settled control; armed force remained the last – and often the first – resort of the colonial power when faced with domestic unrest.

But the Indian Army was itself an *example* as well as an *instrument* of colonial control. Although the army was created to serve colonial ends, and led by a white elite, the men in its ranks were always drawn from local Indian communities. The relationship between British officers and Indian sepoys was a microcosm of the wider colonial order. Drilled, uniformed and quartered in exclusively military spaces, Indian soldiers were the indigenous group perhaps most closely subjected to colonial discipline, regulation and surveillance. Lastly, and most paradoxically of all, the Indian Army was a major potential threat to the Raj which it defended. In 1857, the British were almost driven from the subcontinent by the rebellion of their Indian troops, and the spectre of another mutiny haunted colonial rulers until the end of the Raj.

Because Indian soldiers were essential yet potentially dangerous, their activities were more closely scrutinized and more carefully recorded than those of most other elements of the indigenous population. The written evidence about the Indian Army is accordingly very rich. There are many thousand relevant files in the India Office Library alone (besides other British and Indian archives). Between them, they contain millions of documents, the very quantity of material bearing witness to the central place of the army in colonial concerns. A lack of evidence produced by subordinate groups often hampers enquiry into indigenous perceptions and mentalities during the colonial period. In the case of the sepoys, however, we are more fortunate; we possess invaluable sources generated by the Indian troops themselves. During the Great War, the British high command, worried by depression in the ranks, monitored and extensively recorded the letters to and from Indian soldiers serving in France. The resulting materials have copiously survived, allowing us to glimpse the life of the sepoys more vividly than that of almost any other subordinate Indian group.

The army, however, has yet to make more than a cameo appearance in the textbook literature on colonial India. Judith Brown's elegant study mainly addresses the conflicts and bargains between the colonial elite and the educated nationalists who were to assume the mantle of the Raj in 1947; soldiers and armed force rarely interrupt this delicate story.[1] Sumit Sarkar's more detailed treatment of Indian social and political history more often exposes the coercive face of colonial power; but he still devotes only a few pages directly to the army (although he has made a plea for a closer scrutiny of its workings).[2]

The virtual absence of the Indian army from the relevant textbooks partly reflects the shortcomings of the existing monographs. Our knowledge of the Indian Army in the later colonial period derives principally from three books now twenty years old. Philip Mason's stylish (if rather general) account has all the strengths and weaknesses of a work by a former colonial administrator; it is saturated with the liberal imperialism which he personifies.[3] S. P. Cohen's briefer volume operates largely within the paradigm of a conflict between colonial power and elite nationalism; he shows little interest in questions that do not fall within this rubric.[4] Tony Heathcote's study, perhaps the best of the three, is more concerned with military than with colonial or Indian issues.[5] None of these authors attempts much rigorous scrutiny of the perceptions, hopes and protests of the sepoys; in their accounts, the Indian other ranks are relegated to the margins or serve mainly as an exotic social setting to an essentially British story.[6]

One group of scholars who might have taken an interest in the sepoys have not done so. The *Subaltern Studies* project was begun with the avowed aim of recovering the past of the subordinate or `subaltern' groups in colonial India – above all, workers, tribals and peasants.[7] Yet its contributors (with the exception of David Arnold) have shown little interest in those peasants who sided *with* the Raj. The Subalterns' fascination with moments of resistance and protest has not encouraged them to study the peasant-soldier groups who voted with their feet in favour of the colonial power – as if peasants ceased to be subordinate, or conscious, or potentially dissident once they had enlisted. While often stressing the coercive nature of colonial rule, Subaltern scholars have not taken the next logical step of examining the social structure of the colonial state's military resources. In their accounts of peasant or tribal protest, the Army in India (sometimes casually misnamed `the British Army') plays only a walk-on, repressive part.

Some more nuanced writing on the nature of the colonial coercive power has appeared in the last decade, and many of the questions raised by this work pertain to the army. In particular, David Arnold's fine book on the Madras police has greatly enriched our understanding of the strengths and shortcomings of the colonial security apparatus.[8] (My debt to his work is more pervasive than the Notes to the present volume can show.) David Anderson and David Killingray have edited two useful collections of essays about colonial policing.[9] As these authors point out, the police were the most visible and intrusive manifestation of colonial power, and one which directly touched the life of the people. But the workings of colonial armed force cannot be understood simply by studying its most visible aspects. The army often remained in the background; but the background is an important part of the picture.

There remain many unanswered questions about the Indian Army. Was it gain or glory that inspired several million Indian peasants to volunteer for the colonial armed forces? Which indigenous groups did the British mainly recruit and how did they choose them? Why did the Indian army remain loyal to the Raj during periods of extensive civil unrest? How much dissent troubled the army, what were its causes, and how did the British deal with it? How far did the British Raj rely on military force to sustain its rule? Complete answers to these questions will require many futher volumes; but even the overview contained in this book may illuminate some of the core processes of colonial domination, subordination and resistance.

DAVID OMISSI

1

Recruiting Strategy

It is no use trying to persuade ourselves that the whole of the Native Army is capable of meeting an enemy from Central Asia or Europe; they are not, and nothing will ever make them. It is not a question of efficiency, but of courage and physique; in these two essential qualities the sepoys of Lower India are wanting.

Lord Roberts, June 1882[1]

The duty of a Kshatriya is to die on the field of battle. Who remembers a man who dies in his bed? But it is the duty of us Kshatriyas to kill the enemy, and thus a man becomes a hero.

Havildar Ramji Lal, 107 Pioneers, August 1915[2]

The British empire may have been acquired in a fit of absence of mind, but it was not acquired with an absence of force. Almost every phase of imperial expansion brought its own share of bloodshed. Colonial India was no exception to this pattern of violent dominance. Although the East India Company peacefully absorbed or annexed many indigenous states, it more often conquered them after hard fighting. Between 1757 and 1849, successive campaigns imposed company rule over most of the subcontinent.

The need for force did not miraculously disappear when conquest and annexation gave way to settled colonial control. Imperial armies remained in place to protect the new territories from jealous European or local rivals, and to help crush the sporadic rebellions against the colonial order. Even during long periods of peace in Europe, the British Army was almost always at war somewhere overseas.

The empire could never have depended upon its white soldiers alone, however. A long posting in a torrid and unhealthy colony was usually unpopular with troops who might have been more urgently needed nearer home. And – more importantly – British soldiers cost far more than those raised from the indigenous population. The empire therefore obtained much of its military manpower from local sources. It was easier and cheaper to dominate the world if Asians and Africans could be induced to shoulder much of the white man's military burden. By the mid-nineteenth century, with a quarter of humanity under British sway, colonial armies enjoyed a wide choice of potential recruits. But this embarrassment of human riches posed a further problem; the imperial power had to identify the indigenous communities that would provide the most efficient and reliable troops. The cost of a mistake could be high, for a mutiny in a locally-raised army was one of the greatest threats to the colonial order. Multi-ethnic empires in Europe faced similar problems, but the colonial context made it far more difficult to select the right soldiers. Orientalist assumptions clouded colonial intelligence, and magnified the vast cultural gulf between imperial rulers and their subjects.[3]

Recruiting problems were especially complex in colonial India, where the fissures and fluidities of caste added to the great diversity of language and religion among the local population. These multiple identities provided scope for policies of divide and rule, but also made it harder to select and co-opt military allies. The Indian Army was by far the largest indigenous military force raised under European leadership. This fact alone made it central to broader imperial strategy – and an ever-present danger to the Raj. The sheer scale of military activity in the Indian Empire highlighted the importance of choosing the most suitable military allies; and the ferocious mutiny of the Bengal Army in 1857–58 underlined the dangers of choosing the wrong ones.

This chapter examines how the rulers of British India confronted these problems. It sketches in broad outline the main features of British recruiting strategy from the Mutiny to the 1930s. After a brief survey of British policy before 1857, it will chart the various changes in recruiting patterns which later took place. In particular it will explain why, from the 1880s, the British began to draw more and more soldiers from the north of India and ever fewer from the south. At about the same time, the theory of the 'martial races' began to reflect and direct the selection of recruits. The chapter will analyse the content and assess the influence of this body of colonial discourse. The recruiting patterns of the Indian Army were not the result of imperial strategies alone, of course – they also reflected the interests of those indigenous groups who responded to the call of the recruiting officer. This chapter, however, will mainly focus upon imperial agendas. Later chapters will directly address the strategies and perceptions of those who enlisted.

MUTINY AND MANPOWER

Colonial powers in India had always sought indigenous military allies. The European trading companies had employed local factory guards from the outset. In the late seventeenth century, during the wars against the Mughal empire, whole bodies of Indian troops entered colonial service as irregular auxiliaries. The experience of battle soon revealed, however, that well-drilled European regular units could defeat many times their number of Indian irregulars. Because white manpower was scarce, the next logical step was to drill, train and arm Indian recruits in the European manner. The first Indian *regular* units, led by European officers, were formed by the French on the west coast.[4] Known as sepoys (from the Persian *sipahi*, 'soldier') these troops easily brushed aside the undrilled Indian levies in British service, briefly capturing Madras in the 1740s. After this setback, the British followed the French example and raised their own sepoy companies, grouping these into battalions in Bengal and Madras by the later 1750s.[5] The number of sepoys in British service rapidly increased, from roughly 9000 in 1765 to around 155 000 in 1808. By 1856, the East India Company employed more than 200 000 sepoys in what had become one of the world's largest European-style standing armies.[6]

Strictly speaking, however, this was not one army but three. East India Company rule in the subcontinent had three main territorial divisions, or presidencies, centred in Madras, Bombay and Bengal. Each presidency raised its own armed forces – the Army of Bengal, at about 120 000 in 1856, being much the largest. The three armies were distinct from each other not only in their size. From the late eighteenth century, the presidencies had adopted rather different recruiting strategies. The Madras Army, without access to the fertile military labour markets of the north, obtained most of its men from within its own presidency, drawing on a broad social base as it did so.[7] 'It has been an object to maintain a due proportion, so that no one caste should preponderate over another', observed one officer in 1858.[8] The Bombay Army was similar in this respect. It included around 13 000 (mainly high-caste) men from Hindustan, but no single community dominated its ranks.[9] In both armies, recruits from a variety of backgrounds served together in the same battalion, and British officers showed little deference to caste feeling.

Recruiting and Mutiny in the Army of Bengal

Recruiting policy came to differ in the Bengal Army. By the early nineteenth century, this force drew its soldiers from a very narrow social base. From the 1760s, the Bengal Army began to enlist those groups who had served in the Muslim armies since the fifteenth century – mainly Rajputs and Brahmins from Bihar and Awadh.[10] By 1857, about three quarters of the Bengal Native Infantry were high-caste men from Awadh (perhaps as many as 40 000 of them from the single region of Baiswara).[11] The British officers in Bengal were closer to the centres of power in Calcutta, and appear to have been more sensitive to status, than their compatriots in Bombay and Madras. High-caste men were often taller than average and looked more imposing on parade.[12] As the higher castes came to dominate the ranks, Bengal officers showed more deference to matters of caste, partly because they were anxious not to alienate the men. This attitude encouraged the sepoys to insist on strict observance of ritual prohibitions.[13] High-caste sepoys refused to take orders from men of lower status, who were therefore rarely promoted. Reluctance to break caste was accepted as a valid ground for refusing to serve overseas – only six regiments of Bengal infantry were enlisted for general service.[14] As the consolidation of British rule restricted military employment elsewhere in northern India, high-caste soldiers used their influence to create a closed shop in the Bengal Army.[15] Low-caste men were eventually excluded from its ranks, at first by custom alone then, from 1855, by regulation.[16]

According to some colonial observers, the dependence of the Bengal Army upon a very narrow range of recruits endangered British power. In the 1840s, Sir Henry Lawrence suggested that the Army of Bengal should enlist a more diverse selection of men. 'Our sepoys come too much from the same parts of the country', he warned. 'There is too much of clanship among them, and the evil should be remedied.'[17] Lawrence favoured recruiting various non-Indians, such as Malays, Chinese and Burmese, who would be unlikely to combine with disaffected locals (or with each other). He also believed that the lower castes, and communities without a military tradition, could provide soldiers as effective and disciplined as those who were already serving in the Bengal Army.

The British recruiting base in northern India broadened slightly after the annexation of the Punjab in 1849.[18] The Sikh rulers of the Punjab had created an impressive regular army trained, equipped and uniformed after the European fashion. By the mid-1840s it numbered about 53 000 drilled men, besides irregulars. Its ranks included Hindu and Muslim soldiers, as well as Sikhs. Although the Sikh state eventually fell before the onslaught of the East India Company in the wars of 1845–46 and 1849, its hard-fighting troops earned the admiration of the Bengal Army. After the British annexed the Punjab, the Sikh forces were disbanded, leaving almost one hundred thousand men without military employment. These displaced soldiers might have disrupted company rule if it had not assimilated them. A new Punjab Irregular Force, ten regiments strong, absorbed some.[19] Others joined the armed police. Each Bengal Army regiment that was stationed in the new province was allowed to enlist up to 200 Punjabis, half of whom might be Sikhs.[20] By the time of the Mutiny, just over 30 000 men from the Punjab were serving in the various British security forces. This policy of cooption helped nullify the military remnants of the Sikh state, but the high-caste sepoys of the Bengal Army resented the erosion of their near-monopoly of military employment under the British.[21]

In the early summer of 1857, the disgruntled Bengal regiments began to mutiny. The first outbreak occurred at Meerut on 10 May, after the introduction of a new rifle whose cartridges, greased with animal fats, were rumoured to pollute Muslim and Hindu alike.[22] Within two days the mutineers had captured Delhi. Throughout June and July, further corps joined the uprising which eventually involved nearly one hundred units, almost all from the Bengal Army.[23] The Bengal sepoys had plenty of grievances. A General Service Enlistment Act of 1856, introduced to make the army more flexible, had exposed them to the risk of losing caste by crossing the sea. In the same year, the company had annexed the state of Awadh. Henceforth, sepoys recruited there lost the *batta* they had previously enjoyed for service 'abroad'. The reform of the land revenue system in Awadh after its annexation had compounded the soldiers' economic problems.[24] The military mutiny almost immediately triggered a legitimist and agrarian revolt in the North-Western Provinces and Awadh – the main recruiting grounds of the Bengal Army.[25] After a year's hard fighting, and with great loss of life on both sides, the British crushed the rebellion. The failure of the revolt in Hyderabad freed the Madras Army, whose discipline was mostly undisturbed, to march against the rebels in the north. Only two regiments of the Bombay Army were involved in the rising, both of them drawing their recruits from the same castes and provinces that supported it.[26]

The Punjab was the main British base during this crisis of colonial authority. Although most Punjabis serving in down-country regiments joined their comrades in mutiny, most of the all-Punjabi units did not.[27] The British had ruled the province prudently after its annexation, and now reaped their reward.[28] An initially severe revenue assessment was moderated after 1852, while irrigation schemes mollified the agrarian communities who provided most of the recruits. The Indian soldiers also had their own agendas, to which the British might be peripheral. Many Punjabis resented the sepoys of the Bengal Army for extinguishing the Sikh state, and they hardly relished the prospect of restored Mughal power. They also looked forward to looting the cities of Hindustan. A saying of the tenth Guru, on which the times had bestowed sudden relevance, circulated amongst the Sikhs:

> Then shall the English come and, joined by the Khalsa, rule as well in the East as in the West. Wherever they take their armies they shall conquer, and bestow thrones on those who assist them. Then in every house shall be wealth, in every house happiness, in every house rejoicing, in every house religion, in every house learning, and in every house a woman.[29]

Immediately after the outbreak of the mutiny, Sir John Lawrence began raising new units in the Punjab.[30] There was no shortage of recruits. By June 1858, there were 80 000 soldiers of the Bengal Army under arms, and about 50 000 paramilitary police. Of this grand total, about 75 000 were Punjabis, including 23 000 Sikhs.[31] (See Table 1.1.)

British Policy in the Aftermath of Mutiny

During the Mutiny, the social composition of the military forces under British control in northern India thus profoundly changed. The bias of recruiting shifted away from the higher castes of Awadh and the North-Western Provinces and towards the Punjab and the lower castes of Hindustan.

This situation was reviewed from July 1858, when the British Government appointed a commission under Major-General Peel (the Secretary of State for War) to examine the organization of the Indian Army and to recommend changes to it. The commission

TABLE 1.1
Ethnic composition of the Bengal Army, 1 April 1858

	Regular[1]	Irregular[2]	Others[3]	Total
Christians	511	61		572
Muslims	4 214	5 684	554	10 452
Brahmins	6 549	1 882	95	8 526
Rajputs	6 635	3 460	267	10 362
Low-caste Hindus	4 361	4 002	465	8 818
Sikhs	135	4 337		4 472
Punjabis	192	17 687	495	18 374
Hindustanis		2 115	38	2 153
Cis-Sutlej		2 437	15	2 452
Trans-Sutlej		3 334	5	3 339
Hill Stns of Nepal		377		377
Huzara Tribes		23		23
Afghans		137		187
Goorkhas	590	300		890
Hill Men		3 679		3 679
Mhairs		566		566
Mhairats		915		915
Bhils		803		803
Predatory Tribes		223		223
Total	23 187	52 022	1934	77133
Others				2 920
GRAND TOTAL				80 053[4]

[1] Including light cavalry (1259) and regular infrantry (21 928).
[2] Including irregular infantry (41 828) and irregular cavalry (10 194).
[3] Including artilery (regular and irregular), sappers and miners.
[4] Other witnesses before the Peel Commission give slightly different totals of Bengal troops under arms in the summer of 1858. Appendix 54 gives 72 419 armed Indian troops, with 17 463 disarmed, on 15 April 1858. Viscount Canning (Appendix 55) has 80 000 (excluding troops disarmed) with a grand total of 130 000 including armed police. Of this latter figure, 75 000 were Punjabis and 23 000 Sikhs. Maj-Gen. Birch (Appendix 61) has two sets of figures. The more detailed of these gives a breakdown of 79 207 infantry under arms, 17 769 disarmed, and 25 087 police (including mounted).
Source: Peel Commission Report, Appendix 71, Evidence of Lt-Col Durand.
Note: This blurred snapshot of the Bengal Army suggests how its ethnic and regional composition changed between 1846 and 1859. The regular infantry and cavalry are mainly the loyal remnants of the old Bengal Army. They include a high proportion of Rajputs and Brahmins. The irregulars, of more recent origin, include far more Punjabis. The spellings and contradictory categories of the table conform to the original.

included officers from the forces of the British Crown and from the East India Company, and it heard evidence from 47 witnesses in London between August and December.[32] No Indians were asked to take part. Although the terms of reference did not emphasise questions of recruiting strategy, it soon became clear that these would be important objects of enquiry.

The witnesses before the commission offered conflicting advice concerning the future composition of the Indian Army. Most agreed that less deference should be shown to caste when selecting recruits. 'I should recruit a good soldier wherever I found him, whatever might be his caste', said Sir George Clerk (a former Governor of Bombay).[33] Beyond this, there was little consensus. Many witnesses wanted the higher castes to be excluded from the army: others believed that they made the best soldiers, and should not be alienated. Some believed Sikhs or Muslims to be the most trustworthy and efficient recruits: others warned that it would be 'an enormous risk' to depend on them. Several witnesses thought that soldiers recruited outside India would 'divide and so neutralize' the non-European forces, although some foresaw Malays in this role while others favoured Africans or West Indians. But soldiers from outside might inflame the racial feelings of the Indian population, thought some witnesses, besides displacing social groups who depended on military service. 'The wise policy', according to Sir John Lawrence, was not to push such men aside, but 'to feed, use, and control them'.[34]

Proffered such contradictory advice, the Peel Commission made understandably anodyne recommendations. It rejected, on grounds of expense, the idea of garrisoning India with an all-European army; and it dismissed the plan to employ troops imported from other colonial territories because they might inflame Indian racial feeling. The Indian Army was to remain Indian. But the commissioners made little attempt to advise which Indians should be recruited. They merely noted that 'the Native Army should be composed of different nationalities and castes, mixed promiscuously through each regiment'.[35] They did not specify whether all castes should be enlisted, or merely some; nor did they suggest any province or region which might provide a fertile recruiting ground.

But decisions had to be made. In October 1859, there were still nearly 175 000 Indian soldiers in British service. As the proportion of British troops in the garrison was to be increased, the Indian element had to be reduced to about 110 000.[36] The government adopted the briskly pragmatic policy of keeping those regiments of the Bengal Army which had not mutinied, and making up its numbers by retaining enough of the Punjabi and low-caste units raised in 1857–58. The rest were disbanded. Thus, on the Bengal Army List of 1862, the first eighteen regular infantry regiments were mainly survivors of the old Bengal Army; regiments 19 to 32 were Punjabi units raised in 1857; regiments 33 to 39 were mainly low-caste units raised in Hindustan at the same time; and regiments 41 to 44 were various local corps from other areas.[37] Five Gurkha, four Sikh and six Punjab infantry regiments were also retained, each of these groups numbered in a separate sequence. The Madras Army, which kept 52 battalions, and the Bombay Army, which kept 30, were largely unchanged.

The structure of the Bengal Army, as it emerged from the military confusion of the Mutiny, was 'purely accidental', recalled Lord Ripon in 1881. The British had simply enlisted those men who were prepared to fight for them, and had excluded those whose loyalty was suspect. The reductions which took place after the rebellion were 'as little the result of deliberation' as the expansion which had taken place during it. No defined principle guided British policy, except that the high-caste sepoys of Awadh were widely discredited. New and untried levies were often retained. The Bengal Army, Ripon believed, was 'a mere fortuitous congeries of regiments, raised in haste, brought together in haste, reduced in haste'.[38]

There was much truth in Ripon's remarks. Major decisions of policy are often *ad hoc* responses to immediate demands, and never more so than during an emergency like the rebellion of 1857. But some elements of principle were later invoked to make sense of the largely pragmatic reconstruction of the Bengal Army after the Mutiny. When questioned by the Peel Commission, Lord Elphinstone urged that soldiers of diverse backgrounds should not be mingled in the same regiment. '*Divide et impera* was the old Roman motto, and it should be ours', he advised. 'The safety of the great iron steamers is greatly increased by building them in compartments. I would ensure the security of our Indian empire by constructing our native army upon the same principle.'[39] The practical and reactive nature of British military policy in this period should not be forgotten; but the doctrine of 'divide and rule' was later used to justify the shape of the post-Mutiny Indian Army.

In the first place, there was mutual antipathy between certain parts of the Bengal Army. British officers often noted with approval the contempt in which the Gurkha soldiers of Nepal held the inhabitants of India in general, and the rituals of the higher castes in particular.[40] Many Sikh troops showed similar hostility towards Muslims and to the people of Hindustan.[41] 'It was not because they loved us, but because they hated Hindustan that the Sikhs have flocked to our standards', noted one British major-general. 'They were not attracted by mere daily pay. It was rather the prospect of wholesale plunder and of stamping on the heads of their enemies.'[42] Furthermore, by the early 1860s the Indian Army as a whole was divided into four main elements, recruited in different regions and serving in different regiments. The soldiers of the various parts were unlikely to share the same grievances at the same time, and a mutiny in one portion could be crushed, as in 1857, by the troops of another. In the north, the troops from Hindustan balanced those from the Punjab, while the armies of Bombay and Madras acted as counterweights to that of Bengal.

IN SEARCH OF THE MARTIAL RACES

There matters rested for almost two decades. The desire to maintain a politically secure balance between the four main regional components of the army was the major influence on recruiting strategy in the 1860s and 1870s. Some small changes were proposed, however, and a few carried out. In 1861–65 the 52 battalions of Madras infantry were reduced to 40. In 1869, the Government of India wanted to disband a further eight Madras battalions. They wished to save money; they believed the mainly peaceful Madras Presidency was over-insured against rebellion; and – here they struck a note that would sound more insistently in coming decades – they suspected that the Madras infantry was recruited from 'unsuitable races'.[43] The India Office were sceptical. If further reductions were to be made so soon after the Mutiny, they wished them to fall evenly but lightly on all three armies. After a long and sometimes acrimonious dispute, the proposal fell by the wayside.[44] The four-way balance broadly remained. In 1875, for example, Punjabis made up about 44 per cent of the combined Bengal Army and Punjab Frontier Force; but they accounted for only a quarter of the entire Indian Army.[45] From the early 1880s, however, the bias of Indian Army recruiting started to shift slowly and steadily towards the Punjab and Nepal. (See Table 1.2.)

TABLE 1.2
Regional origin of Indian infantry battalions, 1862–1914

	Year			
Region	*1862*	*1885*	*1892*	*1914*
Nepal (Gurkhas)	5	13	15	20
Hindustan east of the Yamuna (including UP and Bihar)	28	20	15	15
Punjab and NWFP	28	31	34	57
Bombay (including Rajputana and Central India)	30	26	26	18
Madras	40	32	25	11
Total	131	122	115	121

Source: GI Advance Despatch, 27 August 1920, Annexure IIL/MIL/7/5483.
Note: The figures given in this document are very approximate. They differ slightly from those given in the *Indian Army List*, but the broad trends are clear enough. Rajputana and Central India were officially designated as Bombay Army recruiting grounds, which is why they have been included with Bombay. The later Bombay figures are also inflated because, by the turn of the century, that army took many men from the Punjab and the NWFP (see Table 1.5).

The Russian Threat and the Martial Race Strategy

The initial impetus behind this shift came from the growing Russian threat to India's north-west frontier. Throughout the nineteenth century, the Russian Czars had gradually expanded their dominion southwards and eastwards through central Asia. In 1868 the Russians seized Samarkand; in 1880–81 they absorbed the lands which bordered Afghanistan; and in 1885 a frontier incident raised the prospect that they might even invade that state.[46] From the later 1870s it became increasingly clear that the Indian Army might have to defend India against Russian attack. The lacklustre performance of the Indian Army during the Second Afghan (1878–80) and the Third Burma (1885–89) wars had led some British observers to doubt whether it could withstand the troops of a first-class power. 'Many regiments', Lord Roberts grimly concluded, 'are not fit to take the field against a European enemy.'[47]

Russian expansion in Asia prompted reforms to the Indian Army, behind which Roberts was the main driving force. A vigorous personality, Roberts was prepared to override opposition to his plans. He was well-placed to do so, commanding the Madras Army from 1850 to 1885 and the Indian Army from 1885 to 1893. After he left India, Roberts remained very influential, advising Lord Kitchener (C-in-C, 1902–9) on all aspects of Indian Army organization. In response to the Russian threat, Roberts believed that Indian Army recruiting strategy had to change. 'The near approach of a great European power', he argued, 'compels us to have an army composed of very different material from that which was sufficient when we had no external enemy to deal with.'[48] Roberts believed that the peril from Russia was greater than the risk of an army mutiny, so he abandoned the policy of 'balance' which had broadly informed recruiting patterns for two decades. 'We must have the best fighting material the country can supply, and can afford no place in the native Army to a soldier whose only *raison d'être* is that he acts as a check upon another soldier.'[49] This search for the best 'fighting material' – the so-called 'martial races' of the subcontinent – became not merely a colonial strategy, but a colonial obsession.

The new 'martial races' policy had a clear regional dimension. Roberts was the main spokesman for a growing body of British military opinion which held that the peoples of southern India were inherently unwarlike.[50] 'The Madras sepoy can never attain to the Bengal standard', thought Sir Neville Chamberlain (C-in-C Madras, 1876–81). 'The men of Southern India fall far short, as a race, in possessing the courage and military instincts of the men of Northern India.' These views were not confined to a handful of isolated cranks, but were widely shared among the British military establishment in Bengal. 'The Punjab is the home of the most martial races of India and is the nursery of our best soldiers', noted the Eden Commission in their 1879 report to Parliament on the Indian Army.[51]

According to Roberts, his conclusions rested not on mere prejudice but upon a long acquaintance with all variety of Indian soldiers and a most careful study of what he termed 'the native character'. He accepted that south Indian soldiers might do good work against Chinese, Burmese or Abyssinian troops; but hoped that 'when the time comes for us to meet a Russian army in the field, our own force will consist mainly of Europeans, Goorkhas, and the best kind of Sikhs and Dogras'.[52]

Despite his protestations of objectivity, Roberts, like most Bengal Army officers, was prejudiced against southern soldiers.[53] Originally commissioned in the Bengal Artillery, he had served continuously in northern India (including a short spell in command of the crack Punjab Frontier Force) before he moved to Madras in 1880.[54] Bengal officers still smarted over the fact that their high-caste men had mutinied in 1857, while the low-caste sepoys of Madras had remained true to their salt. Anti-southern prejudice diverted attention from this uncomfortable fact, and helped compensate for any residual sense of inferiority.[55] By the same token, Sikhs and Gurkhas were long celebrated in the collective memory of the Bengal Army for having remained 'loyal' in 1857.[56] Bengal officers were especially attracted to soldiers from the Punjab, as many were of high or middling caste but were also lax in their ritual observances.[57] Northern chauvinism was strong: were Bengal officers to be polled 'and their views accepted, the whole army would be composed of Sikhs, Pathans and Gurkhas'.[58] These biases were important, given that Bengal officers had great influence with the Commander-in-Chief, who usually spent most of his time in northern India. Bengal Army views thus carried much weight, and never more so than during Lord Roberts's period as Commander-in-Chief when contempt for soldiers from the south became widely acceptable.[59]

The Shortcomings of the Madras Army

Roberts thus discovered in the Madras Army what he had expected to find. Even after discounting Bengal Army prejudice, however, there remains a residue of evidence that some southern regiments were less efficient than their northern counterparts. Shortly after becoming Viceroy, Lord Northbrook toured India and concluded that 'the native infantry in Madras and Bombay have little or no *esprit de corps*'.[60] Military inspection reports are more ambiguous. The Madras Sappers generally appear in a favourable light, but a few other Madras regiments received damning accounts.[61] Most telling of all, however, was the performance of the Madras infantry in the Third Burma War, when several regiments disgraced themselves.[62] During one attack the men of the 12 Madras Infantry were 'very ready to lie down and extremely difficult to get up', and on another occasion the 10 Madras Infantry were reluctant to advance even though they were not under fire.[63] After a difficult retreat, the same regiment became 'utterly done up and demoralised': on the march, the men had tried to hide behind their baggage animals and had 'fired all the way at nothing from funk'.[64] By the end of the campaign, the Officer Commanding had concluded that 'in all regiments of Madras Infantry there are very many men whom it is an absurdity to call soldiers'.[65]

Many British observers believed 'a want of warlike instinct and manliness' among southern Indians could account for these shortcomings; but the historian must seek social, not biological, explanations. Indian regiments did not normally serve far from their home presidency: with no active frontier like that in the north-west, units from the south had to rust unburnished far from the fighting.[66] Officers in Madras complained for decades that their army was deliberately denied active service.[67] The forces engaged in the Second Afghan War, for example, were almost all drawn from the Punjab and Nepal.[68] Between the Mutiny of 1857 and the invasion of Upper Burma in 1885, the Madras Army saw hardly any action. Without the invigorating effects of occasional warfare, and with only minor police duties to perform, any army is likely to slip into the comfortable routine which dulls its cutting edge. Furthermore, Bengal sepoys were often younger and fitter than those in Madras. Enlisted mainly from communities without much agricultural income, soldiers in the Madras Army tended to remain in the ranks until pensioned. In 1879, only 11 per cent of Bengal sepoys had more than 15 years' service, compared with 23 per cent in Bombay and 37 per cent in Madras.[69] Many of the latter must have been old and tired men, unsuited to the rigours of campaign.

Conventional military wisdom holds, however, that there are no bad troops, only bad officers. The Madras Army certainly found it difficult to attract the best British officer material. Able and ambitious young men did all they could to secure a posting with a northern regiment where there was more chance of winning renown on active service or drawing lucrative emoluments in civil employment.[70] Furthermore, the disbandment of twelve Madras infantry

TABLE 1.3
Madras Army officers by rank, 1862–1881

	Year	
Rank	*1862*	*1881*
Lieutenant-Colonels and Brevet Colonels	40	248
Majors	132	226
Captains	413	60
Subalterns	616	110
Total	1 201	644

Source: GI MD to SSI, 24 June 1881, L/MIL/7/5445; Shibly, PhD thesis, p. 308.

regiments in the early 1860s had created a large surplus in its staff corps. Since the India Office was unwilling to provide extra pensions attractive enough to induce these men to retire, the regimental officers of the Madras Army tended to grow gradually older and more senior in rank, while retaining the same posts.[71] In the 1860s and 1870s, only a trickle of younger officers joined the Madras Army, which therefore lost an important source of new energy and enthusiasm.[72] By 1879, most Madras regiments had four or five field officers, while many had no subalterns.[73] (See Table 1.3.) A middle-aged major would not perform with zeal and efficiency duties which properly belonged to a subaltern fifteen years his junior, and it is not surprising that the quality of the Madras Army declined.[74] It is ironic that the martial-race theory, which focused on the Indian ranks, should emerge in part from the shortcomings of British officers.

The martial-races recruiting strategy dramatically changed the composition of the Indian Army. From 1882, the number of units raised in Madras, Bombay and Hindustan steadily declined, while the number of those recruited in Nepal and the Punjab increased. In 1882, eight of the 40 Madras infantry battalions were disbanded. The new units raised after the war scare of 1885 were mostly Sikh and Gurkha; and the Indian Army reserve, instituted the same year, was on a higher establishment for northern than for southern units.[75] In January 1893, the Punjab and the North West Frontier provided 50 587 soldiers (including 21 966 Sikhs and 21 837 Muslims).[76] Along with the 12 334 Gurkhas from Nepal, these recruiting grounds accounted for nearly 44 per cent of the Indian Army, then 144 020 strong. Between 1890 and 1898, seven of the nine Madras infantry regiments based in Burma were reconstituted, mainly with men from northern India and Nepal. By the turn of the century, only 25 infantry battalions were recruited in Madras, compared with 40 in 1882 and 52 at the time of the Mutiny.

The steady shrinking of the Madras Army shook its morale and discipline.[77] At each stage, Madras officers urged that the current round of reductions should be the last, giving the army a chance to settle down, and making the men feel more secure. 'The Madras Army may be a *damnosa hereditas*', remarked one officer in 1890, 'but we must make the best of it, and that can never be so long as it is distracted by reductions and reorganisations.'[78] Because of the cuts, service in the Madras Army became less popular, and good recruits became harder to find. The shortage merely confirmed the prejudices of the martial-race theorists. The disbandments also threatened public security in the presidency, because discharged soldiers, deprived of their livelihood, were tempted to join the gangs of armed robbers in the countryside.[79]

Martial Races: the Search in the South

It might be argued, however, that this northward drift in recruiting patterns reflected practical military need more than martial-race theory. Given that the Indian Army was deployed more and more towards the Russian threat in the north-west, it might seem only logical to enlist its soldiers from regions nearby. But the shifting pattern of recruitment in south India around the turn of the century shows this to be at most only partly true. Although the martial-race theorists held that the 'ordinary Madrasi' had 'deteriorated', not all thought that replacement recruits could be found only in the Punjab or Nepal.[80] Some believed that southern India has its own 'martial races'. Three Madras infantry battalions were accordingly reconstituted, at least for a time, by tapping two south Indian communities which had not yet provided many recruits to the Indian Army – the Mappilas and the Coorgs.[81]

The Mappilas of Malabar in south-western India were mainly the descendants of Arab traders who had settled in the region since the seventh century, or were Hindu converts to Islam.[82] By the sixteenth century they made up about five or ten per cent of the population of the region, a proportion which conversion, mainly from the lower castes, had increased to roughly one-third by 1921. They had almost no access to modern education, and their literacy rate of 6.2 per cent in 1921 was less than half that of the district as a whole. Mainly petty traders, fishermen, cultivating tenants or agricultural workers, very few Mappilas owned land. Many endured chronic indebtedness or rackrenting, or even suffered arbitrary eviction at the hands of their Hindu landlords. But they were not mere passive victims. In 351 separate rural incidents between 1836 and 1919, small Mappila bands struck back against the landlords and their agents, including elements of the colonial state, killing 83 people. Popular Islam was an important catalyst in the agrarian conflict, although Mappila violence was never directed at all Hindus without discrimination. For much of the nineteenth century, the British regarded the Mappilas as irredeemably 'fanatical' and tried to suppress the rural violence with harsh policy and legislation. Attitudes changed from the 1880s, as colonial administrators began to accept that behind the apparently 'turbulent spirit' of the Mappilas there lay genuine agrarian grievances.

By the 1890s, the army authorities had come to hope that military employment might draw the sting of Mappila agrarian discontent. The Mappilas certainly seemed to possess the warlike qualities that the martial-race theorists thought most southern Indian soldiers now lacked. They had a precolonial tradition of military activity, and their more recent outbreaks had earned them a reluctant respect for their fighting spirit. Their low level of literacy and their dislike of Hindus suggested that they might prove politically reliable on internal security duties. The Government of Madras was sceptical, and agreed to the formation of two Mappila battalions only on condition they were deployed outside Malabar. Raised in 1900, the new regiments were a complete failure. They soon dwindled to 600 men 'quite useless for service'.[83] The sepoys were 'insubordinate and wanting in respect for authority', while the Native Officers were unable to enforce obedience to orders. In 1903 in Bangalore, a party from one regiment even waylaid and assaulted its own Adjutant. During their prolonged struggle against agrarian oppression, the Mappilas had developed an anti-landlord and anti-British mentality, fostered by traditional Islamic intellectuals, which appears to have informed their conduct as soldiers. Besides, the Kola gold-fields, the railways of southern India, and the plantations of Ceylon now offered alternative employment for the able-bodied, landless and adventurous. The Mappila sepoys were also suspected of being 'addicted to unnatural crimes', according to Lord Minto.[84] In 1907, the authorities decided to disband the two Mappila battalions and replace them with a similar number of Gurkhas.

The attempt to incorporate the Coorgs also failed, although for quite different reasons. The tiny and isolated province of Coorg, annexed by the British in 1834, lay in the wooded hills to the south-west of Mysore state. According to the 1931 census, the 41 026 Coorgs were the largest single element in the population of 163 327. A dominant group, unlike the Mappilas, the Coorgs also appeared to be an ideal martial race. They were culturally distinct, few were literate, and they held themselves aloof from the surrounding population. They claimed descent from a Kshatriya – a member of the warrior *varna* second only to Brahmins in the Hindu hierarchy – but were free from prejudices of diet and ritual which might hamper military efficiency.[85] The Coorgs had a martial tradition, having formed the main body of the armies of the Lingayat Rajas in the pre-colonial period. The general orientation of their culture was martial.[86] 'Men should die on the battlefield, and women should die in child-bed', ran a typical Coorg proverb. Their light skin and aquiline noses appealed to British officers who subscribed to fashionable racial theories. In short, the Coorgs promised to be excellent 'fighting material'. The authorities also hoped that a Coorg regiment would bring trade and prosperity to the province, and thus rekindle the feelings of loyalty to the British which recent economic hardship had begun to cool.[87]

A Coorg battalion was accordingly raised in 1901, the men wearing khaki uniforms cut to resemble Coorg national dress. The British believed there would be no shortage of recruits. According to the commissioner for the province, the Coorg population had recently increased out of all proportion to the available land. Work was scarce, and the men feared they would lose status if they became plantation coolies, so, he concluded, military employment was their only alternative to crime. Pure Coorgs would not serve with the aboriginal forest tribes or low-caste men of the province, so the regiment recruited Coorgs alone.[88] According to the census of 1891, the male Coorg population was 25 302 of which only about 5000 were aged 16 to 24, the normal age on enlistment. The British had perhaps over-estimated the degree of economic pressure on the Coorgs, for it was soon found that they were a home-loving people from whom it was difficult to obtain recruits. The patrilineal joint family or *okka*, with its indivisible property, remained strong, and this solidarity perhaps discouraged enlistment. The failure of the experiment was soon apparent, so in 1904 the Coorg battalion was disbanded and yet another unit of Gurkhas was soon raised in its place.[89]

The British experience with the Mappilas and the Coorgs shows that imperial recruiting strategies alone cannot explain the shape of the Indian Army. Military policy might exclude a community from the army, but a community might also exclude itself.

The Martial-Race Strategy Confirmed

The failure to find new 'martial races' in the south merely confirmed the northward drift in the recruiting patterns of the Indian Army. 'I was shocked by what I saw in Madras', observed Lord Kitchener shortly after he took command in India.[90] 'We shall have to reconstitute some regiments and increase our Gurkhas. Good smart officers would sooner go to the Commissariat than join a Madras regiment.'[91] It became easier to impose the martial-race strategy as a general policy after the amalgamation of the three presidency armies in 1893–95 (a move which the Government of India had advocated since 1881) and the renumbering of the regiments on a single list in 1903.[92] At the turn of the century, 25 battalions drew their men from Madras. As Madras supposedly could not supply enough good recruits to keep them efficient, ten were reconstituted, mainly with Punjabi and Gurkha troops, in 1901–3.[93] By January 1904, nearly 57 per cent of the Indian Army (86 841 men) came from the Punjab, Nepal or the Frontier.[94] (See Table 1.4.) Two more Madras battalions were reconstituted with northern troops in 1904, as were the two Mappila regiments in 1907–9, leaving only eleven recruited in that presidency. In 1914, 211 infantry companies were composed of Punjabis and 121 of men from the North West Frontier or Afghanistan. Together with the eighty companies of Gurkhas, they made up almost three-quarters of the Indian infantry, then 552 companies (or 138 battalions) strong.[95]

TABLE 1.4

Class composition of the Indian Army, 1 January 1904

Class	Number
Muslims	
Cis-Frontier	6 835
Trans-Frontier	1 612
Afridis	2 758
Punjab proper including Hazara	21 773
Hindustan and Cis-Sutlej Punjab	10 661
Rajputana and Central India	1 486
Bombay	162
Madras	5 588
Dekhan	2 647
Others	446
Hindus	
Jat Sikhs	23 108
Other Sikhs	7 867
Dogras and Punjabi Hindus	8 669
Gurkhas	14 224
Garhwalis	1 901
Rajputs	10 813
Jats	8 407
Brahmans	2 880
Mahrattas	5 735
Gujars	1 210
Mers	869
Minas	503
Bhils	1 085
Tamils	3 024
Pariahs	1 073
Other Hindus	5 446
Others	
Christians	1 867
Jews (including 1 Parsi)	37
Burmans, Karens, Assamese	161
Total	152 846[1]

[1] Including Indian Officers, NCOs, other ranks and musicians.

Source: Caste Returns, 1 January 1904, L/MIL/7/17084

Notes: This table gives a picture of the Indian Army after the martial races strategy had taken firm hold. It reproduces the numbers, categories and spellings of the original. Detailed returns like this one were assiduously compiled in the 1890s and early 1900s. The simple fact of their existence is itself a window into the nature of colonial military thinking during the imperial meridian. Sikhs are classified here as Hindus. In the returns of 1914, they are classified separately. See Chapter 3 for further discussion of this point.

The bulk of the discussion has so far focused on the growth of the Punjabi and Nepalese portions of the army, at the expense of that from Madras. A similar northward drift àlso affected the Bombay Army. After the mutiny, in accordance with the policy of 'balance', the Government of India forbade the Bombay Army to recruit outside the presidency, even in the neighbouring Indian states of Rajputana. But this principle appears to have been flouted in practice – by 1879, 5032 of the 16 034 Bombay infantry hailed from elsewhere.[96] That year, the Eden Commission officially added Rajputana, Central India and Sind to the Bombay Army recruiting grounds; but from the later nineteenth century the Bombay Army poached more and more of the highly-prized men from the Punjab and the North West Frontier. By 1903, perhaps as many as 82 of the 208 Bombay infantry companies obtained their recruits from those regions.[97] (See Table 1.5.)

The martial-race strategy thus made the Indian Army depend on a very narrow range of communities for its soldiers. But the recruiting methods themselves tended to reinforce this selection and dependence. Until the later nineteenth century, all recruiting was a matter of regimental initiative. A regiment might send a recruiting party into a selected district; British officers might obtain men through their contacts with pensioners of the regiment; or men on leave might bring recruits back with them when they rejoined.[98] In each case, recruiting relied on local connections. Men on leave tended to bring in men of their own family or clan; and a recruiting party would normally be led by an Indian officer or NCO from the district, who would obtain suitable men more quickly than someone who was locally unknown.[99] In practice, regimental recruiting parties tended to return often to those districts that they knew well. The men preferred it that way, as they wanted their families to retain the useful option of regimental employment.[100]

During the Afghan War of 1878–80, however, the Indian Army found it hard to obtain enough men by these methods. Troops even had to be withdrawn from depleted regiments in the front line to go and recruit. Furthermore, the military authorities were concerned that the manpower base was not broad enough. They accordingly set up a series of depots, each headed by a Recruiting Officer who was in nominal control of all recruiting for a particular class.[101] These depots came into being for Gurkhas in 1886,

TABLE 1.5
Ethnic composition of the Bombay infantry, 1903

	Companies
Konkani Mahrattas	24
Dekhani Mahrattas	30
Rajputana and Central Indian Musalmans	12
Punjabi Musalmans	27
Jats	26
Gujars	12
Dekhani Musalmans	14
Rajputs	12
Pathans	15
Sikhs	8
Hazaras	4
Khatteks	2
Mahsud Wazirs	1
Wazirs	1
Baluchs and Brahnis	8
Mers	6
Hindustani Musalmans	6
Total (26 Battalions)	208

Source: Memo by Roberts, 23 June 1903, CID 27-D, CAB 6/1.
Note: This list gives a rough idea of the regional pattern of Bombay Army recruitment at the turn of the century. The Konkani and Dekhani troops were the main elements from the Bombay region itself. The Jats and Rajputs were overwhelmingly from Rajputana and the Punjab. The Pathans, Hazaras and Wazirs were from the North West Frontier. The Mers were from Central Rajputana and the Sikhs were from the Punjab. The categories and spellings of the table conform to the original.

for the rest of the Bengal Army in 1892, for the Bombay Army in 1896, and for the Madras Army in 1900.[102] But they did little to broaden the range of recruits.[103] Recruiting Officers still tended to concentrate on a few well-known districts that had produced good men in the past; and regimental parties, often ignoring the new system, still did more than half the work.[104] (See Table 1.6.)

TABLE 1.6
Source of Indian Army recruits, 1905–14

	Year	
Source	*1905–6*	*1913–14*
Recruiting Officers	10 275	7517
Regimental Parties	13 814	7686
Total	24 089	15 203

Sources: GI Advance Despatch, 27 August 1920, Appendix II, L/MIL/7/5483; Brief, MPhil thesis, p. 132.

Thus, by the early twentieth century, the Indian Army left many districts, even in the Punjab, entirely untapped.

COLONIAL DOCTRINE AND COLONIAL STRATEGY

The first parts of this chapter outlined British recruiting strategy up to 1914. We should now break off the narrative and examine in more detail the martial-race discourse that informed policy from the mid-1880s.

The Origins of the Martial-Race Theory

Some elements of the martial-race theory can be traced back to the second half of the eighteenth century. In those decades, the earlier accommodation between Europeans and Indians gave way to more distant relationships; racial attitudes sharpened and harsh stereotypes emerged. Theories of historical change imagined clear hierarchies of development, from the stage of primitive nomadism to that of high European culture.[105] From the 1830s, the twin impact of utilitarianism and evangelical Christianity further reinforced notions of racial inequality and Indian depravity.[106] This thinking began to affect military policy. The assumption that some communities possessed inherited traits which made them better soldiers informed British recruiting efforts in northern India.[107] These efforts in turn drew upon military experience in the British Isles themselves. From the mid-eighteenth century, the British Army had enlisted distinct units of supposedly warlike Scottish highlanders; and by the early nineteenth century, Irishmen, seen by some commentators as a martial race, were overrepresented in the ranks.[108] Many High Victorian ideas about the warlike races of India thus had an earlier pedigree.

Despite these precursors, the ideas which emerged in the 1880s differed markedly from those which had gone before. In the first place, as the earlier sections of this chapter have shown, they had much more influence upon policy. By 1914, the martial-race enthusiasts had radically reshaped the Indian Army. Secondly, the new discourse was such more systematic. From the late 1890s, martial-race theory was codified in a series of official *Recruiting Handbooks* for the different 'classes' of the Indian Army, most of them written by British officers long acquainted with the troops concerned. Published by the Government of India, the handbooks appeared in successive and often expanded editions until the eve of the Second World War. Thirdly, the new martial-race discourse received much wider currency, mainly through the writings of popular military commentators like George MacMunn. 'It is one of the essential differences between the East and the West, that in the East only certain clans and classes can bear arms; the others have not the physical courage necessary for the warrior', ran a typical passage from his work.[109]

The idea that some Indians were more martial than others was not a pure figment of the colonial imagination.[110] Had it been so, it might still have generated a workable recruiting strategy – although this is unlikely. The martial-race discourse had at least some basis in the customs and self-image of the many Indian communities who had a martial tradition quite independent of the colonial encounter. In response to Mughal oppression in the early seventeenth century, for example, the later Gurus had militarized the Sikh religion.[111] Muslim identity sometimes asserted itself in relation to military matters.[112] The British regarded both Sikhism and Islam as 'martial faiths', and Sikhs and Muslims were each strongly represented in the Indian Army.[113] Mahrattas and Gurkhas also had a precolonial history of military endeavour.[114] British perceptions drew further sustenance from the hereditary stratifications of the caste system, in which each *jati* is traditionally associated with a particular calling.[115]

Some castes saw themselves as warriors. The *dharma* of a Kshatriya required him to overpower or even kill his enemies.[116] The Rajputs – a major subgroup of the Kshatriya *varna* – usually scorned agriculture and saw themselves above all as fighting men.[117] 'We are Rajputs and it is our privilege to fight bravely in battle; and if we are wounded or die, we gain renown and honour', wrote a Dafadar of cavalry in 1917.[118] Many Rajputs were *jagirdars*, originally holding their land in return for military service to a Raja.[119] Other cultivating groups claimed Kshatriya status, even if this was contested by those outside their own *jati*. British parables incorporated Indian proverbs about the martial abilities of various castes. But a martial self-image by no means guaranteed the award of a place in the Indian Army, or even the desire for one. Besides, British ideas had their own logic and served purposes quite different from the self-perceptions of Indian society.

Perfect Soldiers, Perfect Men, Perfect Subjects

One such purpose was to articulate and codify the qualities which the British sought in the perfect soldier. Some of the recruiting handbooks heaped praise upon the more popular classes of troops. 'His proverbial hospitality, courtesy, courage, cheerfulness and loyalty make him an excellent companion and a valuable soldier', noted the handbook for Pathans.[120] The martial-race discourse inverted negative colonial images of barbaric otherness, painting instead a picture of men who added 'to a prepossessing appearance, the charm of simple and unsophisticated manners'. The engaging yet warlike rustics who inhabited the pages of recruiting handbooks reflected colonial desires as much as they described the qualities of Indian subjects. This was especially true when the British were discussing obedience. 'They have a natural respect for authority, and have ever been distinguished for their military fidelity and loyalty', observed the handbook on Dogras, with an air of cautious optimism.[121] Yet the purpose of the martial-race theory was not merely to codify, but to inspire. By putting a positive and disarming gloss on the men's cultural difference, it encouraged officers to trust their troops, to respect their qualities, and arguably to get more from them. As a useful mobilizing myth, the martial-race idea could help sustain the army – for any regiment is likely to work better and fight harder if its officers can be persuaded that they command near-perfect soldiers.

Within colonial parlance, the martial races served as an example of masculine as well as military excellence. The recruiting handbooks are full of references to the 'manly independence' of the favoured recruits, usually contrasted with the 'weakness' and 'effeminacy' of those who were excluded.[122] Fighting was of course a highly-gendered activity, and the British equation of masculinity with martial endeavour reflected this. Indian soldiers saw things in much the same light. 'Men always fling themselves into the fray; those that stay at home are women', wrote one man to his brother in the 2 Lancers.[123] This image of manliness could, however, coexist with homosexual practice. A famous Pathan song, 'Zakhmi Dil' (Wounded Heart), allegedly began with the deathless line 'There's a boy across the river with a bottom like a peach; but alas, I cannot swim'. In the eyes of John Masters, a Gurkha officer, the assertive homosexuality of the Pathans added to their masculinity, rather than detracting from it. He contrasted their behaviour favourably with that of Western 'effeminate' homosexuals. 'They [the Pathans] often wear roses in their long hair, and I frequently wish I could see a Pathan entering a gay cocktail party given by Manhattan fairies.'[124] Here, the imagined sexuality of the Pathans mirrored the hatreds, and perhaps the desires, of a British observer.

While Indian soldiers were admired for their manliness, they earned some contempt for their supposed lack of intellectual agility. George MacMunn spoke frankly of 'the stupider martial races', and recruiting handbooks were sometimes only a little more subtle than that.[125] British officers used to recall the proverbial Gurkha, kicked in the head by a mule. He got a slight headache, but the mule went lame.[126] Stupidity, however, could be seen as a positive virtue in a martial race, given the British fear of soldiers who questioned their authority. 'As a fighting man, his slow wit and dogged courage give him many of the characteristics of the British soldier at his best', wrote MacMunn of 'the Sikh sepoy'.[127] British stereotypes, it should be noted, drew on Indian ones. Baluchi and Pathan proverbs were full of contemptuous references to Jats, a major north Indian cultivating caste which supplied many recruits to the army. 'A Jat is such a fool that only God can take care of him', ran one of their sayings.[128] A similar Punjabi proverb held that 'three things are improved by beating: women, wheat and a Jat'.[129]

It suited the British to believe that their Indian soldiers were stupid. For one thing, it made them feel safer. The belief also reflected and reinforced the sense of superiority that helped run the empire and sustain the morale of its rulers. To this end, the white elite found it useful to suppose that they monopolized the intellectual military virtue of tactical insight, even if the raw courage and muscle of the army were supplied mainly by the Indian ranks.[130] No Indian community had all the desirable military qualities, so the martial-race theory ran, but the right mix – chosen, ordered and led by the British – would make the perfect army.[131] The belief also gave the British a sense of purpose. 'The Gurkha [Indian] Officers were the backbone of the regiment', recalled John Masters. 'Many lacked education, but that was what we were there for.'[132] British officers liked to imagine themselves as the strict but paternal guardians of the supposedly childlike ranks. The best Dogras were thought to possess 'enthusiastic courage and an almost boyish simplicity of character'.[133] The British saw the Mappilas in a similarly dependent light. 'To those who treat them with kindness and consideration they become much attached. But the hand that controls them must be firm' – and, by implication, British.[134] This equation of Indians with children expressed a reality of power. Individual Indian sepoys were comparatively powerless in relation to their officers, and were therefore likely to assume an outward role which fortified the self-esteem of those in authority.

Like most stereotypes, that of sepoy thickheadedness had some basis in fact – if only because Indian Army recruits tended to come from the least literate sections of the population. In the heavily-recruited Punjab (including the North West Frontier), for example, 64 out of every thousand people could read and write in 1901, while in Madras, which sent far fewer recruits to the army, the figure was 119 per thousand.[135] In 1891, male literacy was confined to 53 out of every thousand Muslims (who were over-represented in the ranks) compared with an all-India rate of 87 per thousand.[136] The disparities become more striking when recruiting patterns are examined in more detail. Among the rural Muslim population of Hindustan and the Eastern Punjab, 'scarcely one in a thousand cultivators is able to sign his name', according to the recruiting handbook for those classes.[137] And most Jats accepted into the ranks were 'quite illiterate'.[138]

The low level of sepoy literacy was the result of policy, not of chance. British recruiting strategy showed a marked bias in favour of men from remote regions, unaffected by Western education. For instance, Nepal, which provided twenty Gurkha battalions by 1907, was officially closed to European travellers except at the personal invitation of the Maharaja. More than half its scanty population lived in the hills, and even by the 1930s there were only two main roads in the entire country.[139] The arid region of Rajputana was similar in this respect. Although its railways improved greatly in the first quarter of the twentieth century, camels remained the major form of transport. Ruled mainly by Indian princes, Rajputana retained an 'innate conservatism of ideas, administration and customs'.[140] The preferred recruits from Garhwal came from the isolated and mountainous north-east of the region, rather than the foothills to the south-west which were closer to avenues of commerce or pilgrimage.[141] There were political reasons for this strategy. 'In out-of-the-way districts', believed Lord Roberts, 'the people are much more inclined to accept the authority of the governing race than they are in the large centres of educational enlightenment.'[142] He held that the education of Indians was a danger to the Raj.

The Indian Army also took hardly any men from the towns and cities.[143] The British saw the urban lower classes as mixed, degenerate and potentially threatening. The shifting urban population could not be classified, ordered and 'placed' as easily as that of rural India. 'The inhabitants of Hyderabad City', remarked one handbook, 'are of such doubtful character that it would be dangerous to experiment in enlisting them.'[144] The British shunned the educated urban middle classes, who were seen as corrupted by the myriad temptations of city life and softened by long experience of peaceful British rule.[145] The repulsion was mutual, and until the 1920s most educated Indians would rather become clerks or teachers than serve in the army. In the twentieth century, the growing adherence of these classes to nationalism made the British unwilling to select them. The favoured recruits were often independent peasants, holding the land that they cultivated, such as the Jats of north India.[146] The Sikh Jats of the Punjab were seen as 'the backbone of the province by character and physique – stalwart, sturdy yeomen of great independence, and collectively perhaps the finest peasantry in India'.[147] Jat skill in agriculture was legendary. 'The Jat's son, when as big as the catch of a Persian well wheel, has a plough handle for a plaything', ran one snappy proverb.[148] This positive image of the 'sturdy yeoman' perhaps drew upon popular versions of English medieval military history.

Physical vigour was held to correlate not only with social class, but with local climate. The British had long been impressed by the heat of the Indian plains; and some recruiting strategists came to believe that the enervating effects of prolonged heat, combined with natural abundance, had drained the people of southern and eastern India of all military ardour.[149] 'The inhabitants of the dry country to the North, which in Winter is cold, are comparatively manly and active,' remarked Lord Elphinstone, 'while the Bengalis with their moist climate and their double crops of rice, where the coconut tree and the bamboos furnish all the materials for construction unwrought, are more effeminate than any other people in India.'[150] Recruiting strategists showed a strong preference for men living in the hills. Not only did the British in India adore such scenery and climate, the policy also mirrored the Victorian cult of Scotland.[151] The climatic theory was attractive, for several reasons. It had a pedigree stretching back to Herodotus; and it justified the martial-race strategy of selecting mainly northern recruits, 'whom a cold winter has preserved from military deterioration'.[152] After the Second Afghan War, army chiefs even wondered which troops had best withstood the rigours of the climate. In some regiments, men from different castes or regions had markedly different rates of sickness, but the overall pattern was inconclusive.[153] Nevertheless, in 1883 the Hindustani elements were removed from the Punjab Frontier Force on the spurious grounds that they were less able than Punjabis to withstand the sudden changes in Frontier weather.[154] And, of course, the notion of northern hardiness appealed to the British because they were from more northerly latitudes than any of the Indian population.

Colonial Knowledge and Colonial Power

These more fanciful aspects of the martial-race theory should not obscure the fact that its object was not merely to explain and justify policy, but to exercise colonial control. Although *scholars* had first developed European understanding of Eastern languages in the eighteenth century, *imperial administrators* soon realised the practical value of a skill which weaned them from dependence on Indian subordinates.[155] Linguistic aptitude was merely one aspect of a growing and systematic body of European knowledge about Eastern society – knowledge which not only emerged from the colonial encounter but which reinforced imperial dominance.[156] Behind this search for refined understanding, however, lurked a crude fear of making fateful blunders. 'There is always the dread that something may be done unwittingly by someone who does not understand the native sepoy and thus precipitate a crisis', observed one officer after a mutiny in 1918. 'The Indian Army is such a terribly ticklish thing to deal with.'[157] The Mutiny of 1857 had shown the importance of 'knowing the natives'; and reading handbooks about the various enlisted classes helped the inexperienced British officer to acquire the comforting illusion that he did so.[158] More than half a century after the event, the recruiting handbooks still classified Indian social groups according to the stance they had adopted during the rebellion.[159] Roberts chided Kitchener for not including on his staff more men who were familiar with the 'ideosyncracies of the Natives'.[160] Ignorance brought danger, as surely as knowledge brought power.

Martial-race theory was not only a discursive aspect of domination. Its suppositions positively required detailed knowledge of Indian society. The assumption that 'the fighting capacity of most Asiatics depends upon hereditary instinct and social status' made it 'a matter of supreme importance that the men enlisted should be the very best of their type'.[161] A group might well be a martial race, but some of its elements might be deemed more martial than others. Among Pathans, for example, Khattacks were held to be 'brave, independent and excellent soldiers', whereas some other Pathan tribes were not enlisted because the colonial authorities thought them of poor physique, afflicted with malaria, weakened by internal feuds, prone to gambling, or simply unwarlike. The quest for the utterly martial race therefore generated a copious quantity of ethnographic detail. The handbook on Pathans enumerated every clan, division, section and subsection in a list some 200 pages long. 'A reference to this volume', it was suggested, 'will generally place a recruit. If he is unable to give a good account of himself, it is advisable to reject him.'[162] The handbook on Gurkhas listed all 800 known clans of the Magar, and about 300 clans of the Gurung, the two most heavily-recruited tribes.[163] The colonial authorities feared that would-be recruits from a supposedly unmartial group might try to impersonate more warlike people to gain access to the rewards of military service, leading to friction and indiscipline in the ranks.[164] Recruiters could, therefore, 'commit no worse crime than to attempt to pass a boy of an incorrect tribe'.[165] They were to avoid recruiting at fairs where they might find many adventurous young men who had escaped family discipline, but whose credentials it might be impossible to verify. The handbooks were full of tips, including trick questions, which might help establish a recruit's true identity.[166]

This atomizing ethnographic enterprise existed alongside collective colonial stereotypes. Martial-race theory enumerated Indian society in what were held to be its smallest meaningful social components, each of which had an official collective identity.[167] Although they drew on Indian proverbs and images, these British stereotypes usually failed to accommodate the multitude of individual identities and the fluidities of caste. Instead, official dogmas about the supposed attributes of Indian social groups recurred verbatim year after year in the literature.[168] Collective stereotypes simplified the problem, or at least created the illusion, of colonial understanding. To predict a man's behaviour it was necessary to know only the collective attributes of the group to which he belonged.[169] Thus Brahmins were 'given to intrigue'.[170] Jats were independent, stolid and dense, 'with more dogged courage than dash'; and Gurkhas were playful and funny, yet crazed and bloodthirsty in battle.[171] In the recruiting handbooks, Indians appeared not as individuals but as examples or specimens of a type. The Gil clan of Sikhs in Amritsar District were 'all fine specimens of the Manjha Jat'.[172] By the 1930s, some handbooks even included photographs of suitable recruit types, whose ideal measurements and physique were described as if they were so many breeds of dog or horse.[173] In keeping with this attitude, the British often used the singular when referring to collective social entities.[174] 'The Pallan is a stout, short, jet black man, sturdy, a meat eater, and not overclean in person or habit', noted the handbook on Madras classes.[175]

To be fair, British recruiting officers did develop some awareness of the tension between their fixed categories and the more fluid identities of the population they sought to classify. Dogras are a case in point. The word itself was a corruption of Durgara, the ancient name for Jammu state. Originally of geographical significance, within martial-race doctrine the term came to denote all Hindus enlisted from Jammu, Kangra, Chamba and the other Rajput hill-states of the north-eastern Punjab. 'But no Rajput of the Kangra valley ever styled himself a Dogra, nor to this day will he describe himself as anything but a Rajput', noted the 1928 handbook, which went on to observe that some 'Dogras' had been sent to Rajput regiments 'with which they had no connection whatever'.[176] Ten years later, the handbook on Madras classes was still more agnostic. It cited a recent census to show 'the uselessness of caste enumeration. When caste names are shed like garments there is little point in an enumeration which must perforce go by name.'[177] Nor did recruiting officers always subscribe to 'essentialist' notions of martial ability. They accepted that some men, such as the lower castes enlisted as Dogras, could become as warlike as the martial races simply through long association with the army. But these flickers of a more nuanced understanding appeared only during the last phase of imperial rule. They were not prominent in the 1880s and 1890s, when the martial-race theory began to shape recruiting strategy.

Just as the Indian Army was a microcosm of the colonial encounter, so this martial-race literature was part of a broader body of classificatory and enumerative colonial writing. In the second half of the nineteenth century there appeared not only the massive *Census of India*, published every ten years from 1861, but a flood of settlement and ethnographic surveys, reports on economic activity and accounts of cultural practices.[178] This writing addressed practical problems of administration, and expressed the late-Victorian mania for classifying and counting. It was also an essay in the exercise of power. The growing knowledge of the minute fissures within Indian society aided colonial efforts to manipulate them. Colonial writing thus tended more and more to record caste divisions down to the smallest group cohering around some detail of custom. This drive to fragment was a basic colonial instinct of self-preservation, for no regime could long survive if it treated its subject population as a single, undifferentiated mass.[179]

Racism and Recruiting

The ethnographic detail of the recruiting handbooks could also coexist with cruder racism. Several handbooks opened by claiming that 'the dawn of Indian history discloses two races struggling for the soil. One was a fair-complexioned Sanskrit-speaking people of Aryan lineage, who entered the country from the north-west; the other a dark-skinned race of lower type.'[180] The British saw some of their favoured martial races (especially those of Rajputana and the Punjab) as descendants of these Aryan invaders.[181] Caste was sometimes equated with race, particularly in the case of Rajputs, who – according to the British and to themselves – had maintained their Aryan racial 'purity' through the caste system.[182] Social Darwinism also fed the Aryan races theory, and it encouraged the skull- and nose-measuring habits whose results sometimes found their way into the handbooks.[183] The fair skin and straight, narrow noses of many of the north-western martial races fitted the most common

Indian and British perceptions of beauty.[184] With some justice, this appearance was also held to correlate with high social status. It seemed appropriate to suggest that the Aryan invaders of ancient India were somehow the racial cousins of the Europeans.[185] In the late eighteenth century, scholars had discovered the close affinities between Sanskrit and the European languages. But any potential British embarrassment at the egalitarian implications of the theory could be neatly avoided by assuming that Indian Aryans had gradually degenerated through millennia of contact and occasional interbreeding with the dark-skinned original inhabitants.[186] The Mahrattas had been thus affected, according to the handbook for that class.[187] The German philosopher Friedrich Hegel went further, and argued that the very presence of Sanskrit speakers in the sub-continent proved that the aboriginal inhabitants of India were inherently conquerable.[188] The Aryan races theory neatly confirmed Bengal Army prejudice against the short, dark-skinned, and often low-caste soldiers of Madras; but it does not explain the preference for Gurkhas with their yellow-brown skin, stocky build and Mongolian features.[189]

The Aryan element of the martial race theory was closely associated with notions of racial and ritual purity.[190] If fighting ability was hereditary, then racial mixing would produce only degeneracy and military weakness. British recruiting strategy therefore favoured those groups who followed restrictive marriage practices and who thus promised to be racially pure. 'There is no race in the world of more ancient lineage or purer descent' than the Mians and higher classes of Kangra Rajputs, observed the handbook on Dogras ('with the exception perhaps of the Jews').[191] Jat recruits were favoured because they strictly followed the custom by which a man had to marry within his own subcaste, although not into the clan (*got*) of his mother or paternal grandmother.[192] The British preferred those Sikhs who came from areas where they were in a majority and hence less likely to be 'weakened' by marrying Hindus.[193] This social exclusivity also made for politically more reliable soldiers, since these highly specific and localized identities were unlikely to be touched by the grievances of dissidents in other parts of India, against whom the troops might be deployed. 'Great pride of race usually accompanies those qualities which we look for', noted one handbook.[194] Conversely, a man who migrated from his original homeland might not only 'contract habits and adopt customs foreign to his nature and objectionable in a soldier' but his descendants might become 'effete' through interbreeding with people of another community.[195] The British sought martial races who were as exclusive as themselves.

Martial Races and Criminal Tribes

The martial-race theory also assumed a curious inverted form in the legislation to control the so-called 'criminal tribes'. From the middle of the nineteenth century, some persistently turbulent social groups in north India were collectively labelled 'criminal'. The police tried to register and limit their movements, a policy which eventually gained legal sanction with the Criminal Tribes Act of 1871. Originally applicable only to north India, a new Act of 1911 extended the legislation to all British territory in the subcontinent. Its more far-reaching provisions allowed local governments to declare an entire community 'criminal', deprive it of its rights under the law, and force its members to work on approved sites, often in squalid and degrading conditions. A perceived loss of traditional livelihood was usually pretext enough. Itinerant traders displaced by the spread of roads and railways were hardest-hit by the policy.[196] Permeating this body of repressive law was an assumption of hereditary criminality, akin to that which informed social theory in late Victorian Britain.

Some groups, however, could be labelled 'criminal' and 'martial' at the same time. The Mappilas are an example. A restless and resentful rural underclass, they were the main object of police surveillance in Malabar, but elsewhere enjoyed the status of a martial race, at least for a while.[197] The Minas had a similar reputation for dacoity in their home state of Jaipur, but the army authorities believed they made good soldiers. Recruiting them could be difficult as they all had to register with the suspicious Jaipur authorities; leaving the territory without permission sometimes brought reprisal on their village headman. Many Mers of the mountainous British territory of Ajmer-Merwara, in Rajputana, had also lived by robbery before they turned to service in the Indian Army. Even as soldiers, however, they retained 'somewhat loose notions of *meum* and *tuum*, especially as regards other men's wives', according to the handbook of Rajputana classes.[198] Successful robbers and soldiers both needed to be bold and violent, although not all groups with a criminal reputation were thought suitable for enlistment.[199] Some British observers believed that the Punjab peasantry were good soldiers for the same reasons that they considered them prone to violent crime when unrestrained by military discipline.[200]

CRITICISM AND CONSOLIDATION

Critics of the Martial-Race Policy

Of course there were critics of the martial-race policy. Dissident members of the military elite, educated Indian nationalists, and subordinate groups excluded from the army – all rejected the martial-race theory, either as a whole or in one of its aspects.

Lord Roberts was aware that many in the army establishment did not share his views. 'To those who think that every one who wears uniform must be able to fight, the reduction of certain regiments of the Indian Army must appear suicidal', he wrote in 1884, after advocating the disbandment of some units recruited in the south.[201] At first, he found it hard to get his ideas accepted. Vigorous opposition came from officers of the Madras Army, who resented his slurs on the fighting spirit of southern Indians. 'I cannot admit for one moment that the Madras sepoy is inferior as a fighting man', wrote Sir Frederick Haines, who had served in Madras before he took command of the Indian Army.[202] But from the mid-1880s, broadly speaking, the martial-race theory was Indian Army orthodoxy.

Disagreements resurfaced, however, just before the Great War. A broader recruiting base was needed to provide enough men in wartime, concluded the 1912 Nicholson Committee (the last major pre-war enquiry into Indian Army affairs).[203] Furthermore, there had been trouble in the Punjab among ex-soldiers who were threatened by the 1907 Canal Colonies Bill. The unrest had raised doubts about the wisdom of relying so heavily on men from that province.[204] The Sikhs, who sent many men to the army, had been badly hit by plague, and the government also looked with suspicion on the growing militancy of Tat Khalsa movement among them. 'The glorification of the Sikhs has kept the banner of Sikhism flying to the great advantage of the Government', noted a secret intelligence report in 1911. 'It now appears likely to be used as an instrument to scourge us.'[205] In the event of another major rebellion like that of 1857, there was no guarantee that the Punjab would not rise – and take with it most of the Indian Army.[206]

The martial-race strategy also cut little ice with the educated nationalists – unsurprisingly, since it castigated them as effete, garrulous, and unwarlike. At the second (Calcutta) session of Congress in 1886, for example, Raja Rampal Singh blamed the exclusion of intellectuals from the army 'for degrading our natures, for crushing out of us all martial spirit, for converting a race of soldiers and heroes into a flock of quill-driving sheep. Thank God things have not gone quite so far as this', he continued, amid shouts from the audience. 'There are some of us yet, who would be willing to draw sword and lay down our lives for the support of that Government to which we owe so much.' Another leading critic was the prominent Maharashtrian Congressman and Imperial Councillor G. K. Gokhale, who favoured replacing the 'mercenary' Indian Army with a short-service conscript force. Conscription would be cheaper, and would heal the wounded self-respect of those people excluded from the ranks for allegedly being unmartial. The dramatic success of the Japanese Army in the war with Russia in 1904–5 satisfied some nationalists (Gokhale included) that conscript armies were effective and that all Asians could be warlike.[207] But these criticisms had little impact on Imperial policy.

Some of the subordinate groups excluded from the army also resented this fact and petitioned against it. The Mahars, an Untouchable caste of inferior village servants from Maharashtra, are an interesting example. Some of their traditional occupations had been threatened under British rule, but they regained some of the lost economic ground by serving in the Indian Army. Once the martial-race theory took hold, however, they were excluded. From the 1890s no more Mahars were recruited, and by 1914 there were almost none left in the ranks.[208]

This exclusion provoked a remarkable political mobilization. At the end of the nineteenth century the Mahars began to organize under the leadership of Oopal Baba Walangkar, himself an ex-serviceman. A petition drawn up in 1894 (although not presented) demanded the return of their jobs in the army, and claimed that the Mahars were of Kshatriya origin.[209] This claim was not unusual. Although the position of Untouchables is more fixed than that of the Shudra castes, subordinate *jatis* often assert Kshatriya status (hotly contested by their local rivals).[210] When the 1901 census was being compiled, for example, the authorities were besieged by rival *jati* representatives jostling for position, as the data for that census were to be organized, for the first time, on the principle of ritual status.[211]

The Muslim Merat-Kathats also petitioned the authorities at the turn of the century, claiming they were 'by nature a warlike race', after they were excluded from three mainly Hindu Rajputana regiments because of Hindu–Muslim tension.[212]

But the Mahars went further. The Conference of Deccan Mahars requested admission to the lower grades of public service including the police and army, in a 1910 petition to the Earl of Crewe (the Secretary of State for India). This document, however, was not couched in the language of martial-race theory of Kshatriya origin. Instead, the Mahars appealed to their record of military service, and to Western notions of citizenship:

> And it is most encouraging to know that the Honourable House of Commons, as constituted in these times, is composed, to some extent, of the representatives of the lower strata of English society, the workingmen, who, only a quarter of a century ago were regarded as but Mahars and Paryas by the more educated and affluent classes of the nation. If the Brahminical castes and the Muhamadans have been given the full rights of British citizenship, we must be given the same.[213]

The military service of the Mahars had given them early exposure to Western ideas and institutions, and left them better able to work the new political order than groups otherwise in the same position.

The Mahars were drawn into the army once more during the military crisis of the Great War, and again excluded after the Armistice. They continued to petition, but no major Mahar document of the twentieth century tried to manipulate the *varna* system. Instead they developed an autonomous movement of self-assertion, with their first graduate, Dr. B. R. Ambedkar, as their most prominent speaker. Ambedkar came from a family with a history of military service, and he linked self-assertion to soldiering. He believed that the entry of Untouchables into the armies of the East India Company had made them 'conscious that the low esteem in which they had been held was not an inescapable destiny but a stigma imposed by the cunning contrivances of the priest'. The Mahars' military past served as a mobilizing myth during their militant campaigns of the 1920s and 1930s, when they demanded separate representation within Hinduism, the right to enter temples and tanks, and an end to their traditional services to village chiefs.[214] After failing to obtain satisfaction, the Bombay Mahar Conference voted to leave

Hinduism in 1936, following the example Ambedkar had set the previous year.

The Martial Races in the Great War

The social base of the Indian Army did broaden after 1914, but in response to the demands of war rather than to the voices of protest. The imperial crisis of 1914–18 threatened the established recruiting policy in colonial India. The martial-race strategy had been possible only because the peacetime Indian Army took so few recruits in relation to the Indian population as a whole. In the decade before 1914, annual enlistments averaged only about 20 000.[215] The Great War changed all this. Regiments which had been accustomed to enlist 75 men per year now found that they needed a hundred men a month in the killing fields of Flanders and Mesopotamia.[216] By 1916, the traditional sources of recruits were beginning to run dry. Furthermore, the poor performance of the Indian infantry on the Western Front, when even Gurkhas ran away, had led some officers to question the assumptions of martial-race theory.[217] From early 1917, the army authorities began to seek men with 'good fighting qualities' who did not have a previous record of distinguished military service.[218] Recruiters began to explore areas previously dismissed as 'non-martial'; and by the Armistice they had tried out 75 new classes of men. Some of these were groups related to those already serving, such as Tamang Gurkhas and Saini and Khatri Sikhs.[219] Others were groups like Mappilas, Coorgs and Mahars, who had only recently been dropped from the Army List.[220] Some were men who had not previously served, such as Kanets and Girths – Kangra Shudras of low social status who were taken into Dogra regiments.[221] Additional Madras battalions were levied, and the men of that province, long thought unwarlike, provided 51 223 combatants.[222] The men at the front were well aware that the Empire was hard-pressed for troops. 'Those classes who formerly never entered the Army are now being hustled into doing so', wrote a Muslim of Lyallpur to a *sowar* in France in September 1917.[223]

Although wartime recruiters tapped new districts and classes – especially in the Punjab – the broad regional balance of the army remained roughly the same. (See Table 1.7.) The Punjab and Nepal continued to supply the bulk of recruits. The quota system

TABLE 1.7
Enlistment in the Indian Army by region, 1914–16 (combatants only)

Region	Year			
	1914[1]	1915	1916	Total
Punjab	14 000	46 000	50 000	110 000
Nepal	3 000	14 000	15 000	33 000
North West Frontier Province	3 000	6 000	5 000	14 000
Rest of India	8 000	28 000	32 000	68 000
Total	28 000	93 000	104 000	225 000

[1] Last four months only
Source: O'Dwyer, *India As I Knew It*, pp. 216–17.
Note: The figures have been rounded to the nearest thousand, and therefore do not exactly add up. Those for the NWFP include Transfrontier Pathans.

introduced in 1917, by which each province had to produce a given number of men, merely confirmed the long-standing northern bias in recruiting strategy, even if the Punjab Government had to enlist men from new districts in 1917–18 to meet the heavy demands placed on the province.[224] By the Armistice, the Punjab had provided some 360 000 recruits – more than half the total combatant enlistments during the war.[225] These included 136 000 Muslims, 88 925 Sikhs and 23 000 Dogras.[226] Another 97 063 Gurkhas also enlisted.[227]

The good performance of some new classes prompted a few observers to question the martial-race theory. 'The less conspicuous types have made good', noted the Lahore *Civil and Military Gazette*.[228] 'The war has proved that all men are brave, that the humblest follower is capable of sacrifice and devotion', commented another British author shortly after the Armistice. 'These revelations have meant a general levelling and the uplift of classes hitherto undeservedly obscure.'[229] Where new enlistments were not a success, however, they merely confirmed existing stereotypes. A single regiment of supposedly 'effeminate' Bengalis was formed in July 1917, but its already shaky reputation plummeted when some men, motivated by personal grievances, shot three of their officers at Basra the following June.[230] 'The Bengali regiment was about the worst we ever had in our Army. No General could possibly use it for any operations. I have never seen reports on any regiment so bad as theirs in the whole of my thirty-eight years' service', declared Sir Claud Jacob – who, incidentally, had 'nothing but praise for the Sikhs'.[231] Given these diverse responses, the Great War arguably proved very little about recruiting policy except that, in Kitchener's words, 'the Army system in India will have to go into the melting pot for drastic and radical improvement'.[232]

Postwar Policy

The years after the Armistice brought major change to the Indian Army. As in the period following the 1857 rebellion, its strength was greatly reduced – from a wartime total of about half a million in 1918 to 120 000 by 1923. This time, however, almost all the cuts fell on those classes who had been newly recruited during the war.[233] The Government of India wanted a broad manpower base, to allow easy and rapid expansion in time of war, so their original plan for a 185-battalion peacetime army kept many of the new classes.[234] But, because of financial retrenchment, only much smaller forces could be maintained, and martial-race theory guided the choice of those to be cut from the *Army List*.[235] The Madras infantry were of 'no real military value', thought Sir Claud Jacob; and, given the current financial climate, Austen Chamberlain agreed it was 'intolerable' they be retained.[236] After much reorganization, the Indian Army in January 1923 included only six battalions from Bombay and nine from Madras. There were five from Burma, but 20 from Nepal and no less than 73 from the Punjab and the North West Frontier. Thirty-six battalions were recruited elsewhere – mainly in Rajputana and Hindustan.[237] The northern bias of the army was even more marked in 1923 than it had been in 1914. The peacetime return to 'real soldiering' marked a return to ingrained habits of mind, in racial as well as other matters.

The drift away from the south continued into the 1930s. Further reductions, motivated by cost, made it necessary to 'concentrate on those classes which provide the best fighting material'.[238] The last Madras infantry battalion disappeared in 1928. The Madras Pioneers went the same way in 1933, leaving Queen Victoria's Own Madras Sappers and Miners as the sole remnant of the old Coast Army that had conquered Bengal – once 52 battalions strong.[239]

The martial-race discourse also regained its vigour. The recruiting handbooks went into new editions, and more popular works continued to appear. 'The mass of the people of India have neither martial aptitude nor physical courage', claimed George MacMunn in one of these. According to him, this state of affairs was the effect of 'prolonged years of varying religions, of early marriage, of premature brides and juvenile eroticism, of a thousand years of malaria and hookworm, and the deteriorating effect of aeons of tropical sun on races that were once white and lived in uplands and on cool steppes'.[240] His book *The Martial Races of India* was published the year Hitler came to power.

The atavistic dependence of the postwar Indian Army on a narrow range of recruits brought with it some political dangers. In the 1920s and 1930s, nationalist and communal unrest troubled the Raj, and army chiefs sometimes feared that this might disturb the discipline of the Indian regiments. Their fears had some foundation. Because the army recruited so heavily from a few provinces, the General Staff had reason to be anxious whenever there was unrest in those vital areas. In April 1930, for example, there was extensive rioting in Peshawar – a Frontier city which was not only close to the Pathan recruiting grounds, but which also lay athwart the strategic routes leading to the Khyber Pass. Although the Frontier province was overwhelmingly Muslim, Congress had strong support there. But it was upon the Punjab that the military authorities kept their most watchful eye. The Akali movement in the early 1920s sometimes threatened to affect the discipline of the important Sikh component of the army, and the Khilafat agitation posed similar dangers with respect to the Muslim. Furthermore, the Punjab was a province divided by religion, and fears were sometimes voiced that its growing communal troubles might touch the ranks. Nationalism was also a potential problem. During the campaigns of civil disobedience and non-cooperation, the Congress leaders often threatened, and sometimes tried, to create disaffection in the army, their efforts being focused on the Punjabi recruiting-grounds.[241] As it happened, the troops scarcely wavered; but the fact that half the army came from a single province made the Raj seem especially vulnerable to a surgical strike.

The communal divisions of the Punjab were, however, as much an advantage as a danger to the army. The 1901 census estimated the population of the Punjab, including its princely states, at 24 million. Of these, 12 million were Muslims, 10 million were Hindus and two million were Sikhs. Five major classes of the Indian Army were recruited from the province – Dogras, Sikhs, Hindu Jats, Hindu Rajputs and Punjabi Muslims.[242] Chronic tension, intermittently acute, separated most of these groups, especially Sikhs and Muslims. The British did not welcome communal violence, which posed a public-order problem, but they noted with approval these fissures of caste and religion.[243] 'The equal division of the province between Hindus and Muhammadans helps greatly to preserve its political tranquility and prosperity, which is not likely to be seriously disturbed until they combine under some great national movement', noted a prewar strategic survey.[244] These communal divisions were also cited, along with the martial-race theory, as an argument against Indian nationalism. India, so the theory ran, was not really a nation, but a mere collection of races of widely different religions and martial aptitudes, held together only by the British. If the latter withdrew, the martial races – especially the Muslims – would sweep down once more to dominate and suppress the less warlike peoples.[245]

Understandably enough, Indian nationalists rejected this colonial reasoning out of hand. After the Armistice, they kept up a steady barrage of protest against the martial-race theory and the recruiting strategy to which it gave rise. The Legislative Assembly (established by the 1919 Government of India Act) was a useful forum in which to air nationalist views. In March 1921, the Assembly urged the government 'to introduce in the Indian Army a system of short colour service, followed by a few years in the reserve'.[246] Speeches and resolutions in a similar vein were a recurrent feature of the interwar political climate. 'When God Almighty created this world, he did not take the map of India and say "Take out the Army brains from these people"', noted M. Ghiasuddin (Punjab, Landholders) in a debate held the day before Hitler annexed Bohemia in March 1939. 'This artificial distinction between martial and non-martial races is the guiding policy of the Government. They want to create differences so that a particular section may retain the exclusive right to military service', added the Bombay Congress leader, N. V. Gadgil (Bombay Central Division, Non-Muhammadan, Rural).[247] Men like these thought that all Indians could be soldiers, and that India, as befitted a true nation, should have a national army which represented all its people. As an all-India organization, Congress sought to unite the country behind a single nationalist banner, and the rejection of the apparently divisive martial-races theory fitted well with their purposes.

The Government of India conceded little to the nationalists in the matter of recruiting. The martial-race strategy remained firmly in place until the Japanese onslaught in the Far East from 1941 caused a military crisis so deep that a broader recruiting strategy became imperative. But some small cosmetic changes occurred before then. For the purpose of answering questions in the Assembly, the term 'martial races' gave way first to 'martial classes' and finally, by the 1930s, to the more neutral 'enlisted classes'. The continuities of policy combined with the semantic shift to produce some remarkable doublethink. The Indian Government 'do not say and *have never said* that some classes only enjoy the monopoly of courage and the military virtues', claimed C. M. G. Ogilvie (the Defence Secretary) in reply to the remarks of Ghiasuddin and Gadgil quoted above.[248] He thus denied the very existence of the huge body of official doctrine which had helped mould the Indian Army for the past sixty years.

CONCLUSION

In the early years of colonial activity, the East India Company had to seek soldiers wherever it could find them. Although the company sometimes linked up to precolonial military labour markets, its armies, broadly speaking, recruited whoever was willing to serve. By the early nineteenth century, recruiting patterns could be more selective; and the composition of the three presidency armies began to diverge. The forces in Bombay and Madras took a wide range of recruits, while the Army of Bengal came to depend almost entirely on high-caste Brahmins and Rajputs from the Indian state of Awadh. The very selective policy had its critics, who appeared to be vindicated when most of the Bengal Army mutinied in 1857.

The mutiny dramatically altered the composition of the imperial military forces in north India. The Punjab was the main British base during the crisis, and it was there that most of the new levies were raised – for Punjabis, especially Sikhs, proved willing to serve the British against their old Hindustani enemies in the mutinous Bengal Army. After the Mutiny, the British followed a mainly pragmatic recruiting strategy: most of the regiments that had mutinied were disbanded, and many of the new levies raised in 1857–58 were retained. Yet this essentially practical and reactive policy was not inconsistent with a strategy of divide and rule; and most of the military elite believed it correct to keep the Indian Army separated into 'watertight compartments'. By the early 1860s the Indian army had four main regional components, recruited respectively in the Punjab, Hindustan, Bombay and Madras – an *ad hoc* system of 'balance' which broadly remained for twenty years.

This recruiting pattern began to change from the mid-1880s. As the Russian Empire gradually expanded eastwards, it seemed the Indian Army might have to fight the troops of a first-class power on the Frontier. Under Lord Roberts the policy of 'balance' was abandoned and a search for the most warlike recruits began. A growing body of Indian Army opinion came to believe that southern Indians were unmilitary, so units raised from the 'martial races' of the north more and more replaced southern regiments. Some circumstantial evidence, particularly from the Third Burma War, suggested that Madras regiments were indeed less efficient than those from the Punjab or Nepal. After 1857, the southern units saw little fighting, so the most capable and ambitious British officers preferred service in the north. But the martial-race strategy was also driven by sheer prejudice, since many influential Bengal officers still resented the fact that their army had mutinied in 1857 while those in the south had remained firm. Once the martial-race strategy was established, recruiting methods tended to reinforce it, because the regimental recruiters who supplied at least half the men tended to comb areas with which their units had close personal links. By 1914, about three-quarters of the Indian infantry came from the Punjab, Nepal or the North West Frontier Province.

A large body of colonial writing grew up to articulate and perfect this martial-race policy. Like many effective colonial strategies, which made shrewd use of indigenous material, it drew heavily on existing Indian stereotypes; but it also voiced colonial assumptions and served colonial ends. It boosted officers' morale by suggesting that they commanded the perfect combination of men, whose presumed warlike qualities were bound up with perceptions of their manliness. But the British also liked to believe that their soldiers were stupid, for it made them feel safer and made their leadership seem more necessary. The belief also reflected the lower rate of literacy among sepoys compared with the Indian population as a whole. This was no accident. The British deliberately excluded urban India from the army in favour of recruits from the more isolated communities whom Western education and political ideas had yet to affect. The preferred soldiers were mainly independent peasants, such as the north Indian Jats. In the search for the most martial races of all, the British collected a mass of enthnographic detail about the different communities in the recruiting grounds – detail which coexisted with collective stereotypes about the groups concerned. Some of the categories used in these British classifications were largely invented, although by the 1930s some observers seem to have developed a better understanding of the fluid nature of Indian identities. At some points, martial-race theory became linked to a more explicit racism: the British liked to imagine that their favoured soldiers were of Aryan descent and thus their (slightly contaminated) racial cousins. British policy certainly favoured communities who were socially exclusive, and hence more likely to be 'racially pure'. The martial-race theory also existed in inverted form in the 'criminal tribes' legislation, by which entire communities were branded criminal, just as others (or even the same ones) were labelled warlike.

There were dissenters – within the imperial establishment, among the ranks of those excluded by the martial-race strategy, and among the Indian nationalists who saw the entire policy as an affront to Indians in general and themselves in particular. These criticisms had little impact on Imperial policy; but the demands of the First World War forced the army to broaden its recruiting base regardless. After the war, most of the new classes were once again excluded, and the army of the 1920s was even more heavily weighted towards the Punjab, Nepal and the Frontier than it had been in 1914. This bias in recruiting policy made the army potentially vulnerable to political unrest in the recruiting grounds, although in the event no major problems of military discipline occurred. The nationalists kept up their steady steam of criticism, although without much impact on policy.

But the shape of the Indian Army was not simply the product of British recruiting strategies – as the failed British attempts to incorporate the Mappilas and the Coorgs clearly show. British policy might explain the exclusion of a community from the army; but it cannot by itself explain its inclusion. Not only did the British choose their soldiers, the soldiers chose the British. To fully understand the form of the Indian Army, we must also understand the objectives and perceptions of the Indian recruits. It is to these that we now turn.

2
Enlisting Strategies

soldier (cf. Med. L. *solidarius*)
1. a. One who serves in an army for pay.

The Oxford English Dictionary,
Second Edition, XV

The Indian Army has often been described as a mercenary force. Its peasant-soldiers left the land to escape poverty, and served in the ranks to supplement their meagre income from the soil. They enlisted and fought, so this argument runs, not to win honour or from selfless loyalty to the Raj, but for the tangible gains of pay, pensions and land.

Plenty of contemporaries held this view. 'To preserve the efficiency of a mercenary army, and to secure its loyalty, it is necessary to bind the individual members of it to the Government by ties of self-interest', remarked the Commander-in-Chief in 1875.[1] George MacMunn, for all his talk of 'martial races', recognized that 'regular pay, due sympathy and prompt justice appeal to the mercenary soldier'; he considered it futile to hope for genuine loyalty from the Indian Army, which would only ever fight for pay. 'To expect more is to ask the impossible', he wrote.[2]

Educated nationalists, for other reasons, liked to portray the army in a similiar light. Excluded from the ranks by the martial-race policy, they generally looked askance at a force that was both the epitome and the mainstay of colonial rule. Calling the army 'mercenary', given the negative nuances of the word, was a veiled attack on British policy in India, and on the British presence itself.

But it also furthers our analysis to note the mercenary character of the Indian Army, and to stress the element of contract between the soldier and the state.[3] Doing so reminds us that the social basis of the Indian Army was not simply the product of *British* objectives. Military service was also the deliberate choice of the Indian recruits, made after weighing up the benefits and drawbacks of enlistment. Except briefly towards the end of the Great War, the Indian Army relied on volunteers. It acquired men only when the recruiting strategy of the high command intersected with the enlisting strategy of the troops. When examining the Indian half of this equation, however, it is useful to think in plural terms. The government, whatever its internal divisions and debates, had a single recruiting policy; but the recruits came from a variety of regions and communities, had very diverse fortunes, and entered the army for many different reasons.

This chapter explores in some detail the mercenary dimension of the Indian Army. It will explain why some men left the land to join the ranks – considering the agrarian pressures which pushed them in this direction, along with the material attractions of military life. The sharpest focus will be upon the Indian soldiers. But it must be remembered that a central concern of the Government of India was to secure the contentment of its troops. Therefore the chapter will also consider how British policymakers deployed material incentives to attract recruits and to purchase their quiescence while they served.

LEAVING THE LAND

Since the martial-race policy barred townsmen from the ranks, this enquiry must begin in rural India. Broadly speaking, the Indian Army relied on peasants who could not or would not subsist on agriculture alone, and for whom a martial self-image or the lack of more lucrative non-agricultural employment made enlistment agreeable or imperative.

'It is very noticeable', remarked the handbook on Sikhs, 'that the proportion of recruits forthcoming from the different districts varies in inverse ratio to the prosperity of the land.'[4] Many recruits came from areas with poor soil or where pressure of population had led to extensive subdivision of holdings.[5] The peoples of the north-western and north-eastern Punjab both sent a steady flow of recruits to the Indian Army since they faced similar agrarian problems, although they differed radically in religion and culture.[6] These soldiers would normally remit much of their pay to their families, who might therefore be able to survive or even buy luxuries. In areas of erratic rainfall, men might enlist and save their wages to tide them over a bad harvest. Many peasant-soldiers wanted to buy land; others set themselves up as moneylenders upon discharge.[7] From the 1880s, landless Punjabi recruits might hope for a plot in a newly-irrigated canal colony when they left the army. Conversely, in more prosperous regions where holdings were larger, the land more fertile, or irrigation more widespread, fewer men sought to enlist.[8]

This close correlation between agrarian structures and enlistment was typical of peasant armies.[9] But the great diversity of enlistment strategies in colonial India makes it necessary to look at some districts in detail to clarify the overall picture.

Rural Hardship and Military Service

We can begin by examining some areas where the population was growing, land was scarce and holdings small. In the hill areas of Kangra, in the north-eastern Punjab, the size of the average farm fell from 4.93 acres in 1855 to 3.9 acres in 1897. Families with barely enough land had to find another source of income to avoid debt, and for some castes enlistment was the only choice their culture would accept. Ludhiana District in the Punjab, one of the recruiting grounds favoured by Sikh regiments, was not agriculturally poor, but the growth of its population led to subdivision of holdings. In the eastern parts of the district, irrigation with wells was comparatively easy, yields were high, and cultivators could resort to more intensive agriculture in response to population growth.[10] They thus had little incentive to enlist. In the less well-irrigated western parts, however, the Sikh clans, such as the Garewal Jats, readily embraced military service in order to supplement their income from unproductive farms.[11] Some groups for whom tiny holdings were the rule came to depend upon the army. For instance, the Satti – a Punjabi Muslim clan – had sent as many as 1689 of their 9730 males into the ranks by 1914. 'Without military service they could not live. They make first-rate soldiers and are always in great demand.'[12] Pressure of population in the mountains of Almora District, in the Himalaya, also induced migration and enlistment.[13]

In some recruiting grounds the land under the plough, or the available waste, would yield little. This was true of the three districts of Attock, Jhelum and Rawalpindi, in the north-western Punjab. Together they formed one of the most heavily-recruited areas of the province, and were the main source of Punjabi Muslim troops. In 1914, about 20 000 men from the area were serving in the army, making up roughly one-eighth of its strength. In the Great War, 87 000 men from these districts enlisted, including 40 per cent of all males of military age in Jhelum and Rawalpindi. These large numbers are not surprising. Though often potentially fertile, the land was arid. The water table was too deep to make wells worthwhile, so irrigation depended almost everywhere on the unreliable monsoon rains. Crops often failed to mature. Tangled ravines, steep ridges, and hills broken with boulders made ploughing difficult and commerce rare, especially in Rawalpindi.[14] In response to a growing population, the area under crops in Jhelum was increased by more than half between 1865 and 1900; but much of the freshly-turned land, even at the outset, was so poor that cultivation hardly repaid the effort.[15]

Further east, conditions were similar for the Sandhu Jat Sikhs, the strongest clan of Amritsar District. They inhabited the south-west corner of Tarn Taran *tehsil*, a 'bleak, treeless tract with deep, brackish wells, a soil sometimes poor and sandy, but generally hard and uncompromising, and an uncertain rainfall'. They took eagerly to military service, not only in the Indian Army, but further afield – in the Burma Military Police, in the Straits Settlements, even in China.[16]

Many men therefore joined the army because their kin were short of fertile land. Indeed, some soldiers enlisted because their families had no land at all – particularly in the Madras Army, but also in the Mazhbi Sikh regiments in the north, who were recruited among a community descended from Untouchable converts.

But landless recruits were not the norm, especially in Punjabi regiments. More typical were the men who enlisted to help their families develop an existing, if inadequate, holding. One or two sons of an extended family might join the army to raise cash, while the others remained at home to work the farm.[17] While the younger brothers of a Jat family often enlisted, the eldest usually stayed on to cultivate.[18] Most Jats depended on agriculture for their livelihood, so their young men were reluctant to join the army unless they had brothers or other near relatives to whom they could entrust their cattle and land while they served in the ranks.[19] Jat sepoys often had to leave the army and return home to look after the family interests upon the death of their father or an elder brother. The government was sympathetic to their needs, although it remained anxious to retain them, with their military skills, as reservists.[20] There were political reasons to prefer landed to landless recruits, especially with the growth of popular protest after the Great War. The General Staff rightly considered landholding soldiers generally immune to the influence of radical movements such as the Kirti Kishan, the Nau Jawan Bharat Sabha, the Ghadrites, 'and other parties with Bolshevik tendencies'.[21]

Annual and Seasonal Rhythms of Enlistment

Even some men with land, however, joined the army through fear of temporary destitution. They came from districts where the success of the harvest depended upon erratic rainfall, and drought and hunger were intermittent hazards of peasant life. In areas with military connections, the pattern of years of plenty and years of dearth was also a pattern of enlistment; and every failure of a harvest yielded its own crop of recruits.[22] The Mers, from the British district of Ajmer-Merwara in Rajputana, faced 'incessant hardship owing to the precarious rainfall of their country and the consequent difficulties of cultivation'.[23] The famine which afflicted them in 1899–1900 bore in its wake many hungry men seeking pay and food in the ranks.

Some communities used army pay to insure against years of hunger. Uncertain rainfall and occasional famine afflicted most of the south-eastern Punjab, in which Rohtak District was the most important recruiting ground, supplying half of all Jat sepoys in the late 1890s. Rohtak suffered a famine every decade from the 1860s – not surprisingly, since it had an average yearly rainfall of only twenty inches, when nineteen were needed for a good crop. The district was a major cattle-raising area, but the famine of 1877–78 reduced the herds from 418 000 to 240 000 head. Most recruits came from the arid south rather than the irrigated north, and entered the army to gain the security that land and cattle alone did not provide. They normally stayed in the ranks only until they had acquired enough wealth to see them through a year of hunger. They were most reluctant to take their discharge during a famine.[24]

Any peasant army is also likely to show a seasonal pattern of enlistment.[25] In colonial India, the rhythms of recruiting kept time with the agricultural calendar. When the cultivators were busy in their fields, the recruiting depots had little to do, for parents were unwilling to part with the labour of a son during the months of ploughing, sowing and harvest.[26] In the slack season, however, the army soon found work for idle hands. But this theme was played with regional variations according to the pattern of the weather, the timing of the harvest, and the nature of the crop.

The best period for recruiting Pathans was from the middle of December until the end of April, when there was little to be done in the fields. Between the middle of April and the end of May, and from early October until the end of December, the men were gathering the harvests; they would not enlist during the fast of Ramazan until the Id was over; and they were reluctant to leave the cool of the mountains for the heat of the plain in July and August.[27] Gurkhas seldom enlisted after March, for similar reasons.[28] Further south, in the Maratha recruiting grounds of Konkan, the south-west monsoon made migration all but impossible between June and October, which were also the busiest months in the fields. Recruiting parties were usually sent off in October, to return in mid-May when the sea began to rise and storms cut communications by steam along the coast. As the monsoon approached, the fields had to be prepared for the rice crops, and recruiting slackened.[29]

The close links between agriculture and enlistment become clearer still if we approach the problem from a different angle, and examine those districts and communities which did not send many recruits to the army (even if the British hoped they might prove martial). In these cases, it is clear that agricultural prosperity deterred enlistment. In the Punjab, for instance, the better-off cultivators of Lahore, Lyallpur and Gujranwala districts usually provided far fewer soldiers than those who tilled poor soils or small farms in Rawalpindi, Jhelum or Kangra.[30] In Kangra itself, the Girth Shudras, who held most of the best land in the accessible valleys, were reluctant to leave their homes when the army was opened to them during the Great War.[31] Sahranpur district, in the United Provinces, gave fewer Jats to the army than other areas east of the Jumna, mainly because its prosperous inhabitants, living close to the foothills, enjoyed an unfailing rainfall on good soil, and had no canal dues to pay.[32] And the introduction of canal irrigation in a previously arid area could undermine an established tradition of military service, as could a change to more profitable cash crops.[33]

Rajputs: Economy and Status

Agriculture, although clearly crucial, cannot alone explain the decision to enter the army, since some men enlisted despite having an economic alternative. For many soldiers, joining the army was also an assertion of identity. A martial self-image or a community tradition of military service could influence the choice between different economic strategies.[34]

This was particularly true of Rajputs, whose identity and social status depended upon their image as warriors.[35] The Rajputs of the Punjab – Muslim in the north-west, Hindu in the north-east – often suffered economically under Sikh and British rule. Traditionally dominant in many places, they used to extract revenue from cultivating tenants, but lost out when the new states refused to accept their authority as revenue-gathering intermediaries and began to deal directly with the cultivators. Many Rajput villages stood on hills for defensive reasons, leaving the most fertile land to tenants of lower caste. With few resources to meet the new conditions under British rule, Rajputs were also culturally ill-equipped to adapt. Many had a strong prejudice against handling a plough, which they regarded as the mark of low social status. In Kangra, for example, a Mian Rajput would not give his daughter in marriage to a man who had followed a plough, nor eat with him at ceremonies.[36] Some were forced to till the soil themselves, but would yoke their oxen at night and try to work unseen, so hard did the prejudice die. For related reasons, Rajputs also made poor rural entrepreneurs.[37] They preferred to keep their wives in purdah, and thus lost valuable outdoor labour; they consumed conspicuously on ritual occasions; and their deep aversion to the plough, which put them in a weak bargaining position, often forced them to accept a poor deal if they rented their land to low-caste cultivators.

So they became soldiers. More and more Rajputs enlisted in the later nineteenth century.[38] The number of Dogras (mainly orthodox Hindu Rajput sepoys from the Kangra hills) increased from 3453 in 1875 to nearly 9000 by 1910. Army remittances were vital for those Rajput groups which had lost out after the annexation of the Punjab, most of whom were represented in the ranks. Service in the army was well-established for some groups by the twentieth century; in 1921, out of 17 200 Gakhars (who had been particularly hard-hit by change) no less than 2255 were soldiers. Joining the army was a culturally acceptable way of maintaining the living standards which political and economic change had undermined. Indeed, for many Rajputs, the cultural values and practices which went with their warrior status had themselves helped to create the hardship which left them with little choice but to enlist. Their fortunes and their identity reinforced each other.

Those Rajputs who had weathered the political changes, and who felt no economic pressure to join the army, illustrate the importance of warrior status as a motive for enlistment. The 1500 Tiwanas of Shahpur district are an example. Although they owned over 157 000 acres of land, much of it irrigated, over half of their men were soldiers. They enlisted not for pay, but to bear arms as true Rajputs should.

THE TANGIBLE REWARDS

A mixture of material need and martial identity usually prompted the decision to enlist, the exact combination of motives varying between communities according to their relative wealth and status. But military service could be an effective strategy for securing non-agricultural income only if the army offered material rewards. Of these, pay in cash was the most compelling.

Army Pay

The irregular cavalry were paid the most. In the later nineteenth century a sowar, or Indian trooper, received 27 rupees a month, increased to 31 in 1891. But deductions to pay for his horse, fodder, food and some equipment meant that in real terms he was little better-off than an infantryman. The basic pay of a sepoy was seven rupees for most of the nineteenth century, rising to nine in 1895 and 11 in 1911.[39] Gunners usually received one rupee more than this, and regular troopers two. Wartime bonuses, and *batta* paid on overseas or frontier service, were an important additional source of income. With these, a sepoy could earn 20 rupees a month by the last years of the Great War.[40] But pay-differentials between officers and men were enormous. In 1859, the 1000 sepoys of an Indian battalion at full strength received between them Rs 7000 a month, whereas its 26 European officers earned a total of Rs 9861.[41] It is, however, the comparison between what a sepoy could earn in the army and what he was likely to earn elsewhere that is relevant to understanding strategies of enlistment.

As might be expected, the number of men seeking to join the army tended to fall when more lucrative employment was available. In the second half of the nineteenth century, recruiting became more difficult because military pay remained static while the cost of living and other wages rose. For example, a sepoy's average monthly supplies of atta, dhall, ghee, sugar, salt, firewood and tobacco cost Rs 3.6.8 in 1848 but had risen to Rs 4.11.3 in 1875.[42] Private soldiers found it harder to live on their wages, and by 1885 it had become difficult to replace even peacetime wastage.[43] Successive increases in pay from the 1890s eased the situation.[44]

Some local examples also show a correlation between high civilian wages and declining numbers of willing recruits.[45] The docks and growing industries of Bombay drew much of their labour from the nearby hinterland; and they competed with the army for men, especially in Konkan.[46] Many Marathas preferred to seek well-paid work in the city rather than enlisting, which perhaps explains the slight decline in their martial reputation by the early 1900s.[47] In the 1920s, Sikhs with mechanical skills or education proved reluctant to enlist because they could obtain better pay elsewhere.[48] These economic correlations were by no means exact, however. Gurkha migrants to India seem to have preferred military to other employment, but for cultural rather than economic reasons.[49]

The British believed that the prospect of relative wealth might tip the balance in favour of the decision to enlist. They therefore preferred an Indian soldier to appear affluent when he was sent to find new recruits. 'Forty rupees is the minimum which he should take on his first trip', advised the handbook on Gurkhas.[50] Men about to depart for the hills to find volunteers received their back-pay at the depot before they left. Married men with families in the cantonments were less likely to recruit successfully, since they would give most of their pay to their wives and children with the regiment. But the army authorities did not believe that many men would enlist for pay alone, and sometimes expressed suspicion of those that seemed to have done so. 'The appearance of well being, and the tales of life in our service, attract the potential recruit just as much as the fact that all soldiers appear to have plenty of money.'[51] Experience during the Great War suggested that soldiers who had been in the ranks for only a few months also made good recruiters, since they returned to their villages 'full of enthusiasm and self-esteem' and looking better for good food, regular exercise and a smart uniform.[52]

It was not just the amount of pay that attracted men to the Indian Army, but its certain and regular arrival. This simple fact was central to the ability of the East India Company to dismantle or defeat pre-colonial polities. Most Indian states did not have a system of revenue able to pay an army and keep it in the field for long. Tipu Sultan's regime in Mysore, and the Sikh state in the Punjab were possible exceptions; for this reason they caused the company far more anxiety than did, for example, the Maratha kingdoms.[53]

The British stood out from other polities in the Indian subcontinent because they could maintain well-paid armies in the field almost indefinitely.[54] This was originally because they collected the vast revenues of Bengal.[55] The military importance of regular and reliable pay hardly diminished when Britain became the paramount power in India, however. Evidence from the Great War shows that soldiers drew comfort from being able to trust their paymasters, even if they died in battle themselves. 'You are continually asking me to send you more money', wrote a Muslim sowar to his father. 'You think that perhaps I shall be killed and the money lost. Do not be disturbed. If I die the Sircar will make up my account to the very *pie* and will remit the amount to you.'[56] This sense of security, which survived the hazards of war, rested on a belief that the British Raj was bound to endure. 'My friend, as long as British rule lasts, my money is quite safe; it cannot be lost', remarked one man.[57] 'It is next to impossible for the British Raj to pass away', thought another.[58] There were occasional discrepancies in the pay books – 'dogs' ears on cats' heads', according to one trooper – and these caused great irritation; but they were very rare.[59]

The Indian soldiers often referred to their pay as 'salt', and when they received wages they called it 'eating salt'. This harked back to the time when salt was used as currency. Like gold or cowries, salt was of high value and easy to carry, and was hence able to function as money – denoting price, storing wealth and acting as a means of exchange. According to the troops, to 'eat salt' was to incur an obligation to a paymaster or person from whom salt was taken. For soldiers, this duty was to fight, and if necessary to die, in government service. 'Who is there whom this war has not saddened and depressed?', wrote a Muslim trooper in April 1917. 'But one is bound to discharge the obligation laid on him. It was for this that for generations our family have been eating the salt of the Sircar. Therefore this is no time to be disturbed in mind and for turning one's face away from duty. Rather it is the time for showing valour.'[60] (He went on to ask God to end the war in a few days.) There are many similar examples of soldiers saying that they had incurred an obligation as a result of eating salt. Sometimes they detailed the benefits they had received – such as pay, pensions, freedom from hard labour, and an easy life in a peacetime cantonment.[61]

The duties of the soldiers, however, were part of a system of deepening reciprocity. The troops believed that taking salt incurred obligations, but they also held that discharging these duties entitled them to ask more favours of the authorities, or to refuse to perform other tasks – especially in wartime. When the grandfather of a Jat lancer lost face after being denied the right to own a breech-loading rifle, a relative told the trooper, 'You are in a position to remove the disgrace. The Sircar gives ear to the complaint of soldiers. I feel confident that he will not deny you, seeing that our family are getting their heads cut off for the Sircar and have done so for generations. Will the Sircar then continue to deny us this trifling concession?'[62] Other soldiers told their families not to give money to the War Loan or buy War Bonds, because they had given the government enough help already by sending a son to fight.[63] 'Tell them that your son has spent three years under shell fire, and this is your contribution. No other subscription is necessary', said one.[64] Taking salt or pay was only the visible and legal element in a more complex implicit contract involving a series of rights and duties.

The British went along with this system of reciprocal obligation in order to avert unrest in the army or the recruiting grounds. Soldiers thus gained privileged access to authority, enabling them to appeal over the heads of oppressive Indian officials to a British superior. District officers on tour made a point of talking to soldiers, and were often met by uniformed bodies of pensioners with petitions. The number of such requests grew during the Great War, as serving soldiers realized that they could use their position to bargain concessions from the government. In the first six months of 1916, Rawalpindi district alone received 2388 petitions from men in the ranks.[65] Most were demands for patronage for their relatives – jobs as local officials, release from debt or imprisonment, or free grazing on government land. The local administration usually looked into their requests. Soldiers had similar access to politicians of the Punjab Unionist Party, in office after 1937. Since the franchise was biased in favour of veterans, the party had to listen; and its agrarian laws and spending usually favoured the enlisted classes.[66]

Wartime Incentives and Pressures

The normal inducements of pay and privilege were attractive, but on their own were not enough to maintain a steady flow of new recruits in wartime. During the unpopular Afghan campaign of 1879–80, the rate of enlistment was too low to replace losses at the front. The army introduced a bounty of 25 rupees on enlistment and a further 25 rupees on discharge after three years, but even this produced only 1422 more men between April and September 1880.[67] According to the 1912 Nicholson Committee, recruitment would decline in a serious war unless the conditions of field service were improved.[68]

When a serious war did come, in 1914, there was at first no lack of volunteers; but the face of battle on the Western Front came as a tremendous shock to the sepoys. By early the following year many had come to regret enlisting.[69] 'My friend, bread [soldiering for pay] has sent me here, alas my belly has destroyed me', wrote one.[70] Tales of squalor, carnage and biting cold began to appear in the soldiers' letters, and soon circulated freely in India. With men writing things like 'do not let Sher Baz Khan so much as hear the words "military service"', it is not surprising that enlistments fell – from 14 201 in February and March 1915, to 10 397 in April and May.[71] This was far more than in peacetime, but still not enough. Standards were lowered. The minimum height for Sikh recruits was five foot nine before the war, but men of five foot three were taken.[72] The new recruits did not always impress. 'They are very stupid and many of them upwards of thirty years of age', wrote a disillusioned Lance Dafadar from a cavalry depot.[73]

Recruiting remained a problem, so more temptations were offered.[74] All troops on active service in Europe received a pay rise of 25 per cent. Uniforms were issued free. From January 1917, all combatants and some auxiliaries received free rations even when not on active service, while pay and pensions were also improved.[75] From mid-1917, all new recruits received a bounty of 50 rupees, which made families much more willing to part with a breadwinner.[76] A further war bonus of four rupees a month was issued from April 1918.[77] The most active recruiters and fundraisers were granted land. The villages and districts which produced the most men were given remissions of revenue.

But material incentives alone failed to bring forward enough volunteers, so a quota system was introduced. Each province or district was instructed to provide a given number of men over a specified time. 'But it was clearly laid down that there was to be nothing savouring of compulsion', recalled the Governor of the Punjab, Sir Michael O'Dwyer.[78] In practice, however, policy was less scrupulous than this. Local Indian officials were made responsible for obtaining the men. Fearing the loss of their jobs if they failed, they resorted to intimidation, bribery and even kidnapping.[79]

After the Armistice, the quota system was ended, but several of the material emoluments remained. Although the General Staff feared that high rates of pay might 'attract those who became soldiers for purely monetary motives as opposed to the better classes, which have supplied recruits for several generations', the basic pay of a sepoy was raised to 16 rupees a month in 1921.[80] There were several reasons for this. During the war and its aftermath the Indian soldiers had encountered the wider world – their ideas of comfort had changed, they had acquired new tastes, and they were more apt to compare their pay with that of British troops.[81] Industrial development and agricultural prosperity weakened the incentive to enlist; the population was war-weary, and would-be soldiers were loath to spend long periods overseas on garrison duty.[82] Furthermore, the widespread political unrest in India immediately after the war made it essential to keep the army loyal. 'No one can possibly say whether there will be any Government in India within a few years', remarked a pessimistic Lord Sydenham in February 1921. 'Authority is at a very low ebb over large areas of the subcontinent.'[83] The troops had to be paid well, thought one Conservative MP, 'for we must have a contented army, or we are indeed undone'.[84] The policy seemed to work, for the upheavals of the 1920s and 1930s never greatly disturbed military discipline.[85]

Army Pay and the Rural Economy

The soldiers sent much of their pay to their families, often to help them survive on scanty holdings. Men who did not send any pay home were often scorned by their village.[86] 'Shame on your pretensions to bravery while you leave your children to be fed by charity!', wrote one irate neighbour to a parsimonious havildar. 'Today your wife was about to commit suicide by throwing herself into a well owing to your neglect of her.'[87] Soldiers who received angry letters like this often complained that their remittances had simply not arrived; but the British authorities preferred to believe that they were just lying to disguise their meanness.[88]

In general, the soldiers had plenty of opportunities to save, especially on active service when rations were free and there were few temptations to spend. The significance of this flow of military money into the villages is not clear from the all-India picture, however. The geographical pattern of recruiting was very uneven, and its local impact varied greatly between different communities. During the Great War, Kangra district sent 16 000 of its 401 109 males to the army; but 12 000 of the Kangra soldiers were Rajputs from a Rajput male population of only 56 400.[89] Some villages depended almost entirely on military income, most of their able-bodied men having joined up. In Jhelum, Rawalpindi and Attock districts in the heavily-recruited North-Western Punjab, soldiers and pensioners received 14 million rupees from the Government of India in 1939.

Remittances home were in steady decline in the nineteenth century, as military wages fell in real terms. They were higher between 1919 and 1939, but were highest of all during the Great War, when recruits received special bounties.[90] Apart from pay, military activity in the broadest sense was a welcome stimulus to the economy of the Punjab. Army camps, military contracts and strategic communications – all provided scope for peasant initiative. The economic life of some peasants came to centre on the cantonments, which offered new outlets for market gardening, mule-breeding and the carriage of goods. Cantonments also led to urban growth. Some towns were largely the product of the military presence. Rawalpindi, for instance, grew from being a small fort at annexation to become the third largest city of the Punjab. (In 1921, 46 000 of its 101 000 inhabitants lived in the cantonment.) By then, the nine largest cities of the Punjab all contained garrisons. These military centres attracted clusters of European settlement, which created new markets for local goods. Cantonments were partly the product of improved communications, which enabled troops to be held in masses and moved to where they were needed, instead of being scattered across the country. Excellent military roads and strategic railways also helped to generate trade and brought the agriculture of the Punjab into closer touch with the world economy. Nepal also benefited greatly from soldiers' earnings; until the advent of mass tourism, Gurkha pay was the country's main source of foreign currency.[91]

Army pay and military markets brought about social change.[92] In the Punjab, this strengthened the middle peasantry in the recruited tracts and weakened the hold of landlords, moneylenders and officials. Middle-ranking cultivators such as Jats and Gujars were the most responsive both to the new markets and to military service. Peasants who had gained wealth through association with the army preferred to invest it in land – partly for cultural reasons, but mainly because the real value of land did not decline. Income from military sources could redeem mortgages on land or repay other debts. Some landless or sharecropping groups entered the land market for the first time as a result of having access to the army. There was a steady drift of land away from landlord groups such as Gakhars and Janjuas towards the cultivators. The army also loosened the grip of moneylenders, since some peasants could now earn cash elsewhere. Once they had amassed some capital, cultivators sometimes took to lending money – often at more attractive rates than those offered by traditional moneylending groups.

Peasants with military links clearly improved their long-term economic prospects. By 1939, men with fewer than 15 acres owned three-quarters of all cultivated land in Rawalpindi – one of the most heavily-recruited districts – compared with one-third of that in the Punjab as a whole. The houses of peasant-soldiers reflected their improved fortunes. Among the Garewal Jats, who held 75 villages in Ludhiana district, 'the complete change from mud huts to "pukka" houses, testifies to the money which the sepoys' savings has brought to their villages'.[93]

Leave, Food, Health and Clothing

While military service often improved the lot of a recruit's dependents, the conditions of service also had to be attractive enough to induce him to join. For this reason, the authorities granted generous paid leave and furlough to allow soldiers to take part in the harvest or in domestic ceremonies.[94] In peacetime, up to 30 per cent of a unit could be absent at once in the seven-month furlough season, and up to 10 per cent in the drill season, according to the 1923 regulations.[95] If a unit was destined to serve overseas, all ranks would normally receive three-and-a-half months' furlough before departure. The rules concerning leave were most attentive to the mens' ritual and religious needs, to avert the problems of discipline that were otherwise envisaged.[96] Muslims from the Deccan, for example, normally had 12 days' leave to attend ceremonies of birth, 15 or eight days to attend the marriage of close or distant kin, and 12 days after the death of a relative – although there was no fixed length for circumcision.[97] In practice, leave was much longer than this, for it also allowed for travelling time, and the distance of a soldier's home from a railway. Service overseas posed a problem, since it was not usually compatible with the preferred policy. During the Great War, some men had been away from their homes for almost two years before leave was first granted in September 1916.[98]

Obtaining plenty to eat was a further material incentive to join the army, particularly for less prosperous cultivators; but it was also a potential area of conflict, since cooking and eating carried much ritual significance. For most of the nineteenth century, soldiers bought their own rations from local suppliers. Before 1857, Brahmin sepoys in the Bengal Army prepared their food individually, paying great attention to its ritual purity; but they often made do with one meal a day, since such preparation was a lengthy process. When cooking was impossible they lived 'for days together on parched grain and sweetmeats, for they are a most frugal and abstemious race'.[99] Men from poor backgrounds, such as Mazbhi Sikhs, were found to 'improve physically in a marvellous manner after they have been a few months in the service', because they could now afford enough to eat.[100] The same was true of Garhwalis from impoverished areas, and of poorer Mian Rajputs who had a prejudice against agriculture.[101] Recruits acquired a liking for a more varied diet, which helped keep food prices buoyant in the Punjab, as veterans had enough money to satisfy the more diverse tastes they had picked up on service. Tea-drinking in particular became a habit in the rural areas before the Great War.[102]

Matters of health and medicine were a related area vital to the morale and cohesion of the army. Before the twentieth century, diseases like cholera and malaria killed far more soldiers than warfare ever did. There was a close connection between cholera and military power in colonial India – troops crowded in poor sanitary conditions were especially vulnerable to the disease; and as they marched about the country they were one of its main vectors.[103] Any cholera attack was likely to devastate morale. Its onset was sudden, those who contracted it usually died, and it claimed its victims in an especially violent and distressing manner.[104] In the early nineteenth century, when very little was known about the origins and spread of the disease, effective measures against cholera were few. Afflicted regiments would normally disperse from the affected site into 'cholera camps', and there await the end of the attack. This policy could work, since it unwittingly took the troops away from the water that bore the disease; but it could also infect the hapless people of the country through which the soldiers marched.

Once something was known of the origins of cholera, the colonial authorities had more incentive to act when it afflicted soldiers than when it struck the civil population. Cholera in the army weakened a vital prop of colonial rule; but the government feared religious unrest if they imposed measures to curb its spread among the civil population, because one of the main vectors was the water which Hindu pilgrims carried back to their villages.[105] It was far less contentious to improve army sanitation; and from the 1860s a programme of barrack-building did much to reduce the death toll from cholera. Nevertheless, by the eve of the Great War, many men still had to build their own huts; and it was not until the early 1930s that most Indian soldiers were housed in 'comfortable and airy barracks and in healthy sanitary surroundings'.[106]

In the nineteenth century, these improvements in living conditions did more than advances in medicine to combat disease in the army (although quinine began to be used to prevent malaria). The Indian Medical Service was formed in 1896 from the three military establishments of Bombay, Bengal and Madras.[107] Its leading lights made some important contributions to the study of tropical disease; but the service remained rudimentary. Until the Great War, there were no hospitals for Indian troops, other than regimental medical centres. Indian soldiers wounded on the Western Front were sent to hospitals in the south of England; and their letters show that they warmly appreciated the efforts that were made to ensure their comfort.[108]

A smart uniform has often attracted a young man to military service; but had he joined the nineteenth-century Indian Army he might have been dismayed to learn that he had to pay for it. Deductions were made from the wages of a recruit until the cost of his uniform had been recovered. Soldiers even had to buy their own shoes, rather than being issued with army boots. 'A good type of boot is one of the greatest needs of the Native soldier of the present', reported the Eden Commission in 1879.[109] From the Great War, to attract more recruits, uniforms were issued free. The soldiers seemed to be impressed. 'If a sepoy chooses, he can get as much clothing as he likes', wrote one. 'If he wears out four pairs of boots a week, he can do so. But no one takes any account of these admirable and expensive things. It is as if the government had resolved to think nothing of expense in this campaign.'[110]

Sex and Marriage

Material incentives may have attracted many men into the ranks; but the thought of leaving wives, or of remaining unmarried, could act as a deterrent to prolonged military service, especially in the North. British policy tried to take account of this.

The status of soldiers' wives in India varied from army to army. In the late-nineteenth-century Madras Army, married soldiers could bring their wives and children with them to the cantonments at their own expense, even when their regiments were posted to Burma.[111] This policy had its advantages: the men would regard the regiment as their home, and hence be more content; they would serve for longer, and perhaps settle nearby when they left the army; and their sons might join the regiment when they came of age.[112] The presence of their loved ones was also thought to give the men a stake in the system: or as one British observer cynically put it, 'the wives and families act as hostages for the good behaviour of the men – no small consideration with a mercenary army'.[113] The Madras Army did not mutiny in 1857 partly for this reason, thought George MacMunn.[114] But families encumbered the army, slowed its movements, and – according to Lord Roberts – drained the 'martial spirit' of the soldiers. Roberts tended to favour military effectiveness over political safety, so he tried to reduce the number of wives in camp when he commanded at Madras in the early 1880s.[115]

In the Bengal and Bombay Armies, the soldiers' wives normally stayed in the villages, although a quota of men were allowed to have their families with them. The troops usually served for a shorter time, and used their frequent leave to visit their homes. This system also had its problems. Good soldiers might quit the regiment after a few years' service to rejoin their loved ones: others visited prostitutes and picked up sexually-transmitted infections. Stationed at Almora in the midst of 'a hopelessly diseased population', 1/3 Gurkhas suffered badly from this problem.[116] In 1891, as a trial, the men were given financial inducements to bring their wives to the cantonment. The number of venereal cases fell sharply, and the discipline of the battalion greatly improved. Only a lack of money prevented the policy from being more widely adopted. By 1921, however, married quarters were routinely provided for about 9 per cent of Indian Army ranks, except Gurkhas, who were given 27 per cent.[117] The Gurkha regiments needed more, as their men usually served longer, and often settled in their permanent Indian stations.[118]

The sexual needs of the soldiers became more of a disciplinary problem when the Indian troops were sent to Europe in the Great War. Much contemporary popular culture saw soldiers as sexy. To outsiders at least, a military life might appear glamorous, dealing as it did in the currency of violence with its subliminal sexual content.[119] The soldier embodied an especially strong masculine ideal, while military drill and discipline, with their connotations of domination and submission, invested a uniform with a powerful sexual aura. Many cultures link military with sexual prowess, and imperial soldiering had the romantic advantage of association with distant and unknown lands. The frequent separations and dislocations of military life might easily disrupt established sexual mores, while encounters between white women and Indian troops could be charged with the heightened curiosity of racial and cultural difference. It is not surprising that, soon after they arrived in Europe, Indian soldiers began to enjoy the most tangible of all rewards.

Indian troops at Base Camp in Marseille were 'able to obtain access to the women of the neighbourhood', and some illicit sex took place.[120] Men recovering in Brighton or Bournemouth from wounds received on the Western Front also used to walk out with white women.[121] Brighton 'is covered with girls who make a lot of the natives. They are very fond of coloured people', noted a British medical subordinate.[122] The women in question do not appear to have been prostitutes: according to a Maratha soldier, eager French women paid Sikh troops between six and eight francs a time to have sex with them – although this may simply be a rumour reflecting the dim view Marathas took of Sikhs.[123] Letters written by French women to troopers of the Indian Cavalry Corps were often of a 'violently amatory nature'.[124] The authorities regarded these encounters as 'prejudicial to good discipline', and did their best to keep Indian troops under strict surveillance.[125] Sex with English women was considered 'detrimental to the prestige and spirit of European rule'.[126]

Some Indian troops also thought these liaisons were distasteful. Two Muslim sepoys believed that young women were 'the proper task for young men'. But they had reservations about pork-eating Frenchwomen. 'They are all Kafirs. And their food is very vile; that is to say they feed upon that thing whose very name we cannot take.'[127] A Sikh soldier had similarly mixed feelings about French 'water drawing machines' [women]. 'The sight of them delights us, but we are ashamed to touch them lest we lose caste.'[128] Pathan soldiers were less ambivalent about their homosexual relationships. One man, pining in Milford-on-Sea for a comrade who had been transferred to

France, sent him a large selection of amorous postcards. 'I was very much annoyed at your departure', he wrote. But he managed to ease the pangs of separation: 'now I have a beautiful white boy. He is my mess-mate, and I am very happy'.[129]

As the war dragged on, some of these temporary liaisons became more stable. Indian soldiers often wrote home to praise the independence, courage and intelligence of European women; and sometimes they married them.[130] In the winter of 1916–17 the authorities decided to sanction marriages between Muslim soldiers and French women, although permission was not extended to Hindus.[131]

Several unions did take place, but comrades and relatives of the Indian party often expressed doubts, especially if the man intended to convert from Islam to Christianity.[132] Even when the girl promised to convert, the Indian family might still disapprove. One anxious husband-to-be, trooper Mahomed Khan of 6 Cavalry, felt 'ashamed and unable to hold up my head' because he had not asked permission of his kin before he agreed to wed.[133] He was reduced to claiming that the girl had secretly obtained the sanction of the King, and he could not refuse her. 'But do not be anxious', he continued. 'God will protect us – and she has plenty of money.'[134] A Hindu supply and transport agent, Mehta Deoki Nandan, got short shrift from his father when he told him he wanted to marry a French girl. 'Have you no shame? Could a man be so perverted as to lose his religion for the sake of a woman? It is the greatest disgrace for a Hindu to become a Mahomedan or a Christian; do not therefore blacken your face before the whole world. Take care how you bring such a woman to my home, for she will be beaten on the head with a shoe a thousand times.'[135]

Some betrothed couples had to endure the anguish of separation when the soldier was sent back to India. 'Whatever you have written about Bernadette is entirely false', wrote one anxious lover to a comrade who had remained in France. 'She has given me her youthful promise that she will never look at another man. Further, my actual seal remains imprinted on her, and no one has the power to break it. Don't you even contemplate breaking it yourself, or in place of bread you will eat sawdust.'[136]

INCENTIVE STRUCTURES

We must now leave affairs of the heart, and return to matters of the pocket. It was British policy to make enlistment as attractive as possible; but the authorities also structured the material rewards of soldiering to give the men an interest in conforming to military discipline. A soldier who gave years of obedient service would gain higher status and income.

Incentives of Cash and Status

Good conduct pay, introduced in 1837, was the simplest of these incentives. Men who had kept a clean sheet for two years received an extra rupee a month after 16 years' service, and two rupees a month after 20.[137] These terms were far from generous, and were gradually made more attractive over the next half-century.[138] In 1877, for example, the scales were changed so that obedient sepoys received an extra rupee a month after three years' service, two rupees after nine years, and three rupees after 15.[139]

Pay differentials between the Indian ranks were probably more important, however. An infantry havildar (or Indian sergeant) received fourteen rupees a month – double the basic pay of a sepoy before 1895.[140] The income of Indian officers was the most attractive of all. The four senior subedars of an infantry battalion each earned no less than 100 rupees a month, according to the 1877 pay scales. As early as 1861, the six troop commanders of an irregular cavalry regiment each received between 120 and 300 rupees.[141] It was not surprising that an Indian officer was often highly successful at recruiting. 'His position is a sufficient guarantee to all he comes in contact with, that service in the Army is honourable and paying.'[142] The prospect of promotion was a major incentive to stay in the army, and to adapt to its discipline.

Men would normally become officers only after long and loyal service, since the authorities usually took the view that promotion by merit rather than seniority might threaten discipline. The motives behind enlistment also influenced the length of time a man remained in the army. Men who had joined to buy more land or to insure against famine might leave when they had saved enough money to do so; but those who had joined to stave off long-term economic decline would be more likely to stay until pensioned. Soldiers normally remained fit until they were 40 or 45, when they might have served for 20 or 25 years. In the second half of the nineteenth century, however, few men stayed in the army that long, especially in the north. In 1885, veterans with 20 years' service made up only 3 per cent of the Bengal infantry, and 7 per cent of the

Bombay Army. Only in the Madras Army, where 14 per cent of men had served for 20 years or more, was long service at all widespread.[143]

The pension structure also influenced the typical length of service, the decision to enlist, and soldiers' attitudes to military service.[144] The regulations of 1864 allowed a man to retire on a full pension of seven rupees a month after 40 years' service, or of four rupees if invalided after 15 years.[145] The system proved to be 'unpopular' and 'radically defective'. A pension after 40 years in the ranks was effectively no pension at all, since very few men could expect to serve, or even live, that long.[146] Decrepit and senile men stayed on; many others malingered after completing 15 years, in the hope of retiring on the lower pension. The 'stout, hearty fellows, who turn out to be pensioned sepoys' on invalidity benefits were a noted feature of some recruiting grounds.[147]

Reforms were needed for several reasons – to eradicate malingering, to allow the timely removal of the ineffective, and to ensure that men who had given long and loyal service to the government were clearly seen to be well rewarded.[148] In 1876, the full pension requirement was reduced from 40 to 32 years.[149] Even this proved to be too long. Only about one hundred men of the Bengal Army and the Punjab Frontier Force served on to their full pension every year; but about 4600 – many of them malingerers – left with the benefits due to invalids. From 1886, a man could retire on full pension after only 21 years' service, while any soldier discharged as an invalid after 15 years merely received a bounty of one year's pay.[150] Men discharged as a result of wounds suffered on active service received a pension, as did their dependants if the soldier were killed. By the end of the Great War, however, inflation meant that the widow's pension of four rupees a month hardly kept her and her children from starvation, so it was raised to eight rupees with a further two for each child she had to support.[151] Further problems occurred when addresses in the regimental rolls were vague or incorrect, and pensioners or heirs could not be traced.[152] By the early 1920s this was 'the only real cause of discontent among the military classes', according to the General Staff.[153] The authorities worked hard to trace all beneficiaries because it fostered contentment and reacted favourably on recruiting.[154]

The authorities also tried to enhance the civil status of soldiers. This improved the image of military service, stimulated recruiting, and encouraged cooperation with the government. In 1899, Lord

Roberts revived a dormant order granting soldiers precedence in the hearing of civil suits.[155] Five years later, Lord Kitchener persuaded the Prime Minister of Nepal to exempt former Gurkhas from corvée works. 'This greatly improves our position as it gives our men on their return great *izzat* in their villages', he told Roberts with delight.[156] Former soldiers could also be honoured on public and festive occasions. At the Delhi Durbar of 1903, the surviving Mutiny veterans – both British and Indian – shared with Lord Curzon and the Duke and Duchess of Connaught the privilege of entering the arena along the road leading to the Viceroy's dais. The soldiers were old men; some were blind, and others lame; many had to be helped along – but all received a magnificent ovation as they completed their sedate lap of honour, proudly wearing their red and white medal ribbons.[157] The Great War induced further measures to win respect for soldiers. They and their relatives gained preferential treatment in Punjab government appointments; the children of the dead or disabled received free primary education; and Gurkhas who had fallen behind in revenue payments were secured against the seizure of their lands.[158] Those who had marched with the Indian Army were to walk tall when they went back to their villages.

The Longing for Land

While peasant soldiers were glad to win prestige and pensions, they desired nothing so much as land. The grant of a fertile plot was always the most popular reward for long and loyal military service, and the government was in the happy position of being able to repay its most devoted servants. Much more government land became available in the later nineteenth century, as the Public Works Department undertook vast irrigation projects in the Punjab, in the Western United Provinces, and in parts of Madras.[159] These schemes aimed to increase land revenue and to improve the condition of the people. Modern irrigation methods made the water supply predictable, and helped prevent the crop failures that sometimes occurred when agriculture depended on shallow flood channels. The works were especially extensive in the interfluvial tracts, or *doabs*, of the Punjab.[160] The valleys of the Sutlej and the Indus, which had once supported flourishing settlements, had long since become arid or reverted to pasture. From the 1880s, large tracts were restored to agriculture and repopulated. The Lower Chenab Canal was built between 1892 and 1905; and the area watered by the Lower Bari Doab Canal, completed in 1917, was colonized by 1922. The increase in the irrigated area was prodigious. In 1880 there were a little over one million irrigated acres in the Punjab, but by 1917 more than four million were artificially watered.[161]

Soldiers clamoured for their share.[162] 'Were the whole of India turned into a Garden of Eden and portioned out amongst ex-soldiers, there would still remain the demand for grants of land', noted the General Staff in 1923.[163] Parcels of land were used as rewards for loyal military service before the canal colony development – after the Mutiny and the Second Afghan War, for example – but not on a large scale.[164] The recruited groups gained large amounts of state land only after the major irrigation projects had begun. The canal colonies were gradually militarized, as the government sought to bind the enlisted classes closer to the Raj.[165] Grants of irrigated land were originally made to officers as they retired. Similar opportunities were rarely offered to the other ranks, but the prospect of promotion and resettlement must have been a powerful incentive to those who planned to serve for long. By 1911, the government had adopted the principle that any canal colony scheme had to make provision for the military.[166] During and after the Great War, far more land was set aside for soldiers. Sir Michael O'Dwyer, the Governor of the Punjab, reserved 178 000 acres in the Lower Bari Doab for officers and men who had served with distinction in the field. 'This was the most effective of all inducements to the Punjab peasant', he said.[167] The land was parcelled out in a little over 7000 'rectangles' of twenty-five acres each – officer-grantees received two of these, and other ranks one.[168] Given that the average holding in the Punjab was a mere eight acres, the plots were highly desirable. Between 1919 and 1939, the Punjab Government gave one-third of a million acres of prime irrigated land to military grantees.[169]

The allocation of land to soldiers could create geographical and social mobility – as in the case of the Mazhbi Sikhs, a group of mainly landless menials, descended from Hindu Untouchables and despised by their Jat co-religionists. Numbering about 21 500 in 1911, they normally made up about a fifth or a quarter of the population of the Jat-majority villages in which most of them lived. The Mazhbis served in their own infantry and pioneer units. Their British officers suggested, and Lord Roberts sponsored, a scheme to make grants of land on the Chenab Canal to Mazhbi soldiers with more than 15 years' service. Officers received 50 acres and other ranks 20 in Gujranwala district, which it was hoped would become 'a really valuable recruiting ground'.[170] Thus the military connection transformed some impoverished menial groups into prosperous cultivators.

The canal colonies strengthened the ties between the army, the government and the vigorous middle peasantry of the Punjab. Grants of land made the government seem worth serving, while the settlements helped foster a collective military identity.[171] Paternalist legislation protected landholders from the encroachments of commercial and trading groups.[172] The alliance between the army and the enlisted classes sometimes shouldered the civil authorities aside, and military needs usually won priority.[173] These policies were prudent. It was a long time before nationalism made much headway in the Punjab; and the canal colonies normally remained pro-British, supporting the Punjab Unionist Party into the 1940s.[174]

For the Government of India, incentive structures such as good conduct pay, pensions and land had one great advantage – they could be withdrawn. The knowledge that hard-won privileges could be lost gave the high command important influence over present and former soldiers. The authorities were prepared to use this lever. In 1910, for example, sepoy Kunwar Singh lost his mark of good conduct for wearing the *jamu* – the sacred thread of the Brahmins affected by the adherents of the supposedly subversive Arya Samaj.[175] In the Bengal Army in 1865, 17 465 men had served for less than six years, and hence did not qualify for good conduct pay; 19 371 received the privilege; and 292 had lost it.[176] In the early 1920s, when there was much civil unrest, some pensioners and old soldiers who had received land in return for good service in the Great War indulged in 'seditious activities'.[177] Such men had influence on the ranks, so the government ordered that those convicted of sedition should lose their pensions or land, or both, with no hope of restoration. These harsh measures worked, discouraging the subversive and satisfying the loyal. They were revived in 1930, during Gandhi's campaign of civil disobedience.[178]

The Silladar Cavalry

Incentive structures were especially important in the silladar cavalry. In the irregular silladar regiments, men were originally accepted into the ranks only if they could provide their own horse, arms and equipment. They were paid the high wage of 20 or 30 rupees a month, but from this they had to find the money for food, clothing, arms, fodder and perhaps a grass cutter or servant.[179] If their horse was killed on active service they received free compensation; but if the animal died of natural causes, they drew on a regimental insurance fund to which they had to contribute.[180] There were problems with this system. The pay was too little, and the men fell into debt; they bought cheap and flimsy weapons of no standard pattern; and they were often poorly mounted since they could rarely afford the sort of horses which the regular cavalry rode.[181] By degrees the system changed in the third quarter of the nineteenth century.[182] Recruits began to turn up with a deposit, or *assami*, of about 250 rupees in cash. For this they would receive a horse bred on a regimental stud farm, a government rifle, and equipment of regimental pattern. Since the total value of these items was about 500 or 550 rupees, they would have about 50 rupees deducted from their wages each year to insure and pay for them. When a man had cleared his debts, he could leave the regiment, trading in his horse and equipment for an *assami* of about 500 rupees in cash.[183]

The silladar system had several advantages for the government. In the first place, it was cheap.[184] The government did not have to find rations for the men or fodder for the horses except in wartime; nor did they have to look after the sick or provide transport. This cut down the cumbersome and expensive 'tail' of the army; and it proved economical and effective in Frontier war. The system also encouraged the independence, self-reliance, and responsibility of the men, who knew they had to shift for themselves.[185] The silladar cavalry enjoyed great *izzat* in their villages, for a discharged trooper might return with a very impressive 500 rupees in his pocket. This made the army more popular, especially among men of higher social status than was typical of the infantry.[186] The troopers were also likely to take good care of their horse and equipment if they knew that they had to replace them. Above all, the *assami* was a bond for good behaviour. A man honourably discharged would receive his *assami* in full; but a man discharged in disgrace lost all the credit he had accumulated on the regimental funds.[187] The threat of dismissal was therefore a major deterrent to disgraceful behaviour; and 'the fact of a man having a stake in this regiment, and consequently in Government, is a political advantage'.[188] The *assamis* of soldiers killed on active service were returned to the next-of-kin, which saved the trouble and expense of providing pensions.[189] For these reasons, the silladar system was extended until, by 1903, 36 of the 39 cavalry regiments were run along these lines.[190]

The silladar system worked well in peacetime and in Frontier skirmishes, but it could not deal with the many casualties of a lengthy conflict.[191] The Great War exposed its shortcomings. Heavy losses meant that regiments had to accept men who brought no *assami*.[192] By 1918, the average recruit joined with only 50 rupees, and would remain in debt to the regiment for many years.[193] The basic incentive underlying the silladar system had therefore ceased to operate. Regiments could no longer remount their men from their own stud farms, owing to the enormous wastage in horses. If a unit suffered heavily in battle, the regimental funds might not be enough to repay *assamis* to the relatives of all the dead.[194] The 15 regiments serving in France each had their own pattern *talwar* and scabbard, and soon exhausted their reserves of these.[195] Because the regiments could not meet their wartime needs in horses, equipment and clothing, the government had to take control of most sources of supply. Most officers felt that the peacetime organization of the cavalry ought to resemble that which had proved most effective in modern war.[196] The silladar officers also complained that they were overburdened with non-military duties to the detriment of their professional skill and efficiency.[197]

In August 1916, a committee of silladar officers unanimously recommended that the system be abolished, not reformed: 'we regard it as fundamentally unsound to continue a system which practically ceases to exist on the outbreak of war, since it is axiomatic that an army must be organised in peace with reference to its obligations in war'. The government postponed the change until after the Armistice, as they did not want to unsettle the men at the front.[198] The Great War also exposed the declining usefulness of horsed cavalry – by 1917 the regiments on the Western Front were sent into the trenches to fight on foot. Accordingly, in 1921, the Government decided to reduce the cavalry by amalgamation from 39 regiments of four squadrons to 21 of three, and to abolish what remained of the silladar system. Regiments with historic associations and similar ethnic composition were combined into new corps which adopted as much as possible of the titles and distinctions of the old. Troopers who agreed to transfer received a bonus of 50 rupees; and men for whom no vacancy could be found were discharged with 25.[199] The Government paid off all outstanding *assamis*, and engaged the sowars at the new rate of 18 rupees a month, without deductions.[200] Henceforth, incentive structures in the cavalry closely resembled those in the regiments of regular foot.

CONCLUSION

British recruiting strategy alone did not dictate the social composition of the Indian Army. Enlistment was mainly voluntary, and Indian recruits would normally join the army only in the conscious pursuit of their own economic objectives. For many men, the decision to enter military service was partly one of deliberate self-interest. Peasants usually left the land for the army because they could not make a good living from agriculture alone – their holdings were too small, their soil was poor, or their crops periodically failed. A martial identity also helped men choose between the army and other non-agricultural options, although it could sometimes induce enlistment on its own.

Military service offered plenty of tangible rewards. Army pay was attractive and regular, although the supply of recruits might fall short when more lucrative work could be found nearby. Receiving pay – or 'salt' as they termed it – made soldiers feel obliged to the government; but the troops also believed that discharging their duties earned them further rights, such as privileged access to British officials. Soldiers saved much of their pay and sent it home, which benefited the military communities and stimulated the economy of the recruiting grounds in the Punjab. Apart from pay, the peacetime army (at least by the twentieth century) offered attractive conditions of work – including generous leave, plentiful food, a smart uniform and clean barracks. In wartime, when the hardships of campaign deterred enlistment, the authorities introduced further material incentives to make military service more attractive. For men serving in France during the Great War, sex with white women was another bonus – unlooked for at enlistment, but often taken up when available.

With good conduct pay, pensions and the prospect of promotion, the material rewards of soldiering were structured to give the troops a clear incentive to conform to military discipline. Successful efforts to enhance the status and well-being of veterans improved the image of the army, and made men more likely to volunteer. Grants of irrigated land in the canal colonies satisfied a deep yearning among peasant-soldier communities, and strengthened the relationship between the enlisted classes, the army and the Raj. The incentive structure of the silladar cavalry produced well-disciplined regiments for Frontier service, although the system did not long survive the strain of heavy losses in the Great War.

In these respects, the Indian Army was a mercenary force. Indian soldiers can be seen as a group of labour migrants, like those who left their rural homes to work in the mines, on the railways, or in the factories of Bombay, Calcutta and Madras. But rational self-interest only explains so much. The analogy between civilian workers and those in uniform breaks down as soon as any army goes to war, for then soldiers face the supreme test of their trade – their willingness to fight, and if need be to die. Soldiers had much in common with other migrant labourers; but the duties of a coolie on a tea plantation did not include laying down his life. Homo Oeconomicus never won a battle. We must now examine the forces of honour, identity and loyalty which sustained the Indian Army, not only in peacetime, but during the arduous trials of war.

3

Fighting Spirit

May God put victory into your grasp, and may the enemy never see your back – this is my constant prayer. Write your name in the list of heroes, that is the greatest honour. My lord, enter my name also, for I, too, long to join the strife. I am no coward.

I have but one request, which I beseech you to grant. I hear that five thousand women have been recruited for service in France, and I beg you to send in my name also. My heart is not made of glass. It throbs at the thought of war.

Letters to Prayag Singh, 2 Lancers, from his Rajput wife, 17 and 19 May 1917[1]

Motives are rarely simple, often mixed, and sometimes downright contradictory. There is clear evidence that economic pressures to leave the land, and the tangible rewards of military service, induced most Indian recruits to join the army. These peasant-soldiers seemed to pursue goals of material self-interest, entering the ranks after balancing the costs and benefits of the various options open to them. But the Indian Army did not fight just for pay. Although men may have enlisted to secure a living wage, they did not then face death in battle simply because the army had lined their pockets. Embattled armies deal in the currency of courage and loyalty, which cannot easily be reckoned in cash.

Experience taught the British that pay was not enough to motivate even a mercenary army. 'There can be no question that a contented servant is better than a discontented one. Unfortunately we have tried too much to purchase the contentment of our Native armies by increased pay. This has not answered its purpose', noted a committee under Sir John Lawrence in 1858.[2] 'It has enriched the sepoys, but not satisfied them.' Many believed that Indian soldiers fought for a complex of motives, of which money was only one.[3] Badly-paid mercenaries might well mutiny, but not all well-paid ones would fight. It is rarely an act of rational self-interest to risk death in battle, and it would be a feeble army indeed whose soldiers were motivated by nothing more than cool calculations of profit and loss.

This chapter discusses the intangible motives of the Indian ranks. The first section examines the workings of shame and honour. The second part considers the vital matter of identity (without which a military unit is little more than a fragile agglomeration of individuals). After explaining how *esprit de corps* was created and sustained in a very diverse army, it explores the relationship between regimental and other identities. The third section examines the attitudes of Indian soldiers to the various founts of colonial and military authority – regimental officers, the Commander-in-Chief, the government and the monarch.

HONOUR AND SHAME

Honour

Some soldiers joined the army not for economic reasons, but because it was the honourable and fitting thing to do. The Tiwanas, a group of wealthy Rajput landlords from Shahpur District in the Punjab, are one prominent case.[4] Even those groups who served mainly for pay, however, often had other less material incentives for enlisting. For example, the Garewal Jats, the leading Sikh clan of Ludhiana District, still looked upon military service as a matter of honour.[5] A naik (Indian corporal) of pioneers vividly expressed these mixed motives in a letter written from a Brighton hospital during the Great War:

> Today the sword of the Gaekwar, belonging to the Saria family, though for so long rusting, has at last been discovered. The inhabitants of Nepal, the Punjab, the Deccan, Satara, and Kolhapur, who have entered the service and given their names and are fighting against the enemy, can never be said to have done so merely

for the sake of pay. Anyone who makes such a statement becomes a liar before God.[6]

The Indian sepoys often enlisted for very different reasons from those of the men conscripted by hardship into the ranks of the nineteenth-century British army. 'The English soldier does not always come to the ranks because it is the most honourable career he knows', noted George MacMunn. 'In India', on the other hand, 'military service is a source of much honour and prestige.'[7]

Most of the men who chose the Indian Army as a career had a strong sense of honour, which the process of recruitment tended to reinforce. The Indian Army was very selective. Before 1914, it needed only about 20 000 recruits per year, and a regimental recruiting party would normally bring in only seven or eight men a month.[8] Because the peacetime manpower needs of the army were so small, the authorities could exclude all groups they suspected of being dishonourable – defined as unwillingness to react to a slight or to take part in a vendetta. Those groups who failed the test of honour risked losing a valuable source of employment, besides damaging their local reputation. Military policy therefore encouraged faction-feuds and violent reprisals in the recruiting grounds.[9]

Although recruits with a strong sense of honour were preferred, the army did not necessarily seek grown men whose values were already clearly formed: they might have proved resistant to the military ethos. Recruiters enlisting Marathas, for example, were warned against obtaining big, tall men, as these would normally be near the informal upper age-limit of 25 years. 'Such men, when they join, are more or less "set"; there is little room for further development, and they do not improve. The guiding principle should be "catch the recruit young. Feed, train and develop him yourself."'[10] The age of choice for recruits was about 17 or 18 years.[11] These impressionable youths could more easily imbibe military values and mores.[12]

The values of an army are put to a crucial test when it goes into battle. When sent to France during the Great War, some Indian soldiers took clear delight in the fierce fighting they encountered.[13] 'The Sikhs did not turn even their noses', wrote one wounded sepoy. 'They were keen for the fight, and where one man fell, another from behind stood in his place. And we took pleasure in the battle.'[14] One man found an almost aesthetic joy in watching the Indian troops advance during the battle of the Somme:

One forgets the achievements of Bonaparte when one sees what our men have done. How our heroes have gone forward, quite regardless of life, and crushed the head of the enemy on the ground! Battalion after battalion follow their music, filled with enthusiasm, just as a snake dances to the pipe of the charmer and darts forward to strike. Battalions go forward with even step, steadily and firmly, just as an elephant moves along the road swaying slightly from side to side, to show the worth of their valour. Truly even from the enemy's lips they must have wrung applause. Even the heavens do not cease from shedding tears on our warriors, so great is their valour.[15]

Another trooper, languishing in Baluchistan after having fought in Mesopotamia, missed the excitement of battle. 'I cannot describe how great fascination there is in fighting at the front. He who has never been present in action has seen nothing.'[16] He longed to return to the fighting. Several men expressed their delight when the Indian cavalry finally saw mounted combat on the Western front in April 1917.[17] But joy in battle was often mixed with fear and depression. Responses to so momentous an experience were rarely simple.

For most soldiers, fighting was not joyous or delightful in itself. A far more important motive for combat was the hope of winning honour and fame by taking part in battle and performing deeds of valour. When discussing these matters, men often spoke of *izzat* – an Urdu word which roughly translates as honour, reputation, credit and prestige.[18] Men gained or lost *izzat* in their own eyes and those of their fellow-soldiers according to a widely understood but informal code of conduct. Fame was closely linked to *izzat*.[19] If a man performed deeds which increased his *izzat*, he might be spoken of and remembered even after his death.[20] 'This is the time to show one's loyalty to the Sirkar, to earn a name for oneself. To die on the battlefield is glory. For a thousand years one's name will be remembered', wrote one sowar.[21] Several men regarded an undying reputation as compensation for physical death in battle.[22] 'Fighting is the work of brave men. Such men have passed away from this earth, who, although their bodies are dead, their name and fame live forever. Be therefore unconcerned.'[23] For others, behaving in a manner worthy of *izzat* gained them a more limited but perhaps no less important renown. 'You went to the war in 1914 and are still fighting the King's enemies on the field of battle', wrote one mother to her son, serving in France in 1917. 'I am heartily grateful to you for this faithfulness and loyalty, and will remember it to my dying breath.'[24]

The military authorities were well aware of the power of *izzat*, and therefore tried to structure rewards accordingly. In 1837, they founded two orders to recognize distinguished Indian soldiers. The first, the Order of British India, rewarded long, faithful and honourable service, carrying with it the title of Bahadur ('chief', or 'brave one'). The second, the Indian Order of Merit, was open to any Indian soldiers who showed conspicuous gallantry in the face of the enemy. The most elevated decoration for bravery, the Victoria Cross, was instituted in 1856, but Indian troops were excluded from the award until 1912.[25]

A political purpose informed the grant of some decorations. After heavy fighting in the early months of the Great War, the commander of the BEF, Sir John French, wanted to give more medals to the sepoys. Growing sedition among the Indian troops on the Western Front had made him anxious, and he thought that the army would be more likely to hold together if acts of courage gained wide publicity – sometimes combined with grants of land.[26] To emphasize the honour that went with decorations, they were to be presented, whenever possible, 'on parade with befitting ceremony'.[27]

Medals brought wealth as well as honour to those who earned them. By 1938, the award of the Military Cross carried with it an income of up to 40 rupees a month, and the Victoria Cross of up to 525 rupees a year.[28] It could pay well to be honourable. Conversely, dismissal from the service might also bring dismissal from a prestigious order, and the loss of valuable income.[29]

The military authorities judged the sepoys well. Ample evidence shows that Indian troops took great pleasure in receiving medals, especially if the King-Emperor presented them himself.[30] 'You may judge my delight at having received the Order of British India from the Sacred hand of His Majesty', wrote one risaldar.[31] 'I have some good news', commented another. 'For my work in the trenches I have been fortunate enough to get the Military Cross. All my trials are forgotten now after the grant of this great distinction.'[32] Others relished the opportunity which the Great War provided for winning several awards. 'Heretofore a "one medal man" has been accustomed to swagger amongst us, even though his medal was pinned to a shirt of coarse home spun cloth', wrote a Sikh sowar. 'You will understand [our worth] when we return with rows of medals on our breasts.'[33] Several men received letters from comrades and relatives in India, urging them not to return until they had won an award for courage – preferably the Victoria Cross.[34]

But even the award of a Victoria Cross did little to salve the pain of wounds. Subedar Mir Dost won a VC in the summer of 1915. 'The men who came from our regiment have done very well and will do so again. I want your congratulations. I have got the Victoria Cross', he wrote to a comrade on the North West Frontier.[35] But the brave Subedar had been wounded in the hand, losing the use of two fingers, and he also suffered badly from a gas injury. The pain clouded his joy over his decoration. 'The Victoria Cross is a very fine thing, but this gas gives me no rest. It has done for me', he said. The King sent for him to come and receive the award. Mir Dost then announced that he would ask of His Majesty that no wounded man should be sent back to the trenches when he had recovered – a widely-shared grievance.[36] Other men did not wait until they had won a VC before seeking a respite from the battle. 'The time for getting honour has passed', wrote one disillusioned sowar. 'I am trying hard to get back.'[37]

The mixed response of Mir Dost to his VC reveals some of the ambiguities which informed the Indian soldiers' feelings about honour. Many men sought to win honour so they could escape the fighting and return home to their loved ones in a socially acceptable way. As a homesick trooper remarked, towards the close of the Somme offensive: 'The time is near when the echoes of victory will be heard, and we, wearing the medals which are the reward of bravery, will be restored to the bosom of our beloved mother India.'[38] Notions of honour could also complicate bereavement. 'The news of the death of Munsha Singh was a great shock to me and I grieved greatly', wrote a Sikh lancer. 'But grief for such losses is unseemly, as they occurred in the Field of Honour.'[39] His belief that it was honourable to die in battle helped him bear the loss of a loved comrade, but his sense that he should not mourn such an honourable fate made him reluctant to grieve openly. For another trooper, the main attraction of death with honour was the thought that it would be quick and fairly painless. 'To die in battle is a glorious end. It is not well to die in one's bed wrapped up in a blanket. Better a bullet and then oblivion in ten minutes.'[40]

In each example discussed so far, Indian soldiers spoke of honour as something that was won or lost by individuals on their own behalf. But the troops talked far more often in collective terms – their actions would win *izzat* for a corporate body of which they were part. Occasionally, that collective entity was India itself. 'Our King will conquer his enemies very soon', wrote a Jat lancer. 'He will say "My brave sepoys have done splendidly and have gained great fame for India."'[41] Some at home urged the soldiers to fight bravely 'so that the Europeans may realize how gallant, loyal and self-sacrificing are the people of India' – perhaps with winning future political concessions in mind.[42] But these references to the concept of 'India' were very rare. Soldiers talked more often in terms of the 'great name' which a particular regiment had won for itself in battle.[43] Most common of all, however, was the language of family, clan and caste.[44] 'If we get any chance we will show the stuff our caste is made of', hoped a Jat cavalryman.[45] 'Before this war no one thought anything of our clan', wrote another Jat. 'But now it is definitely recognized as very warlike. Truly it has done excellent work.'[46] A Muslim jemadar neatly summed up the relationship between caste and *izzat*. 'Our caste has got to win a name by serving Government. We get our livelihood here all right, but what about our *izzat*? The whole object of military service is to raise the reputation of one's caste.'[47]

Shame: The Concomitant of Honour

Honour, whether individual or collective, could not exist without shame. Men who could not feel ashamed would never fight and die for their *izzat*. Soldiers often remarked in passing that desertion, cowardice and disloyalty were shameful.[48] For many, these beliefs were deeply held. For instance, the father of a Muslim sowar asked his son to obtain leave and come home from the trenches in France.

> It is sad to think [his son replied] that you served for twenty-five years, and yet you are unable to understand the present state of affairs! Moreover, you say all this on a post card and the consequence is that people ridicule me for what you say. Give my compliments to the writer of the card! Is it possible that anyone could go home on leave at such a time as this. Never write me such a letter again.[49]

Yet shame, being the mirror of honour, was equally ambiguous. Men expressed fear of disgrace and fear of physical punishment almost in the same breath. 'If you betray any cowardice, weakness or disloyalty you will be for ever dishonoured and disgraced', one cavalry officer told two friends. 'The man who fears on the battle-field is sure to be killed', he added.[50] Another man confided similar worries to his mother. 'I have no fear of death; but I am greatly concerned about my honour', he wrote. 'How could I say to anyone here that I do not wish to remain in France? If I were to say such a thing I should be shot.'[51] His words speak for all those confused and frightened men who feared dying honourably as heroes only a little less than they feared dying shamefully as cowards.

For soldiers, shame almost always originated on the battlefield as a result of an act of cowardice or disloyalty. But it could be experi-enced within a variety of relationships. A cowardly soldier would almost certainly feel ashamed in front of his immediate comrades. A battalion which had done badly in battle might collectively feel ashamed in relation to other units.[52] In December 1878, for instance, two Muslim sepoys of the 29 Punjab infantry fired shots at night to warn the Afghans of the regiment's secret approach. A Gurkha battalion was selected to lead the march instead, and as a result of this incident the Punjabis felt disgraced.[53] Soldiers who had behaved dishonourably might also feel shame when they returned home. Not all did so, however. Risaidar Faiz Mohamed Khan escaped the trenches in 1916 by feigning madness and trembling when he appeared before a medical board. 'The people in the village who saw him in good health were disgusted to see him shamming in this way but he had no shame at all.'[54]

Shame was infectious, and could be passed from the soldier to his immediate family. 'I shall be well pleased with you, if you do not turn your back on the enemy, so that our neighbours may not taunt us', wrote the mother of trooper Ahmed Khan of the Poona Horse.[55] A soldier who failed in battle knew that he might eventually have to face the scorn of his entire village, as well as the contempt of his comrades and the displeasure of his immediate superiors.[56]

The Indian soldier's sense of shame was bound up with his masculine identity. Because fighting was such a gendered activity, soldiers who behaved with dishonour were held to be imperfectly male. 'I met Gulam Shah', reported a Pathan sepoy, 'and he told me that Nur Shah was trying to make [men] desert. I think this is a very shameful matter, and not a man's work.'[57] Some men, like Ganga Singh, a Rajput trooper, thought that cowardly or disloyal soldiers had made themselves like women. He lamented that he had not been able to return to India to visit his mother during her recent mortal illness. 'Leave is impossible to get,' he wrote, 'and I would not go by practising deception as so many have done, by making themselves ill or by injuring themselves. Such conduct is fit for women only.'[58] One havildar identified betrayal as an especially female vice, after nearly two hundred men of the 26 Punjabis deserted. 'These were men who had eaten the salt of the Sirkar all their lives', he wrote. 'They acted treacherously as a woman would. This is not the conduct of a man. It is the business of men to fight. Now the Afridis have become like women.'[59] Cowardice had homosexual as well as effeminate connotations. 'He has blackened his face by enlisting in a regiment which does not go to the war', wrote a Rajput trooper of a timid acquaintance. 'He is doubtless a chicken hearted sodomite.'[60]

Shame was not always beyond redemption, however. The authorities sometimes gave disgraced soldiers a chance to redeem themselves through exemplary conduct. After Turkey entered hostilities against the British Empire in 1914, some Pathan units in Egypt and Mesopotamia began to waver. They were reluctant to fight against their fellow Muslims near the Holy Places of Islam. Some battalions had problems with discipline, but the men of at least one company 'expressed their desire to proceed on service and so wipe out any shame on their class by the behaviour of their comrades'.[61] Even mutineers were sometimes given the opportunity to restore their military honour.

But some crimes, at least in the eyes of the authorities, blackened the name of a unit for ever. In November 1938, after suffering a religious slight, a Muslim sepoy of 4/2 Punjabis ran amok with a rifle. His fellow-soldiers did nothing to stop him until he had murdered four British and two Indian officers. After this, the unit was disbanded, 'since it is certain that the reputation of no battalion could survive the wholesale slaughter of its officers and that it has incurred disgrace which can never be lived down'.[62]

IDENTITIES

For a battalion to incur shame and lose its reputation, its members must have had a collective identity in the first place. Indeed, without some such corporate consciousness, a military unit might not work effectively at all. According to Karl von Clausewitz, the professional military as a body possessed this self-awareness. 'Those who follow the trade of war', he wrote, 'come to look on themselves as a sort of guild in whose ordinances, laws and customs the military spirit is incarnated. One who is seeking a profound understanding of the fundamentals of war, therefore, must understand "esprit-de-corps". This spirit is the cement which binds together all qualities which give the military its value.'[63]

Indian soldiers certainly possessed a sense that they were different from civilians, but military identities in so diverse an army were mainly embodied in much smaller units – regiments, battalions and companies. Men who were mostly unconcerned with the larger political scheme of the Raj, and of the army's place within it, might still be enthusiastic soldiers who strongly identified with a unit in which they knew every other man by sight.[64] John Masters, a Gurkha officer, eloquently recalled his devotion to his regiment. '"Fourth" – an honourable number. I soon came to believe with a passion worthy of a religion that there was no other regiment on earth like it.' Other Gurkha units were far inferior to his own, he thought.

> As for the rest of the Indian Army – well, the Guides weren't bad, but even they were not what they used to be in the old days. The British Army, lock, stock and barrel, was useless. But we – we were wonderful! We were stiff with battle honours.[65] We had fought from France to China. We were witty, happy, carefree, tough, efficient, wise. It was no bad state of mind to be in, and not inaccurate. The 4th Gurkhas would not have been even good unless we had believed it to be the best.[66]

This strong sense of identity did not always emerge unprompted, especially in peacetime when men were not drawn together by the common experience of danger and loss. Identity could be fostered in several ways. Competitive team games between units reinforced pride in the regiment and encouraged individuals to submit to a code of conduct in which their personal advantage was subordinated to a common purpose.[67] Games had other advantages. Officers and men of the same unit could mix more informally on the playing field than they did on duty.[68] Many sports promoted skills which might be useful in battle, such as accurate shooting, physical fitness and quick reactions.[69] Several senior British officers were staunch advocates of sporting excellence. 'There is no surer indication of a good soldier than that he is likewise a good sportsman', thought Henry Rawlinson, 'for the one is the corollary of the other. It was "playing the game" that won us the Great War, and I ask all

ranks to see that they "play the game" in peace.'[70] Lord Kitchener
was a great believer in using competitions to foster collective pride,
so he began an elaborate inter-unit contest in all aspects of training
and drill.[71]

The bonds established on service lasted after troops had left the
army, as regiments were normally keen to stay in touch with former
soldiers who had served for many years. British officers were
accordingly encouraged to tour the recruiting grounds to meet pensioners and listen to their grievances, 'fancied or otherwise'.[72] Regimental magazines helped to reinforce unit identity. (They were also
a valuable instrument for disseminating pro-government news,
because soldiers were more inclined to believe what they were told
by their regiment than by Army Headquarters.)[73]

Identity and Military Organization

Regimental identities were, of course, not the only ones that Indian
soldiers carried with them. Religious, caste, regional and linguistic
self-perceptions could all assert themselves in different contexts,
often working more powerfully than simple *esprit de corps*, since
they usually tapped more deeply-rooted aspects of a soldier's mentality. The military authorities spent much time and effort trying to
discover the ideal way to structure the relationship between regimental and other identities. Their aim, broadly speaking, was 'to
organize the Army in such a way as will be least likely to admit of
combination, and lead to contentment and efficiency'.[74]

There were three basic ways of structuring the identity of an
Indian Army regiment. In a 'general mixture' unit, recruits from a
variety of castes and provinces served alongside each other in the
same company. The recruiting basis of a 'class company' unit was
similar, but its men served only with others of their kind in the same
company. A typical 'class company' battalion might have four companies of Muslims from the Punjab, two of Sikhs and two of Hindu
Rajputs. In a 'class regiment' the men were all of the same religion,
caste and language.[75] Each method had its strengths and its weaknesses, and there was much to be said for using a combination of all
three. 'There is safety in a variety of systems, and the Army should
be no more homogeneous in system than in race', opined the influential Punjab Committee shortly after the Mutiny.[76] It was not then
clear which method would turn out to be the best.

The general mixture system was the most widely used in the 1860s. It was employed by all battalions of the Madras Army, most of the Bombay Army, and about half the Bengal Army. Soldiers were less likely to combine for political purposes if men of different backgrounds served together in the same company and regiment, argued the supporters of general mixture (among whom were the Peel Commission).[77] They also thought that caste would cause fewer discipline problems in these regiments, because less deference would be shown to it. 'But excellent as this theory seems', argued the Punjab Committee, 'it does not bear the test of practice. Different races mixed together do not long preserve their distinctiveness; their corners and angles, and feeling and prejudice get rubbed off.'[78] Soldiers serving together in a single unit became 'linked together by a strong feeling of regimental brotherhood, which quite dominates any race or caste animosities'.[79] This might seem desirable, but it posed a political danger to the Raj. If a feeling of comradeship spread throughout the army, then its soldiers might all turn against the British if any portion of them bore an especial grudge. 'The counterpoise of natives against natives' would thus be lost. This seemed to have happened in the Bengal Army in 1857. As one witness before the Peel Commission put it: 'By mixing the castes in one corps they make common cause, which they never do if kept separate. Hindoos and Mussulmen are natural enemies, the same with Sikhs; yet the result of mixing them in one corps has been to make them all join against government. *Divide et impera* should be the principle.'[80]

For these reasons, the class company system gradually replaced the general mixture in the later nineteenth century.[81] In a class company regiment, each company (or group of companies) was drawn from a different community. The companies therefore mutually competed in military excellence, since the pride of each one reflected that of the community which it embodied.[82] Class company regiments preserved antagonisms of caste and religion.[83] They were therefore less likely to mutiny as a body, since the different parts of a regiment would rarely share the same religious or political grievances.[84] The Eden Commission of 1879 recommended eventually converting most mixed regiments to the class company formula. By 1883 the general mixture had been abolished in the Bengal Army, and in 1895 all the Madras infantry were reorganized along class company lines.[85]

There were problems with the new class company system. It heightened friction between the different castes and religions, and the companies of a given community tended to make common cause after any insult to one of their number.[86] This led to numerous discipline problems. Class company regiments could also be difficult to use for internal security work, since 'few corps can be employed on service against any enemy or rebel without having in their ranks some clansmen of the men they are engaged against'.[87]

This problem did not affect homogeneous units, or class regiments, which became more and more common from the 1890s. Regiments of men from a single religion, caste and region (such as Gurkha or Muzbhi Sikh battalions) usually developed greater *esprit de corps* than those that were more diverse.[88] Wider social identities overlapped with and reinforced the military identity of the unit. Men preferred serving with people like themselves, and they could be promoted anywhere in the battalion regardless of their caste or religion. Jealousy between different companies might interrupt the working of a class company unit; but tension between different class regiments was useful to the Raj, since it caused few discipline problems and hampered mutinous combinations.[89] British officers could get to know the habits and prejudices of their men more easily if they were all of one religion. A homogeneous regiment was also more of a known quantity than a class company unit during civil unrest, for its simple composition was 'a ready index of its reliablity in the event of internal disturbance'.[90]

Given all these advantages, it is not surprising that many experienced officers wanted to reorganize the entire Indian Army into class regiments.[91] Some steps in this direction were taken in the late nineteenth century. (See Table 3.1.) Between 1890 and 1893, twenty of the class company units in the Bengal infantry were converted to class regiments, mainly by switching entire companies between battalions.[92] By 1914, 52 of the 136 battalions in the Indian Army belonged to class regiments and 84 to class company ones.[93] Homogeneous regiments did have one slight disadvantage. It could be difficult for British officers to discover what was happening in the ranks, since men of a single community were unlikely to inform on one another.[94] A conspiracy was therefore easier to foment and more difficult to detect.[95]

In units drawn from a single community, kinship networks tended to form in the ranks. Some groups of neighbouring villages, often inhabited by the same clan, sent their sons to the same regi-

TABLE 3.1
Internal structure of Bengal Infantry regiments, 1864–97

| | Year | | | | | |
Composition	1864	1883	1890	1891	1893	1897
General mixture	20	–	–	–	–	–
Class company regiments	16	32	43	39	23	22
Class regiments	7	12	21	25	41	42
Total	43	44	64	64	64	64

Sources: Lansdowne to Cross, and MD Minute, 7 June 1892, L/MIL/7/7052; Memo by Roberts, 23 June, 1903, CID 27-D, CAB 6/1; GI Advance Despatch, 27 August 1920, L/MIL/7/5483, Annexure II; *Indian Army List*. Figures differing only in minor details appear in Braun, *Die Verteidigung Indiens*, p. 162; Heathcote, *Indian Army*, pp. 95–101; and Shibly, PhD thesis, pp. 361–3.
Note: The figures for 1864 and 1886 do not include the Punjab Frontier Force.

ment for generations.[96] This was a natural result of standard nineteenth-century recruiting methods which relied on personal contacts and local knowledge.[97] Native officers in charge of recruiting parties, or sepoys returning from leave, tended to bring in their own relatives as new recruits.[98] This gave them more influence and *izzat* in the regiment.[99] Recruiters could also be under pressure from their families to find jobs for young men of military age.[100] A local community linked to a particular regiment often wanted its young men to enlist to help retain its lucrative status as a martial race. The recruits thought they were more likely to gain advancement if they joined a regiment dominated by their relatives.[101] Men seemed to like serving with their neighbours and kin. 'All of us from one village at home are assembled together and are very pleased with ourselves and always joking', wrote one lancer from the trenches in

France.[102] These kinship networks reinforced the cohesion of the unit, although cohesion did not work automatically in the British favour – men could cohere in dissidence as well as obedience. Ties of kin within the regiment tended to loosen in the 1920s and 1930s, however, as more recruiting was done through the formal channels of depots and British Recruiting Officers.[103] 'The old order is changing with the times and the parochial spirit with all its sentimental and practical advantages is rapidly declining', noted the Military Department in 1932.[104]

The military authorities conferred titles to emphasize the relationship between caste or religion and the collective identity of the regiment. In 1887, for example, the 35 and 36 Bengal Infantry were given the title 'Sikhs'; and in 1893 the 9 Bengal Infantry were renamed the 9 Gurkha (Rifle) Regiment of Bengal Infantry to foster their *esprit de corps*.[105] By 1914, seven infantry regiments were known as Rajputs, 13 as Sikhs, two as Brahmins, two as Jats and six as Marathas.[106] These titles indicated the community from which a regiment drew its recruits and, it was thought, made enlistment more popular. Some units had appropriate regional names, like regiments 24 to 31, which were all known as Punjabis. Many of the remainder had honorific designations, such as the 101 Grenadiers, or the 17 Infantry, called The Loyal Regiment. Several units carried colours, for similar reasons. According to senior British officers, the Indian soldiers cherished 'insignias around which they have rallied in hours of danger, and followed on the tide of victory. It is well to nourish such feeling and add every accessory incentive to increase *esprit-de-corps*'.[107]

The strength of regimental identity became clear when it was threatened. There was some anxiety in 1903 when Lord Kitchener planned to renumber the Bombay and Madras regiments to place all Indian Army units in a single sequence for ease of administration. Lord Roberts had grave misgivings. 'It goes against my feelings', he wrote. 'I am quite sure that many regiments will dislike intensely losing their old numbers. I am very pleased that the Gurkhas are not included.'[108] In the event, the renumbering went very smoothly, perhaps because regimental titles and composition were unaffected.[109] More serious were the heavy losses in the Great War which, combined with new drafts, changed the character of some regiments. After a few months at the front, more than half the men with most Indian Army units in France were replacements from outside.[110] The cohesion and gallantry of these scratch formations at first surprised some British observers; but by July 1915 it was clear that the Indian infantry would not survive another winter on the Western Front, in part because the regiments were 'no longer effective units but conglomerations of drafts'.[111] The loss of identity upset some men. 'Two hundred police have joined the regiment – such a dirty, mean rabble that no one knows any of them. That is why I am unhappy in the regiment', wrote one rifleman.[112] 'I have never even heard of the villages from which our recruits now come', lamented a Sikh officer. 'Truly, confusion and chaos have entered the regiment. Nothing is safe.'[113]

While the British authorities were keen that Indian soldiers should identify closely with their unit, they were much more cautious about fostering military *esprit de corps* in formations larger than one-battalion regiments. In the 1870s, several officers suggested grouping similar battalions in threes, so that one could supply trained drafts to the others in wartime.[114] But 'it would be contrary to our policy', thought the Commander-in-Chief, 'to provide an union of feeling and a common interest in so large a body as three regiments, because disaffection in any one portion would be certain to pervade the whole'.[115] The demands of modern warfare, however, made it imperative to have regiments larger than one battalion if units at the front were not to waste away, as the Afghan campaign of 1878–80 had made clear.[116] In 1885, the infantry regiments of the Indian Army were combined into ethnically similar groups of three.[117] From 1888, each group had a regimental centre. In the early 1900s, Lord Kitchener wanted to extend the principle, and form homogeneous 'class brigades' for active service. Although he had some supporters, his scheme was dropped because it posed political dangers.[118]

The system of three-battalion groups served well enough in Frontier campaigns; but the feeder units in India could not find enough recruits from the right communities to replace the grievous losses of the Great War.[119] To maintain the strength and identity of a regiment in such a conflict, a larger and more formal grouping of battalions was needed; but unrest in a corps this size might disturb the internal security of the Raj. The authorities, it seemed, had to choose between military weakness and political danger. Such are the dilemmas of Empire. It was decided that the Indian Army had to be made more fit to fight a major war.[120] In 1920, the Commander-in-Chief prepared a scheme to combine all Indian infantry units into twenty regiments, usually of four active and one training battalion each.[121] The active units were to give up all work with depots, reservists and recruits. The training battalion was to concentrate on training drafts and sending them to other units of the regiment. Beyond providing cadres for internal security, it had no active service tasks. The scheme was introduced in 1922. The same year, the cavalry regiments were reduced to 21 and combined in seven groups of three. The ten regiments of Gurkhas, each of two battalions, were not affected by the changes.[122]

The internal organization of the battalions had still to be decided. Most senior officers favoured the class company system, as the Great War had shown it to be more efficient in a major conflict.[123] Several class battalions, unable to replace all their losses from their parent community, had been forced to recruit new elements to the unit. Class company battalions had encountered fewer problems, since they each drew their recruits from several communities and the supply from all was unlikely to fail at the same time. A shift towards the class company system, however, was bound to be unpopular, as it would mean breaking up several class battalions which had a strong sense of identity, and scattering some of their companies among other units. Sikh regiments in particular were likely to be hurt by the changes, and political agitation was feared. 'But questions of sentiment cannot be permitted to prejudice the introduction of changes designed to ensure the maintenance of the Army in the field and its expansion in times of emergency', noted the Government of India. In the aftermath of the Great War, the ability of the army to fight the forces of a major power seemed more important than regimental *esprit de corps*. The General Staff also calculated that the soldiers would remain quiescent in the end, even if they grumbled at the time.

In the event, the changes carried out were less drastic than those suggested. Apart from the Gurkhas, four regimental groups retained class battalions with their attendant strong sense of identity. Hillmen from Garhwal and Dogras from Kangra, in North-Eastern Punjab, each formed one homogeneous regimental group, as they had 'little or nothing in common with the classes recruited in the plains of India'.[124] In deference to Sikh feeling, and in honour of their contribution to the Imperial victory in the Great War, one regimental group of infantry and one of pioneers were recruited exclusively among Sikhs. The reliability of these class battalions could be more easily judged during civil unrest, and the units also formed 'a useful counterpoise to the other classes in the Indian Army'.

Uniform and Identity

Military identity was also classically embodied in the idea of uniform. This was primarily an attribute of drilled, regular forces rather than irregular ones, which were agglomerations of individual warriors in a sartorial as well as social sense. Uniforms served several purposes. Lavish costume could impress an onlooker. 'Some military display is necessary in an oriental country', observed Lord Kitchener. 'If the Amir of Afghanistan came to India, our troops in khaki would not impress him as much as if they were in red.'[125] A uniform also described its wearer, setting him apart from civilians, and confirming his identity as a soldier from a particular unit. 'The different uniforms have been associated for many years with hallowed traditions of the various regiments', remarked Winston Churchill of British Army full dress. 'Sentiment is of extreme importance in a voluntary army, and the distinctive uniforms of the various regiments have a sentimental hold on the men which could not be replaced.'[126] But as sentiments changed, so too did military uniform. In the early nineteenth century, the sepoys in British service mostly wore red jackets and shakos in the European style. They retained this costume during the first stages of their mutiny in 1857; but as the rebellion deepened, most reverted to an all-white local dress of turban or skull-cap, jacket or shirt, and dhoti.[127] The rebels discarded the fashions of Europe along with its values.

The military were usually skilled in decoding the meanings enshrined in uniform. In the decade after the Mutiny the army authorities carefully adapted the language of military clothing to serve colonial purposes. Several witnesses before the Peel Commission advised that sepoys should be dressed in costume of local inspiration.[128] The European-style uniforms which the mutineers had rejected in 1857 were simply impractical. The tight jackets hampered free use of the limbs, and a sepoy in a really well-dressed regiment could neither stoop to the ground nor take rest in his accoutrements.[129] In the later nineteenth century, more and more regiments adopted turbans, flowing jackets and loose pantaloons.[130] These were well-suited to the climate and, moreover, preserved 'the distinction between the different nationalities and races, which is very necessary for our security'.[131] The authorities used visual language to express and reinforce other useful relationships. The Gurkha infantry, who identified more closely with the British than with Indians of the plains, were usually clad in rifle-green uniforms of distinctly European cut.[132] Astonishing attention was devoted to matters of sartorial detail. Very senior officers, and even members of the Royal family, would busy themselves sounding opinion on coat colours, badges and orders of dress.[133] They were prudent to do so, for these outward marks of distinction reflected their wearers' pride and sense of self.

Identities in Flux

A soldier was the bearer of more than one identity. He could define himself in terms of religion, caste, locality or membership of a corporate military body. These various identities could overlap and reinforce each other, but they could also come into conflict. In some contexts, one particular identity might more readily assert itself and influence a soldier's behaviour. Nor were identities firmly fixed. In civilian life, some *jatis* could assert a higher status (with occasional success) by borrowing the manners and taboos of groups traditionally superior to them – a process known as sanskritization. Something akin to this took place in the army. When Brahmins served in a battalion with other Hindus, the latter began to assume some of the ritual practices of the former.[134] This could hamper military efficiency, for the Brahmins' lengthy food-preparation rituals and their clumsy cooking vessels could impede a regiment on the march. In the early 1890s, to contain the problem, the Brahmin companies of the Bengal infantry were combined into two class regiments from which all other castes were excluded.[135]

The army could also have a more than local impact upon the self-perceptions of a community. Between the 1880s and the 1920s, the Indian Army half-consciously helped to change the nature of Sikh identity. Originally, Sikhism was not sharply distinguished from the main body of Hindu tradition from which it had emerged.[136] The Sikh Gurus probably did not intend to create an entirely separate faith and community; and the rulers of the Sikh state observed many Hindu rituals and practices, as did the members of the militant Khalsa brotherhood, founded by the tenth Guru. For more than four hundred years, Sikh and Hindu identities overlapped and interacted.

In the forty years which followed the the British annexation of the Punjab, the number of Punjabis who defined themselves as Sikhs showed a steady decline. In 1868, for example, there were 511064 Sikhs in the five districts of Amritsar, Gurdaspur, Sialkot, Lahore and Gujranwala; but by 1881 there were only 490 677.[137] The loss of prestige after the fall of the Sikh state, the strong attractions of behavioural Hinduism, and the activities of Christian missionaries had all combined to produce the fall in Sikh numbers.

The pattern changed from the 1880s, when the proportion of Sikhs in the population of the Punjab began steadily to rise.[138] According to the census, there were 1 706 165 Sikhs in the province in 1881, 2 102 896 in 1901, and 3 110 060 in 1921.[139] The numbers recorded as Hindus in the same years slightly declined. The agricultural wealth of Sikh cultivating castes had helped revive the prestige of their religion, and reform movements had injected a new militancy. The success of Christian missions among low-caste Sikhs, and the shock of a number of conversions within the landed elite, encouraged Sikh theologians to renew the vitality of their faith through schools, societies, publications and meetings. Reform focused attention on the nature of orthodoxy. The spectacular advances of the militant Arya Samaj (arguing that a purified Hinduism was superior to all other faiths) also inspired a defensive zeal in promoting Sikh identity.[140] Faced with this threat, Sikh reformers of the Tat (or true) Khalsa drew communal boundaries between themselves and Hindus. Many others followed suit, and began to define themselves as Kesdhari Sikhs (who were more distinct from Hindus than the Sahajdharis). The Tat Khalsa fostered a spirit of internal solidarity and consciousness. By the time of the Great War, those Sikhs who did not observe the outward symbols of the Khalsa were coming to be seen as Hindus or apostates.

The army influenced this process. When Sikhs first entered Company service in the 1840s, the authorities laid down that there should be no interference with their religion.[141] The British then went further, stipulating that no Sikh could enlist unless he observed the outward distinctions of the Khalsa.[142] For recruiting purposes, Sikhs were thus being defined as Kesdharis, which encouraged the distinction from Hindus. Like male converts to the Khalsa, soldiers in Sikh regiments had to wear the *kirpan*, or dagger, and keep their uncut hair wrapped in a turban. The Guru Granth Sahib – the holy book of the Sikhs which contained all the hymns of the Gurus – was carried at the head of the unit on the march, and was prominently displayed in camp.[143] 'One man is so efficient in reciting the Granth, that he is employed on that duty alone', remarked a resaidar. 'Prayer meetings are constantly held, and our Sircar gives us every opportunity for holding them.'[144] British officers were briefed on the content of the Sikh scriptures, and were expected to attend certain ceremonies at their unit gurdwaras, or temples.[145]

The object of these endeavours was 'to preserve intact the distinctive characteristics of their race, their peculiar conventions and social customs'.[146] A strong sense of separate Sikh identity would reinforce *esprit de corps* and bolster morale. There was a further dimension to this strategy. The more that Sikhs distinguished themselves from Hindus, the more reliable Sikh units were likely to be during periods of Hindu civil unrest. The army authorities liked to pose as the protectors of the Sikhs, and preferred to recruit in areas where Sikhs were in a majority and their customs hence less diluted by Hinduism.[147] It was army policy to encourage the Sikh religion in its 'pristine purity', because 'any falling off from orthodoxy not only detracts from the fighting value of the Sikh soldier, but inevitably tends to adversely affect his whole attitude to the British power'.[148]

According to some British observers, Sikhs would gradually have lost any sense of difference from Hindus had not the Indian Army fostered a separate Sikh identity.[149] 'It is the British officer who has kept Sikhism up to its old standard', thought George MacMunn.[150] The British often overestimated their own impact and importance, but MacMunn's hyperbolic statement contains a grain of truth. The army authorities showed a marked preference for Sikh soldiers, and in some heavily-recruited areas there was a distinct trend of conversion to Sikhism.[151]

Sikh identity was asserted with especial vigour immediately after the Armistice. In the early 1920s, Khalsa militants sought to wrest control of lucrative shrines from government-appointed guardians.[152] This led to a prolonged struggle with the Punjab Government, in which the militants were eventually successful. The Sikh Gurdwara Act of 1925 conceded management of the temples to those Sikhs who declared that they had 'no other religion'.[153] This was a crucial turning point in the evolution of the Sikh community, for it formally recognized the claim of the Tat Khalsa to represent a coherent and separate Sikh identity. Temple management was to serve as the institutional basis for an exclusive Sikh consciousness.

The army may have influenced these developments. During the Great War, enlistment in units which fostered Sikh separateness may have encouraged the assertion of this identity; and the discharge of veterans after the conflict perhaps helped transmit this consciousness to a wider population.

The service of so many Sikhs in the Indian Army also affected their political identity and influence at the highest levels of power.[154] As it became clear that constitutional reform would eventually concede some role to elected Indian delegates, the leaders of the Sikh community began to fear that Hindus and Muslims might squeeze them out of political influence unless they were promised separate representation. Their loyal military service worked in their favour, but the Morley–Minto reforms of 1909 still did not meet their demands. The Great War provided another chance for Sikhs to serve with distinction in the army and to plead for a separate voice in the highest councils of the state. Most Congress Hindus dismissed the claims of the Sikhs, and even denied their independent existence. But by 1918 the British thought differently. 'The Sikhs in the Punjab are a distinct and important people, they supply a gallant and valuable element to the Indian Army, but they are everywhere in a minority and experience has shown that they go virtually unrepresented', noted the Montagu–Chelmsford Report. 'To the Sikhs, therefore, and to them alone we propose to extend the system [of communal representation] already adopted in the case of the Muhammadans.'[155] This concession was a great victory for the separatists, and a grave blow to Congress, which claimed to speak for all Indians. Yet the 1919 Government of India Act allowed the Sikhs a smaller percentage of elected seats than most of them had hoped for. Many felt betrayed. The inaugural session of the Sikh League in December 1919 approved the act, but regretted that 'the Sikh community has been denied that substantial representation to which it is entitled by reason of its political status and its military achievements and sacrifices for the King-Emperor'.

Muslims were in an analogous position to Sikhs. Communalist politicians cited the large number of Muslims in the Indian Army to support their demand for separate electorates. In 1906, an elite Muslim deputation asked the Viceroy, Lord Minto, for separate electorates and representation in excess of their numbers, because of 'the value of the contribution' that Muslims made 'to the defence of the Empire'.[156] The British were rarely reluctant to seize a chance to divide and rule, so by the Indian Councils Act of 1909, at least eight of the 27 elected members of the Imperial Legislative Council were to be Muslims.

Military service also affected the outward signs of Muslim identity at a much more fundamental level.[157] Army pay helped to finance Islamization in the core Muslim recruiting grounds of the Punjab. Money from the troops helped fund the building of mosques, and pious soldiers began to pay for their sons to receive a Muslim education. The *pirs* – holy men who had inherited religious charisma from their ancestors – received higher incomes as their followers became more wealthy through their army connection. Military wages paid for more pilgrimages to Mecca and visits to local shrines. Military pay and pensions also encouraged more widespread purdah. The strict seclusion of women gained *izzat* for themselves and their families; and service in the army made men more conscious of their honour and better able to afford the labourers to do the outdoor tasks previously performed by unsecluded females. In Attock, Jhelum and Rawalpindi, military wages helped fund an Islamic revival a generation before the demand for Pakistan.

By making men more conscious of their religious differences and caste status, military service could occasionally fuel communal conflict. Such was the case in Merwara, a hilly enclave of British territory in Rajputana.[158] The Mers were 'inclined to hold themselves aloof from the inhabitants of the surrounding States' and looked on themselves 'as the especial soldiers and retainers of the British Government'.[159] They used to make a living by raiding the adjacent territories, but in the colonial period they turned to regular military employment to relieve their poverty. The military authorities regarded them as good soldiers. They were certainly willing enough to enlist – during the Great War about 40 per cent of the male Mer population between the ages of 18 and 40 served in the ranks. While most Mers were Hindus, and were known as Rawats (a petty title of nobility), one clan, the Merat-Kathats, regarded themselves as Muslims. Religious practice in Merwara was far from rigid. There were no mullahs to instruct the Merats in Islam, and they had no desire to proselytize; the Hinduism of the Rawats was vague and undefined; and there were no stately mosques or temples. Most unusual of all, Hindu and Muslim clans interdined and intermarried, and had done so for centuries.

Military service changed these casual customs, by bringing Mers into contact with a wider world. An infantry battalion had been raised in Merwara as early as 1822. Composed entirely of Mers, it existed under various names into the twentieth century. From 1887, however, three Rajputana class company battalions each added two companies of Mers to their existing two companies of Rajputs, two of Gujars and two of Muslims from Hindustan.[160] Service in these units brought the Merwara clans into closer contact with more orthodox Hindus and Muslims, and the Mers of both religions started striving to be accepted as such. The minority of Merats, who sought to be treated as Muslims, did achieve a limited recognition from orthodox followers of the Prophet, and were allowed to dine with them.[161] But Rawats who interdined with Merats were excluded by orthodox Hindus and Muslims alike. Tension arose between the two Mer communities, at first in the Rajputana regiments, later in the Merwara infantry. In 1902, a meeting of Rawats proposed that they should cease giving their daughters in marriage to Muslims. Later the same year, when a detachment of the Merwara infantry went to England for the Coronation ceremonies, Rawats who claimed to be Rajputs were snubbed by orthodox Hindus for dining with Muslims. The quarrel spread to the villages which supplied men to the army, and the previous harmony between the Merwara clans was upset. In 1903, a Rawat meeting decided to cease socializing with Muslims and urged men to dress their wives and daughters as Rajputs. As the tension in the recruiting grounds became acute, the discipline of the Merwara infantry suffered; so in 1904 the men of the battalion were segregated into six Hindu and two Muslim companies. The Indian Army had thus been the unwitting and reluctant vehicle for the creation of local communalism.

Military Policy and Religious Practice

Developments such as those in the Merwara infantry underlined one crucial lesson of 1857 – that military discipline could be preserved only if the authorities understood the religious needs of the men.[162] 'Everything should be done to secure the contentment and loyalty of the Native Army by a scrupulous regard for their customs and their religion', urged Lord Roberts.[163] Many experienced officers believed that 'the first qualification of a leader of Native troops is that he should be intimately acquainted with and known to his men, and that his value increases in proportion as this object is attained'.[164] There were various ways in which a British officer could gain some understanding of the Indian ranks. Most importantly, he was expected to tour the recruiting districts at least once, preferably early in his service.[165] By doing this, he would gain a knowledge of the localities from which the men were drawn, and 'obtain greater insight into their habits, customs and peculiarities'.[166] British officers were also expected to take counsel from their Indian colleagues on cultural matters that might affect discipline. 'On any point of Gurkha custom, tradition or religion it was these Gurkha officers' duty to give me the opinion and feeling of the enlisted men', recalled John Masters.[167] Lastly, the recruiting handbooks included brief introductory surveys of Indian religions for the benefit of the new subaltern.[168] Some educated Indian officers considered the British overscrupulous in these matters. Lacking an easy familiarity with the customs of the men, they tended to err on the side of caution in their efforts to avoid giving offence.[169]

The British authorities certainly tried to be sensitive to the feelings of the troops, and did much to include customary practices in the routine of military life. Religious teachers, appointed to each unit, blessed the weapons and colours of the regiment.[170] Commanding officers were urged to take these men into their confidence, because they could be of great help in sustaining morale, and, if alienated, 'they constitute perhaps the greatest danger of all to the integrity of the troops'.[171] Religious ceremonies were closely integrated with the regimental calendar. In Gurkha units, for example, British officers normally attended the Dusserah festival, which took place within a hollow square formed of the weapons of the battalion, garlanded with flowers.[172] After the sacrifice of animals, the band played the regimental march, and the officers dined and danced with the men and their families. Gurkha customs were also incorporated in standing orders, and domestic disputes in the ranks were settled in traditional manner before a court of Gurkha officers.[173] When military operations threatened to upset the religious sensiblities of the men, great care was taken to soothe any injured feelings. After the revolt of the Sharif of Mecca against the Turks in 1916, for example, the British government issued a pledge that the Holy Places of Islam would be more secure than ever from Christian molestation. Commanders of Muslim units were instructed to keep in 'close and unobtrusive' touch with the feelings of their men, and to hold tactful discussions with selected Indian officers, 'to remove misunderstanding as to the present and future policy of Government'.[174]

Spiritual needs are often embodied in texts or other material objects, and an unfamiliar lack of these might cause disorientation or distress. Indian soldiers serving in France during the Great War keenly felt the need of the comfort provided by scripture and other religious artefacts. 'Here our religion is destroyed', lamented a Sikh infantryman attached to a Gurkha battalion. 'I have omitted the wearing of the *kachhehra* [drawers]. I had none and the cloth for them is not to be had here. When I get back I shall have to be initiated afresh. Here there is plenty of everything, except *kachhehra*, *kanga* [comb], and *kirpan* [sacrificial knife].'[175] The authorities proved sympathetic to these religious needs. 'The Indian soldiers, like most Orientals, value the minute observation of their religion far above anything else', remarked the censor, 'and a few rupees expended on Qurans, extracts from the Granth, kirpans, Brahminical threads, and the like would give more pleasure than a great deal of sweetmeats and tobacco'.[176] A fund was set up in Britain to provide articles of religious importance to Indian soldiers. Three thousand sets of Sikh bracelets and daggers, forged in Sheffield to a design approved by experts, were sent to troops in hospital and at the front. Four thousand *kachhehra* were provided for Sikh troops in France and the Dardanelles. The authorities also passed on large consignments of literature received from India, including 900 Qurans and 1400 other Muslim tracts donated by Her Highness the Begum of Bhopal. Great care was taken to ensure that these scriptures were not damaged in transit.[177]

These and similar endeavours might seem patronizing and manipulative, but there is clear evidence that the troops and their families took them in good faith and responded warmly. 'Colonel Sahib has made excellent arrangements and takes great trouble for us Musalmans' wrote one soldier during Ramazan. 'His arrangements for our food during the fast are very good, and he has put us all together because during the fast it is not easy to live with Sikhs and Dogras. I cannot describe how good his arrangements are.'[178] After the Id in 1917, one Muslim trooper recalled how 'all the Mahomedans of the Division had their prayers together. About 1500 men assembled and prayers were offered for the victory of our King. After that we had sports and such a display of joy that I cannot describe it. All the Sahibs thanked us for what we had done and now at midnight full of happiness I am sitting down to write this letter.'[179] Sikhs were equally pleased with the efforts made to accommodate their religious needs. 'The Sircar has made the very best of arrangements', wrote one.[180] 'Animals intended for the food of Sikhs are slaughtered by a Sikh by a stroke of a sword on the back of the neck, and those intended for Musalmans, by a Musalman in the lawful way, namely by cutting the throat. Our Sircar has made the most satisfactory arrangements in all matters relating to our religion'.[181] The Sikhs of the Central India Horse were able to celebrate the birthday of Guru Sri Nanak 'with great splendour. We all enjoyed ourselves very much.'[182] Families in India were delighted when they learned of this. 'I am greatly pleased to hear that even on field service our brothers have been celebrating the birthday of our Guru Sahib. Thanks, a thousand thanks, to the Government under whose rule, not only we, but the members of every sect, are able to observe fittingly their holy days. May the Guru ever keep over our heads the shadow of this great King.'[183]

Military Isolation

While the troops were usually loyal and obedient, the authorities did not tempt fate by leaving the army open to potentially subversive influences. Letters to soldiers at the front or in hospital were strictly monitored and sometimes suppressed. Any seditious literature enclosed with a letter was removed.[184] Recruiting was normally suspended in an area which had been affected by anti-colonial movements.[185] Soldiers were forbidden to take part in any meeting or demonstration which had a political purpose, nor could they belong to any political association. Even army bands were prohibited from joining public processions.[186] These security measures were stepped up during the Congress-led civil unrest of the 1920s and 1930s, when the nationalists tried to subvert military discipline. A careful watch was kept on all non-combatants, such as clerks or workmen, who had easy access to the lines. Religious mendicants were treated with grave suspicion, as were unknown persons who offered to work as servants.[187] Reservists from disaffected areas were segregated from the regulars. The common purpose of these and other measures was 'to prevent contact of seditious ideas with serving soldiers and to safeguard them from disturbing rumours and suggestions'.[188] But the army could not be kept in total political purdah. The troops, after all, were essentially peasants in uniform who used their frequent leave to affirm their close links with their place of origin. Men returning from leave were closely watched, however, and leave was not normally granted to a currently disturbed area.

The organization of military space aided the seclusion of the army. Barracks were physically isolated as far as possible from 'the contamination of large native centres of population'.[189] Army camps, or cantonments as they were known, were self-contained military townships, usually placed on the outskirts of a city.[190] At Rawalpindi, for example, a river and a railway line separated the military area from the Indian town.[191] Within the cantonment, the allocation of space reflected and reinforced racial and social hierarchies, with British troops segregated from Indian, and officers from men. The well-defined boundaries of a cantonment could be guarded and patrolled, which made it easier to exclude those, such as newspaper-sellers, who might threaten the discipline of the troops. Because a cantonment was a precise space given over to military use, it was easier to identify and remove those who had no business to be there. If need be, city areas could be placed out of bounds to the troops during civil unrest.[192]

The more reflective troops sometimes saw through these security measures. 'Very strict rules have been introduced for us', wrote one wounded soldier from a Brighton hospital, 'because it is the wish of the English that all the Indians should not acquire or learn the ideas of freedom which the people here possess.'[193] When a soldier began to understand the fears that underlay the rules governing his every-day life, then those fears became justified.

SAHIB, SIRDAR, KING

Sahib and Sepoy

British officers, it was widely believed at the time, were crucial to the cohesion and efficiency of the army.[194] 'Sepoys led by a European officer are different men from those not so', thought one British general.[195] 'Deprived of their European officers, native troops are a mere armed rabble'.[196] Many shared these views. It became an article of imperial faith that everything depended on the British officer.[197] 'British leaders are essential to the success of Native soldiery', thought Lord Roberts.[198] According to Lord Curzon, the efficiency of the Indian Army 'was due solely to the British officers serving in it'.[199]

The cult of the British officer partly reflected the tendency of the ruling elite to explain other processes in terms of themselves. It also

suited the British to believe themselves essential. It gave them a
sense of purpose, and inflated their self-esteem. Once they began to
doubt their own necessity, their lack of confidence might betray
itself and damage their prestige.

Elements of this imperial perception inform some modern scholarship. Most commentators start from the assumption that 'the quality of the officer corps will determine the quality of the army'.[200]
Philip Mason suggests that a public-school background enabled
British officers 'to get the best from others by trusting them and
giving them responsibility within a framework of discipline'.[201]
According to T. A. Heathcote, 'the devotion with which the jawans
followed their sahibs, leaders of an alien race from an alien country,
testifies to the achievement of the officers in winning and keeping
the respect and trust of their men'.[202] Interestingly, an Indian general, D. K. Palit, follows a similar line. 'The relationship between the
regular British regimental officer and the warrior peasantry of India
established the steadfast traditions of the Army we inherited', he
writes. 'English society encrusted its young men in values that
made for military leadership.'[203] Jeffrey Greenhut is most blunt of
all. 'The conventional military wisdom of the day was correct: in an
Indian infantry battalion the white officer was essential.'[204]

These arguments must be tested. The Indian Army appeared to
attract more dedicated and professional men than the forces based
in Britain.[205] Until the 1870s all regimental promotion in the British
Army was by purchase, and an officer had to have private means,
for he could not live on his pay. The British Army therefore
excluded the less affluent middle and professional classes from its
officer corps, regardless of their talent. If such men planned a military career, they would have to seek a place in an Indian regiment
where the pay was better and the cost of living low. For this reason,
complained Lord Roberts, 'all the best men at Sandhurst strive to
get into the Indian Army'.[206] Indian Army officers were also
dedicated enough to learn the languages of their men (as indeed
they were enjoined to do by regulation).[207] John Masters studied
Gurkhali fairy tales with a jemadar of his battalion; and D. K. Palit,
who served as a regimental officer in the 1930s, could not recall 'a
single case of a regular British officer not knowing both Urdu and
the language of his troops'.[208]

Yet the Indian Army officer corps had its fair share of problems.
Absenteeism was a major difficulty before the Mutiny. British officers
did not sacrifice their regimental position by taking a more lucrative

and prestigious civil or staff appointment.[209] They therefore spent much time and effort trying to secure detached employment, which reduced the status and efficiency of regimental soldiering.[210] Absent officers would often rejoin their units in wartime to share the glory, but some men who returned to their regiments during the campaigns of the 1840s had been absent for a dozen years, and were quite out of touch with regimental life. Reforms in the 1860s curbed the worst abuses, but many of the best younger officers were still removed from their units.[211] An Indian Army officer also had to spend the first six months or a year of his commission with a British regiment. This was meant to be a good school, but it could engender an initial distaste for Indian troops.[212] 'There are probably no conditions of Indian life less favourable for becoming acquainted with the people of the country and seeing them to advantage than service with a British regiment', thought Lord Ripon.[213] Many British Army officers looked down on the Indian Army as the home of the 'second rate soldier'.[214] Promotion in the Indian Army was by strict seniority, a 'radically bad' system, according to Kitchener, which put inefficient men at the head of the list.[215]

During and after the Great War, the quality of Indian Army leadership declined. After a year in the trenches, most regiments had only one or two of their original twelve officers left.[216] The new officers did not know their men, and sometimes could not speak their languages. 'No wonder the natives think they are fit to have commissions when they see some of the specimens sent to be officers over them', remarked one disillusioned regular in September 1918.[217] Morale was dented by the surrender at Kut in 1916, and by adverse comparisons with the training and equipment of the British Army.[218] The postwar army was considered inferior to that of 1914, owing to this 'officer difficulty'.[219] Furthermore, British Army officers received a living wage by the 1920s, so the Indian Army could no longer automatically select the best of the less affluent but able men. Henry Rawlinson even complained that heavy drinking was becoming a problem, as too many officers acquired 'the cocktail habit'.[220] Small wonder then that John Masters, destined to be commissioned as a Gurkha officer in the 1930s, was reluctant to join the Indian Army. 'I thought myself far too clever to waste my life in that backwater'.[221]

But this evidence is not conclusive. To assess the importance of British officers to the morale and cohesion of a unit, it is perhaps more useful to examine the attitudes of the Indian soldiers themselves. Knowing as they did that their regimental officers read their letters on active service, the other ranks clearly had every incentive to make positive remarks about their leaders. But Indian soldiers in fact hardly ever mentioned their officers by name in their letters, much to the surprise of the army censors. 'It is very much the exception outside a few regiments such as the Guides, the Frontier Force, and, for example, the 15th Sikhs, in all of which esprit de corps is very strong'.[222] When British officers are mentioned personally, it is usually when they have resolved a dispute, awarded a medal, or when a particularly well-liked man has been killed.[223] But such mentions are very rare. Not one British officer appears in any of the many hundred surviving letters written by soldiers between 1 January and 5 June 1917. Indian soldiers, it seems, did not strongly approve or disapprove of their officers, but were indifferent to most of them.

Several intrusions could disrupt this peaceful indifference. The widespread appointment of new and unfamiliar officers made the men uneasy. 'I have my troubles and trials, as the Hindus had in the Musalman reign', wrote one Sikh soldier when serving under men he did not know.[224] In the later stages of the Great War, many men of low social status were commissioned, which sometimes caused resentment in the ranks. 'The officers we have now', wrote one sepoy, 'are men who in India were "Bank Clerks" and "Tea Planters" and did not associate with officers of superior rank. Consequently they are not men whose recommendation would carry much weight.'[225] Insensitive actions by a British officer could provoke mutiny, as the history of dissent in the Indian Army shows. But the fact that mutinies were so few suggests that the British had learned not to disturb the cherished customs of the men.

Although the bond between British officers and Indian other ranks was not as intense as the imperialists liked to believe, it had many of the ingredients of a stable marriage. Both parties accepted that they could never fully understand each other, but each had their own carefully-marked space and well-defined duties, and their mainly peaceful coexistence was warmed by familiarity and reinforced by habit. For the British to have won even the indifference of the troops was no mean achievement.

Sirdar

The Commander-in-Chief in India was the focus for feelings rather different from the usually lukewarm Indian acceptance of

competent and sensitive officers. The British tried hard to make the
C-in-C known to the men, and fostered a sense of allegiance to
him. 'The personal influence of the recognised head of the Army'
was of great importance, 'especially over Indian troops',
remarked the Army in India Committee in 1919. 'The Commander-in-Chief should be looked upon by all His Majesty's
Indian subjects and feudatories as a representative of a personal
authority second only to that of the Viceroy.'[226] Inspections and
reviews therefore received much emphasis. But as military leadership became more complex, the bureaucratic and charismatic
functions of the high command sometimes came into mutual conflict. In time of war, the C-in-C could not take the field with his
entourage at the head of the troops, as this would at a stroke
deprive the Governor-General of contact with his most experienced officers. A council or committee could not easily replace the
post of C-in-C. Such a move 'would be regarded with uneasiness
by the Native Army', thought Lord Roberts. 'They look to the
Commander-in-Chief as their personal head and protector.'[227] But
if the commander paid too much attention to inspiring the troops,
army administration might suffer. Lord Birdwood, who led the
army in the 1920s, 'loved talking to the Indian soldier, the
pensioner and the villager in their own language and had a rare
knowledge of their needs and troubles'.[228] An engaging personality, Birdwood spent too much time on inspections, and neglected
manoeuvres and vital matters of technology.

It is hard to tell how the troops reacted to all this, although the
response of some soldiers to the news of Lord Kitchener's death at
sea in June 1916 may offer some clues. 'Alas! Alas! The ship *Hampshire* conveying Lord Kitchener and his staff was mined', wrote a
Muslim trooper. 'Alas! that the Army should lose such men! My
prayer is that God may give them all eternal rest in Paradise and
that Britain may, thanks to their sacrifice, soon be victorious.'[229] His
remarks are typical, and similiar ones could be cited.[230] They
strongly suggest that the men did feel personally attached to their
former Commander-in-Chief. From these few brief excerpts it is
hard to judge the precise nature of their allegiance. One Sikh Dafadar wrote a more elaborate 17-stanza epitaph which opened as
follows:

Suddenly has disappeared Lord Kitchener, our great hero.
Where has he gone, our great hero?

A trusted leader of the Armies was that soldier.
Where has he gone, our great hero?

Biggest General in the world was he,
To that height had reached our great hero.

All around and everywhere we see Armies of Kitchener,
This is one of the works which he did, our great hero.[231]

(The author, Taja Singh, was unusual for more than being a poet. He sent an English translation of his verses to a British major serving at the regimental depot – one of the few occasions on which an Indian soldier corresponded with a British officer.)

The King and his Enemies

The British made similar efforts to enourage the personal devotion of the soldiers to the King-Emperor, to his immediate family, and to his Viceroy. With this in mind, many units were granted permission to include a Royal name in their honorific titles. By July 1914, 11 of the 116 Indian infantry and pioneer regiments, three of the ten Gurkha regiments and 13 of the 38 cavalry regiments had been awarded this mark of distinction.[232] Titles grew ever more elaborate. A unit listed unassumingly as 1 Bengal Cavalry in 1861 was officially known in 1914 as 1 Duke of York's Own Lancers (Skinner's Horse). The King was its Colonel-in-Chief, as he was of six other Indian cavalry regiments. Visiting Royals liked to inspect regiments with which they were personally associated. Members of the Royal family were also closely involved in army ceremonial, presenting new colours to regiments and sometimes making short and hastily-learned speeches in an Indian language.[233] Indian Army pensioners were assembled in camps to meet the Prince of Wales during his tour in 1921–22.[234] Over one thousand former Indian Officers gathered at the Delhi Race Course, and 'HRH must have shaken hands with nearly all of them.'[235]

Most spectacular of all, however, were the three great Durbars, held in 1877, 1903 and 1911 to celebrate, respectively, the proclamation of Queen Victoria as Empress of India, the accession of King Edward VII, and the visit and Coronation of King George V.[236] Staged at Delhi, the ancient seat of Mughal authority whose mantle the British hoped to assume, the Durbars were intended to legitimize British rule, to generate pro-imperial sentiment and to bring the sovereign or the Viceroy into communion with the people. They employed lavish ritual and feudal imagery to express and realize imperial power. In the words of Lord Lytton, they were 'like those parts of an animal which are no use for butcher's meat, nor even suited to scientific dissection, but from which augurers draw the omens that move armies and control Princes'.[237]

The troops of the Indian Army played a prominent part in every stage of these ceremonies. At the Durbar of 1903, Lord Curzon had a personal escort of one British and one Indian cavalry regiment; a Guard of Honour at his dais presented arms as he entered the amphitheatre; and a salute of 101 guns marked the conclusion of the National Anthem and the hoisting of the Royal Standard. Along the road from the Viceregal camp to the Durbar, and on the plain opposite the entrance to the amphitheatre, were drawn up no fewer than 37 000 soldiers, and their carefully-orchestrated cheers echoed the speeches, the trumpet flourishes and the patriotic music. A week later, there was a long-rehearsed and almost faultless military parade. Before the march-past, rain had damped down the dust which must otherwise have risen in choking swirls from the feet of 29 616 soldiers, the hooves of 8096 horses, and the wheels of 124 guns.[238]

The Royal family it seems, were in earnest. 'The thought that I leave India as Colonel-in-Chief of ten of its Native regiments is especially gratifying to me', remarked the future King George V in 1906. 'I shall always take a keen interest in their welfare.'[239] There is also clear evidence that Indian soldiers felt a strong sense of loyalty to the monarch.[240] Meeting the King was usually considered an honour and a delight. 'Oh my friend, what a thing it is to be an Indian Officer!' remarked one jemadar after a visit to London. 'It is full of pleasures. Above all to see His Majesty, and speak to him and stand in his presence for three hours, what greater pleasure can there be than this?'[241] Royal visits to the wounded, and letters of condolence to the families of the dead, earned warm approval.[242] Some soldiers spoke of the King in spiritual terms, and talked of 'worshipping' his presence.[243] 'It is a noble fate for us to be allowed to sacrifice our bodies for our King', remarked a wounded Garhwali sepoy. 'If we die on the battlefield in the service of our King, this is equal to entering heaven.'[244] Other letters imply a more secular perception of Royalty. One man spoke of the King as a 'father'; another hoped that 'our King may get relief from his arduous toil and, victorious, may be able to devote himself to the care of his subjects'.[245]

Attitudes to the King-Emperor emerged rather more clearly in the early months of 1917, after each soldier received a little portrait of King George V as a New Year's present. 'May God grant long life to the generous-hearted sovereign who has deigned to think of his humblest soldiers', remarked a Sikh lancer.[246] The picture was a poor likeness, which several soldiers took to mean that the King was grieving for the trials of his subjects.[247] 'Owing to the war this is the condition of his picture, that is to say he is suffering from anxiety for his people.'[248] For some men, the portrait assumed religious significance.[249] One Pathan sowar sent the likeness to a friend in the North West Frontier Province. He was told that 'the Mir Syed saw the card, took possession of it and said he would put it up in his shrine'.[250] A Sikh cavalryman sent the portrait to his wife, accompanied by the following message:

> I have sent you thrice before pictures of His Majesty. As you framed those and put them up on the wall opposite the door, so do the same with this picture after framing it. Worship it every morning when you get up. This is an act of religious merit. Every morning pray to the Guru that he will give victory to the King.[251]

Indian soldiers not only showed great affection for the King, they expressed hatred for his enemies. British troops in the trenches during the Great War developed something like affection for their German counterparts who shared the hardships of the front line and who echoed their contempt for shrill patriots safe at home.[252] The Indian soldiers, however, seemed to dislike the Germans more as the war progressed, their initial respect for the fighting spirit of the German Army gradually giving way to disgust at what they regarded as its brutality. 'The Germans are being trampled underfoot', wrote a Sikh sowar in October 1916. 'The day is at hand when the tyrant will receive the reward of his villainies and the ideas he had of world domination will be scattered far and wide and his dreams of playing the part of Napoleon will be dissipated.'[253] Indian feelings ran very high in the early summer of 1917, when they advanced over ground from which the Germans had recently retreated. For military reasons the Germans had scorched the earth, and the Allied soldiers entered a wasteland in which every house had been reduced to dust and ashes, every fruit-tree cut down and every road destroyed. 'This is the act of a wild beast', remarked one man.[254] He spoke for many Indians who were 'overwhelmed with grief' to see 'ruins which represented buildings costing thousands of rupees'.[255] Indian soldiers, often drawn from hard-pressed cultivating communities, were greatly distressed by the devastation of once-prosperous French farmland. Some urged revenge. 'We hope soon to give the German his just reward', wrote a Sikh lancer. 'His country will be destroyed in the same way. Neither the British nor the French will be content till they have entered Berlin.'[256]

CONCLUSION

Indian soldiers clearly did not fight just for pay. Most had a strong sense of honour, which induced some to enlist and encouraged others to act bravely in the field, usually with the aim of winning renown. The British were well aware that honour was important to the ranks, and tried to ensure that those who behaved honourably received suitable distinctions. Yet there can be no honour without shame; and the fear of being ashamed in front of comrades, kin or neighbours (along with a fear of physical punishment) was the main deterrent to desertion, malingering or running away.

Military identity, or *esprit de corps*, is essential to keep a unit coherent on the battlefield. The authorities did much to foster the *esprit de corps* of Indian Army regiments, mainly by trying to make extra-regimental identities underwrite those of military formations. Companies and regiments recruited from a single community, bound by ties of kin and locality, had better morale and *esprit de corps* than a mixed body, besides being less likely to combine in mutiny with other units. For reasons of internal security the British were reluctant to foster a single identity in units larger than the battalion; but heavy losses in Afghanistan and in the Great War meant that regimental groups of three or five battalions had to be formed to feed replacements to the front in a major conflict. Regimental titles, customs and details of uniform encouraged the fusion of military with other identities. The regimental calendar incorporated the main religious festivals of the ranks. The army's assiduous concern with identity had a wider social impact, and separatist or communal feeling in several recruiting grounds probably owed something to regimental structure and policy.

Nevertheless, the British still liked to believe that European officers held the army together. Contemporary observers perhaps protested too much, and their constant reiterations of what became an imperial litany may have disguised deeper insecurities about the competence of the officers and the attitude of the troops to them. There is scant evidence that most Indian soldiers felt much more than indifference to capable British officers, and active hostility to those that disrupted their familiar habits and cherished customs. The Commander-in-Chief was an exception, for Indian troops seem to have warmed to British efforts to foster a sense of personal attachment to him. Whatever their attitudes to British officers, the letters of Indian soldiers confirm that many were intensely loyal to the King-Emperor. The army was involved in most aspects of Royal ceremony, and the troops showed a devotion to the King that was at times spiritual in nature.

In general, the British were able to manipulate the Indian soldiers' sense of honour and identity to serve colonial and military ends. But honour and identity were two-edged swords, and they sometimes threatened to cut the ties that bound the sepoy to the Raj. Honour and identity may have fostered the cohesion of the army, but the ranks did not always cohere in loyal quiescence to the British. Although the discipline of the Indian Army was good, it was not perfect. The next chapter examines the occasional breakdowns in military discipline, and the strategies which the British employed to contain them.

4

Dissent

To say that a society functions is a truism; but to say that everything in a society functions is an absurdity.

Claude Lévi-Strauss[1]

I have often thought before I joined the Army how true were the words of the poet. 'Oh bee, how often have I warned you against sipping the honey of the flowers, because one day or other you will get caught and yield up your life writhing in agony.' This is the situation in which I find myself.

Sobha Ram, 2 Lancers, January 1917[2]

'Disaffection', remarked the Commander-in-Chief in 1875, 'is the greatest evil we have to guard against.'[3] He was half right. A major mutiny in the Indian Army would indeed have placed the Raj in grave peril. A large military rebellion would have been a serious problem in itself, and perhaps beyond the power of the British Army to suppress.[4] Furthermore, British rule in the subcontinent relied heavily upon the Indian Army, and the failure of this linchpin of colonial control might have fatally weakened the hold of the Raj over the civil population – for the policy of British India as a whole was closely connected to the constitution and discipline of its armed forces. 'An army of 120 000 men could not mutiny without dragging a large part of the country with it', commented a British general, wise after the event, in 1858. 'And if wide provinces strike for freedom', he added, 'the soldiers who spring from them are sure not to forget the claims of race, religion and brotherhood.'[5]

Imperial anxieties, however, tell only a partial story. A major mutiny was always a fearsome potential threat, and the white elite never forgot the atrocious lessons of 1857; but in the eighty years after the rising there was very little active dissent in the army. The Indian Army was a notably well-disciplined body, surviving the Great War with a more impressive record than the forces of several

major European powers.[6] The material and moral incentives
described in the previous two chapters were usually enough to keep
the Indian ranks in line. The British appeal to the interests and the
honour of the sepoys was for the most part rewarded with loyalty of
a kind.

But there were occasional problems. The material interests and
moral imperatives of the soldiers sometimes failed to prevent dissident behaviour, or could even work against the Raj. The Indian
Army, like most others, had intermittent outbreaks of desertion or
malingering. Depression and self-inflicted wounds made the
authorities anxious at certain stages of the Great War; after the
Armistice, political unrest in the recruiting grounds threatened
the discipline of some units. There were also more than a dozen
mutinies between 1886 and 1930. Most of these were minor, and
easily contained, but a few raised the spectre of a widespread
military uprising like that of 1857.

This chapter will explain why the material and ideological
incentive structures of military service sometimes broke down. It
will also show how the British were able to defuse or contain these
spatterings of military dissent.

FROM DEPRESSION TO DESERTION

The first section of this chapter will discuss forms of dissent other
than mutiny. It will focus upon the Great War and its immediate
aftermath for two reasons – because the conflict imposed great
strain upon the discipline of the army, and because the documents
for that period are especially rich.

The Failure of Morale on the Western Front

Upon the outbreak of war in 1914, an Indian Army Corps of two
infantry and two cavalry divisions was sent to France to help
stem the German onslaught. The troops saw heavy fighting, and
suffered great losses. Their spirits sank during their first winter
at the front.

Men in battle often become frightened and depressed, especially
if they have been wounded; but the collapse of morale among the
Indian soldiers in France in 1915 was at times unusually complete.
The sepoys seemed enthusiastic enough at first. 'The condition,

health and spirit of Indian troops now in France is excellent', reported their commander shortly after they had landed.[7] 'All realise that it is their duty to serve the Sirkar to death.'[8] The men were anxious to show that they could fight as well as Europeans, and they regarded the war much as a Frontier campaign on a larger scale.

After the troops had been at the front for only a few weeks, their confidence began to give way to an intense despair. The British General Staff grew anxious, and appointed a censor to secretly monitor the soldiers' correspondence, to report on their morale, and to watch for imminent signs of mutiny or panic. More and more letters from men in the trenches betrayed 'undeniable evidence of depression', while those written by the wounded from British hospitals were often hopeless in tone.[9] 'Many of the men show a tendency to break into poetry', remarked the censor, 'which I am inclined to regard as a sign of mental disquietude.' Of 220 letters from injured soldiers examined by the censor in January 1915, only fifteen displayed what he termed 'an admirable spirit'. Twenty-eight had been written by despairing men who clearly regarded themselves as good as dead already; many of the remainder gave a 'melancholy impression of fatalistic resignation'. Morale picked up a little in the summer of 1915, but another general collapse was clearly imminent in the autumn as the weather cooled and victory seemed as distant as ever. Rather than expose the troops to a second morale-battering winter on the Western Front, the authorities sent the two infantry divisions to Mesopotamia where the fighting was arguably less fierce and its outcome less vital. The cavalry, which had seen little action, remained in France.

There were various reasons for these failures of fighting spirit. Homesickness was a major problem. Indian troops disliked serving far away, and the General Staff had long recognized that this would hamper the maintenance of an army in Afghanistan.[10] Service in France was even more disorientating. Many men praised the education and admired the wealth of the French, but still pined for their loved ones. 'I am like a flower withering under a fierce sun. If only I could see you my heart would be like a bud opening in the fresh morning air.'[11] The French habit of keeping pigs disgusted some Muslims, and others resented celebrating the Id far from their homes.[12] 'Without one's family one might as well eat mud.'[13] Bad news from India compounded the worries of the men. They learned of the plague which afflicted the Punjab in the spring of 1915.[14] Men grew anxious for the well-being of their families when they heard, second-hand, that 'the rain has spoiled the crops, and in the Doab the dacoits have ruined the place'.[15] One soldier's wife told him bluntly, 'I have been starving for lack of food.'[16] Long separations strained marriages, and by July 1915 many letters were filled with conjugal reproaches.[17] One man was warned, 'your honour is in danger. If you are a Pathan, and have any pride, look to your wife.'[18] Betrothals were broken off, and some wives, despairing that their men would ever return, took new husbands.[19] 'When our thoughts turn to our homes our hearts become soft like wax', wrote one Muslim trooper.[20] Distance denied men the power to prevent their domestic affairs slipping out of their control. The Armistice did not lift these burdens all at once. In July 1920 there were still 100 000 war-weary Indian troops overseas, many of whom had not seen their homes for many years.[21]

The British authorities liked to use the weather to explain the poor morale of the Indian troops in France. Spirits had sunk, some argued, because Indian soldiers needed a warm climate if they were to fight well, and could not stand the cold, wet winters of North-West Europe. Morale certainly plummeted in the rain and sleet:

At night we wonder whether we shall see another morning; but morning comes all right and with it fresh trials to endure [wrote an Indian lancer]. One day we slept in the open with one blanket only and it snowed the whole night and we lay shivering. In the morning we expected to be dead but we got up all right and shook the snow off our blankets. We are in a regular hell and tired of life, yet our souls are so shameless that they do not leave our bodies.[22]

The British concern with the weather may, however, have misrepresented the feelings of the troops. Indian soldiers admittedly sickened at a higher rate than the British, but that rate was still only 2.5 per cent.[23] Furthermore, even though morale deteriorated in winter, depression also occurred in warm weather. The high command made a public issue of the unfamiliar European climate partly because they wanted to evade other awkward questions about the performance of the Indian troops in France.[24]

Transferring two Indian infantry divisions to the baking plains of Mesopotamia did not completely solve the problem of their morale. During the disastrous siege of Kut in 1916, General Townshend noticed that the Indian soldiers of his force lost heart much more quickly than the British. His explanation was simple. 'Indian troops', he thought, 'are not constituted by nature to stand misfortune and hardship with the same courage as Europeans.'[25]

Judging from their letters, Indian soldiers were troubled less by inclement weather than by the prospect of being killed. Losses in the West were heavy.[26] One of the first Indian regiments to see action, the 57 Rifles, suffered nearly 300 casualties in the last week of October 1914 alone. Two months later, the Germans exploded a series of mines under the Indian trenches, wiping out an entire double company of 1/4 Gurkhas. The following March, during the three-day battle of Neuve Chapelle (considered a major Imperial success) the Meerut Division lost 19 per cent of its Indian soldiers and 27 per cent of its British officers. Some regiments suffered especially hard. The 47 Sikhs once lost 575 men, nearly 80 per cent of their strength, in two days' fighting. Casualties on this scale, month after month, were quite unknown in the brisk Frontier skirmishes that had been the staple fare of Indian Army soldiering for the past half-century.

British troops were familiar with industrial society if not industrial slaughter, but Indian troops had seen nothing like it before. They tried hard to describe the battlefields of the Western Front in familiar terms, and their letters to their home villages are accordingly rich in animal and agrarian imagery. 'The men are dying like maggots. No one can count them – not in thousands but in hundreds and thousands of thousands', remarked a Sikh.[27] The death of a human being 'has become of as much account here as the death of an insect', commented another.[28] 'The enemy's guns roasted our regiments even as grain is parched.'[29] For one Gurkha, the war was 'like a huge mutiny'.[30] A wounded Muslim soldier tried to convey the astonishing destructive power of the German forces:

> God has made them fowls of the air, dragons of the earth, and poisonous crocodiles of the sea, and he has given them such skill that when we encounter their deceitful bayonets they set light to some substance which causes a suffocating vapour and then they attack. How can I describe this?[31]

One Rajput summed up his impressions in a single, telling remark. 'This is not war. It is the ending of the world.'[32]

The source of the most profound dismay, however, was the policy (without precedent in the recent past of the Indian Army) of returning wounded men to the front once they had recovered.[33] 'There is no hope that I shall see you again', wrote a Sikh soldier to his father. 'For we are as grain that is flung a second time into the oven, and life does not come out of it.'[34] The Indian troops thought that a man had amply discharged his duty if he had fought in the trenches and been wounded, and regarded it as most unjust to expect him to risk death or disablement a second time.[35] Because no end to the war was in sight, and because losses were so heavy, some of the wounded were reduced almost to despair. 'No one has any hope of survival', wrote a Muslim soldier, recovering in a British hospital. 'Only those who have lost a leg or an arm or an eye will see the Punjab again.'[36] Fighting spirit among the recovered sick and wounded in camps in France was understandably low. 'Their one object is, by any means, to avoid return to the front. These men undoubtedly contaminate fresh arrivals from India.'[37] Although expressions of anti-Imperial sentiment were rare, some men urged their relatives back home not to enlist.[38] The kinship networks which made Indian regiments so cohesive thus began to impede the strategies of the military elite.

Exit Options and Acceptance

The Indian troops occasionally translated their dismay into collective behaviour on the battlefield. By early November 1914, after fierce fighting during the recent First Battle of Ypres, the average strength of Indian Army battalions was less than 550, compared with 764 when they landed. Units which suffered notably large casualties became less reliable in action than British units which had endured comparable losses. A general pattern soon emerged. Indian Army regiments performed their ordinary duties well enough, but broke more easily than their British counterparts when under severe pressure.[39]

More common than these collective breakdowns of battlefield discipline, however, were acts by individuals seeking to escape the rigours of military service. Malingering had a long pedigree in the Indian Army. The pension regulations of 1864 allowed a healthy man to retire with pay after 40 years' service, while one unfit for further duty could obtain a smaller pension provided he had served for 15 years or more. These terms encouraged 'constant and successful malingering' until they were changed in the later nineteenth century.[40] Men who had served 15 years, but who were reluctant to wait another quarter of a century for a pension, took to feigning illness in the hope of a financially satisfactory discharge.[41]

During the Great War, some men – 'hundreds of thousands', according to one sepoy – took to malingering in the hope of saving their lives.[42]

> Many men, who can hear, pretend to be deaf; and those who can speak to be dumb [remarked a wounded soldier]. Some complain of pains in the loins, knees or body; others say they have giddiness in the head, or something the matter with their lungs. Each one gets before some committee and is sent back to the Punjab, thus saving his life. Otherwise it would be difficult, for there is no sign of the war stopping, and the whole world is being destroyed.[43]

Soldiers occasionally received letters from home urging them to report 'sick', and some men serving in France wrote to sepoys in India suggesting that they malinger to avoid the trenches.[44] Some reacted with horror at the idea. 'If I were to act according to your suggestion what explanation could I give to God and his prophet?' wrote one Muslim lancer.[45] The extent of malingering is difficult to measure; but the rate of sickness – real or feigned – did not much trouble the authorities.

Self-inflicted wounds were a different matter. In the autumn of 1914, medical officers began to remark on the large number of men who had been wounded in the left hand. It was thought at first that enemy fire was responsible, and men were warned not to expose their hands above the parapet. But senior officers soon realized that the injuries were self-inflicted. A study showed that 1049 (or 57 per cent) of the 1848 wounded Indian soldiers admitted to hospital by 3 November were injured in the hand.[46] While the Indian Army Corps was in France, the problem was mainly confined to those units which had endured the first shock of battle. British and Gurkha regiments were mainly unaffected. The number of self-inflicted hand wounds soon declined as the British authorities took firm action against the culprits. Officers threatened soldiers with a court martial and the death penalty for the offence. Some executions were carried out, but other men escaped with a long prison term.[47] Self-inflicted wounds could normally be distinguished from others by scorch marks on the flesh, even when a soldier had wrapped a piece of cloth around his hand to disguise the burn.[48] Nevertheless, errors of judgement occurred. 'My brother Johan Singh was hit on the hand the first night', wrote a disconsolate sepoy to a comrade in India. 'The Doctor declared he had shot himself, and the Doctor had him killed. You must not volunteer for service here. On no account must you come.'[49]

Sepoys soon found more subtle ways to make themselves unfit for military service. Several letters from 1915 and 1916 refer to *bhalwa*, a vegetable substance used by dhobis to mark clothes.[50] When made into a mash, heated and applied to the body or the inside of the mouth, it produced inflamed weals which lasted for ten days.[51] A Muslim from the United Provinces advised a sowar to apply the ground seeds of the *rand* plant to his eyes two or three times a day to redden them. 'By the Grace of God,' he added, 'no harm will be done.'[52] Applying earwax to the eyes with a blunt needle obtained similar results. He also suggested drinking a mixture of white lead in curds to become feverish, or placing a piece of copper in a knife-wound in the foot. He clearly had his friend's best interests at heart. 'The first and most important thing is to have yourself sent to hospital as soon as possible', he urged. 'Do not think of a pension.'

When soldiers in France were depressed, they injured themselves or malingered more often than they deserted. A disenchanted soldier was most likely to abscond when serving near his home.[53] The authorities were keen that battalions in India should do regular duty at their regimental centre near the recruiting ground, which shows that peacetime desertion was not considered a major problem. During the Great War, there was more incentive to quit the ranks, but in Europe the would-be deserter had no obvious place to go.[54] The distinctive appearance of Indian soldiers meant it would be difficult to find safe refuge in Britain or in France. The prospect of going over to the Germans was neither safe nor appealing – for it would be hard to get back to India, and severe punishment awaited those who were caught. Officers took a sympathetic attitude to temporary desertion in peacetime; but those who absconded in the face of the enemy would be lucky to escape the firing squad if recaptured.

There were two main exceptions to the overall pattern of low desertion rates. From early 1915, letters written by Pathan sepoys often show that they were willing to consider absconding.[55]

Many did so. When the 46 Punjabis were ordered to find drafts for France, more than fifty Afridis left the regiment.[56] A smaller party of Afridis from 58 Vaughan's Rifles went over to the Germans in March 1915. 'If any Pathan goes on leave', remarked a havildar serving in Karachi, 'he never comes back.'[57] The reasons were partly religious. Pathan attitudes to the war changed when Turkey entered hostilities at the end of 1914. Pathans were uneasy about serving an empire that was in open conflict with the temporal embodiment of Muslim authority, and they had especially strong scruples about fighting against their fellow Muslims near the Holy Places of Islam.[58] Some deserted for less elevated motives. When the 26 Punjabis went on leave, 168 Pathans did not return after their kinsmen induced them to join the rival factions in a clan feud.[59] Pathans also had a more attractive exit option than most other Indian Army soldiers, since their territory was not under direct British administration and they were likely to escape punishment if they ever got home. Some Afridis do appear to have made the journey back to the North West Frontier after deserting to the Germans in France.[60] Aware that Trans-Frontier Pathans were not wholly reliable, the British stopped recruiting them at the end of 1915.[61] Later in the war, all Pathans were excluded from field service in Mesopotamia for fear they might affect the rest of the Muslim sepoys in the region.[62]

The second spate of desertions came in 1916, among the force besieged at Kut, in Mesopotamia. 'Many' men went over to the Turks, even though the authorities took 'every precaution' to prevent them.[63] Food ran short during the siege, conditions were hard, and the trenches of the Turks were invitingly close. For Muslim sepoys, the fact that their enemies shared their religion further strained their loyalty. After the capitulation, the Turks put the deserters in with the prisoners, perhaps to demoralize the captives.[64]

The depression of the soldiers, and their desire to escape the fighting, gradually eased as the war progressed. After the first shock of battle had subsided, and the first two winters had passed, the troops seemed to adapt to the new conditions of warfare, and to accept that the conflict would last a long time. The morale of the cavalry on the Western Front remained consistently high from 1916, even though they were sent into the trenches to fight on foot.[65] There were some hints of war-weariness early in 1917, as the soldiers endured their third winter in the West. 'How long, how long can we stand all this! It would be a good thing if my soul were to quit my body. Oh God! turn thine eyes upon us sinners and forgive us', cried a despairing Muslim trooper.[66] Many soldiers could achieve happiness of a kind only by accepting that they were fated soon to die.[67] 'Except for resignation there is no remedy. I have met you and have eaten and drunk of India. Now I am ready to die, and it is best that I should die in the service of the Sircar', a Sikh cavalryman told his mother.[68] Others smoked opium or cannabis to soothe their worries.[69] But the winter of 1916–17, although much more severe than the first two of the war, did not inspire anything like the same outpourings of misery.[70] By July 1917, 'gloomy' letters were 'very much the exception'; and the censorship at Boulogne was soon ended, so confident were the authorities that morale was high.[71] The troops, it seems, were getting used to the war. 'Of course, when we have to go into the trench we do suffer some inconvenience', remarked a nonchalant Sikh trooper. 'But when you consider that we are soldiers and that a great war is on, the inconvenience is nothing much, nor novel. As regards life and death, that is all in the hands of God.'[72]

Nevertheless, the bewildering experience of fighting in an alien continent led some soldiers to question their assumptions about the world and their place within it. Their letters bear eloquent testimony to their astonishment at the splendour of European homes, the vast size of cities like London and Paris, and the cleanliness, fine clothes and orderly conduct of their inhabitants.[73] India seems to have suffered by comparison. 'The Creator has shown the perfection of his benevolence in Europe, and we [Indian] people have been created only for the purpose of completing the totality of the world', remarked a Muslim sepoy.[74] 'The man whom God wishes to punish is born in India.'[75] Indeed, the soldiers occasionally compared Europe to paradise.[76] The high level of European literacy, even among women, greatly impressed them, and it was to education that they most often attributed the achievements of European civilization.[77] Several urged their kin or caste-fellows to follow the European example. 'When they ask us here why our women are illiterate, we cannot give them any answer. Learning is an excellent thing; make arrangements for my daughters to be taught', instructed a Sikh cavalryman.[78] Contact with European mores encouraged Indians to question their own, particularly as Europeans seemed more affluent and successful.[79] Several soldiers noted with approval the modest French expenditure on religious display, and began to doubt the need for poor Indians to spend lavish sums on ceremonies of marriage or circumcision.[80] By serving in France, the Indian soldiers learned a little about Europe, but they began to understand a lot more about India and about themselves.

Modern war is also a great leveller, and soldiers who served in the field broke certain taboos.[81] One Sikh described a trip to Paris which he had made with two Muslims, two sweepers and two cooks – the men ate together, and he confessed that he 'often' consumed food and drink prepared by Muslims. Others began to doubt the importance of religious distinctions after talking with French Catholics. 'God is not the God of any particular religion', commented Fateh Mohammed Khan of the 19 Lancers. 'It is only in India that there is a *lakh* of Gods each with his own particular arrangements. This is clearly due to the ignorance of religious leaders and to them is due the fact that India is a depressed country and the laughing stock of the world.'[82] But military experience could encourage a rough egalitarianism that might have troubled the guardians of the colonial hierarchy. 'Sirdar Azmat Ullah wrote that we have no *izzat* here', remarked a Muslim lancer. 'This is a lie, for in a war like this, all men are equal. All the English suffer equally with us and sleep on the bare ground.'[83]

The Great War and Civil Unrest in India

These men, of course, went back to India after the Armistice, subtly changed by their experiences. They possessed a rare cultural commodity, for they had seen the homeland of the Sirkar, and had fought his enemies in France, Africa and Iraq. Their tales must have found ready listeners in their home villages; and in ways perhaps impossible to measure, the returning soldiers imparted new and broader perspectives, just as India was about to undergo its greatest civil unrest since 1857.

The soldiers came back to a country that the war had already deeply affected.[84] Grain and raw materials had been pumped out of India to supply the army. High military spending and the wartime disruption of transport pushed up prices to nearly double their prewar levels by 1919. Taxes rose. The most painful burden was the army's seemingly endless demand for young men.[85] Even during the Second Afghan War it had proved difficult to replace

losses, but that conflict was minor compared with the conflagra-
tion of 1914 to 1918. There were already six Indian expeditionary
forces serving overseas by the end of 1914. Recruitment became
much more intense in the middle years of the war, as the traditional methods failed to keep pace with the losses in an ever-
expanding conflict. By 1918, India had supplied 826 855 combatants, of whom 683 149 came from territory under direct British
rule.[86] Pressure was most heavy in the last months of 1918, after
the massive German offensives in the spring. Between June and
November, 98 869 men were enlisted from the Punjab alone.
Indeed, the Punjab remained the mainstay of army manpower
throughout the war; by the end of 1918, one male Punjabi in
twenty-eight had been mobilized.[87]

The British offered honours and grants of prime irrigated land
to those men of local influence who helped attract recruits. At
first, this produced willing help; but from the middle of the war
these methods failed to provide enough men. More Indian troops
were needed for the minor theatres to free British and Dominion
soldiers for Europe. In October 1916, the Government centralized
all recruiting under the Adjutant-General. Recruiting by geographical division replaced recruiting by class, so men could
enlist without travelling far from their homes. From the summer
of 1917, a Central Recruiting Board set quotas of men for each
province. The Punjab bore the brunt, being expected to provide
14 000 combatants per month – 40 per cent of the Indian total.
This was still not enough. So the Government promised to find
500 000 men between May 1918 and June 1919, 180 000 of them
from the Punjab. Even General O'Dwyer, the authoritarian Governor of the province, thought this was too much. Purely voluntary enlistment had proved inadequate by 1916, so from that
autumn coercion was tried. Influential men were told they would
lose government patronage if they did not bring in recruits. The
revenue administration was also harnessed to military ends, and
its Indian officials were threatened with the loss of their jobs and
land if they did not cooperate.[88]

The Indian functionaries of imperialism transmitted these pressures to the villages, without, however, directly implicating the
colonial authorities. Fearful of losing their jobs, their land or their
honours if they failed to find men for the army, many Indian
officials resorted to coercion in their efforts to procure recruits. They
threatened to suspend leases on land, or to cut down the supply of

water for irrigation unless a village provided soldiers. Some men were falsely charged, then given a choice between prison and the ranks. In Shahpur District one official made men stand naked in thorn bushes in the June heat until some gave in and agreed to enlist. Recruiting committees occasionally descended on a village and demanded food until recruits appeared. Sometimes men were simply kidnapped, as in Gujranwala District where recruits were pressganged in nocturnal raids, although such outright violence was mainly confined to the Western Punjab.[89]

The British tried to remain in the background to avoid sharing the odium which their subordinates incurred. It suited the authorities to turn a blind eye to over-zealous recruiting, provided enough men appeared. But British officials could not afford to ignore recruiting methods when they provoked resistance. Oppressive officials were sometimes murdered, as in Shahpur District where villagers killed and mutilated a recruiter whom they suspected of interfering with local women. In some districts there was occasional rioting, and in Multan a recruiting party 120 strong ended up fighting a pitched battle with angry villagers.[90] Minor clashes were common; but most of the violent incidents took place in 1918, when pressure to find men was at its most intense. The Gujranwala disturbances of 1919, however, were perhaps also linked to coercive recruiting during the war.[91] In the last year of the conflict, the Punjab Government received 126 petitions complaining of recruitment by force, more than a third of them from Gujranwala alone. Peasants could, however, turn the desperation of Indian officials to their advantage. Some men offered two or three hundred rupees to anyone who would enlist: recruits occasionally joined up on behalf of a village, then absconded with the bounty.[92] But these bribes were sometimes pledged with no intention of paying them, which left a postwar legacy of resentment among those former soldiers who had served without receiving the money or land which they believed was their due.[93]

Civil Unrest and the Indian Army

During the Great War, political dissent within the army itself was most rare. There were a few flickers of sedition in the ranks. 'I have had to hang and shoot a certain number of Indian soldiers', complained the Commander-in-Chief in February 1916. 'But I think I am through the worst of that.'[94] Some of the troops in France used coded letters to convey political information, usually of a fairly innocuous kind.[95]

From the early 1920s, however, nationally-minded Indians made repeated efforts to subvert the Indian Army.[96] Between January 1920 and September 1921, the General Staff detected over ninety attempts on the loyalty of the Indian soldiers. Only four of these succeeded, involving only a handful of men in each case.[97] Army chiefs were usually confident that the political agitation would not greatly appeal to the enlisted classes.[98] When persuasion failed, less delicate methods often followed. On several occasions, the families of serving soldiers were harassed with the object of forcing their menfolk to leave the army.[99] These efforts did not succeed; but soldiers travelling by train were unwilling to arrest civilians who had spoken seditiously to them, as they feared that the resulting publicity might bring harm to their families. They waited until they had returned to their units before reporting such incidents, which made it difficult to secure convictions. The police and magistrates, moreover, had come to view the troops' complaints with some suspicion, since a few men had made false accusations to gratify a personal grudge.[100]

Twice in the early twentieth century, the Government of India made concessions to political opponents when wider currents of unrest began to ripple the discipline of the Indian Army. The first occasion was in 1907, after extensive agrarian disturbances in the Chenab canal colony in the Western Punjab.[101] Founded in 1887, the colony had been settled by carefully-selected cultivators of 'proven loyalty', many of them from the enlisted classes. After initial success, the colony encountered problems. Choice plots soon ran out, subdivision among sons led to small and uneconomic holdings, and it proved difficult to maintain sanitary and residential discipline. The Chenab Colonies Bill of 1906 addressed these issues. It proposed to forbid the transfer of property at will, to make primogeniture compulsory and to legalize a system of fines to maintain discipline. The colonists saw the Bill as an unjustified intrusion into their private lives and an offence against their concept of ownership. A rise in the Bari Doab Canal water rates of between 25 and 50 per cent was the catalyst for widespread rural protest, which urban organizations soon took up.

Some agitators appealed to the martial traditions of the peasantry in attempts to foment anti-British feeling. Ajit Singh, a revolutionary Jat leader from Lahore, wrote in a widely-circulated pamphlet:

Oh! brave soldiers of the Khalsa you are lost to all sense of national honour. Give up the British service and permit the Feringhees no more to disgrace you. If you are brave enough, expel the English from your land.[102]

A local newspaper editor coined the slogan 'Pagri Sambhal Jatta' [Oh Jat! guard your turban]. This sort of language tried to tap the powerful military and religious identities that the British had hitherto successfully harnessed to colonial purposes in the army. Indeed, as Kitchener remarked, 'the agitators openly state that they can do nothing unless they do get hold of the Army'.[103] The government grew concerned for the discipline of the troops. Some sepoys went to seditious meetings at Ferozepur.[104] Kitchener admitted he was 'anxious' about agitators reaching the ranks, where he thought there was 'plenty of tinder'.[105] The close connections between the colonies, the districts and the regiments of the Punjab made the agrarian unrest more widely important. The crucial military role of the Punjab peasantry tied the hands of government in the province, forcing the Viceroy, Lord Minto, to veto the Canal Colonies Bill and reduce the water rates.[106]

The Sikh Gurdwaras Act of 1925 was the second political concession provoked partly by worries over army discipline. In March 1919, the new Sikh League announced its plan to liberate all *gurdwaras* from the control of government-appointed guardians or *mahants*; and in November the following year, a meeting of 10 000 Sikhs elected a group of temple-managers known as the Shiromani Gurdwara Prabandhak Committee. The SGPC, aided by the Akali Dal (formed at Amritsar in December 1920 to coordinate the local bodies of volunteers, or Akali Jathas) launched a successful movement to bring all *gurdwaras* under its own control on behalf of the Sikh people. The struggle began in earnest early in 1921. Within a year, defiance of law and order had become 'widespread' among Sikhs. The militants agitated mainly without violence; but police repression was fierce, and by the end of the five-year campaign some 4000 people had lost their lives. About 30 000 more were arrested. The campaign had various foci, including the Golden Temple; but the best-known confrontation took place from August to October 1922 at the Guru-ka-Bagh [Garden of the Guru] near Amritsar. Akali *jathas* marched there daily, courting arrest yet remaining peaceful in the face of severe police beatings.

The movement soon began to affect the army. Retired and demo-bilized Sikh soldiers were employed to inspect the *jathas* as they set out; and one body which marched to the Guru-ka-Bagh was com-posed entirely of veterans, led by a former Subedar Major.[107] The Akalis appealed to Sikh troops to leave the army; and in the early 1920s recruiting officers found it harder to persuade Jats to enlist.[108] The discipline of most Sikh units at first remained good, but the General Staff doubted whether the army would ignore the agitation for long. Sikh troops began asking the advice of the SGPC on regimental matters, and the possible behaviour of some Sikh units in an emergency was thought to be uncertain.[109] The 14 Sikhs and the 52 Punjabis showed 'signs of contamination'.[110] Akali Dal and SGPC activity had encouraged some Sikh soldiers to wear black tur-bans or *kirpans* of greater than regulation length; and of the 45 Indian other ranks punished for disaffection in 1922, 39 were in con-nection with the *kirpan* agitation.[111] Not all the militants remained peaceful. In 1922, the Babbar Akali Jatha was formed to intimidate British officials. This gang of 800 men, including many former soldiers, carried out a series of political murders in 1923 before the army broke it up.[112] In 1925, the government acknowledged the SGPC as the lawful guardian of all *gurdwaras*, partly because the authorities feared that the discipline of Sikh units might not hold if the campaign continued. A legacy of mistrust remained. The 1928 recruiting handbook included a long review of recent Sikh history, 'in order to show that the Sikhs are not immune from disloyal influences'.[113]

British propagandists did what they could to counter political subversion in the military. Late in 1922, for example, a senior mem-ber of the Indian Civil Service toured Sikh units to present the gov-ernment's view of the Guru-ka-Bagh affair.[114] British officers were sent into the recruiting grounds to redress the grievances of pensioners, to show support to soldiers' families, and to dispel the 'absurd rumours spread by seditionists'.[115] British counter-propaganda became more active during the Civil Disobedience movement of 1930–31. Recruiting officers made it known that the government would punish 'disloyalty' among former soldiers with a loss of pension or land. The army newspaper *Fauji Akhbar* pub-lished articles contradicting 'the false statements of agitators' and showing 'what we are doing for the country and what would happen if we left'. The Commanding Officer of each unit prepared a weekly news sheet which presented 'the true situation from a regimental point of view'. These were sent to men on leave, to influential former soldiers, and to the families of those still serving. The men were fed a pro-British line on the current political situation before they visited their homes. The Chief of the General Staff, 'Butcher' Deverell, hoped that 'every soldier of the Indian Army' could become a loyal government spokesman. 'All must remember that the present revolutionary propaganda is unsound because it is untrue', he added.[116]

Islam and Indiscipline

The conflicting appeals of Islam and Empire were a further threat to army discipline. Wars with Afghanistan and the campaigns against the Frontier tribes tested the loyalty of Muslim troops from time to time.[117] Pathans in particular disliked fighting the Amir, whom they regarded as 'their big man'.[118] Many Pathans deserted during the Second Afghan War of 1878–80. According to Lord Roberts, 'the Mahomedan element in my force gave me considerable anxiety'.[119] In view of these worries, no Muslim troops were employed in the Frontier campaign of 1897–98.[120]

The presence of large numbers of Muslims in the army affected the attitude of the Indian government towards some broader political questions. In particular, the authorities kept a watchful eye on the pan-Islamic movement, which emerged in the later nineteenth century in response to the global retreat of Muslim temporal power before European imperialism.[121] Pan-Islamic feeling ran deep, and during the Great War the British grew worried that the Anglo-Turkish conflict might unsettle Muslim sepoys. The military defeat of Ottoman Turkey did not immediately end these concerns. By 1919, almost all Indian Muslims supported a lenient peace for Turkey – one which kept the Anatolian provinces intact, guaranteed Muslim protection of the Holy Places and, crucially, retained the Khalif at Constantinople (for he was seen by many Muslims as the temporal and spiritual head of Islam).[122] 'If hostilities are prolonged we cannot say how the additional blow of Turkey's ruin may affect our Moslems, including those in the Army', remarked an anxious Government of India in May 1919.[123] As if that were not enough, the Amir of Afghanistan declared *jihad* against the British the same month. 'Great Britain has Islam against her,' he announced, 'and is weakened by having to trust to troops whose hearts are not with her.'[124]

Although the Afghan Army was quickly beaten, Congress and the Khalifate politicians made what they could of Muslim grievances during the civil unrest of 1919–22. In February 1923, a conference of Muslim theologians (Jamiat-ul-Ulema) issued a *fatwa* declaring it to be a sin against the Prophet to give help of any kind to the Government of India, for such aid would 'only be used to destroy the faithful Turk'.[125] In the event, these various appeals did not much disturb the discipline of Muslim soldiers, but there was general Imperial relief when the Turks themselves abolished the Khalifate after a revolution in 1924. At times it had seemed a near-run thing, and government anxieties reflected those voiced earlier by George MacMunn. 'It is only necessary for a feeling to arise that it is impious to serve the British', he warned, 'for the whole of our fabric to tumble like a house of cards without a shot being fired or a sword unsheathed'.[126]

While the Indian regular troops never realized MacMunn's deepest fears, the irregular forces proved less resistant to the claims of Islam during the Afghan *jihad* of 1919. These local militias owed their origin to the growing cost of military operations on the North West Frontier which had culminated in the massive campaign to suppress the tribal risings of 1897–98. Lord Curzon sought a cheaper method of control, which would free Indian troops for greater purposes.[127] From 1899, the Indian Army held back from the inhospitable, profitless and ungoverned zone along the Afghan border between the furthest limits of effective administration and the outer edge of nominal British rule.[128] Regular troops, besides being expensive, were thought to provoke the tribesmen. So the army was withdrawn to the administered territory, and tribal levies under the orders of the civil power were put in its place.[129] The new units were recruited among the Pathans themselves, but led mostly by British officers seconded from the army. By 1904, there were 8736 irregulars in Imperial service on the North West Frontier.[130] Lightly-armed, mobile and cheap, they proved effective. No army operations were needed on the Frontier between 1902 and 1914, as the militias checked raiding gangs, arrested 'bad characters' and struck minor punitive blows.[131]

Cheap the militias may have been, and competent enough at their workaday duties, but they failed their makers during the crisis of 1919. When the Afghan Amir declared *jihad* in the spring, the Pathan irregulars began to melt away with the snows. Many men reported 'sick' as soon as hostilities began. Desertion rapidly became a major problem. By early June, 1200 men of the Zhob militia had absconded, leaving only a handful under orders.[132] All the other corps were also badly affected. The militias were staunch enough until ordered to withdraw from forward posts. This they regarded as a great victory for the Afghans, and large groups began to slip away during the retreat.[133] The Afghan *jihad* subjected the loyalty of the men to a strain the militia system was never meant to bear.[134]

The former militiamen showed no reluctance to exchange fire with government troops, and they attacked isolated posts or ambushed imperial columns – sometimes with other hostile tribesmen in support.[135] Many still wore their khaki uniforms, and were from time to time mistaken for Afghan regulars.[136] They moved in bands sometimes several hundred strong, occasionally waylaying Hindu moneylenders.[137] Some even joined the Afghan Army.[138] Five hundred men of the Waziristan Militia formed a battalion in Afghan service, and 120 trained signallers went to Kabul as instructors.[139] After the war, tribal deputations tried to persuade the Amir to obtain amnesty for all deserters; but isolated raids by former militiamen went on at least until May 1920.[140] The British response was often heavyhanded. Cavalry swept across the plains in search of absconders, and the RAF bombed other parties who had taken refuge in the hills.[141] The British clearly did not set much store by Pathan life. They were more concerned to prevent militia weapons from falling into the hands of hostile tribesmen, and threatened violence against those communities who did not return government firearms.[142]

Military policy on the Frontier changed radically after the campaign of 1919–20. Regular troops occupied Waziristan and built roads to conduct Imperial power far into the hills. With the return of the army, the militias were no longer so vital. Most were disbanded, or converted to armed police and stationed far from their homes.[143]

MUTINY

For the British, the desertion of the militias was a disappointment, but a mutiny of the army would have been a disaster. The military uprising of 1857 nearly broke colonial power in the subcontinent, and, in the years that followed, the white elite still feared the sepoys. 'There are many discontented people amongst the 300 millions of India', remarked Lord Roberts in 1907, 'and the native troops may

again be led astray.'[144] During the Great War, the Viceroy worried
that a military disaster in Mesopotamia might 'seriously affect' the
discipline of Muslim troops elsewhere.[145] The enemies of the Raj
were conscious of these fears and sought to turn them into facts. The
Ghadrite leaders, for example, were well aware that 'without the
active cooperation of the troops, their plans for revolution in India
are doomed to failure'.[146] In 1915, British agents in Persia discovered
leaflets, printed by the Germans, urging the sepoys 'to shoot down
their English officers, to massacre the English soldiers and share
with us the glory of becoming a free nation'. After the Armistice,
both Congress and the Afghan Amir tried to subvert army discipline.[147] By then, however, the British authorities were more confident of their troops, some of whom had endured four years of
imperial war with only murmured protest. Demobilization, military
reforms and political unrest did prompt some anxiety in the early
1920s, as did the Civil Disobedience campaigns ten years later; yet
the Government of India still held that a widespread mutiny was
'improbable'.[148]

But not impossible. Only the most imprudent of colonial governments would ignore the risk of a rebellion among indigenous
troops; and if 1857 had taught the British anything, it had taught
them prudence. For example, in 1936 they did not chance sending
Indian troops to Palestine to suppress the Arab Revolt.[149] They also
made it a matter of policy to keep a large European garrison in India
to guard the guardians of the Raj. On the eve of the Mutiny, there
were 232 224 Indian and 45 522 European troops in the subcontinent
– a ratio of more than five to one. (See Table 4.1.) After the rising,
most British officers urged an increase in the European portion. 'If
we have a large native army,' one remarked, 'we must also have a
[British] army to keep it in order.'[150] The Peel Commission in 1859
recommended a permanent European garrison of 80 000 men, outnumbered only two to one by Indian troops in Bengal and three to
one in the southern Presidencies.[151] In practice, however, the abso-
lute number of British troops usually remained a little less than this,
but they formed a larger proportion of a much-reduced military
establishment. From the Mutiny until 1914, there was normally one
British soldier to every two sepoys.

During the Great War, British soldiers were urgently needed in
Africa and Europe, and at one point their numbers in India dwindled to 15 000.[152] As it turned out, there was no extensive wartime
unrest in the subcontinent, but the General Staff grew anxious.[153] 'I

TABLE 4.1.
Ratio of British to Indian troops in British India, 1794–1905

| Year | Number of troops | | Indian soldiers per British soldier |
	British	Indian	
Before the Mutiny			
1794	16 000	82 000	5.1
1808	24 500	154 500	6.3
1857	45 522[1]	232 224[2]	5.1
After the Mutiny			
1863	62 000	125 000	2.0
1878	66 343	123 254	1.9
1901[3]	66 086	142 831	2.2
1905	78 370	150 410	1.9

[1] Bengal 24 366; Madras 10 726; Bombay 10 430. These figures are slightly higher than some estimates. The Eden Commission Report gives 39 375 Europeans for 1856.

[2] This figure comes from a detailed breakdown in the Peel Commission Report (Appendix 15) giving the totals on the eve of the Mutiny (Bengal 135 767; Madras 51 244; Bombay 45 213) with 45 522 Europeans. It includes 4 241 veterans. The Eden Commission Report gives 214 985 (for 1856), a slightly low figure which perhaps excludes artillery. Shibly (PhD thesis, p. 32) has 311 038 Indians, which must include many paramilitaries and armed police. On the other hand, Viscount Canning (Peel Commission Report, Appendix 55) gives 200 000 as the Indian total (Bengal, 119 000; Madras 50 000; Bombay 31 000). For the Bengal Army alone on 1 January 1857, Maj-Gen. Mansfield (Peel Commission Report, Appendix 62) has 15 570 Europeans and 170 000 Indians. The former figure closely agrees with that for the British regular regiments given in Appendix 15 of the Peel Commission Report. It perhaps excludes artillery and the Company's Europeans. The latter figure explicitly includes irregulars, drivers and gun lascars.

[3] Actual strength. The establishment on paper was 75 970 British troops and 155 935 Indian.

Sources: Eden Commission Report, 15 November 1879, L/MIL/7/5445 (1794, 1808, 1878); Peel Commission Report, Appendix 15 (1857); Mason, *Matter of Honour*, pp. 318–19 (1863); Report of Committee on Military Defence of India, 24 December 1901, CAB 6/1; Establishment of the Army in India, 10 March 1905, CID 90-D, CAB 6/3.

want every white soldier in India that I can get', the Viceroy told Kitchener in 1915. 'I cannot gamble with the lives of loyal Indians and Europeans.'[154] After the war, the nationalists urged the abolition of the formal ratio between British and Indian troops, on the grounds that it was a costly insult to the loyalty and fighting spirit of the Indian people. In 1921, Henry Rawlinson agreed. 'We have decided to trust the Indians, and we cannot justify an army of occupation', he wrote.[155] But little changed.[156] British troops were still thought necessary to guard against sepoy disaffection.[157] Their numbers declined, but only slightly – from 57 080 in 1925 to 51 669 in 1938.[158] And although the memories of 1857 faded, they did not die. Even in the 1930s, British soldiers still took their weapons to Church parade on Sunday, just in case.[159]

Defining Mutiny

These elaborate precautions were never fully tested, perhaps because they were taken. There were, however, a number of minor Indian Army mutinies which this section will discuss. Before analyzing their origins and their form, we must define the term 'mutiny'.

Military law is a good place to start. The 1879 Army Act regarded mutiny as 'collective insubordination, or a combination of two or more persons to resist or to induce others to resist lawful military authority'.[160] This definition contains several noteworthy points. First, a mutiny must be collective. A single soldier, no matter how he might defy military authority, cannot commit mutiny by himself, at least not according to the terms of the 1879 Act. Secondly, a mutiny need not be violent. A body of soldiers who peacefully refuse to obey orders have, in law, committed mutiny. And thirdly, the authorities expected soldiers who shared a grievance to present their complaints one by one to their immediate superiors or company officers, rather than collectively to the commander of their unit. If they assembled to present their grievances, the authorities might regard this as a mutiny, especially if it involved even an implicit refusal of duty.

The problems of defining a mutiny, however, begin rather than end with military law. Men peacefully engaged in mutiny, legally defined, might resist the suggestion that they were mutineers. To accept the label, and the associated stigma, might undermine the legitimacy of their protest. Most soldiers acknowledged collective violence as mutiny; but they sometimes hinted that peaceful collective protest was a legitimate way of drawing attention to a grievance. Regimental officers were sympathetic to this view. No officer liked to admit that his men had mutinied, since his own conduct would probably then be in serious question. 'The men's action was not mutinous except in the technical meaning of the word, the matter being merely a regimental grievance and a passing outburst of temper', remarked one commanding officer after he had delayed reporting a mutiny in his unit.[161] Moreover, officers and men shared a concern for the reputation and standing of their regiment, which gave them a further reason to play down the mutinous character of any protest. The higher military authorities were also reluctant to admit in public that a mutiny had taken place. They perhaps feared it might be imitated, or that public knowledge of an army mutiny might damage the prestige of the Raj. So they sometimes charged mutineers with a lesser offence such as 'disobeying lawful commands'. After one such incident, a British general remarked that 'the disturbance was nothing more than a "sudden fit", which natives sometimes take'.[162]

Nevertheless, the authorities did not want soldiers to conclude that collective disobedience was an effective and legitimate way of getting grievances redressed. They were therefore reluctant to flatly deny the legally mutinous nature of these protests. Some remarks of Lord Birdwood illustrate this ambivalence towards peaceful mutiny. 'One cannot help having the very greatest sympathy for them', he said in 1930 of some Garhwali soldiers who had refused to perform riot-control duty. 'But even so, it must be impossible to overlook what technically amounts to mutiny.'[163]

According to this broad 'technical' definition, there were at least fourteen mutinies in the Indian Army between 1886 and 1930. (See Table 4.2.) Unlike the military uprising of 1857, they were all relatively minor affairs. The smallest incident involved as few as twenty men, and the largest only a battalion. A company or two was usual. Furthermore, most of them were isolated incidents, without direct links to civil unrest or to other military protests. And only one – the Singapore mutiny of 1915 – involved sepoy violence against their officers.

The following discussion will reflect the widely-drawn distinction between peaceful and violent military unrest. It will first address the origins and pattern of non-violent mutinies before examining the transition to violence.

TABLE 4.2
Indian Army mutinies, 1886–1930

Date	Unit	Place	Troops involved
12 April 1886	3 Gurkhas	Almorah	most of the battalion
3 May 1894	17 Bengal Infantry	Agra	A and E companies
Oct. 1894	25 Madras Infantry	Shwebo (Burma)	4 Hindu companies
13 Sept. 1897	14 Bombay Infantry	Bareilly	170 Konkani Mahrattas
1 Nov. 1897	17 Bombay Infantry	Bhuj	one company
18 Sept. 1897	27 Madras Infantry	Moulmein (Burma)	30 men
11–12 April 1910	76 Punjabis	Tientsin (China)	200 men
Jan. 1915	130 Baluchis	Rangoon (Burma)	three Pathan companies
15 Feb. 1915	5 Light Infantry	Singapore	half the battalion
23 Feb. 1916	15 Lancers	Basra (Mesopotamia)	429 men
2–4 April 1917	3 Brahmans	Mesopotamia	120 men
22 June 1918	18 Infantry	China	20 men
1–3 July 1918	38 Dogras (depot)	Jhelum	Hill Brahman companies
24 April 1930	2/18 Royal Garhwal Rifles	Peshawar	two platoons

Sources: Mainly L/MIL/7/7266-84 (Collection 159). Also L/MIL/7/7156-7, 7191, 18327 and L/MIL/17/19/48. And see Notes to Chapter 4.

Symptoms and Outbreaks

Peasant rebellions in colonial India were often preceded by warning signs – coded messages, rumours that something was 'in the air', or symptoms of unease like the chapattis that passed from village to village in North India just before the rising of 1857.[164] Similar noises sometimes sounded in advance of military discontent, and the antennae of colonial intelligence were occasionally sensitive enough to detect them.[165]

British intelligence did score one notable success – against the Ghadrite conspiracy early in 1915.[166] The Ghadrites were a body of revolutionaries active mainly among Sikh expatriates in North America. The migrants retained close links with their homelands, and many returned to the Punjab after the outbreak of war in 1914.[167] Encouraged by the Germans, the Ghadrites took advantage of the conflict to plan an uprising against the Raj. They tapped potential support among Sikh units in North Indian cantonments.[168] But the British had penetrated the organization, and moved fast to forestall the revolt. They raided the Ghadrite headquarters, arrested the leaders of the movement, and disarmed the doubtful regiments.[169]

British intelligence, however, was normally much less alert than this. The Indian officers were supposed to give timely warning of discontent, but they rarely did so.[170] In 1857, and later, most of them mutinied with their men because they shared the sepoys' grievances or feared their violence.[171] The senior Indian officer of a unit – the subedar-major (or risaldar-major in a cavalry regiment) – was held responsible for keeping its British commander 'acquainted with every occurrence, circumstance, or condition among the native ranks which may be prejudicial to the general good feeling or interests of the corps'.[172] But even this source of information sometimes ran dry. The Subedar-Major of the 10 Jats, for example, had become an opium-eater by 1910, 'and was probably too dulled to know what went on in the regiment'.[173] A detective assigned to the unit also failed to discover the pervasive influence of the Arya Samaj.[174] The commander of the 25 Madras Infantry attached Muslim sepoys to the Hindu companies of the regiment to act as informers; but the Hindus regarded this as an insult, and it did not prevent their mutiny in 1894.[175]

The first that most British officers knew of a mutiny was the outbreak itself. This was despite the fact that the most common trigger for collective protest was a British action. These triggers seemed very varied – they included the introduction of new messing arrangements, a partial judgement in a caste dispute, the with-drawal of a customary rice *batta*, the arrest of a spokesman, and an order to fight the Turks near the Holy Places of Islam.[176] But they had one thing in common. In each case, a British action broke the tacit bargain between officers and men which informed the discipline of the Indian Army. The troops reacted to the loss of a right which custom had sanctioned – the right to non-interference in matters of religion, to unbiased judgements in regimental disputes, to a given level of pay and allowances, to representation through a chosen spokesman. Most mutinies began when an officer breached the implicit contract between the sepoy and the Raj.

Deeper Causes: Political and Religious

A particular action by an officer could trigger a mutiny, but sometimes there were underlying tensions which predisposed the troops to dissent. Philip Mason argues that a mutiny usually has two ingredients besides what he calls (following convention) 'a spark to touch off the powder'. One of these, he suggests, is a history of poor relations between officers and men; the second is 'widespread discontent outside the army among people with whom the soldiers are in sympathy'.[177] In Mason's view, mutiny is not a purely military or regimental event, but one linked to broader social and political currents.

There is certainly ample evidence that Indian troops were aware of the world outside their regiment and the army.[178] There is no need for complex theories of transmission to explain this. Soldiers' letters contain frank references to recent mutinies in other units, from which the politically dissident drew comfort.[179] The British watched this correspondence closely but did little to suppress it. The soldiers also wrote about current political events, such as the Arab Revolt of 1916, sometimes encoding their letters in attempts to outwit the censor.[180] The military censor drew attention to some of these cryptic messages, if only 'to show the impossibility of preventing these people from communicating any news which they have a mind to spread'.[181] Ghadrites, Bolsheviks, Congress nationalists and others tried from time to time to pass political literature to the troops, sometimes with success.[182] Men returning from leave also brought back news of events at home.[183] Given all this, it is not surprising that British enquiries into the origins of mutiny tried to uncover any links to Indian political dissent.[184]

They did not find many. The mutiny most often thought to have political content was that of the 2/18 Garhwalis at Peshawar in April 1930, at the height of the Civil Disobedience movement.[185] On 23 April, two platoons of the battalion deployed across a road, facing a hostile Congress and Redshirt crowd about 1500 strong. For an hour or two, the rioters taunted the soldiers, struck them with staves and pelted them with bricks, bottles and stones, often from very close range. Many men were injured, a few seriously. But they were under orders not to shoot, even in self-defence, except on the express instructions of their British officer; and he was badly wounded and taken to hospital early on. Only when the crowd had seized a rifle did the soldiers open fire to disperse the assembly. The following day, two platoons were ordered into the city for further riot-control duty, and – they thought – for more of the same treatment. The troops refused, gave up their weapons without a fight, and were peacefully disbanded.

Several commentators thought the Garhwali mutiny was political in nature. Fenner Brockway (the Independent Labour Party MP), a few Indian nationalists and some British trade union branches claimed that the soldiers had refused 'an order instructing them to shoot down unarmed Indian demonstrators'.[186] This was quite untrue, as was their implication that the troops sympathized with the crowd.[187] In fact, the rioters taunted the soldiers with shouts of 'when we have our Government, we will make the Garhwalis and Gurkhas into sweepers'.[188] There had, however, been a history of dissent in the Garhwali recruiting grounds, which in 1937 voted solidly for Congress.[189] Since the late nineteenth century, the peasants of Garhwal had resisted the intrusion of commercial forestry, which was eroding their customary right to use the resources of the woods.[190] Soldiers on leave and former sepoys were prominent in these protests. By 1930, however, this peasant activity was still largely independent of formal political movements such as Congress, and there is no evidence that it influenced the behaviour of the troops at Peshawar. The Garhwalis mutinied simply because they had been mishandled and 'subjected to treatment which no soldier should be asked to stand without retaliation'.[191]

Mutinies more often had a religious than a political background, although the two were never completely separate. British officers did not normally interfere in regimental religious practice, considering this a matter for the Indian officers and men to arrange for themselves. The British would, however, judge communal disputes, which often had a religious content, but it was vital for discipline that such arbitration was seen to be fair. The Hindu companies of the 25 Madras infantry mutinied after a dispute with the Muslims of the regiment over the cooking plans for the Dusserah festival.[192] The tactless and indecisive Commanding Officer contributed to the mutiny, for he was thought to be under the influence of the Muslim Subedar Major.

Many Pathans had strong religious objections to fighting the Turks, which resulted in at least one mutiny. In January 1915, three Pathan companies of the 130 Baluchis refused to embark at Rangoon when they learned that their regiment was destined for Mesopotamia.[193] The men did not resist arrest and the remainder of the regiment duly sailed, but its destination was changed to Mombasa. A similar protest occurred in one non-Pathan Muslim regiment. In February 1916, the 15 Lancers were ordered to march from Basra up the Tigris to join the forces at the front. Most of the regiment refused, owing to their 'very strong religious scruples against fighting in the vicinity of the holy places of Baghdad and Kerbela'.[194] There was no hint of cowardice – the regiment had fought well in France the previous year, and several men had been decorated only the day before the mutiny. Nor did the unrest have any broader political content. The men admitted their oath of allegiance and pleaded that 'they were willing to fight any enemy, including Arabs or Turks, in any other place except Arabistan, which they considered from their religion as holy ground'.[195]

Workers in Uniform

Most mutinies, however, were highly localized affairs over less elevated matters than this.[196] Pay, allowances, promotions and the conditions of service – these were the staple fare of peaceful collective insubordination.

The 3 Gurkhas, for example, mutinied in 1886 when their Colonel reduced their customary rice *batta*.[197] The protest of the men brought to light a whole range of related grievances. Food and fuel were costly; there was nowhere to cook in the barracks, so the men had to go hungry when it rained; there had been no furlough for nine months; the Native Officers did not heed the men's complaints; and the new Colonel was unpopular. Two companies of the 17 Bombay Infantry mutinied for similar reasons. The men were told they had to mess in sections instead of with their friends. A rumour soon went round that further changes would be introduced, by which the men would lose financially. 'The Sircar first started section messes, then will start company messes; finally, a bania will be put over us, and we shall be cut 8 or 9 rupees monthly and then how will our families live?', lamented their anxious spokesman.[198] A thwarted desire for promotion lay behind two mutinies. The hill Brahmins attached to the 38 Dogras, and the Rangur sepoys in two companies of the 17 Bengal Infantry, resented the domination of the higher ranks by the majority castes in the regiment.[199] These protests all involved attempts by the men to defend or gain what they regarded as a just material return for their services.

Unusually, the mutineers of the 3 Brahmans went further than this.[200] Brahmins were accustomed to messing individually but, because this arrangement was unsuitable for service in the trenches, the regiment had been confined to communications duty during the campaign in Mesopotamia in 1917. When a system of group messing was introduced, 120 men mutinied. The authorities suspected that the main concern of the mutineers was not to preserve their caste, but to exploit the system of individual messing to avoid front-line service. (The food which was introduced was in line with Brahmin practice, and was later freely eaten by the regiment.) The customary rights of the men here conflicted with their customary duties; but the authorities would always be reluctant to absolve the soldiers of their obligation to fight.

The Forms of Protest

We should now consider the form that mutinies took. The *way* in which soldiers mutiny reveals much about their attitudes to military authority; and the way in which the authorities react can further illuminate the workings of Indian Army discipline.

A mutiny was by definition collective in intent. But it was also usually collective in form. In an age in which orders were given to the troops by word of mouth, it was almost impossible for the men to be collectively insubordinate unless they were also physically assembled. Most mutinies therefore began with an unauthorized gathering, or with a refusal to disperse after an authorized assembly such as a parade. The mutiny of the 14 Bombay Infantry, for example, started when 170 Konkani Mahrattas gathered and began marching to see the commander of the regiment.[201] The Sikh Jemadar-Adjutant appeared, and reminded the men that they were not supposed to present grievances collectively, but to pass them on individually via their non-commissioned and company officers. The 3 Gurkhas started their mutiny with 'a strong mustering throughout the companies; even the men about to parade for guard and other duties joining with their rifles in their hands, *all evidently acting in concert*'.[202] Any prior coordination of a mutiny might occur in a place such as a temple, mosque or *gurdwara* where the men could congregate without arousing the suspicion of their officers or attracting their attention.[203]

The unauthorized assemblies which began most mutinies were not normally accompanied by physical disorder. The insubordination of the 3 Gurkhas was unusual in that it started with a gathering 'in a tumultuous manner'.[204] The 15 Lancers were more typical. 'During the whole sad crisis the regiment was quite orderly and behaved in an exemplary manner', reported their commander after the incident.[205] There was perhaps an element of special pleading to his judgement; but accounts of other mutinies are similar. When elements of the 17 Bombay Infantry protested about new messing arrangements, a subedar selected ten men and marched them to the Commanding Officer to make a formal complaint. As the official party moved off, a further 42 men fell in behind them and marched down in good order, ignoring instructions to disperse.[206] Scenes of drunkenness or looting were quite unknown during peaceful mutinies. Insubordinate soldiers may have rejected specific actions by the military authorities, but they did not reject with them the physical signs of discipline and unit cohesion. The outward orderliness of a mutiny showed that the men still adhered to military values. It may also have served the men's interests to make their protest in an orderly manner, since by doing so they evoked a visual language with which officers could emphathize.

The British reacted in a calm and prudent way to this orderly disorder. They used several strategies in attempts to peacefully resolve the dispute and prevent a repetition. Their first recourse was usually persuasion. The form of most mutinies made this understandable enough, since the men often assembled with the object of finding a seni˙˙officer and bringing their grievances to his attention. When addressing the men, a British officer would normally first try to deter them by emphasizing the significance of their actions and the possible penalties if they persisted. He would then offer the men a way out by assuring them that their grievances would be considered or by promising to look leniently on the matter if they desisted.

'You know it is against orders to assemble in a large body like this, and to come down to this office to make complaints, when you have been ordered to dismiss in the lines', remarked the commander of the 17 Bombay Infantry to mutineers of the regiment after hearing their spokesmen. 'You are all old soldiers and cannot plead ignorance of Regulations.'[207] He promised to assemble a Court of Enquiry, and meanwhile confined the men to the lines. Occasionally, an officer was able to disperse mutineers by sheer force of argument.[208]

If persuasion failed, the British then usually tried to fragment the mutiny by identifying, arresting and confining those whom they held to be the 'ringleaders'. Ringleaders were normally defined as those who shouted back at the officers, who openly encouraged the men, or who were 'most ardent and excited in their manner of giving expression to their grievances'.[209] It suited the officers to believe that the mutineers were not acting entirely on their own initiative but 'had been led astray by bad advice'.[210] This assumption implied that there was nothing fundamentally wrong with the discipline of the regiment, and that removing a few especially mischievous individuals would restore harmonious relations between officers and men. This was not altogether far-fetched. The arrest of a few men ensured that the British did not seem totally powerless, and reminded the mutineers that insubordination would not go unpunished. The confinement of a few also suggested to the remainder that they could escape without penalty if they quietly returned to duty. The arrest of ringleaders might therefore defuse the situation. It was not always easy to pick individuals out, however. One colonel concluded that 'there were virtually no ringleaders' in his mutinous regiment and that 'no one man was more implicated than his comrade'. For this he was severely censured. The authorities thought that he should have made an example of some men, 'even if no actual ringleaders existed'. He could have arrested the Native Officers for not reporting the imminent disturbance, and the senior soldiers for failing to show 'that good example and submission to discipline which was to be expected from them'.[211]

Indian soldiers, however, did not passively accept these efforts to fragment their collective action. The men were aware that the force of their protest lay in its solidarity, since military discipline works most easily when the rebels are clearly out of step with the rest. Mutinous soldiers often tried to maintain their cohesion in the face of British attempts to break it by arresting ringleaders.[212] When several mutineers of the 3 Gurkhas were imprisoned, a party of 50 men went to the quarter-guard to try and rescue them. 'We desire the release of these prisoners (for their cause is ours) or else, that we, who are equally guilty with them, may also be confined', the men said to a general who went to meet them.[213] The arrest of a prominent individual could occasionally intensify the solidarity of mutineers, at least for a short time. When a sepoy spokesman of the 25 Madras Infantry was marched away as a prisoner, the remaining men of his company followed in military formation and refused to disperse. The Commanding Officer then confined the entire company, which he regarded as a sort of collective ringleader of the mutiny. Upon hearing of this, the three remaining Hindu companies of the battalion refused to parade. 'They sent answer by the Native Officers that they had committed the same offence [refusing to attend parade] as B company and that they therefore were prisoners too.'[214]

The men sometimes took secret oaths before a mutiny to help maintain the solidarity of their action. The night before the disturbance in the 3 Gurkhas, two sepoys toured the barracks encouraging or pressuring the men to wish aloud that, if they did not join the mutiny, their mothers would be 'dishonoured seven times'. Another man took around the Gurkhas' book, or *Shuksagar*, giving soldiers the chance to touch it, to swear that they would mutiny, and to curse all the female relatives of those who did not. Once the men were assembled, the book was placed on the ground, and the men took an oath with their arms extended towards it.[215] Waverers among the would-be mutineers of the 17 Bombay Infantry were sworn to stay with their comrades on pain of drinking their wives' urine.[216] These preparations only came to light after the mutinies. Other units may also have used oaths, without the British ever discovering the fact. The men certainly had a vested interest in keeping their oaths secret, since the authorities took a dim view of these alternative foci of loyalty.[217]

Ceremonies which strengthened the determination of a regiment in battle could also be inverted to serve mutinous ends. Before marching up to the trenches in France, the 15 Lancers had customarily observed a ceremony known as *oman manga*, in which the men passed under the Quran and asked God to grant His protection. They did the same before their mutiny in 1916, when they pledged not to fight in the holy land of Iraq.[218] The inversion perfectly illustrates how the religious cohesion of a class regiment, which the British so carefully fostered, could become dissident cohesion in another context.

Outcomes and Punishments

Once the troops had made their protest, they seem to have calmly accepted their fate. There was very little prolonged resistance to the workings of military justice. Soldiers protesting about pay or conditions, or about some specific act of bias, usually returned to duty within a few hours or a day. Those who were unwilling to serve in a particular theatre of war, or to perform particular tasks, became almost passive once the authorities recognized the force of their objection. The 429 mutineers of the 15 Lancers, for example, were disarmed, marched on board a steamship and tried by court martial the day after their protest. One or two men fired shots during the mutiny, but no one was hurt, and beyond this there was no resistance.[219] The men of the 2/18 Garhwalis acted in similar fashion.[220]

At first sight, it might seem strange that soldiers who were prepared to mutiny were also prepared to peacefully submit to the penalties for doing so. But most mutinies involved an appeal to a higher military authority, not a rejection of it. The act of mutiny was enough to bring the grievances of the men, and their strength of feeling, to the attention of the authorities. Mutineers might also successfully avoid an especially painful military duty. If this was their object, there was little point continuing their protest once it had achieved its immediate goal.

One party of mutineers did try to resist military justice. They got short shrift. The mutinous Hill Brahmins of the 38 Dogras threw stones at their Punjabi escort and tried to run away as they were being led for court martial. The escort opened fire, killing 33 prisoners and wounding 57. 'I daresay it will have a salutary effect', one British officer remarked.[221] But no orders to fire appear to have been issued, and some of the escort were themselves court-martialled for their hasty and violent reaction.

For the most part, mutineers judged the authorities well, and were wise to trust to their clemency. Death penalties were very rarely imposed after a peaceful mutiny, and these were almost always commuted to long terms of imprisonment. Only two non-violent mutineers appear to have been executed between 1886 and 1930, the period discussed in this section.[222] Prominent 'ringleaders' normally received sentences of transportation, ranging from seven years to life; and those who were judged to have taken less initiative were typically sentenced to between three and seven years, or were dismissed from their regiments.[223] Many mutineers escaped punishment altogether. The Army Department suspended the sentences of five years' rigorous imprisonment passed on 82 mutineers of the 3 Brahmins, because the offence was thought to be a mere 'display of childish insubordination'.[224] And of the 170 sepoys who mutinied in the 14 Bombay Infantry, no less than 141 received no penalty of any kind.[225] The authorities were reluctant to impose collective punishments, and preferred to 'make an example' of a few men to deter any repetition.

Even mutineers who had been severely and collectively punished were not beyond redemption, as the example of the 15 Lancers shows. All 429 of the men who mutinied in 1916 were tried by court martial. Sixty-four were each sentenced to three years' rigorous imprisonment, and the remainder received long terms of transportation, some for life. The mutiny was the subject of much comment in the ranks of the Indian Army. Soldiers wrote freely about it in their letters, apparently without interference from the censor. One civilian was grieved to learn that a relative was among those sentenced, but he hoped that the authorities would show eventual clemency:

> It is very sad that fate should have dealt this cruelly with this regiment in the end, after they had done such good service and gained so much renown elsewhere. Now they are all imprisoned. My idea is that the Government have acted in this way simply to indicate their authority, and that after the war all these unfortunates will be released.[226]

He was right about the clemency, but wrong about the timing. A year after the mutiny, and well before the end of the war, the Secretary of State for India advised that men who were 'not ringleaders or instigators of mutiny' should be given 'an opportunity to retrieve their character'. The men had been sorely tried before the incident, and not very tactfully handled during it, he thought.[227] And the convicts had behaved well.[228] So, on the King's birthday in the summer of 1917, after they had served a little over a year of their sentences, the mutineers of the 15 Lancers were offered their freedom in return for service in the remount depot of the regiment. All agreed.[229] The men were grateful, but not always repentant. 'We have arrived safely in India, having been released. The King has been very gracious to us', wrote one. But, he added, 'we were blameless. After having seen the face of Hell, and after having in fact lived there for one year and three months, we have returned in safety. God has been merciful to us.'[230]

Whatever the costs, some mutinies achieved their ends. Soldiers who mutinied to avoid particular tasks were usually successful, since the authorities were prudent enough not to provoke dissident soldiers by trying to force the issue. 'As it was quite clear that the men thoroughly understood the certain consequences of any refusal to march, and in spite of this firmly persisted in their intention, there seemed no object in testing them further', remarked the CGSI of the 15 Lancers. The mutiny in the 2/18 Garhwalis ensured that the battalion was released from unpleasant riot-control duty. The 3 Brahmans even managed to avoid front-line service in Mesopotamia during the Great War, as the high command transferred the mutinous regiment to another theatre. Unpopular commanding officers were also removed on at least two occasions.[231] The authorities did not wish to give the impression of surrendering to other-rank pressure, so in each case the ostensible cause of removal was 'insufficient firmness' or 'weakness and indecision' in dealing with mutineers.[232]

The Transition to Violence

Having looked at the thirteen peaceful mutinies, we should now consider the transition to lethal violence. It should be noted in passing that in otherwise peaceful mutinies, the soldiers sometimes resorted to symbolic violence. On one occasion they threw stones which broke windows near an officer.[233] A gesture like this emphasized the strength of the mutineers' feelings, without risking the dire penalties that would have surely followed lethal violence. In two other mutinies, the sepoys threw their belts rather than stones.[234] The choice of missile is interesting. A soldier's belt carried his military equipment – such as ammunition and bayonet – and was a potent symbol of his military status. Soldiers donned their belts before going on duty, so to discard their belts implied at least a temporary rejection of duty – a visual symptom of the loosening bonds of military discipline.

Lethal violence was not necessarily mutinous, just as mutiny was not necessarily violent. Disenchanted soldiers sometimes took fatal revenge on their officers, but this was not normally regarded as mutiny if they were acting on their own.[235] A court of enquiry heard in December 1938 that the most common reasons for murdering officers included disputes over promotion or caste, interdistrict feeling, bullying, abuse or sodomy.[236]

The court was sitting to investigate a shooting affray that had recently occurred in the 4/2 Punjabis. The men of the two Muslim companies had been looking forward to a day's holiday to attend the Id prayers and the end of Ramazan. At short notice, their commanding officer moved the holiday forward by 24 hours, so the men could attend an air-cooperation parade.[237] This was a clear slight to religion, unusual in the Indian Army after 1857. On the night when the moon rose, indicating the end of Ramazan, a sentry decided to take matters into his own hands.[238] He shot and killed four British and three Indian officers, and severely wounded two others. The authorities decided to disband the battalion. No other Muslim troops were involved in the shooting, but equally they did nothing to apprehend the man, who was at large in the camp for an hour before he was killed. The two Muslim companies clearly sympathized with the man's action, even though they did not take part in it.[239] Furthermore, the court of enquiry met a 'conspiracy of silence designed to defeat the ends of justice'.[240]

But to qualify as a mutiny, insubordination had to be collective. And in the period under discussion there was only one Indian Army mutiny which involved lethal violence – that of the 5 Light Infantry at Singapore in February 1915. The regiment was raised mainly from Muslims of the Eastern Punjab.[241] In early 1915, it was stationed at Singapore, but was scheduled to sail for Hong Kong. The mutiny began shortly after an address by the Commanding Officer, which left the men uncertain as to their final destination. Rumours went round that the regiment was due to sail for Europe or for the Middle East where they would have to fight the Turks near the Holy Places of Islam. Violence soon followed, involving four out of the eight companies. The men made first for the regimental ammunition, then went to a nearby camp to free German prisoners who, however, showed little interest. The mutineers then attacked any Britons they could find, including their own officers, those of the Malay States Guides and local civilians.[242] By the end of the first day they had shot dead 34 people. Although the British were muddled and indecisive at first, they soon declared martial law, summoned a naval landing party, formed a body of European volunteers and evacuated white women and children. The mutineers seemed to lose direction after the initial outbreak. Most made off in small parties for the jungle, the mainland or the sanctuary of local mosques. By the end of March, all but 51 had been recaptured.[243]

The mutiny had much in common with other Muslim protests against fighting the Turks, such as that of the 15 Lancers. But none of the other disturbances took a lethal form, so this unique feature of the Singapore mutiny must be explained. The regiment was unhappy and divided even before it had arrived in the Far East. The new commandant was deeply unpopular with some British officers, who thought he undermined their authority in the eyes of the men.[244] They had formed two rival cliques, as had the Indian Officers, who were divided over a dispute about promotion.[245] These problems at the top of the regiment must have undermined discipline further down. The men had also come into contact with local dissidents. A holy man at a mosque frequented by the troops preached against the British and urged a sepoy uprising.[246] Pan-Islamic influences were also at work. On the Friday before the mutiny, one sepoy ended prayers with 'a blessing for the success of the armies of the faithful'.[247] The declining visibility of local British power suggested that the Empire was in global retreat. The sole British battalion at Singapore had been recalled to France; and the destructive cruise of the German raider *Emden* – which had sunk Allied ships in the Penang roads in October 1914 – had damaged British prestige, and seemed to lie behind the promise of local Turkish sympathizers that a warship would soon arrive to help the mutineers. The men followed German successes with interest, and some Indian Officers predicted 'there would soon be a German Raj instead of a British Raj'.[248] The men's letters reveal that they knew thousands were dying in Europe every day.[249] Some believed that the German Emperor, and many of his subjects, had converted to Islam.[250]

This uniquely potent combination of regimental grievances, political dissent, fears for religion (fuelled by rumour) and an act of apparent bad faith explains the transition to violence at Singapore. The British reaction to the unrest was far more severe than in any mutiny without violence. Over 200 men were tried by court martial. Most of these were sentenced to long periods of transportation (64 of them to life). No less than 65 men were sentenced to death, of whom 43 were actually executed.

Although the mutiny at Singapore was uniquely violent, it shared several features with other collective protests. First, it happened outside India. Of the 14 Indian Army mutinies discussed in this chapter, two took place in Mesopotamia, two in China, one in Singapore, three in Burma, and only six in India proper. Given that the soldiers of the Indian Army spent the vast majority of their time in India, this shows they were more likely to mutiny when serving abroad. Then they were homesick, disorientated and more likely to heed disturbing rumours. Secondly, like two others, the Singapore mutiny took place at a point of departure, which seems to have been an especially delicate moment in matters of discipline. The troops at Singapore believed they were being sent to France or to fight the Turks; the mutineers at Rangoon knew they were about to sail for Iraq; and the 15 Lancers mutinied when they were ordered to leave Basra for the front. In each case, the mutiny occurred when Muslim troops feared they were about to take one step closer to fighting the Turks.

The episode at Singapore was also typical in its timing. Six of the 14 mutinies occurred during the Great War, when the equilibrium of the Indian Army was under especial strain. The other cluster of Indian mutinies took place in the 1890s. Four of the five in that decade occurred in the two Southern armies, which may reflect the problems they faced as the British began to recruit more and more men from the Punjab. These peaks of mutiny in the army do not coincide with the main phases of Indian political unrest – the few years before the Great War and the one-and-a-half decades which followed it. Civil disturbance did not produce sepoy mutiny, which remained very much a military matter.

CONCLUSION

In some sense, any dissent in an army reflects a failure of military leadership. Indian Army protest reached a peak during the Great War, when the troops suffered unusually heavy losses far from home. The soldiers serving in France, and their wounded comrades in Britain, grew deeply depressed as it became clear that the war would last a long time, many men would die, and even those who had been hurt would have to return to the trenches if they recovered. Desertion rates remained low, but many despairing Indian troops wounded themselves before the British took stern measures to stamp out this practice. The authorities, however, could treat only the symptoms not the cause of the widespread depression; and Indian Army morale began to plummet once more at the end of 1915. The infantry had to be transferred to the less arduous and less important Mesopotamian front, although the cavalry saw out the war in France. Morale appeared to recover by 1916 as the troops grew more used to the conditions of modern warfare, and the intense disillusionment of the first winter was not widely repeated.

The decline of Indian Army morale in the Great War was largely a response to heavy losses on an unfamiliar battlefield; it was not linked to civil unrest at home. But military dissent could emerge from disturbances among civilians with whom the soldiers were in sympathy. Indeed, the main fear of the British authorities was a combined military mutiny and civil rebellion, like that which had nearly driven them from India in 1857. For this very reason the sepoys were kept under close surveillance, and were guarded by a large British garrison. Civil unrest troubled the peacetime discipline of the Indian Army at least twice – during the Chenab Canal Colony disturbances of 1907, and during the Sikh Gurdwara campaigns in the early 1920s. In each case, agitators appealed (with some success) to the values and martial traditions which the British had hitherto harnessed to serve colonial and military ends. In the event, the Government of India made concessions rather than risk further alienating the groups upon whom the army depended. International religious politics also brought problems during the Great War, when the reluctance of Muslim troops to fight their Turkish fellow-believers was the main cause of three mutinies and of heavy desertion among Pathans.

Yet the history of dissent in the military forces of the Raj perhaps bears witness to British success rather than to British failure. The level of indiscipline in the Indian Army remained remarkably low. Nationalism had little impact on the ranks, and attempts by Congress to subvert the army got nowhere. There were fifteen minor mutinies in the Indian Army between the 1880s and the 1930s, but in only one of these did the troops fire on their officers. Even during the Great War, there were no large-scale breakdowns of discipline among Indian soldiers – a record which compares very well with that of the French or Russian armies, or the German Navy. None of the Indian mutinies involved more than a single regiment. Most were very local affairs, the result of grievances confined to a particular unit..The mutineers usually conducted themselves in an orderly manner, even when they were publicly refusing to perform a particular duty. Far from rejecting all military authority, they often sought redress by appealing to their Commanding Officer or to a higher rank. Most mutinies lasted only a few hours, and the British were accordingly very selective in their punishments. These affairs should not be seen as miniature versions of 1857. They bore much greater resemblance to the strikes and protests of industrial workers, just as peasant-soldiers had much in common with other labour migrants. These small, occasional and local mutinies may even have helped to avert a larger and more widespread military rebellion. Every mutiny in the army was a tap on the collective British shoulder – a useful, if chilling, reminder that the loyalty of the troops, so vital to the Raj, had to be earned, not taken for granted.

5

Indian Officers and Indianization

Our subjects, of whatever race and creed, shall be freely and impartially admitted to offices in our service, the duties of which they may be qualified by their education, ability and integrity duly to discharge.

Queen Victoria's Proclamation upon the Dissolution of the East India Company, 1858[1]

So far as the Army is concerned, the Queen's proclamation is a dead letter.

Sir George Chesney, 1894[2]

In England, the young officer of the grenadiers constantly leads his veteran men to victory; but I am certain that the young, educated, university Indian will never do it.

Henry Rawlinson, 1921[3]

The British ruled India, but never by themselves. A few thousand whites could not have dominated a fifth of humanity without extensive help from at least some of the subject population. The colonial authorities always depended upon Indian allies to exercise their political control.[4] These servants of the imperial cause, often men of influence in their own right, acted as intermediaries between the colonial elite and the Indian masses. They picked up the signals of European authority, and retransmitted them – both for imperial purposes, and for their own.

The military elite relied no less than the civil power upon the efforts of local allies. The structure of the Indian Army was a microcosm of the entire colonial encounter, and its internal patterns of authority resembled those in the country at large.[5] A handful of regimental officers could not have commanded their units without Indian assistance.[6] The interpreters of colonial military

153

authority were the Viceroy's Commissioned Officers – the ageing and whiskered jemadars, subedars and subedar-majors so fondly recalled in British military memoirs of the period. Imperial in their functions, yet Indian in their language and outlook, they helped bridge the great cultural gulf between British officers and Indian other ranks. The VCOs were also an essential safety-valve for dissent. The best of them were in close touch with the ranks, and could tactfully pass on the grievances of the men, thus helping to preempt open mutiny by alerting British officers to otherwise inaudible murmurings of discontent in the lines.[7]

The relationship of Indian officers to the Raj was, however, deeply ambiguous. The Indian officers were essential collaborators, but they were also a potential weak link in the chain of imperial authority. A Viceroy's Commission could be an outlet for an able and ambitious sepoy, or it could be a reward for long and loyal, if undistinguished, service. Either way, its bearer could create problems of military discipline. Young and energetic Indian officers, promoted for merit, would lead effectively in battle. They could prevent mutinies by giving timely warning of the first signs of discontent. But if the troops ever did mutiny, there was a grave risk that talented VCOs would provide them with dangerously efficient leadership.[8] It might therefore be prudent to promote older and weaker sepoys, of proven loyalty, in return for faithful service.[9] Such men could not replace British officers during an uprising, but they might also be less than competent when fighting on behalf of the empire.[10] They might not always command the respect or confidence of the ranks, which might make indiscipline more likely and incipient mutinies harder to detect.[11] As so often happened in the Indian Army, the demands of political safety conflicted with those of efficiency for war.

From the later nineteenth century, nationalism brought another element into the equation, which further complicated imperial policy. Nationally-minded Indians looked down on the Indian Army as an instrument of colonial oppression. They wanted the officer corps to be opened to Indians – especially to the western-educated elite like themselves. Their demands could hardly be satisfied without changing the Indian Army into an embryonic national force, perhaps less than amenable to purely imperial purposes. But the military ambitions of the articulate could not be thwarted without adding to the already formidable list of Indian political grievances.[12] The British could hardly maintain a permanent monopoly over the management of violence without eventually harming the legitimacy of the Raj.

INDIAN OFFICERS BEFORE 1918

The British had always recognized that they needed Indian intermediaries. Indeed, when Indian manpower was first tapped, the East India Company did not enlist soldiers directly into British-led units. Instead, whole military communities were taken into company service as auxiliaries, complete with their own officers. But the British feared that this autonomy might undermine their power. As colonial rule became more established, the British sought to impose their own authority and methods of organization on the military apparatus.[13] In the regular sepoy battalions raised from the 1740s, Indian officers were placed directly under British officers permanently assigned to each unit.[14] Indians remained influential at company level, but formal power in the battalion was concentrated in British hands. By the early nineteenth century, each regular company (or cavalry troop) was normally led by between one and three British officers (typically a captain and a lieutenant). They were assisted by Indian officers, of three main grades. The subedar-major was the senior Indian officer of an infantry battalion. He personally advised the commanding officer on all matters concerning the morale and customs of the men. His counterpart at company level was the subedar, with the jemadar directly beneath him. Further down the chain of command were the Indian NCOs – havildars (or sergeants) and naiks (or corporals).[15]

Under this system, the rank of subedar-major was the highest that an able or experienced Indian soldier might achieve. His entire career would normally be spent in a single battalion, and even its most junior British lieutenant would always outrank him.[16] He could never command European troops. Not every British observer thought this cautious policy was wise.[17] According to Colonel John Biggs of the Madras Army, Indians should have been allowed to exercise higher command. In 1836, he suggested setting up an Indian military college for the sons of Indian officers. Trained and loyal Indians could then gradually replace British officers, freeing the latter for political tasks. Henry Lawrence argued a similar line in the 1840s:

There is always a danger in handling edged tools but justice and liberality forge a stronger chain than suspicious and niggardly policy. No place or office should be absolutely barred to the Native soldier. Legitimate outlets for military energy and ability in all ranks and among all classes *must* be given. The question is only whether justice is to be gracefully conceded or violently seized. Ten or twenty years *must* settle the point.[18]

These liberal recommendations were not followed, and the avenues of promotion for Indian soldiers remained very limited in regular units.

The Mutiny and Reconstruction

The mutinies of 1857 were taken as evidence that Indian officers had failed in their tasks. Although intended to act as a channel of communication between the sepoys and the British, many Indian officers failed to report the first stirrings of discontent. As a result, the mutinies took the British by surprise. Either the Indian officers did not know of the disaffection, or they were too weak or too frightened to divulge it.[19] Their age partly explains this.[20] The sepoys of the Bengal Army were normally promoted by strict seniority as a reward for long service rather than for merit.[21] The senior havildar could expect to become a jemadar when there was a vacancy, unless there was a very good reason to the contrary. Old age and 'failure of mental qualities' did not prevent promotion.[22] Many men were worn out when they reached the higher ranks. A sepoy who had enlisted at 19 might be as old as 40 before he was promoted to naik, and most jemadars were in their fifties when they were appointed.[23] The Subedar-Major of 7 Cavalry, who died at Cawnpore in 1858, was a smart and sprightly man of 71, but he was 'one of a thousand who had his energies about him'.[24] Indian Officers did not have to pass examinations, and many could not read or write.[25] They often had little influence over their men. 'The native officer', thought one British colonel, 'is a cypher, and has not been of any benefit to the service'.[26] This evidence comes almost entirely from the accounts of British officers, and some allowance must be made for their keenness to blame others for the Mutiny. But aged Indian officers were probably not the equal of British sergeants in the prime of life.[27]

As a result of the Mutiny, many British observers concluded that the standing of the Indian officers ought to be enhanced. In 1857, the typical regular regiment had two dozen British officers, of whom up to two-thirds might be absent on other duties in peacetime (although many would rejoin in war).[28] There were also twenty Indian officers, whose responsibilites were closely circumscribed. Matters were different in the irregular corps, which made up 18 of the 28 regiments of Bengal cavalry, including such crack units as the Scinde Horse under Sir John Jacob.[29] These drilled and uniformed regiments, irregular in name only, differed from the regulars by normally having only three British officers – a commandant, a second-in-command and an adjutant – seconded from regular units.[30] The Indian officers of an irregular regiment commanded their own companies and squadrons. They therefore had to be good, and were selected mainly for their merit and energy.[31]

According to the supporters of the irregular system, the Indian officers in these units took more interest in the men under their command because they had more responsibility for them.[32] Indian officers wielded greater influence in the irregular regiments, and were therefore more proud of their unit and of their rank.[33] Admittedly, they might provide younger, fitter and more efficient leadership during a mutiny, but their attachment to the service made insurrection less likely.[34] The events of 1857 seemed to bear this out. Only 10 of the 18 irregular cavalry regiments mutinied, compared with almost all the regulars in Bengal.[35] Irregular regiments were also cheaper, since they had far fewer British officers, whose generous emoluments made up half the cost of a regular unit.[36]

Critics of the irregular system warned that a large and influential body of efficient Indian officers could pose a danger to the Raj.[37] Promotion by seniority rather than by merit was less risky, they thought, and was also a just way of rewarding long service in the ranks.[38] They felt that an irregular unit, with only three British officers, was more likely to scatter on the battlefield.[39] 'In action you cannot have too many British officers', remarked a sceptical regular captain.[40]

Supporters of the irregular system strongly pressed their case in the discussions and enquiries which followed the Mutiny. The circumstances ensured them a sympathetic hearing. Most of the Bengal regular regiments had disappeared or been disbanded in 1857. Only 15 of the old infantry regiments had survived, while almost all of the regular cavalry had gone over to the rebels. Most of the new units raised to replace them in 1857–58 had been formed as irregulars.[41]

From January 1861, all Indian regiments were reorganized on a modified irregular basis.[42] Each unit was to have only six British officers, all of whom were to remain with their regiment. This policy had several advantages. In the first place, it was cheap. Secondly, giving well-defined regimental duties to a smaller body of British officers reduced their opportunities to seek lucrative staff or administrative posts. Thirdly, it was hoped that Indian officers might become more efficient as a result of acquiring more responsibility. The changes were introduced in Bombay and Bengal in 1861–63.[43] The 40 foot and four horse regiments of the Madras Army, all regulars, were reorganized in 1865–66.[44] There was some opposition, but most of the displaced regimental officers were posted to the staff or the administration, or retired on full pay.[45] Under the new arrangements, Indian officers commanded each of the eight companies of an infantry regiment and the six troops of a cavalry regiment. British officers led the two infantry wings or three cavalry squadrons into which the smaller units were grouped.

The Indian officers warmed to their new responsibilities.[46] They proved competent to command companies and troops, and acquitted themselves well on detached duties.[47] They developed and improved as a result of being given greater authority. Some regimental commanders came to prefer veteran Indian officers to inexperienced British subalterns because the former exercised more effective sway over the men.[48]

Some problems still remained, however.[49] Since 1857, there had been little change in the methods of selecting officers.[50] Promotion by seniority was still the norm, as it was very difficult to disappoint a senior and loyal NCO who had every hope of higher rank.[51] The advanced age of Indian officers thus remained a cause for concern.[52] The subedars of the Madras Army in 1879, for example, had each served for an average of nearly 33 years.[53] Most of these men were in their early fifties, and their retention at the head of the list retarded the promotion of younger soldiers.[54]

Although Indian officers were generally alert and efficient, the number of British officers with each regiment was gradually increased in the later nineteenth century. In 1865, the sanctioned establishment was changed from six to seven per unit.[55] Ten years later, one or two 'probationers' (junior officers in the first year of their appointment) were added to each regiment to replace those absent or on furlough.[56] Military reverses in the Second Afghan War showed that casualties to British officers could create problems in the field, as Indian officers were not trained to take over the full range of leadership duties.[57] In 1882, the Government of India sanctioned an additional British officer per unit, bringing the total to eight (not including the 'probationers').[58]

From the Later Nineteenth Century to the Great War

The rise of the Indian National Congress from the later 1880s raised greater questions than these tinkerings could resolve. Congress passed annual resolutions demanding – among other things – Indian access to higher military rank.[59] The Government of India was cautiously receptive to this idea. The emergence of an articulate opposition encouraged their search for collaborators at higher levels.[60] In 1885, the government proposed to raise one regiment of foot and one of horse, officered entirely by Indians, a plan intended to give the most distinguished Indian officers the chance of an extended military career.[61] Lord Roberts found, to his mild surprise, that British officers were not averse to the proposal.[62] But the British government thought that such a cautious measure would encourage the demand for change, rather than satisfying it, so the scheme was dropped.[63] Memories of the Mutiny remained fresh, and it was not forgotten that the lack of trained leaders among the mutineers had served the British well in 1857. To create such a class of men would have been a pointless military risk, unjustified by political pressure.

The issue surfaced again at the turn of the century. In 1901, Lord Curzon created an Imperial Cadet Corps to give Indians of princely or noble families the chance of prestigious military service. The aim of the new body was to satisfy the political aspirations of the Indian aristocracy of birth, not to add to the military strength of the empire.[64] There was no intention of appointing commissioned cadets to regimental posts; they were merely to perform (unspecified) staff duties. The corps, dressed in a gorgeous uniform designed by Curzon himself, acted as the Viceroy's bodyguard at the Durbar of 1903.[65]

Kitchener was hostile to the entire project, and not merely because it was Curzon's idea. Since the ostensible military functions of the corps were entirely bogus, ambitious cadets were doomed to resentful frustration. Furthermore, gentlemen who previously would gladly have served in the Indian Army as jemadars or even as private soldiers now held back, because they did not want to seem inferior to those admitted to the cadets. The main benefit of the corps, thought Kitchener, was its discipline, which might help to reform otherwise hopelessly dissolute young aristocrats. 'This combination of the Borstal system with a military college does not commend itself to me', he drily remarked.[66]

Some senior Indian Army figures were unwilling to completely bar all paths of higher military advancement to Indians. In 1908, General O'Moore Creagh (the C-in-C) advised giving Indian officers more senior positions and greater responsibilities. As a first step, he suggested turning over three battalions of foot and one regiment of horse to mainly Indian command. The proposal was rejected, largely for fear that it might become the thin end of a very broad wedge. 'Sooner or later the preponderating influence in the Army would be Indian instead of British', remarked Kitchener. 'When that point was reached, our position in India would be one of sufferance, terminable at any moment when the people so desired it.'[67]

In the meantime, the number of British officers per regiment continued its gradual increase. The importance of Indian officers underwent a corresponding decline. The development of long-range precision weapons meant infantry fighting-formations became more dispersed and harder to control. During the manoeuvres of 1885–86, the men often became scattered and out of hand. It proved very difficult to keep them advancing together and to control their fire (two of the most important elements of battlefield success).[68] Skirmish lines tended to spread out and dissolve, while their supports lost their way. Lord Roberts thought that at least 13 British officers were needed to exercise effective leadership over a regiment in these new conditions of battle. In 1901 the officer strength was fixed at 10 or 11 in peacetime and 12 in wartime; but the C-in-C believed that 15 British officers were needed in the field.[69] Most Indian Army regiments went into action in 1914 with 14 British and 16 Indian officers.[70] By then, subedars normally commanded platoons rather than companies.[71]

The Great War

During the battles in France, Indian officers did not acquit themselves especially well. When British officers took heavy casualties, their Indian subordinates were rarely able to replace them efficiently. General Wilcocks (the OC Indian Corps in France) explained this in racial terms:

> Immediately you touch on this point you strike the bedrock of the reason we own India [he wrote]. The Indian is simply not fit to lead his men against Europeans; he will lead a charge or cover a retirement, but if he has to think he fails. It is the presence and natural instincts of the white man which the Indian officer can *never* replace. The Indian has not the instincts which make leaders in modern war. There is in fact no solution; the European and the Indian are built on different lines, the one to command men, the other to wait for guidance before he issues commands.[72]

Sir John French offered a more generous and persuasive account of these failings. The diminished status of Indian officers was, he thought, largely responsible for their shortcomings. The lower commissioned ranks, by then paid little more than the average civilian clerk, were not accorded much recognition in civil life. This weakened their commitment to military duty.[73] Furthermore, Indian officers were strictly subordinated to British officers within their regiments, which impaired the initiative they had once shown.[74]

Despite this, the war brought growing pressure to award King's Commissions to deserving Indian candidates. Educated Indians had long resented their exclusion from the higher military ranks, and the war gave them ample opportunity to advance their case.

During the conflict, the political influence of the nationalists grew as never before. By the Lucknow Pact of December 1916, the Muslim League and the Indian National Congress created a brief but effective alliance. They organized their agitation mainly through the Home Rule League of B. G. Tilak and Annie Besant. Formed in April 1916, the League had an all-India membership of 32 000 by early 1918.[75] The veteran nationalist Tilak clearly saw that Indians could make political capital out of their contribution to the Imperial war effort. 'If you want Home Rule be prepared to defend your home', he urged in a recruiting speech at Poona. 'You cannot say the ruling will be done by you and the fighting for you. Had it not been for my age,' he added, 'I would have been the first to volunteer.'[76]

The Imperial authorities saw that it was not prudent to thwart the ambitions of those on whom they depended during a severe military crisis. Accordingly, in August 1917, Edwin Montagu (the

Secretary of State for India) made his famous vague but liberal-sounding declaration in the House of Commons:

> The policy of His Majesty's Government, with which the Government of India are in complete accord, is that of the increasing association of Indians in every branch of the administration, and the gradual development of self-governing institutions with a view to the progressive realization of responsible government in India as an integral part of the British Empire.[77]

India's great material and human contribution to the war also won some minor military concessions. From 1917, ten vacancies a year were reserved at Sandhurst for 'suitable Indians' – defined as 'selected representatives of families of fighting classes which have rendered valuable services to the State during the War'.[78] The move was not planned as a step on the road to self-government, but was simply intended to reward loyalty and sacrifice. Places were granted mainly to conservative Indian aristocrats, few of whom were expected to pursue a military career after the war.[79] A few Viceroy's Commissioned Officers and a handful of NCOs were also granted King's Commissions. Most of these men, however, were elderly, and would retire before reaching high rank.[80] In 1918, an Indian Cadet College was opened at Indore. Its graduates received a temporary wartime commission, some of which became permanent. The college was a wartime expedient, and it lasted only a year.

By 1918, the cause of Indian political reform had gathered further strength. Edwin Montagu's declaration of liberal intent was followed in April 1918 by a report written jointly with Lord Chelmsford (the Viceroy). The Montagu–Chelmsford Report advised important concessions to educated Indian opinion. Political awareness in India was growing as a result of the war, which was being portrayed more and more as a struggle between liberty and despotism, argued the authors of the report. The British could hardly deny to India the liberties for which they claimed to be fighting in Europe.[81] But the aim of reform was to buttress rather than to weaken the Raj. The British sought to buy the loyalty of key Indian groups at a crucial point in the war. As Montagu observed, 'it is important to avoid a state of things in India which would not only impair her war effort, but might also place new burdens on the military resources of the Empire'.[82]

INDIANIZATION: THE FIRST PHASE

After the Armistice, it would have been imprudent to thwart the hopes raised by the report. The Government of India Act of 1919 gave shape to the principles outlined by Montagu and Chelmsford. It established a Legislative Assembly of 145 members, and a Council of State of 60. A majority of the delegates to both houses were to be elected, rather than appointed. The right to vote was extended to more than one million Indians at national level, and to five-and-a-half million in the provinces.[83] The Act also enshrined the principle of 'dyarchy', by which some areas of administration – such as education, health and agriculture – were handed over to provincial ministries responsible to the legislature, while the remaining subjects were 'reserved' to the Government of India.[84] The army was 'reserved', and its budget was not subject to vote or amendment; but members of the Assembly became skilled at embarrassing the government with questions, and could thus exercise some influence over military policy.[85]

In the 1920s and 1930s, one issue dominated military debate – Indianization. This could hardly be discussed without questioning the fundamental purpose of the Indian Army, or the future of the colonial state which it defended.[86] The officer-corps could not be Indianized without transforming the army from a colonial garrison into the embryonic national self-defence force of an emergent dominion. In the early 1920s, the recruitment, equipment and organization of the Indian Army faithfully reflected its colonial role. For this reason, Indian nationalists often castigated the army as the mercenary agent of an unpopular foreign autocracy. They wanted to abolish the 'martial races' policy, so that the recruiting base of the army reflected the national make-up of the Indian population. They attacked the costly and demeaning presence of British troops in the subcontinent. And, above all, they wanted the higher ranks of the army to be fully open to Indians.[87] Conservatives argued in reply that British troops and British officers could not leave India until India could defend itself. This was not possible immediately, they suggested, because India was not yet a nation. Only when the constituent Indian communities had settled their differences and forged a common national identity could they be trusted with the command of their own armed forces. Until then the British could not leave, nor could India proceed to responsible government. These debates about Indianization were of more than military significance.

They reflected the desire of both sides to control the Indian Army, and by implication to control the political destinies of India itself.

The Creation of Part-time Forces

The British began the 1920s by making some very limited concessions which did not affect the regular forces. The Indian members of the Legislature voiced a widespread feeling when they urged that all Indians should have the chance to bear arms in the defence of their country.[88] As matters then stood, only the 'martial races' could enlist in the regular army, while membership of the Auxiliary Force was confined to Europeans and a handful of Indian Christians.[89]

To meet this demand for military service, an Indian Territorial Force was set up in 1920 as a 'safety valve' for the martial ardour of the politically articulate and as a harmless sop to nationalist opinion.[90] Each territorial battalion was linked to a regular infantry regiment, to which it could supply drafts of men in time of war. Units were embodied for training on 28 days of the year.[91] At all other times their arms were secured in British-controlled arsenals. Between four and six British officers were assigned to each battalion to direct training and to watch for signs of 'disloyalty'. The territorials were officially liable for general military service, but they were unlikely to have been much use in the field. They could, however, help out during internal security work.[92]

By July 1922, enlistments had reached over 6000. There was some talk of a Territorial Force of 100 000 strong, but the authorities were reluctant to entertain this notion. They feared that the force might come under the control of 'extremists' or be used for 'political ends' – by which they meant political ends other than those sanctioned by the Government of India.[93] Part-time soldiers could not imbibe the spirit of devotion to the Raj shown by the long-service regulars, nor attain similar military value.[94] But the authorities had no desire to stifle the Territorial Force at birth, for this would have only invited more insistent calls for the genuine Indianization of the regulars. Furthermore, the British were anxious to seem sincere in their fulfilment of wartime pledges. The territorials were, however, restricted to a strength of 20 battalions, or a total of 20 000 men.[95] The authorities wanted to nip in the bud any idea that the Territorial Force could grow to become a national rival to the regular army. In fact, there was little danger of this. The new force attracted recruits mainly from rural communities already accustomed to military service.[96] Even in urban areas the territorials were far from being a political liability. In Bombay, the Parsi battalion was formed with the open aim of resisting the non-cooperation movement.[97] Furthermore, territorial units could easily be supervised, and could be disbanded upon showing any sign of dissent.

A similar political purpose informed the creation of the University Training Corps, a branch of the Territorial Force set up in the Indian Colleges. Its aims were primarily 'educational' – meaning it would discipline unruly Indian students and instruct them in an Imperial version of patriotism. The Corps was modelled on the OTC in Britain, from which Indian students in the UK were normally excluded. Like the rest of the territorials, the UTC was in theory liable for general military service. It was seen as a possible future source of Indian candidates for commissions in the regular army, should the latter be Indianized. The British instructors with the corps were regulars on secondment. By 1927, the UTC numbered more than 4000, mustering full battalions in Bombay, Calcutta, UP, Lahore, Madras and Rangoon, and single companies in Delhi and Patna.[98] By 1929, 20 000 Indian students had passed through its ranks. Some British officials feared that the UTC might sympathize with a renewed campaign of civil disobedience.[99] Partly for this reason, its weapons were kept under lock and key, rather than being entrusted to the students. As it turned out, these fears were misplaced. The UTC 'improved the discipline, the character and the physique of University students', reported the Army Department, and the movement had 'the full support of the educational authorities in India'.[100]

Meanwhile, by 1925, the Territorial Force had reached its prescribed strength of 20 battalions. Although these numbers were impressive, few of the urban middle classes had bothered to enlist. The force had therefore failed in one of its principal aims – to 'impart military and patriotic ideals to the non-martial classes'. The territorials had been formed at a time when the regular army was being reduced, and they had therefore attracted many former sepoys.

To redress this imbalance, explicitly urban units were created. These could maintain discipline over graduates as they left the University Training Corps, or make 'better and more valuable citizens' of those who had not passed through its ranks.[101] Two companies of territorials were formed in Bombay, two in Madras and two in UP. Calcutta was at first omitted, ostensibly on grounds of expense. By 1929, the Government of Bengal was keen to form a Calcutta Territorial Force to draw in and discipline the 'respectable people' such as lawyers, doctors and merchants, who were potential sympathizers with nationalism. There was a danger that the plan might backfire, and that the unit would become a 'centre of disaffection', but the Government of India eventually went along with the scheme and formed two companies in the city.[102] To appease local opinion, this body was given the grandiose title of 'The Bengal Battalion, 12/19th Hyderabad Regiment, Indian Territorial Force'. Many remained sceptical. 'I cannot imagine any circumstances under which the Calcutta urban unit would have any military value', wrote the GOC Eastern Command. 'If such a force existed I would not allow it to be called out in the event of local disturbances. The present value of the Territorial Force in Bengal is nil.'

The Indianization Debate

The Government of India must have known, however, that feeble half-measures like these could not satisfy the fundamental military ambitions of the nationalists. As Sir Claud Jacob (the CGSI) remarked, 'a striking feature of all conversations with members of the Legislative Assembly is their keen desire for the rapid Indianisation of the Army. They are particularly anxious to be given greater facilities for obtaining King's Commissions.'[103] Indeed, in March 1921, the Assembly passed a resolution demanding exactly that. They proposed:

> That the King-Emperor's Indian subjects should be freely admitted to all arms of His Majesty's military, naval and air forces in India, and that every encouragement should be given Indians – including the educated middle classes – to enter the commissioned ranks of the Army.[104]

The Assembly wanted a quarter of all new King's Commissions to be reserved for Indians, pending the creation of an 'Indian Sandhurst'. They also sought equal basic pay for British and Indian officers, a reduction in the British garrison, and the introduction of short colour service for the sepoys. The resolution was moved by Sir P. S. Sivaswamy Aiyer, a leading Madrassi moderate interested in military affairs.[105] He was far from being a Congress militant, and he had support among most strands of Indian opinion.[106]

The Government of India amended the Sivaswamy Aiyer resolution, adding a clause by which the number of commissions granted to a particular Indian community would reflect the number of its men serving in the ranks. This policy enshrined the military dominance of the 'martial races', who were closely associated with the British. The amendment passed by one vote, with the strong support of Punjabi Sikhs and Muslims.[107] The debates exposed an enduring split among those who supported Indianization – between the communities that were designated as 'martial' and those, like educated Bengalis, who had long been excluded from the army.

These proposals also caused concern in some British quarters. Imperial conservatives were loath to concede that Indianization could ever work. According to their racially-based arguments – aired repeatedly over the next decade – 'martial' Indians could fight but were not clever enough to lead. British stereotypes had always emphasized the poor education and alleged slow-wittedness of the martial classes.[108] As the Simon Commission was to comment in 1930, 'those races which furnish the best sepoys are emphatically not those which exhibit the greatest accomplishments of mind in an examination'.[109] Part of the reason, of course, was the British policy of selecting soldiers from communities with low levels of literacy, who were still untouched by Western education and political ideas.[110] Conservatives also believed that educated Indians, despite their brains, could never make good army officers. According to them, the *babu* lacked the strength of character, the physique and the self-discipline needed to win the respect and loyalty of the troops.[111] Henry Rawlinson (C-in-C, 1920–25) was one sceptic. An entry in his diary for July 1921 neatly sums up his doubts:

> Will you ever get the young, educated Indian to lead a company of Sikhs in a charge against a sangar held by Mahmuds? Even if he did, would the Sikhs follow him?[112]

Opponents of Indianization believed that only the British had the right mixture of brains, brawn and backbone to lead the 'martial races' into battle.[113]

Conservatives also objected to Indianization on the grounds that Indian officers could never be entirely impartial. This was largely because the national idea in India remained very weak.[114] India, they believed, was home to a collection of very different communities, which were often in conflict with one another. Indian officers, no

matter how sincere their efforts, could never seem utterly aloof from
the inter-communal disputes that troubled the army from time to
time. The other ranks would resent or exploit this, which might lead
to indiscipline or even to mutiny. The communal violence of the
later 1920s added weight to this argument. Indian officers might not
remain strictly impartial when policing communal clashes.[115] For
this reason, the ranks would not trust their officers, and civilians –
especially of minorities – would not trust the army to protect them
from violence. These arguments drew on a basic Imperial justifica-
tion for the British presence in the army and in India itself. Unlike
any Indians, British officers clearly stood above communal division,
which made their authority – in their own eyes at least – acceptable
to all ranks and to all communities.[116]

This cautious reasoning was neither frivolous nor fatuous, and it
must have carried some weight in Government of India circles.
Nevertheless, the government accepted the Sivaswamy Aiyer proposals. In the summer of 1921, they formed a committee under
Henry Rawlinson to discuss plans for Indianization. The committee
accepted that 'responsiblity for defence is the natural corollary of
self-government', and they recommended the early announcement
of a definite Indianization policy.[117] They advised eventually award-
ing all new army commissions to Indians, while reducing by prudent stages the number of British units in India. To make this policy
effective, they recommended immediately reserving for Indians a
quarter of all Indian Army cadetships at Sandhurst.[118] This proportion was to be annually increased, with Indians receiving half of all
new commissions in ten years' time. The Government of India made
no formal commitment to the Rawlinson proposals, but they made
it clear that they were broadly sympathetic to Indianization. Neither
the British government nor British officers in India warmed to these
plans, however.[119] Even Rawlinson had his private misgivings. He
found Sivaswamy Aiyer 'very ignorant' and thought that Indianization would lead to bitter racial conflict and to mass resignations by
British officers:

They will see the bread being taken out of their mouths by
Indians, whose intrinsic value is far below their own; they will no
longer retain the prestige of the white man which made them in
the past highly respected individuals in their districts; and they
will resent beyond measure the changed conditions in which they
have to live.[120]

Given these objections in high places, we must explain the willingness of the Government of India to consider Indianizing the army. Their chief aim was to win support, at a delicate political juncture, for their recent constitutional reforms. The government wanted to satisfy influential Indian opinion that they were sincere in their professed desires to Indianize the army and to reduce the costly British garrison.[121] They feared political trouble over military spending if they did not soon announce a definite scheme with these ends in view. The government did not see Indianization as a direct threat to the Raj, but as a potential prop to its power. As the supporters of Indianization pointed out, British India had always been ruled through Indians – and might always be so in future. Henry Rawlinson, for one, believed that British rule would be eternal, simply because India would 'never' be able to defend itself without the help of British officers.[122] Indians, he thought, could take over all branches of the army 'except those requiring real strength of character and broad-minded leadership'.[123] Some European assistance would always be needed in all departments of state. He was also confident that Indian officers would pose no real threat to the political order. As he remarked in 1923:

I have come to realise what a despicable creature the Indian really is. We are not running serious risks. Except for the inhabitants of the Punjab, the Indian races are nothing but a lot of sheep, and a few thousand British soldiers could conquer Central, Southern and Eastern India today just as they did 150 years ago under Clive.[124]

(His confidence rested upon faulty history. The armies which had conquered under Clive included more Madrassis than Europeans.)

In the meantime, the Secretary to the Military Department, General Alex Cobb ('very deaf and old-fashioned', according to Rawlinson) had put forward a new plan for Indianization.[125] Like many other people, Cobb believed that the demand for Indianization was a 'political' rather than a popular one.[126] The King's Commission would therefore not attract the 'best' Indian material – or, more frankly put, the poorly-educated and politically quiescent. The influx of Indian officers envisaged by the Rawlinson proposals would, he feared, fatally damage the efficiency and morale of the Indian army. His arguments were far from original:

The fighting races of India are the very classes who are most backward as regards education, and, on the other hand, those classes whose educational qualifications are the highest are generally regarded as lacking in martial qualities.[127]

No British officer would contentedly serve under Indians who happened to be his seniors in rank, thought Cobb. Instead, he proposed setting up a dominion force in India, to exist alongside the regular Indian Army.[128] Unlike the Indianization of the regulars, this would not endanger and disorganize India's current defences. The dominion force would be led entirely by Indian officers from the outset, save for one or two Europeans attached to each unit to help it form and train. The Indians would hold a dominion commission, which would confer powers of command over Indian but not British troops. The force would be raised from demobilized soldiers and by voluntary transfers from the Indian Army. If the experiment were successful, the regular army could be reduced as the dominion force were expanded. No British officer would have to serve under an Indian of whatever rank.

The Government of India rejected the Cobb proposals, despite the support of Viscount Peel (the Secretary of State). Cobb's scheme would have created a formation for which India had no real military need and could ill afford, and which might have proved unfit for service in the field.[129] Furthermore, Indian political opinion would not have accepted the creation of another second-rate force as evidence of the government's sincere intention to Indianize the regular army.[130]

It remained politically most desirable to announce a definite Indianization scheme to the Assembly before the budget came under their purview.[131] The military committee which had rejected the Cobb proposals therefore prepared a new plan, which they submitted in January 1922.[132] This abandoned the idea of a separate dominion force in favour of the complete Indianization of the regular army (except the Gurkhas) in three stages of 14 years each, beginning in 1925. (See Table 5.1.) During the first stage, seven cavalry regiments and 20 infantry battalions would each receive two Indian officers per year to replace one British officer and one VCO. During the second stage, a further seven cavalry regiments and 40 infantry battalions would be Indianized in the same fashion; and in the third stage the scheme would embrace the remaining seven cavalry regiments and 34 battalions.[133] The decision to start each stage was to depend upon the success of the previous one. If condi-

TABLE 5.1

Government of India scheme for complete Indianization in three
stages, January 1922

	Stage 1	Stage 2	Stage 3
		Commencing (Year)	
	1925	1934–39	1941–53
Units involved			
Infantry battalions	20	40	34
Cavalry regiments	7	7	7
Indian officers			
Required			
Annual average	81	182	227
Stage total	1 139	2 547	3 178

Sources: Viceroy to SSI, 24 January 1922, IMR.59, and Report of Committee
Appointed by C-in-C, 6 January 1922, IMR.80, CAB 16/38/2; Report on
Indian Military Requirements, June 1922, CID 125-D, CAB 6/4.
Note: By the end of the third stage, 21 Indian cavalry regiments and 94
infantry battalions would have been Indianized. A total of 6864 Indians
would have received the King's Commission.

tions warranted, the second stage could be shortened to nine years
and the third to seven, allowing complete Indianization in 30 years
instead of 42. After stage one, the Indian Army would no longer
offer an adequate career to new British officers, so those who were
needed would be seconded from the British Army, as was the practice in Egypt. All junior Indian officers would begin by serving
under experienced Europeans, from whom, it was hoped, they
would learn discipline and the principles of command. This over-
came one major objection to the idea of a separate dominion force.
And – most importantly – no British officer would have to serve
under an Indian.

The scheme had many other attractions to reforming imperialists.
It was elegant and entirely practical. Existing regimental names,
traditions and structures would survive intact. There would be no

costly reorganization. The plan showed a genuine commitment to Indianization, and, by implication, to Indian self-government. It promised to win the hearts and minds of the Indian political class by offering complete Indianization, but postponed real change for many years. The scheme therefore received the warm approval of the Government of India.

The authorities in Britain gave it a much cooler reception.[134] Winston Churchill (the Colonial Secretary) expressed vehement opposition to the whole idea of Indianization. Churchill was deeply conservative on Indian matters, and he openly doubted the wisdom of 'granting democratic institutions to backward races which had no capacity for self-government'.[135] According to Lord Curzon (the Foreign Secretary), the scheme 'was probably doomed to failure from the beginning; if it succeeded, it would almost certainly endanger our rule in India'.[136]

This hostility bewildered the Viceroy. He confessed himself 'unable to understand' how a practical programme, prepared by his own military advisers, could be interpreted as implying a policy of 'retreat from India'.[137] On the contrary, he protested, the army reforms went hand in hand with the 1917 declaration and the 1918 Montagu–Chelmsford Report. The plan for Indianization merely gave practical expression to a liberal policy already agreed in principle and proclaimed in public.

The Viceroy would have been less bewildered had he overheard one of his chief military advisers, Sir Claud Jacob, speaking to British ministers in February 1922. Jacob clearly assumed that British policy was 'ultimately to hand over India to the Indians and surrender British rule'.[138] Along with most Europeans in India, he saw the proposal to Indianize the army in this light.[139] Lloyd George robustly corrected him. 'There was no question of a withdrawal of the British Government from India', he insisted. 'Any talk in a contrary sense was both mischievous and malignant.' He continued by urging Jacob, on his return to India, 'to let everybody know that it was the fixed and irrevocable intention of His Majesty's Government to see that British ascendancy and British rule in India are maintained'.[140]

In this anxious and uncertain climate, the manifold objections to the Government of India's bold scheme carried much weight. Their plan committed them to a policy that would take thirty or forty years to fulfil. Much might happen in that interval to make the policy unsafe. The experiment of admitting Indians to Sandhurst was not proving a great success, as it was hard to find enough willing and qualified Indian candidates.[141] There was no firm evidence that enough 'efficient and loyal' Indians would come forward to allow the complete Indianization of the army without harming its readiness for war or undermining its political reliablity.[142] Furthermore, the Viceroy himself had earlier implied that the loyalty of the Indian troops could be trusted only if the current proportion of British officers were maintained.[143] There remained the spectre of a mutiny, in which case 'an Indian Army officered by Indians would be a much greater danger than the present Indian Army'.[144] Nor did the unsettled state of India – then in the aftermath of extensive civil disturbances – encourage bold and liberal military policies. 'When authority is widely challenged, and sedition is openly preached, special caution is necessary in all that relates to the armed forces, which are the ultimate basis of the King-Emperor's Government', warned the Indian Military Requirements Committee.[145]

The Eight-Unit Scheme

But the need to 'rally the moderates' remained. To do this, a definite scheme of Indianization had to be announced.[146] It would have been inconsistent with British promises, and politically dangerous, to have made no further progress.[147] The Military Requirements Committee therefore proposed a limited gesture in this direction, suggesting that four units alone should be officered by Indians.[148] They advised no further promise of Indianization until this experiment had clearly proved successful.[149]

There would have been little problem finding enough Indian officers for so tiny a force, and any potential dangers would have been confined to a very small portion of the army. But so limited a concession would have inflamed rather than satisfied Indian political opinion. Henry Rawlinson saw this clearly. The Assembly 'will be furious', he wrote.[150] He feared that they would refuse to vote taxes, unless Indianization were extended. The proposal betrayed previous promises to the Legislature, and it would have damaged British standing with the moderates. As the Viceroy pointed out:

> The Indianisation of the Army is, to Indians, the crucial test of our sincerity in the policy of encouraging India to advance to the goal of self-government. To make an announcement of so restricted a

scope would inevitably carry conviction that His Majesty's Government no longer desires to give effect to that policy.[151]

The Government of India managed to have the scheme extended to embrace eight units – two regiments of horse and six battalions of foot.[152] The units were judiciously chosen to include as many different classes of Indian troops as possible.[153] Commissions were to go by preference to the 'martial races', but the 'non-martial' classes were also eligible. Indians currently holding the King's Commission in other units would be encouraged to transfer. No further British officers would be posted to the Indianizing units. The eight-unit scheme – effectively a 'dominion army' within the Indian Army – had one crucial merit in British eyes: no British officers would have to serve under Indians, and very few alongside them.[154] The recruiting of British officers to other Indian Army units would therefore not be prejudiced.[155] Rawlinson formally announced the scheme to the Legislative Assembly on 17 February 1923. Its aim, he said, was to 'give Indians a fair opportunity of proving that units officered by Indians will be efficient in every way'.[156]

Rawlinson felt that his statement was 'well received', and thought the ensuing debate went very much the government's way.[157] But he had misgivings about the long-term effects of the measure on Indian political opinion. 'It will keep them quiet for a bit, but they will return to the charge when they find it will take 15 years to complete the Indianisations.'[158] The Indian press soon picked up on this very point. The scheme fell far short of what was hoped for, and was taken as evidence that the government had no intention of ever fully Indianizing the army.[159] British opinion was no less critical – unsurprisingly, given that each Indian appointed to a commission meant one less post for a European.[160] The *Daily Telegraph* suggested that the Indian rank and file objected to Indianization 'which is more popular with the political classes than it is with the Indian soldiers'.[161] British observers generally assumed that Indian officers would rather serve alongside British officers than with each other. There was some evidence to support this view. Four of the five Indians already holding King's Commissions in the army proved unwilling to transfer to the Indianizing units, so the decision was made optional. According to the critics of Indianization, the Indian officers were rightly unwilling to go to segregated and socially inferior units. The Army Department had a kinder explanation: 'once an officer has settled down in a particular regiment, has made it his home and found his friends, he is generally very loath to leave it'.[162]

The eight-unit scheme highlighted the problem of finding suitable Indian cadets for Sandhurst. Very few Indians with the right qualifications had come forward, and those that were admitted were often a disappointment.[163] 'The cadets at Sandhurst this year are just as bad as they were last year', lamented Henry Rawlinson in 1922.[164] Most British officers thought that caste, linguistic and religious differences prevented Indian youths from showing a spirit of patriotism or a sense of duty towards the state. Alex Cobb had already urged the creation of a pre-Sandhurst military school in India to inculcate 'those qualities essential to the making of a good officer'.[165]

To foster such officer-like qualities, the Prince of Wales' Royal Indian Military College was founded in 1922 at Dehra Dun, a cool and pleasant station in the Himalayan foothills. The College was run on English public-school lines, with an initial capacity of 70 cadets.[166] Its purpose was to prepare boys for the Sandhurst entrance exam and for the ordeal of their subsequent training there.[167] But the aims of the school were far from being narrowly intellectual. The official objectives of the College included giving all cadets

a social training which will enable them to move with confidence in any society, whether European or Indian, without embarrassment either to themselves or to others

and imbuing them with

a sense of loyalty, patriotism, manliness and a self-effacing spirit of 'service', together with a healthiness of mind and body such as will render them true and useful servants and citizens of India and the Empire.[168]

The ethos of the College betrayed the firmly-held British belief that suitable 'officer-material' could be bred only in the public-school atmosphere. The College accordingly placed great emphasis on games, to prepare cadets to later 'face with fortitude and endurance the hardships inseparable from military life'. The school magazine reflected this bias. Its pages were mainly taken up with sports news, including match reports that contained slightly incongruous comments like 'Jalal-ud-Din is becoming a centre half of real class'.[169] The library, by way of contrast, was little-used, and its books were poorly-treated. The classical writers and works of fiction remained largely unread – the boys' favourite authors were Conan Doyle, Alexandre Dumas, Edgar Wallace and P. G. Wodehouse.

The search for a new maths master in 1927–28 keenly exposed the College's distinctive blend of Imperial racism and public-school snobbery. The appointee had to be excellently qualified in maths because 'the Indian boy requires more and better grounding in mathematics than does the English boy whose mind is far more logical than the mind of the Eastern'.[170] But the man had to be a 'Sahib' – an Indian would not really do because the 'weakening' of the white staff woud be a 'grave disadvantage on the "Public School" side'.[171] A search was begun at Oxbridge.[172] The happy news arrived by telegram on 26 May 1928:

> Believe we have now secured good man. First class mathematical moderation Oxford. Taking finals June. Swimming blue.[173]

The creation of the College did not immediately solve the problem of finding enough officer-candidates. By 1926, there had been only 243 applications for the 83 places reserved for Indians at Sandhurst. Moreover, after initial enthusiasm, the annual number of applicants was in slow but steady decline.[174] Nationalists argued, reasonably enough, that the low application rate reflected the many obstacles which might deter Indian youths – including a possibly daunting interview with a senior British officer or the Viceroy, and the thought of travelling all the way to Sandhurst. More worrying was the very high failure-rate of Indians who actually began the Sandhurst course. Of the 83 who had entered by November 1926, 18 were still there, 44 had passed out successfully, two had died and 19 had failed to qualify.[175] Among Indians who had completed the course, the failure rate was was 30 per cent, compared with 3 per cent for British youths. Results were more encouraging among Dehra Dun graduates, however.[176]

Reports on individual Sandhurst cadets by company commanders and by the Commandant reveal the qualities the British were looking for. Indian cadets were often criticized for learning by rote instead of using their initiative to apply the knowledge they had acquired, suggesting that Indian boys lacked confidence as a result of being thrown into an unfamiliar environment. Several of those who failed to qualify showed 'little aptitude for leadership' or 'power of command'. Many had a poor knowledge of English, which handicapped their studies. Successful candidates, on the other hand, were usually 'keen both at work and play', 'always cheerful' and 'loyal'.[177] Political dissent was not a problem. Almost all the Indian cadets were sons of princes, zamindars, planters or soldiers – classes closely associated with the Raj, and otherwise politically inert.[178]

Upon leaving Sandhurst, the Indian cadet was commissioned as a second lieutenant. He was then posted to a British regiment in India for one year, during which time he could command white troops. After this, he joined one of the eight Indianizing units. This would remain his home for the remainder of his regimental life. The military authorities kept close watch on the Indian officers, and asked the commanders of the Indianizing units to provide regular reports on their progress.[179] The reports revealed a consensus that Indianization had damaged efficiency, or would have done so without extra supervision by British officers. Indians lacked 'a sense of justice' and were 'inclined to treat their inferiors badly', according to the CO of 7 Light Cavalry. The commander of 2/1 Punjab Regiment believed that Indians lacked 'team spirit, power of command, initiative and drive'. Several COs also claimed that the Indian other ranks intensely disliked serving under Indian commissioned officers, whom they feared might show 'caste prejudice' or 'love of intrigue'. These reports must be treated with some caution. A whole series of stereotypes about the 'Indian character' distorted the perceptions of British COs. The latter tended to criticize Indian officers not for anything they had done, but for the future that they apparently represented. Commanding officers also reacted to the damage which Indianization had done to their self-esteem. They stressed that British officers remained essential, and they liked to believe that the Indian other ranks shared their view (although the evidence on this point is not conclusive).

The political decision to admit Indians to the commissioned ranks did not magically remove the social prejudices that had for so long helped to exclude them.[180] In the delicate words of the Montagu–Chelmsford Report, it was 'natural, indeed necessary, that a small and scattered community of European dwellers in an Asiatic country should nurse among themselves a certain communion of their own'.[181] Put more bluntly, most cantonment clubs operated a colour bar, which Indian officers were often the first to break.[182] The ensuing difficulties and embarrassments repeated themselves at every cantonment to which an Indianized unit was posted. Indian officers were a group carefully selected for their loyalty and political reliability, but they everywhere encountered racial prejudice at first hand. The result was a great sense of shock, and much resentment. D. K. Palit joined an Indianized unit at Peshawar in the late 1930s. He was astonished to find that British and Indian officers 'lived in virtual isolation from each other'. Inter-racial friendships were very rare. There was almost no exchange of mess entertainment between Indianized units and others, and Indian officers hardly ever sat and drank with their British colleagues at the Peshawar Club. 'I never once was invited to a British home', recalled Palit. 'Never, during my ten months in the station, was I asked to so much as a cup of tea by my own British CO or Company Commander or any other British officer.'[183]

TOWARDS A NATIONAL ARMY?

The Skeen (Indian Sandhurst) Committee

Despite these social obstructions, the Government of India remained willing to consider further Indianization – partly in response to the pressure of opinion in the Legislative Assembly. In February 1925, the Assembly recommended accelerating the rate of Indianization, and establishing a Sandhurst-type military college in India to train Indians for army commissions.[184] The government proved sympathetic, and set up a committee under Sir Andrew Skeen (the CGSI) to discuss some of these issues. The 'Indian Sandhurst Committee', as it became known, included Motilal Nehru (who soon resigned), M. A. Jinnah, some retired VCOs and other Indian notables.[185] Its terms of reference were less broad than the Assembly would have liked, for the committee were not asked to consider stepping up the pace of Indianization. Instead, they were to examine measures to improve the quality and number of Indian candidates for the King's Commission, and to discuss whether an Indian Sandhurst could or should be created. The committee first met at Simla in August 1925. They interviewed British and Indian experts, military men and politicians, before completing their unanimous report in November 1926.

The report went much further than the Government of India had intended. It advocated measures that would have dramatically increased the number of Indians reaching higher rank, until by 1952 half of all officers would have been Indian. The committee proposed doubling the number of vacancies reserved for Indians at Sandhurst to 20 per year from 1928, with later progressive increases. They suggested setting up an Indian Sandhurst in 1933, initially with 100 cadets taking a three-year course. To prepare enough suitable officer-candidates, the committee suggested expanding the Royal Indian Military College at Dehra Dun, and opening a second and similar establishment elsewhere in India. They also wanted to abolish the restrictive eight-unit Indianization scheme, and make Indians eligible for commissions in every branch of the Army in India, including engineer, signal, artillery, tank and even air force units. In this case, Indian cadets would have to be admitted to the Royal Military Academy at Woolwich, to train as gunners, and to the RAF College at Cranwell, to train as pilots. [186]

The Government of India were taken aback by the liberality of their own officers.[187] The committee, they felt, had 'clearly exceeded their terms of reference'; their demands appeared 'insufficiently considered and in consequence ill-founded'.[188] The government objected to experimenting with the Indian Army as a whole, and wanted to confine Indianization to the eight units already earmarked. The committee's proposals, they complained, were 'merely a time-table, which depends on an unascertained supply of entrants of unproved quality'.[189] Lord Irwin (the Viceroy) was privately hostile to an Indian Sandhurst.[190] But, expecting criticism, the Government of India advised some movement. They suggested reserving 25 places a year for Indians at Sandhurst, with a further eight at Woolwich and two at Cranwell. The Legislative Assembly, on the other hand, warmly welcomed the report when it was published. After debating it in August and September 1927, they recommended its full and immediate adoption.[191]

The Skeen proposals would eventually have placed Indian officers in command of mixed British and Indian formations. They were therefore a matter for the British Cabinet, which set up a committee under Lord Balfour to consider them.[192] The Balfour Committee were broadly hostile to Indianization in any form, but felt that the British government was 'irrevocably committed' to 'the policy which had been embarked on in the post-war atmosphere'. Winston Churchill (the Chancellor of the Exchequer) feared that a future Labour government would adopt an 'even more undesirable policy' if some limited progress were not made. The committee advised a strategy of flexible conservatism; they wanted to make small concessions to avoid being forced to make larger ones later. The Government of India's proposals, they believed, were the 'most innocuous'[193] that could be devised, and they recommended that they form the basis of policy. They remarked:

> We do not for one moment believe that, by adopting them, we shall satisfy Indian aspirations. But we shall be keeping the ground fully occupied, and we shall be able to reply with truth for many years to come that we are doing our best to meet Indian susceptibilities.[194]

The Balfour Committee rejected the Skeen proposals partly because they would eventually have placed British officers under the command of Indians.[195] As it was, the limited Indianization so far undertaken had already caused an 'alarming and growing short-age' of British officer-candidates of the 'right stamp'.[196] In 1925, a lecturer at Sandhurst felt obliged to reassure his British audience that there was almost no chance of a British officer having to take orders from an Indian.[197] Most of the Indian officers were old and due to retire, while the remainder were confined to the eight Indian-izing units. Under the Skeen proposals, however, Indian commissioned officers would have been accepted in all units of the Indian Army. Within a few years, incoming British subalterns would have had to take orders from their Indian seniors, probably with 'disastrous' results for British recruitment. The eight-unit scheme had originally appealed largely because it confined all newly-commissioned Indians to a small portion of the army, in which they could give orders only to each other and to the men. Henry Rawlinson neatly summed up the attitude of the British military caste in this matter when he concluded that 'the only solution is the creation of certain *wholly* Indian units, otherwise we shall have white officers serving under Natives, which will never do'.[198]

The objections to the Skeen proposals also drew on the traditional catalogue of racial stereotypes.[199] Claude Jacob frankly thought that Indians could never be 'efficient'. There were lingering fears of political and communal bias – 'it was impossible to send an Indian officer to settle a dispute in a village, since they could not be trusted'. The demand for Indianization did not come from the ranks, thought Lord Birkenhead, but from a 'small minority of agitators of the non-martial classes' – perhaps the lowest form of life in the Imperial demonology. Winston Churchill was being uncharacteristically progressive when he suggested that some Indians might make good officers. Indians of what he called 'the polo-playing class' did not need paper qualifications because they already 'had many of the attributes of a good junior officer – horsemanship, nerve and courage'. Yet hostility to Western-educated Indians also informed *his* comments. 'A young Rajput would probably make a far better officer than the more nimble-minded Bengali', he thought. He differed from his colleagues mainly in believing that the well-bred but poorly-educated Indian could lead in war – a view which probably reflected his own class background and his unhappy experiences at Harrow.

In place of the Skeen proposals, the Balfour committee advised maintaining the eight-unit scheme as an isolated experiment in Indianization.[200] But they wanted to increase Sandhurst vacancies for Indians to 25 a year (conveniently obviating any immediate need for an 'Indian Sandhurst'). The committee also advised reserving a few vacancies at Woolwich to train Indian officers for the sappers and for the mountain artillery; and they recommended sending two Indians a year to Cranwell, provided they did not command RAF units when they graduated.[201] This proposal implied the eventual formation of an Indian air force.[202] The Cabinet approved these generally cautious steps in December 1927, and soon obtained the broad agreement of the Government of India.[203]

Of the 25 places at Sandhurst, five were reserved for VCOs. The other 20 were to be filled by open competition, rather than by selection as had previously been the case. Competition would advertise the prospect of an army career more widely in India, and perhaps encourage more youths to consider it. The test by interview was retained 'to make sure that the candidate should have a backbone of character as well as brains'.[204]

Increasing the number of Indian places at Sandhurst created a further problem. The eight units selected for Indianization could not between them absorb 25 new King's Commissioned Officers each year. But the Cabinet were reluctant to immediately Indianize other formations to soak up the surplus. Instead, they decided to abolish the Viceroy's commissioned ranks in the units selected for Indianization.[205] In future, these units would have a homogeneous leadership of between 23 and 28 King's Commissioned Officers, as in the British Army.[206] Other units of the Indian Army would retain their two-tier system of command, with 19 or 20 VCOs and 12 to 14 British officers.[207] The measure effectively diluted the authority of a

King's Commission held by an Indian. New Indian subalterns would now lead platoons rather than companies, and they would have a much smaller chance than their British counterparts of ever commanding their own battalion or regiment.[208] The change was justified on the grounds that there was no need for an intermediary between the Indian other ranks and officers who were themselves Indian.[209] The real motive was transparent, however, and Indian officers naturally resented it.[210] Promotions to VCO formally stopped in the Indianizing units from January 1935.[211]

The Round Table Conference and After

In the meantime, India's political progress had come under renewed scrutiny. The Montagu–Chelmsford reforms had allowed for an investigation into their workings within ten years. In 1928, a parliamentary commission of enquiry was appointed under Sir John Simon, a prominent Liberal barrister and politician. The Simon commission did not include a single Indian, which provoked widespread and prolonged protest in the subcontinent. It was against this disturbed background that the commissioners toured India to collect material. Their report appeared two turbulent years later. Its anodyne political recommendations – redundant before they were made – are not our concern. In the military sphere, however, the commission accepted that India could not obtain self-government without achieving self-defence. The indefinite presence of British officers and troops was incompatible with autonomy, however helpful it might be to Indian defence. The Simon Report proposed that the Imperial government take control of the Indian Army, and pay half its cost, during the transition to self-government. The Commander-in-Chief would be an Imperial soldier, responsible to the War Office. Alongside the regulars, a dominion army would be created under an Indian ministry and paid for from Indian funds.[212]

The plan met with little enthusiasm.[213] The nationalists did not want a second-rate dominion force – they wanted to gain control of the Indian Army, which they correctly saw as one of the vital levers of power. An Indian Army made over to the Imperial government would have been in an invidious constitutional position, while the War Office were reluctant to assume the burden of administering the Army in India. Despite this lukewarm response, the Simon Report showed a genuine commitment to broader Indianization, which encouraged moderate Indian politicians.

Gandhi, however, had other ideas. Early in 1930, he persuaded a reluctant Congress to reject Irwin's offer of dominion status – made in October 1929 – and to demand complete *swaraj* instead. But Irwin persisted in his attempts to 'rally the moderates'. He aimed to win legitimacy by creating a form of government in India which reflected the consensus arrived at by men of goodwill after rational discussion. The First Round Table Conference, which assembled in London in October 1930, had this ambitiously reasonable end in view. The British representatives included eight from the Labour government, along with some Conservatives and Liberals. The Viceroy nominated 58 delegates from British India, and the Indian Princes sent 16. (Congress was not represented.) As a result of the conference, the Cabinet accepted that 'responsibility for the government of India should be placed upon Legislatures, Central and Provincial. The alternative', they decided, 'was trouble of a most serious character.'[214]

Future military policy was the work of a subcommittee including M. A. Jinnah, who openly favoured complete Indianization within a specified period of time.[215] Most delegates, however, eventually came round to the government view that an exact timetable for Indianization was undesirable. Instead, they recommended immediate steps to greatly increase the rate at which Indianization took place.[216] The discussions exposed differences of opinion between Western-educated Indians and those from the 'martial races' (who wanted most new King's Commissions to be reserved for the communities which provided the troops).

On 25 February 1931, the Commander-in-Chief announced to the Council of State that the British and Indian governments had agreed to more rapid Indianization.[217] The details remained to be worked out. An essential part of the policy was to be the gradual creation of Indianized war formations, able to take their place alongside the British and Dominion armies in an imperial field force.[218] The Government of India presented their plans in April 1931.[219] The Indianization of eight units was to give way to the Indianization of an entire war division – including 12 infantry battalions, three cavalry regiments, 13 artillery batteries, and two armoured-car companies – a total of some 15 000 men, or about one-eighth of the entire Indian Army.[220] The policy increased the rate of Indianization, while also extending it to the technical arms and to the ancillary services.[221] The scheme still confined Indianization to a particular portion of the army, so that British officers would not have to take orders from Indians. British company and squadron officers already serving in the units destined for Indianization were to be given the option of transferring to another unit of the same regimental group.[222] There was bound to be 'some heartburning' in the units earmarked for Indianization, thought the Military Department, but they believed their proposals to be 'logical and quite impartial'.[223]

The Round Table Conference had also advised the creation of an 'Indian Sandhurst'. The idea had been around for a while – Sivaswamy Aiyer, the Skeen Committee, and the Simon Commission had all put it forward at one time or another. By 1931, British political opinion had swung cautiously in favour. During the Round Table discussions, the Labour administration had accepted the idea in principle. This had been announced, then taken as settled policy, which left it difficult for the incoming National government to postpone the issue further.[224] The war-division scheme required more Indian officers than Sandhurst could produce, without changing the racial character of the institution. Moreover, the results of sending Indians to Sandhurst had not been encouraging.[225] By August 1931, 157 Indians had been admitted, of whom no less than 23 had resigned or failed the course.[226] It was clearly an ordeal for Indian youths to come to a strange country and to settle down in a college among mainly British cadets.

In May 1931, the Government of India set up an expert committee to work out the details of an Indian Sandhurst.[227] They published their report in September. The plans of the expert committee were adopted more or less completely. The Indian Military Academy – as it was known – opened at Dehra Dun on 10 December 1932.[228] It ran a five-term course lasting two-and-a-half-years.[229] The termly intake was 40 cadets – 15 selected by open competition, 15 chosen from the Indian Army, and 10 from the Princely States.[230] The Indian Army cadets studied free, while the others paid Rs 3850 to offset the Rs 10 775 which it cost the government to send a cadet to the Academy.[231] On graduation, cadets became Indian Commissioned Officers (ICOs) in His Majesty's Indian Land Forces. Allowing for wastage, the Academy turned out some 56 officers each year.[232] Incoming cadets proved weak in English, geography and elementary mathematics. All were physically unfit at first, except those coming from the Indian Army or from the Military College at Dehra Dun. There was a great divergence in academic skills between the best cadets chosen by competition and the worst from the Indian Army. Otherwise the cadets were impressive. 'Their conduct leaves

TABLE 5.2
Extent of Indianization, 1932

| | King's commissioned officers | | | |
| | 14 March 1923 | | 30 June 1932 | |
Regiment	British	Indian	British	Indian
2/1 Punjab	20	–	8	8
5/5 Mahratta	16	2	9	8
1/7 Rajput	19	2	9	10
1/4 Punjab	20	–	10	8
4/19 Hyderabad	16	–	10	10
2 Madras Pioneer	20	–	10	8
7 Light Cavalry	18	–	7	10
16 Light Cavalry	20	–	8	10
Totals	149	4	71	72

Source: Legislative Assembly Debates, 16 September 1932.
Note: Most regiments had about 19–20 VCOs at both dates. This table lists
only the regiments of the eight-unit scheme. A handful of Indian officers
served with other units.

nothing to be desired, and the majority should make useful and
responsible officers', reported the Commandant at the end of
1933.[233]

   The cadets from the Princely States were an exception to this
generally happy picture. The representatives of the Indian States
had lobbied hard to have places reserved for them at the IMA. Their
cadets had to pass the same educational test as those from the
Indian Army, as well as convincing a brigade commander that they
had a working knowledge of colloquial English. But the cadetships
reserved for the Indian States did not attract many applicants. The
well-to-do in the Indian States showed little inclination to serve in
the inefficient, under-funded and poorly-equipped Princely armies.
They saw no need to waste money sending their sons to Dehra
Dun.[234] Their attitude reflected that of the Princes themselves, who

were often more keen to train their soldiers for ceremonial duties than for war.[235] There were often fewer qualified candidates than places available, which left no margin for selection. As a result, most of the cadets from the Princely States were of a much lower standard than the others. By February 1936, the Academy had accepted 36 candidates from the Indian States. Of these, 10 had failed to pass or complete the course – a far higher failure-rate than that for Indian Army cadets or for those entering by competition.[236]

The cadets who came from the Indian Army were drawn from the whole range of its units (except the Gurkhas) and reflected its regional and religious composition.[237] There was a predictable preponderance of Sikhs and Muslims, who accounted for 50 out of 63 Indian Army cadets admitted to the Academy by March 1934.[238] But the 'martial races' also dominated the competition for the remaining places. Sikhs and Muslims made up nearly half of the cadets who entered the Academy through competition. The regional bias was just as strong as the religious one; 75 of the 130 admitted by competition up to February 1936 were from the Punjab and the North West Frontier Province.[239] Indianization did surprisingly little to undermine the military predominance of the 'martial races'.

After graduation, cadets spent a year with a British regiment in India, before joining a unit in the Indianizing war division. When they arrived at their unit, many newly-commissioned Indian officers must have felt excluded from the arcane and elaborate rituals of British mess life.[240] D. K. Palit, commissioned in 5/10 Baluchis at the end of the 1930s, was struck by the lavishness of it all – the silver loot from the Boxer rebellion, worth *lakhs* of rupees, the velvet and gold table mat, 20 feet long, and the full mess kit, worn with all the 'jungle jangles'. (And all this on mess charges of less than three rupees a day.) Many Indian officers reacted by becoming more British than the British. Palit closely followed the strict decorum of the mess – no smoking pipes before dinner, no touching the silver, no talk about politics, religion or shop. 'We talked mostly about the day's social activities – there was a lot of shikar', he recalled. 'A certain amount of professional discussion did creep in, but if it got too dull for the senior officer present he would say "alright chaps, no shop"'.[241] Palit joined in the boisterous games in the ante-room, and kept pace with the heavy drinking of his British mess-mates. Hostile British critics saw this adaptability as another example of Indian

TABLE 5.3
Religion of Indian Military Academy cadets, 1932–34

	Muslims	*Sikhs*	*Hindus*	*Others*	*Total*
Competitive Cadets					
Admitted	20	11	25	8	64
Removed	–	–	1	–	1
Withdrawn	1	1	–	1	3
Indian Army Cadets					
Admitted	30	20	10	3	63
Removed	1	1	–	–	2
Withdrawn	–	1	–	–	1
Total					
Admitted	50	31	35	11	127
Removed	1	1	1	–	3
Withdrawn	1	2	–	1	4

Source: Macdonald to Brown, 1 March 1934, L/MIL/7/19145.
Note: The figures do not include the 30 cadets (four removed, one withdrawn) admitted from the Indian States' Forces.

routine imitation – a demonstration in a social context of the supposed lack of initiative that had handicapped Indian cadets at Sandhurst.

As the 1930s progressed, fewer and fewer Indian youths appeared to want an army career. In 1932, 274 Indians had entered the competition for a place at the Indian Military Academy. By 1938, this number had dropped to 128.[242] (See Table 5.4.) According to some Indian nationalists, this was the result of social discrimination against Indian officers who were 'treated as an inferior class'.[243] Progress towards Indianization remained very slow, and the Indian elite sought much faster results. In September 1938, the Legislative Assembly recommended the immediate creation of a mainly Indian committee to consider increasing the pace of Indianization.[244] Congress went further, demanding complete Indianization in 15 years, and denouncing the Government of India's more cautious plans as a fraud. Criticism of the government was expecially vociferous during an Assembly debate in March 1939, on the eve of

TABLE 5.4

Number of candidates for the Indian Military Academy (entry by
open competition only), 1932–38

Year	Number of candidates	
	Competed	*Qualified*
1932	274	162
1933	326	126
1934	292	85
1935	260	74
1936	215	72
1937	189	54
1938	128	21[1]

[1] Excludes October 1938 admission, for which the results were not then
known.
Source: Legislative Assembly Debates, 1 December 1938, L/MIL/7/19156.

Hitler's invasion of Czechoslovakia. 'We want the Indian Army to
be officered by Indians alone in the shortest possible time',
remarked Sardar Sant Singh (West Punjab, Sikh) to widespread
applause.[245]

These proposals generally met with a lukewarm British
response. But in 1939, the Government of India bowed to
nationalist pressure and set up a committee under the Adjutant-
General to examine the progress of Indianization.[246] The committee included some Members of the Legislative Assembly,
although Indians were in a minority. The Defence Department
put forward a scheme to enlarge the Royal Indian Military College, which would then become the main channel of entry to the
Indian Military Academy. Candidates for the College would be
selected at 13. Promotions from the ranks had not been proving
a great success, as primary education had made too few inroads
into the rural communities from which the army drew its
recruits.[247] Places at the College would therefore not be reserved
for candidates from army families, but military schools would
be improved to allow the sons of soldiers to compete on equal

terms.[248] The outbreak of war prevented the committee from reporting on this and on other proposals.[249]

CONCLUSION

In the military as in other spheres of colonial activity, the British always depended upon Indian subordinates to transmit and to interpret their authority. This dependence created a dilemma for the Raj. Young, vigorous and effective Indian officers would be highly dangerous if ever they led an army mutiny. But old and worn-out men, promoted as a reward for long and loyal service, might be a fatal handicap in war.

During the nineteenth century, the British never really resolved this problem to their own satisfaction. The elderly Indian officers were widely seen to have failed in their duties during 1857, although allowance must be made for the British desire to find scapegoats for the disaster. Later in the century, the development of long-range precision weapons changed the character of military leadership on the battlefield. Troops had to scatter to survive, which meant that decision-making devolved more and more upon the heads of junior officers. The military authorities responded cautiously, increasing the number of British officers in a unit, and reducing the authority of Subedars and Jemadars. They paid the price for this in the Great War, when the Indian officers – their initiative long stifled – proved unable to replace British captains and lieutenants killed in action.

The rise of nationalism presented the British with a different, but no less difficult, problem. Nationally-minded Indians deeply resented the colonial structure of the Indian Army. Many were critical of the 'martial races' policy, which excluded the educated and the urban from the ranks. They were especially hostile to the British monopoly of higher military command, which was an obvious practical impediment to self-government, and an insult to Indian strategic skill. India's impressive contribution to the Imperial cause during the Great War handed nationalists a powerful weapon in political debate. Indians could hardly be denied the right to excercise some military command after they had died in thousands fighting for the Empire.

Some movement in the army had to follow, especially after the Montagu–Chelmsford political reforms, but the British response was usually to offer the smallest concession that they thought they could get away with. They wanted to retain control of the army – the bedrock of British power – even if they had to give important ground in other areas of Indian political life. The British government tried to follow a policy of flexible conservatism, giving a little in the hope of avoiding being forced to concede even more. Ambitious schemes for sweeping Indianization usually got no further than the debating chamber. In practice, Indianization was confined to a very small portion of the army.

British reactions to the demand for Indianization exposed some of the fundamental assumptions of the Imperial governing elite. Few believed that educated Indians could ever replace British officers. For at least four decades, the influential doctrine of the 'martial races' had caricatured Western-educated Indians as effete, garrulous and incapable of making war. The 'martial races' themselves, on the other hand, were seen as bellicose but slow-witted, able to fight but not to lead. Only the British could do both. The British also liked to believe that only they could arbitrate impartially in caste and communal disputes. Plans for Indianization clashed with these cherished assumptions, and were often privately greeted with a mixture of ridicule, hostility and fear.

The Labour Government of 1929–31 proved more sympathetic to nationalist demands. As a result of the First Round Table Conference, Indianization was extended to a full war division, or about one-eighth of the Indian Army and an 'Indian Sandhurst' was created. There were no other major concessions before the Second World War. By the later 1930s, the slow pace of Indianization was producing increasing resentment and frustration among the Indian political class.

When war came, the Indian Empire did not have a large indigenous body of educated and trained officers on which to base the much-needed expansion of its army. In October 1939, there were only a few hundred Indians in an officer-corps of several thousand. Faced with pressing military need, selective Indianization was immediately abolished, and all regiments were opened to Indian officers. The College at Dehra Dun and the Indian Military Academy were both expanded. But these concessions came far too late, and were too obviously forced by circumstances, to win the British much gratitude. As Claude Auchinleck remarked in October 1940:

We have been playing a losing hand from the start in this matter of 'Indianisation'. The Indian has always thought, rightly or wrongly, that we never intended the scheme to succeed and expected it to fail. Colour has been lent to this view by the way in which each new step forward has had to be wrested from us, instead of being freely given. Now that we have given a lot we get no credit, because there was little grace in our giving.[250]

Between 1940 and 1945, mass Indianization fundamentally altered the character of the Indian Army officer-corps. Many of the new officers were sympathetic to nationalism. Partly because of this, British power in postwar India rested on very fragile military foundations. But this change lay in the future. In 1939, the colonial structure of the Indian Army remained largely intact, whatever concessions the nationalists had won in other spheres. For eighty years the British had successfully retained a virtual monopoly over the management of organized violence in India. The next chapter will assess the importance of that monopoly to the power of the Raj.

6

Military Power and Colonial Rule

So long as the Army and the Native Chiefs are with us, all should go well.

Roberts to Kitchener,
9 September 1907[1]

Our rule must depend on the morale and loyalty of the Indian Army, and that we can confidently put our trust in it.

Court of Enquiry, Proceedings,
28 April–7 May 1930[2]

The earlier chapters of this book showed how the colonial authorities rebuilt the Indian Army after the shock of 1857, and how they maintained the military system of the Raj in the eight decades that followed – despite world war, civil unrest and recurrent financial problems. The Government of India made sure that military service was well rewarded, thus cementing its vital alliance with the communities that provided the bulk of army recruits. The Raj was safer if the men who defended it won honour and made a profit. They did, and the discipline of the troops usually remained steady. The authorities had learned the lesson of 1857, and paid careful attention to the needs and the grievances of the ranks. They also tried to shield the army from influences – such as nationalism and militant religious movements – which might disrupt its impressive cohesion. There were occasional mutinies, but these were mostly minor affairs, easily contained and quickly settled.

It is not surprising that the Government of India took so much care of its army, for that is where much of its money went. In financial terms, military matters were absolutely central to the activities and concerns of the colonial state. Even in peacetime about 40 per cent of all central government revenue was normally spent on the Army in India.[3] In 1921, the figure was no less than 59 per cent.

These are remarkably high proportions. In 1900–1, a typical year, the Government of India spent nearly three times more on the military than it did on famine relief, irrigation and education combined – which gives some idea of the order of colonial priorities.[4] Some of the other major items in the government budget, like railways, also had clear military applications. Most of the lines in north-western India were built for strategic reasons, could support only light civilian traffic, and ran at a loss.[5] The Raj, however, was not a military autocracy, as nationalists sometimes claimed: military spending remained firmly under civilian control.[6] But in financial terms at least, the army was by far the most important element of the colonial state. This high level of military spending is unsurprising, given that the Army in India usually numbered around a quarter of a million men in peacetime. If money was the measure, the British Raj was a garrison state.

Nationally-minded Indians were far from happy with this situation. Excessive military spending – as they saw it – came in for unrelenting criticism, first from Congress, and later from the Legislative Assembly (which was able to vote on taxation).[7] Nationalists resented Indian money being spent on an army that served Imperial as well as Indian purposes. 'Surely no self-respecting nation will pay for a mercenary army in order to remain under control by an alien government', cried Motilal Nehru in 1928. In particular, nationalists disliked having to fund British battalions, which cost more than four times as much as a comparable Indian unit. Some were attracted by cheaper options, such as short-service conscription or a mass army of Indian volunteers, raised during moments of crisis. Nearly all wanted to see less money spent on the military and more on nation-building projects such as dams and canals.[8]

They did not get their way. The army remained a major financial burden for the entire period of this study. Indeed, high military spending at times threatened to become 'a grave political danger'.[9] The Government of India feared that the taxation needed to maintain the army, combined with low spending on socially useful projects, formed 'a ready weapon for the agitator', and might lead to internal unrest.[10] The political risks of high military expenditure sometimes threatened to undermine the very security which the army was there to preserve.[11]

But noting the military character of the Raj does not by itself measure the contribution of the Indian Army to the process of colonial domination. The Raj was highly militarized, but for three rather different purposes – defending the British Empire, protecting the frontiers of India, and sustaining the colonial order.[12] The exact weight given to each of these various duties was not always immediately clear.

This chapter is mainly concerned with internal security, since it addresses the relationship between military power and colonial rule within India itself. The first section measures the relative importance of the police and the army in protecting the Raj from domestic disturbance. The second section relates the changing deployment of the army to the changing threats to the Raj from within and without Indian frontiers. The third section looks at the use of the army 'in aid of the civil power'.

THE POLICE AND THE ARMY

Contemporary Imperialists never doubted that force was central to the security of the Raj. As the Governor of Bombay frankly remarked in 1875, 'we hold India by the sword'. Throughout the colonial period, British policy worked upon the assumption that violence was an instrument of government especially suited to the colonial context. Colonial thinking supposed that Indian society saw might as right, and stressed the need for the British to adopt some of the methods of the 'Oriental despotisms' they had rudely replaced.[13] Authority had to be visibly and quickly enforced, for the Indian people would interpret any hesitation as a sign of weakness.[14] 'Against Orientals it was essential to show force at once', remarked a British general in 1921.[15] At the root of this strategy lay a belief that 'the black man is fundamentally different in his mentality to the white'.[16] According to Sir Henry Rawlinson, 'the semi-educated native as well as the entirely stupid coolie takes clemency as proof of weakness. Ninety-nine per cent of the natives of India are children and must be treated like children. If they are patted and spoiled when they do wrong instead of being well smacked, they will only ruin themselves. Families brought up on these lines always come to grief.' He longed for 'a good strong Viceroy with a birch to smack the naughty boys'.[17]

The Civil Police and their Limitations

It was, however, the police rather than the army that did most of the 'smacking' in colonial India. Admittedly, the British acquired India largely through military conquest, and early administrators were keenly aware of their dependence upon the army.[18] But from the mid-nineteenth century, the state appeared to free itself from over-identification with the military. The civil police became more import-ant as conquest and revolt gave way to more settled administration. Numbers alone ensured the police were a prominent feature of the colonial state: in 1879 there were nearly 158 000 police regulars in India.[19] The duties of preserving order, quelling unrest and pro-tecting property normally rested with the police.[20] They were the first line of defence of British rule, the most visible expression of colonial power, and often the first target of popular anti-colonial protest. Few instruments of colonial authority, in the words of the 1902–3 Police Commission, 'so nearly touched the life of the people'.[21]

There were also plenty of objections to employing the army on routine internal security duties.[22] The military authorities preferred to hold the troops in reserve to isolate them from dissidents, and to magnify their powers of intimidation when they at last appeared on the streets. Soldiers were normally concentrated for mobile opera-tions, so they were less readily to hand for minor troubles. They were also more costly to equip and maintain than the police.[23] Nor was the army a very refined political instrument, for it offered little choice between passivity and armed intervention. Regular troops were trained primarily to direct maximum force against well-armed enemies, rather than in the more delicate duties of crowd control and surveillance. Mechanization and improved firepower made the army more effective in battle, but not always more capable of inter-nal security work.[24] Splitting the army into 'penny packets' to pro-tect civilian life and property undermined the discipline and cohesion of its units.[25] Troops assigned to internal security also had to remain on hand to reinforce the Frontier if an emergency arose in that quarter.

But the police had their limitations. Slackness and indiscipline were rife, and desertion rates were high, at least in the nineteenth century, when rates of pay and conditions of work were poor.[26] The police could never be fully subjected to colonial regulation and dis-cipline. The very nature of their work brought policemen into daily contact with the population, often while operating in small groups that could not be as closely supervised as soldiers in barracks or workers in a factory.[27] Even ordinary police duties required more intelligence than those of private soldiers, so policemen were usually more literate than their counterparts in the army.[28] Because they lived and worked among their own communities, policemen and their families were much more vulnerable than soldiers to popular pressure or violence. Congress volunteers made persistent efforts to subvert the force, and tried to persuade or compel individual men to resign.[29] In the early 1920s, the police constantly faced intimidation and social boycott, and the authorities grew uncertain how far they could be trusted in a crisis.[30]

The vagaries of Indian politics also undermined the police as an instrument of colonial control. During the last decades of the Raj, the provincial forces came under the scrutiny of the Legislative Assembly, which could try to obstruct spending. More importantly, Congress ministries assumed office in seven Indian provinces after the elections of 1937, thus gaining control of their respective police forces. As a result, the authorities felt that soldiers – particularly British ones – were needed all the more for internal security work.[31]

Alternatives to the Civil Police

The army, however, was not the only alternative to the unarmed constabulary. Armed police were a convenient middle way between military and civilian force, and it was often debated whether the colonial police should be a centralized paramilitary gendarmerie or a lightly-armed provincial body.[32] Colonial police forces always had a more violent disposition than those in Great Britain, and drew greater inspiration from the Royal Irish Constabulary than from the unarmed metropolitan model. This tendency partly reflected the coercive inclinations of Imperial administrators; but it also mirrored colonial security problems, which seemed to have much in common with those in rural Ireland.[33] Armed police, based in barracks, could be more easily supervized and separated from the indigenous population than ordinary civilian forces. The Indian civil police were normally confined to the prevention, detection and investigation of crime, the usual maintenance of order, and duties connected with the courts. A more heavily-armed body was needed to escort treasure and prisoners, to protect magazines, to control troublesome frontier tracts – for example, in Burma and Assam – and for the messy business of suppressing riots.[34]

Armed police units could relieve the military of much of this internal security work.[35] Army chiefs regarded the maintenance of public order as 'a most distasteful duty' which undermined the discipline and morale of the troops who performed it.[36] They wanted the army to aid the civil power only in 'a grave emergency', whereas the armed police were intended from the outset to enforce the commands of the magistrate.[37] Armed police could easily disperse a demonstration or a riotous assembly; but if they mutinied, the superior firepower of the army would quickly crush them. Paramilitary police were formed in Sind and the Punjab shortly after those provinces were annexed in the 1840s, and by 1904 there were 47 925 armed constables in the subcontinent. Only between 3000 and 4000 of these men had rifles – the remainder carried smoothbores. Despite this, they proved more effective than the military at some tasks, such as preventing and punishing raids among tribal peoples.[38] They were also intended to contain any major rebellion long enough to allow troops to appear on the scene. As the legitimacy of colonial rule declined in the twentieth century, so the armed police became more numerous and more military in character.

The Indian Army was closely involved in the militarization of the police. The army was one of the few sources of trained military manpower in India, and many former sepoys joined the police, especially in south India where the martial-races recruiting strategy began to reduce army employment. The police were normally inspected by Indian Army officers; and, particularly in the third quarter of the nineteenth century, many police officers were military men on secondment.[39] It was hoped that this would impart a martial discipline to the police; but it was also feared that the loss of able officers might weaken the regiments from which they were drawn.[40]

But the armed police also had their limitations, and they could never have taken over the entire burden of the army's internal security work. Troops were always needed as a last resort. Impetuous demonstrators might seize police weapons, so troops had to be available to overpower them.[41] The armed police often fired over the heads of a crowd instead of straight at them as they were enjoined to do – evidence perhaps of a common humanity which the superficial disciplines of the police could not entirely suppress.[42] The army – quarantined in barracks from daily contact with the people – was usually far more dependable than the police. Indeed, the police sometimes took part in crime or riots themselves, and could become more of a threat than the disorders they were supposed to contain. Lord Kitchener thought the armed police were 'more dangerous than useful'.[43] The fear of mutiny was a constant theme in British discussions of the police, and troops were kept on hand to check any signs of indiscipline.[44]

The introduction of an all-British paramilitary gendarmerie might have avoided many of the problems associated with the Indian police. A European force would be impartial during communal riots, and loyal to the Raj during anti-colonial unrest. It could relieve highly-skilled British troops from irksome police duties, freeing them for more fitting military tasks on the Indian Frontier or elsewhere in the Empire. British regular units could more easily be modernized if they were not burdened with internal security work. The idea of a British gendarmerie was superficially attractive, and periodically mooted between the wars. Basil Liddell Hart was a keen supporter of the idea.[45] He believed the British garrison of India could be reduced by more than half if a gendarmerie were formed.[46] Others, more hopeful, thought that British regular troops could be removed altogether.

But the costs of the scheme outweighed its potential benefits. Near-permanent Indian service would hardly appeal to British other ranks, so the gendarmes would have to be paid even more than British regulars to attract recruits.[47] A gendarmerie raised to police India would have been less flexible than all-purpose army battalions. It could not go overseas in an emergency, nor act as a general reserve for the Frontier.[48] It could not deal with a mutiny among the better-armed and better-trained Indian regular regiments. And there were clear political objections to the idea.[49] Indian politicians would probably accuse the government of attempting to saddle the country with an expensive all-British force to maintain colonial, rather than Indian, interests. Therefore the necessary funds would not easily come forth.

The Need for the Army

Because the power of the police was so limited, and an all-British gendarmerie was impractical, the Indian Army had to perform internal security tasks. 'The aid of the regular troops must be counted upon in the last resort to maintain internal order', noted the Military Department in 1904.[50] Contemporaries were remarkably consistent in their belief that the military were essential to the colonial domination of the subcontinent.[51] Indeed, the army was so important that a principal aim of goverment policy was to secure its loyalty and contentment, without which the Raj could not have survived.[52] As the Governor of Bombay remarked in 1875:

> If we cease to maintain our military ascendancy, our rule will speedily come to an end. Thus the maintenance in the highest state of efficiency of everything connected with the army becomes most binding on the British Government. The omission to remedy defects in the Native army must speedily bring about its own punishment.[53]

Many nationalist observers agreed, although they put a different political gloss upon the facts. 'Our army is a mercenary army employed by foreigners to put down their own countrymen, and to keep them under foreign heels', complained Motilal Nehru in 1928.[54]

Thus British rule in the subcontinent relied on the army as its final sanction, even if the police were its first line of defence. The police were the primary force for preserving order, protecting property and quelling minor disturbances.[55] But they could only do so much, besides being barely trusted themselves. Troops were normally held as an armed reserve collected at convenient stations; and in the event of a major rising, the police were expected to hold on only until soldiers could arrive.[56] The army remained the final argument of the Raj.

ARMY DEPLOYMENT

The deployment of the Indian Army from the early 1860s until the mid-1880s reflected the need to protect the Raj from the enemy within. There was no serious threat from beyond Indian frontiers, so domestic security dominated the disposition of the troops.[57] 'The Indian Army is required to maintain internal tranquility rather than for employment against external foes', noted the Military Department in 1881.[58] Indeed, some well-known Indian Army units were originally raised solely for internal security work. The Central India Horse, for instance, were formed by merging several units which had been engaged in suppressing dacoits and rebel chiefs. From 1861, they were collected into two regiments based 130 miles apart.

Their tasks were to clear Central India of bandits and to protect the Grand Trunk Road from Bombay to Delhi.[59]

Communications and Deployment

The 1857 rebellion had shown the need for many small bodies of troops ready to take the field at short notice in different parts of the country.[60] Before the coming of the railway, armies could move only on foot or on horseback at around a dozen miles a day. This restricted pace of operations had important implications for internal security. Slow communications made it necessary to occupy a large number of key points – the so-called 'obligatory garrisons' – to insure against a general rising. Nineteenth-century India was there-fore dotted with isolated military stations so troops were on hand to deal with local outbreaks. 'As centralization is necessary to meet a foreign enemy, so dispersion is requisite for the maintenance of peace in a country which has been occupied', noted one British gen-eral in 1858.[61] The fragmentation of the army also made it harder for mutinous troops to combine.

The development of railways undermined this policy. Rail-ways multiplied the military force of the Raj, enabling masses of troops to be swiftly moved against any outbreaks of rebellion. The amount of track in India quickly increased – from 432 miles in 1859, to more than 5000 miles in 1869 and nearly 25 000 miles in 1900.[62] By 1910, India had the fourth largest network in the world, almost entirely geared to British commercial and strategic interests.[63] Improved railway and telegraph communications made it much easier to crush a rebellion.[64] Railways were 'a real addition to the military strength of the country', according to the 1879 Eden Commission. 'So long as we hold our main trunk lines, a successful insurrection, or any real display of military power by the native states, is out of the question.'[65] The exclusive pos-session of railways conferred freedom of movement upon the Imperial forces, while denying it to rebels.[66] If the British could hold the main rail lines, arsenals and important centres, then they could easily form flying columns to overawe the surround-ing countryside and smash any remaining centres of rebellion.[67] Railways therefore provided an incentive to concentrate troops at a few points, rather than scattering them about the country. In any major rising, the first effort of the British would be to hold the vital lines from Bombay to Delhi.[68]

Securing the railways, however, was no easy matter, since many bridges, tunnels and stations were vulnerable to sabotage.[69] Special measures were needed to safeguard the lines. Many jobs on the Indian railways were reserved for Eurasians – often the descendants of former British soldiers who had married Indian wives – because people of mixed race often strongly identified with European society (which rather looked down upon them) and were likely to side with the British during a revolt.[70] Railway workers would be crucial in a rebellion, for trains were essential to move troops, stores and munitions. The main task of the railwaymen would be to keep the trains running, but in an emergency some could also safeguard installations and track, protect the families of railway workers, and man armoured trains.[71] They were therefore organized into volunteer units, and given arms and military training. The railway battalions would be valuable for internal security work, not least because they were familiar with the installations they would have had to defend. Their very existence bore witness to the strategic importance of the railways to the Raj. The units, 12 681 strong by 1904, also provided the vital Anglo-Indian community with the opportunity for military service, together with the status this conferred in a society in which the right to bear arms was severely restricted.[72]

White society in the subcontinent was also highly militarized for reasons of internal security.[73] In 1857, many bodies of European volunteers were formed to help suppress the Indian rebellion. Often sneered at by the regulars as too old, too fat, or too drunken, they nevertheless performed with credit. Volunteers did not defend any city on their own, but they helped free some regular troops from static defensive tasks. Most units stood down after 1858, but many revived in the 1860s, as public-spirited citizens of European descent, and, encouraged by the volunteer movement in Britain, formed themselves into a variety of volunteer corps. By 1879, these totalled 7000 men, including 2500 who worked on the railways.[74] Their numbers had risen to 24 000 by 1893. But Lord Roberts was still not content. 'We must not rest satisfied', he wrote, 'until every [white] man capable of bearing arms is enrolled in an organization which adds so materially to the stability of our position in India'.[75] By 1907 the Indian Volunteer Force, as it was then officially known, included 34 000 men in 61 corps. These units were intended to maintain order in India during wartime, for example by guarding essential bridges to cover the mobilization of the army. During the Great War the volunteers were occasionally embodied to take over garrison duties from the regulars.

From 1917 all European and Anglo-Indian males were obliged to serve locally in a new Indian Defence Force, which absorbed all the existing volunteer units. In 1920, this in turn was replaced by an Auxiliary Force (India) formed on a voluntary basis.[76] The new corps enshrined the right of European and Eurasian subjects to bear arms in the defence of their life and property, it being thought better that they did this in an organized and supervised manner, sanctioned by law, rather than 'as the wishes of private individuals may dictate'.[77] The Auxiliary Force was also a European balance to the recently-formed Indian Territorial Force, then 20 battalions strong.[78] The Auxiliaries were not liable for general service, but were intended to protect European lives and property in their own neighbourhood. They could not replace regulars for routine internal security work, since they were mainly professional and business men closely involved in the ordinary commercial life of their locality, but they could still be of some value in time of internal disorder.[79] Regular army officers were attached to each unit to help them train. Totalling 30 000 men – including ten railway protection battalions – the force was concentrated in centres of European business such as Calcutta, Bombay and the planting districts. The Auxiliaries saw action from time to time – 125 men, for example, went in with the bayonet when they quelled strikers at Kharagpur station, 70 miles west of Calcutta, during the 1927 strike on the Bengal–Nagpur railway.[80]

Communications by water were much less vulnerable than railways but only a little less valuable to the security of the Raj. Bengal, for example, was crossed from end to end by excellent waterways 'that nothing can destroy and along which troops can be poured from India and Burma'.[81] Because of these useful arteries, the strategic environment in Bengal was very favourable, giving the Raj 'many natural advantages which cannot be taken from us, whatever the attitude of the population'. In Burma, the difficulty of moving troops over the poor country roads, through hills, thick forests and marshy ground merely underlined the importance of river communication. The Irrawaddy and Chindwin were navigable all the year round, and could transport soldiers deep into the interior of the province. It was vital for Imperial strategy to hold the port of Rangoon in time of rebellion because it could always receive reinforcements by sea.

Rangoon was merely one of the many cities that were nodal points of British power in the subcontinent. The major centres of population were knots of railway communication and valuable prizes in their own right. Retaining Calcutta, for example, would have been one of the first aims of British strategy in the event of a rising in Bengal or the United Provinces. Calcutta was the seat of the Government of Bengal and the residence of the Viceroy during the cool season, and therefore of great political importance. It contained an arsenal, railway workshops and a dense concentration of Europeans. Its universities and High Court extended its political influence. It was the greatest seaport in India, of immense commercial significance, and would have been the probable gate of entry for military reinforcements. If a rising took place in the Punjab, on the other hand, holding Delhi would be of central importance to the British. The retention of Delhi would have great symbolic weight, for it had been the capital of the Mughal empire before becoming the site at which the accession of British monarchs was proclaimed, amid great pomp, before governors, princes and chiefs. 'Among so conservative a people its possession is still regarded, by the majority of the Indian races who count in war, as the emblem and symbol of power in Hindustan.'[82]

The Russian Threat

The British were normally confident they could deal with internal unrest, unless it was produced or complicated by outside troubles.[83] In the 1860s and 1870s there were no major external threats to the Raj, but the advance of the Russian Empire to the borders of Afghanistan by the later 1870s seemed to herald new dangers to British power in India. In 1885, 10 000 British and 20 000 Indian troops were added to the army establishment to counter the Russian threat to the North West Frontier. Geography and logistics placed major obstacles in the way of a Russian invasion of Afghanistan, but British planners seem to have taken the danger seriously enough.[84] As Lord Roberts once pointed out, India had been invaded from the north-west at least 21 times since the twelfth century BC. 'No one can have any doubt as to Russia's real intentions', he warned. 'Unless we are able to arrest her further progress, she will inevitably overrun Afghanistan.'[85] The Russian Empire could then attack India, 'an advance', Roberts thought, 'which is absolutely certain to be made some day'.[86] The Indian Army, it seemed, might have to defend the Indian frontier against the troops of an expanding imperial power.

The threat to the North West Frontier increased the internal security duties of the Indian Army, for the internal and external security of the Raj were closely linked.[87] A war on the Indian frontier would make a popular rising more likely and more dangerous. An enemy power might try and foment unrest in India, the appearance of a hostile army on the Frontier would undermine the prestige of the Raj, and any delay in dealing with the military threat would severely try the loyalty of British subjects and allies.[88] Local rumour would quickly transmit, and probably exaggerate, any news of an Imperial reverse.[89] The stress and hardships of war would increase robbery and dacoity.[90] Fewer troops would be available to check unrest, the Field Army would be fully occupied on the Frontier, and the garrison of India would be reduced to a bare minimum.[91] Military communications would therefore become harder to protect from sabotage, so every local disturbance would add to the problems of the army in the field. The troubling prospect of facing war and rebellion at the same time greatly perplexed Imperial strategists and complicated British security policy until the end of the Raj.

Invading India through Afghanistan, however, would not have been easy.[92] The harsh conditions severely limited the number of troops that could be maintained there. Water was scarce, agriculture was poor and communications were primitive. Attempts to live off the land were likely to provoke ferocious tribal resistance. During the campaign of 1879–80, the British could keep an average of only 12 000 men in the north of the country, and even this small force proved hard to supply.[93] If a large army invaded Afghanistan, it risked starvation: if a small army did so, it risked defeat.

Undeterred, Russian planners drew up schemes to invade India from the north-west. They did so believing that decisive military victory would not be needed to cause the downfall of the British Raj – a brief campaign, followed by a popular uprising, would be enough.[94] 'The very appearance of even a small force on the frontiers of India is sufficient to kindle a rebellion, and to ensure the overthrow of the British dominion in Hindustan', wrote one Russian general.[95] A Russian army plan, which fell into British hands in 1886, envisaged a two-stage advance towards India. A single campaign would absorb the northern provinces of Afghanistan. After a pause of two or three years to rest the army and administer the country, a second campaign would close with the capture of Kabul, Kandahar and Kashmir.

> There is no occasion to speak of a third campaign [the document continued], because after our first advance the English would be in a pitiable state in India, and fifty per cent of their influence would have gone: and after our second advance the English would find themselves in the same state as they were in 1857, with this difference – that the natives would have our support.[96]

These Russian plans might have seemed the stuff of pipe-dreams, but British generals took them in fearful earnest from the 1880s until the early twentieth century. British power in India, they often repeated, depended upon its prestige – which was colonial shorthand for the secure appearance of invincible superiority. As Lord Roberts wrote in 1885:

> The whole secret of our successful rule in the East is that our supremacy has never yet been doubted, either by our own subjects or by our neighbours. For close on 200 years Russia's dream has been to gain possession of India. During the last decade she has made such vast strides that the prize must now seem almost within her grasp. The time has come, however, when she must learn that between her and the fulfilment of her ambition lies a barrier that may not be passed – the might of imperial England.[97]

Behind the rhetoric lay fear. If Russian troops crossed the Afghan frontier unchallenged, British prestige in India would be destroyed.[98] The British had pledged to stand for no external interference with Afghanistan.[99] If they then failed to protect the country against Russian aggression 'the whole Eastern world would assume that we were unwilling or unable to risk a conflict with Russia'.[100] The Afghans, the border peoples and 'the more warlike races of India' would turn against the Raj to seek the best terms they could with the Russians.[101] The rest of the Indian population would soon become disaffected. 'They are not our own flesh and blood, and we should make a fatal mistake if we were misled into believing that we could rely on their loyalty under all circumstances.'[102] The army would be barely able to

hold India down – if indeed military discipline did not crumble
as the troops lost confidence in British power to resist attack from
outside.[103] 'In short,' Roberts wrote, 'without being defeated, we
should experience all the moral and political effects of defeat.'[104]
The danger from Russia made external defence seem more
important than internal security, but it also made sure that the
internal security of the Raj depended more and more upon the
strength of its armies in the field.[105]

The Imperial Response

In some respects the Government of India was slow to prepare
the army against the threat from the north-west. As early as
1878–80, the Second Afghan War had shown that the existence of
three separate presidency armies hampered the conduct of operations.[106] The Government of India did administer all the Indian
armies, but in a cumbersome and roundabout way.[107] It was only
in 1893 that the presidency forces were amalgamated and that the
Indian Army was treated formally as a single whole for
operational planning.[108]

More far-reaching reforms took place under Lord Kitchener in
1904–5.[109] Upon taking command of the Indian army, Kitchener discovered that its organization was 'based much more on the assumption that we have to hold India against the Indians than with regard
to possible danger from outside'.[110] The army was scattered over the
subcontinent in numerous military stations, many of which held
only a brigade or even a single regiment.[111] Opportunities to hold
manoeuvres or train all arms together were rare. Almost every
major town had its obligatory garrison to guard against internal
unrest, thus tying down 129 000 British and Indian troops and 226
guns.[112] After deducting the sick and the depots, only 73 900 men
were left to form the Field Army. 'Our available strength is dissipated and sacrificed instead of being economised and concentrated', complained the Military Department.[113] In the event of war
it was unlikely that more than four divisions could be sent across
the Afghan frontier, a force quite inadequate to meet the Russian
threat.[114] Even these divisions would have to be created *ad hoc* from
units unfamiliar with each other, since no higher tactical formations
existed in peacetime.[115]

Kitchener hoped to have a much larger and better-organized force
for campaigns beyond the Frontier. Redistributing the army could

reduce the number of troops tied to local defence and increase those available for war.[116] Kitchener therefore abolished many minor and isolated military stations, freeing their units for the Field Army.[117] He reorganized the Indian military administration, creating divisional areas to each of which he allotted troops for local defence and a single fighting division. The latter could be assigned as needed to the Field Army or to help suppress an internal rising.[118] By these simple measures he roughly doubled the size of the Field Army to a possible maximum of nine infantry divisions and eight cavalry brigades. Including corps troops and units supplied by the Indian Princes, a total of 149 000 men could take the field in wartime.[119] Realistic training was easier when troops of all arms were massed in large divisional garrisons.[120] The new permanent divisions could also take the field more quickly than the previous *ad hoc* formations because they were organized in peace much as they would be in war. In an emergency, field army troops could be used against Indian rebels. The development of the rail network meant that large, mobile columns were better able to dominate the country than small, scattered posts, which were always in danger of being surrounded and overwhelmed by a major rising.[121] Kitchener assigned 85 566 troops to internal security – far fewer than had been usual in the nineteenth century, although still a formidable mass of men and firepower.

The threat of Russian invasion declined after the Russo-Japanese war of 1904–5 and still more after the Anglo-Russian understanding of 1907, bringing great relief to the problem of Indian defence.[122] The revolution of 1917 and the Bolshevik repudiation of Tsarist treaties did not cause immediate alarm, as the fragile Soviet state was beset by internal problems and no longer disposed of formidable military power. The Russian bogey intermittently revived in the 1920s, especially after Russian troops seized an Afghan island in the river Oxus in 1925.[123] Some commentators still held that a Russian occupation of Northern Afghanistan would lead to civil rebellion in India and the loss of the Raj.[124] The war of 1919 had certainly damaged British influence over Afghanistan. But that remote and mountainous state, which still lacked railways, remained impervious to a Russian advance. The Red Army was also in no fit state to mount a full-scale invasion, even after Soviet military strength began to revive in the 1930s.[125] Nevertheless, the Committee of Imperial Defence accepted that Britain would declare war if the Russians violated the Afghan frontier.[126]

The Enemy Within

Civil unrest was a more immediate trouble in the 1920s, not least because internal disorder increased the risk of external aggression and the chance of its success.[127] The Bolsheviks seemed likely to try to spread their influence in the region through subversion and propaganda rather than by armed force.[128] This they were well-placed to do, since they added to the traditional expansionist drive of the Russian Empire a potent revolutionary doctrine of hostility to colonial rule.[129] The Bolsheviks, according to British planners, saw the British Empire as the main obstacle to world revolution, and the chief enemy of the Soviet Union.[130] 'The road to London goes through Kabul and Delhi', Lenin was rumoured to have said in 1920. The 1931 Report on the Army in India concluded that 'the real object of the Soviet was to destroy the British Empire by causing an upheaval in India'.[131] The most likely cause of an Indian uprising, British planners thought, was a pan-Islamic movement fomented by the Bolsheviks, or a *jihad* preached by the Afghans while the British Empire was at war elsewhere.[132] These perceptions perhaps reveal more about Imperial fears than Bolshevik plans; but British strategists still came to believe that maintaining internal security was the most pressing duty of the army, particularly when unrest, encouraged by Congress, began to affect many Indian provinces.[133]

By 1921, there were 56 000 troops deployed primarily on internal security duties, besides others assigned to guard the lines of communication to the Frontier. Units of the Field Army could also help quell serious unrest, provided (at least in theory) that this did not impede their preparations for war.[134] Some educated Indians, including many in the Legislative Assembly, thought that too many troops were assigned to internal security. Recent political concessions and moves towards self-government, they argued, would encourage the political militants and the masses to cooperate with the Raj and to work for change within the established political framework. Colonial officials were much less confident that unrest would die down, and believed they had plenty of evidence to support them in the form of the Non-Cooperation, Khilafat and Sikh Gurdwara reform movements, besides industrial and agrarian disturbances in several provinces. Most provincial governments wanted more troops to back them up, as they feared the Indian 'underworld', especially in the larger towns.[135] The colonial authorities were very reluctant to hazard the security of the Raj, so the number of troops on hand to aid the civil power stayed much the same throughout the 1920s and 1930s.

All units had to train for internal security duties such as street-fighting and the dispersal of crowds. Officers heard lectures on this aspect of their work, and were expected to be conversant with the relevant sections of Indian law.[136] During the 1920s and 1930s, however, the growing number of troops needed to check civil unrest threatened to hamper training for war, as Field Army units were drawn more and more into police duties.[137] By 1938, 28 of the 45 British battalions in India were occupied in containing threats to the colonial order. Police-work also encouraged technical conservatism, since large numbers of men and horses were usually more effective than modern weapons for controlling crowds.[138] Cavalry, for example, could 'show the flag' more easily than armoured vehicles, which were often too heavy for rural bridges or too unwieldy to work in the narrow and cluttered streets of an Indian town. Much of the low-key police-work involved splitting battalions into small detachments with little opportunity for realistic military training. After three or four years on internal security in India, a battalion was 'almost useless as a military force', according to General Edmund Ironside.[139]

Ethnic Security

As the twentieth century wore on, the authorities showed a growing preference for British over Indian troops for internal security work. There were not enough British units to spare, however, and the Indian Army retained an important domestic role until the very end of the Raj. Nevertheless, the changing ratio of British to Indian troops allotted to different tasks reveals much about imperial anxieties. In 1905, for example, the internal security forces included 17 British and 46 Indian units – a ratio of nearly three to one in the Indian favour.[140] (See Table 6.1.) The Russian threat still loomed in the north-west, and most British troops were posted to the Frontier.

By 1922, however, British soldiers slightly outnumbered Indians on internal security duty. On the Frontier the balance was reversed – Indian troops outnumbered the British two-and-a-half to one in the Field Army and six to one in the Covering Troops.[141] These prescribed ratios remained roughly the same throughout the 1920s and 1930s.[142] (See Table 6.2.)

The Sepoy and the Raj

TABLE 6.1

British and Indian units assigned to internal security, 1905–21

	Year			
	1905	1911	1913	1921
British	17	21	22	31
Indian	46	38	36	28
Total	63	59	58	59

Source: Memo by Jacob, 10 May 1921, CAB 16/38/2.
Note: The figures refer to troops assigned to internal security east of the Indus. They probably include units guarding lines of communication. A unit is a cavalry regiment or an infantry battalion. Slightly different figures, showing the same general trend, appear in Report on Indian Military Requirements, June 1922, CID 125-D, CAB 6/4, and Jacobsen, PhD thesis, p. 52.

The growing domestic dependence on British troops reflected the increasing civil unrest in India, which the authorities sometimes feared might affect the Indian Army itself. Indeed, Indian rioters often hoped that Indian Army units might remain neutral or actively join them.[143] They hoped in vain, but planners were unwilling to take risks with lines of communication that would be vital in war. The higher proportion of British troops assigned to internal duties also reflected the growing communal violence of the period. To contain this, local governments normally preferred British or Gurkha units to Indian ones.[144] As outsiders, they were less likely to succumb to religious or ethnic bias when policing conflicts between Hindus and Muslims. Indian troops always proved reliable on such duties, but the authorities disliked putting their discipline to such a test if it could be avoided.[145]

British troops were not only useful for policing communal disturbances. Their appearance was thought to be a more imposing deterrent than that of Indian soldiers, largely because no rioters would ever make the mistake of assuming that British units could be won to their cause. All local governments attached especial importance to the British military presence, which was felt to have a particularly impressive 'moral effect' upon would-be dissidents.[146] In time of

TABLE 6.2
Distribution of the Army in India, 1931

Units	Establishment	Covering Troops	Field Army	Lines of Communication	Internal Security	Burma	Grand Total
Cavalry Regiments							
British	5	–	4	–	1	–	5
Indian	21	5	7	7	2	–	21
Pioneer Battalions	7	1	5	–	–	1	7
Infantry Battalions							
British	45	5	12	22	4	2	45
Indian	100[1]	37	36	12	11	2	98[2]
Total	178	48	64	41	18	5	176

[1] Excludes two battalions overseas.
[2] Two battalions to be reduced.
Source: Report on Army in India, June 1931, CID 138-A, CAB 6/6.
Note: Units assigned to guard lines of communication were intended primarily for internal rather than external security, and were deployed mostly in the Punjab. Field Army troops were drawn into internal security work, but were intended mainly to prepare for war. Covering troops were stationed on the North West Frontier, and on campaign worked in conjunction with the Field Force.

war, thought Lord Roberts, extra British troops should be sent to India, 'whether they be wanted at the front or not, to lend support to our moral position in the eyes of the native population'.[147] British units guarded the main political and industrial centres, with detachments at a few other places of importance. In case of a widespread anti-colonial rising, they would be the last line of defence for European life and property.[148] But India was vast and populous, and the white line was thin indeed. In 1938, discounting units on the Frontier, there was only one British soldier to every 88 square miles of country and every 20 000 inhabitants.[149] The British army could never have maintained the colonial order without extensive help from Indian sepoys.

Some nationally-minded Indians, however, resented any use of British troops within Indian frontiers. From the early 1920s, a growing body of educated Indian opinion wanted the internal security forces to include more Indian and fewer British units.[150] There were sound financial arguments in their favour.[151] A British battalion cost more than four times as much as its Indian equivalent, which made it seem an extravagant form of insurance against unrest.[152] There were other less material, but not less powerful, objections to European soldiers.[153] The use of British troops to keep order seemed to be a slur upon the excellent discipline of the Indian Army.[154] Most sepoys disliked acting in aid of the civil power, but between 1857 and 1930 not one Indian regiment refused orders to put down a public disturbance. Nationalists who aspired to dominion status wanted to see Indians more closely involved with the defence of their own country.[155] Any use of British troops seemed to them to be an implicit and insulting denial of Indian fitness for self-government. The 1931 Round Table conference did accept the need to reduce the number of British units engaged in police work.[156] But this public statement was merely a salve to the wounded self-esteem of the nationalists. The colonial authorities would not undermine one of the foundations of their power, or reduce a force that would remain usefully impartial during communal violence.[157]

The internal security troops, both British and Indian, were not evenly distributed throughout India. The main concentrations were in the Punjab and the United Provinces, for two reasons. First, the gateway to India lay in the north-west, and the strategic lines to the Frontier ran through those regions. These vital communications had to be well guarded. Second, the Punjab provided most of the 'fighting material' for the Indian Army, and its inhabitants were thought to be more warlike, and hence more dangerous, than those from elsewhere in India. 'The Sikhs are in a very nasty mood', noted Henry Rawlinson at the end of 1920. 'We may have a very difficult time with them as they are a fighting race and very tenacious.'[158] The British hold on the rest of India was thought to depend largely upon the prestige derived from dominating the warlike peoples of the Punjab and the power derived from enlisting them.[159] The inhabitants of the east and south were seen as less martial and hence less dangerous than those of the north.[160] 'In the Madras Presidency there is no real danger of anything beyond mass rioting; and as the Madrassi is being eliminated from the Army because he is wanting in soldierly instincts, so the same Madrassi, in the form of a rioter, will not be very dangerous', remarked a complacent 1904 strategic study.[161] The far south was virtually denuded of troops by the early twentieth century, and the Government of Madras complained several times that the local security forces had been reduced below the margin of safety.[162] Their fears seemed to be confirmed in 1921 when the Mappilas rose in revolt, shortly after yet more troops had been withdrawn from the region.

The British tried to avoid using Indian soldiers to police disturbances within their own particular community.[163] 'It is out of the question to ask them to attack their own brothers', thought Sir Claud Jacob. 'It is a crime to expect them to do it.'[164] Thus Afridi units did not serve in the 1897 Frontier campaign, and the Malabar revolt of 1921 was suppressed mainly by British, Gurkha, Garhwali, Chin and Kachin troops.[165] The highly localized composition of most Indian Army regiments aided this policy. The needs of internal security sometimes overrode the demands of economy or swift mobilization for war when troops were being assigned to their peacetime stations.[166]

Gurkha regiments were thought to be particularly suitable for containing civil unrest in India.[167] They were recruited in Nepal, had few cultural links with India, and could be used almost anywhere without endangering their discipline.[168] Gurkha troops had no particular biases that might make them partial during communal conflict, but regarded all Indians alike with mild disdain.[169] For this reason, the civil authorities preferred Gurkha to Indian troops for quelling unrest. Roberts, Kitchener and Rawlinson all considered Gurkhas – along with Garhwalis and Kumaonis – as politically reliable as British troops.[170]

The Indian masses resented the loyalty of these hill-soldiers to the British Raj. In 1930, an angry Peshawar crowd, sympathetic to Congress, taunted Garhwali soldiers with shouts of 'when we have our Government we will make the Garhwalis and Gurkhas into sweepers'.[171] Some educated nationalists also disliked the use of Asian troops from beyond the borders of India, and from time to time voiced their concern in the Assembly.[172] They wanted a genuinely national Indian Army, and resented the Gurkhas for symbolizing its colonial nature.[173] This, however, did not prevent the newly-independent Indian state from absorbing half the Gurkha battalions in 1947.

THE ARMY IN ACTION

The earlier parts of this chapter showed that the deployment of the Indian Army reflected its importance to the defence of the colonial order. But the precise internal security role of the army remained uncertain. Were troops there to prevent the breakdown of public order in the first place, or were they to come to the rescue of the civil administration only after rebellions had begun? Was the army an ordinary instrument of colonial government, or was it an exceptional last resort?

Military Display, Civil Disarmament

These questions were not merely theoretical ones: they had important implications for policy. Their practical ramifications emerged in the early 1920s, after the reduction of the Madras garrison and the subsequent rebellion in Malabar, to take but one example. The Government of Madras felt that the south was under-insured and they wanted more troops to be stationed there.[174] They asked for 'a sufficient backing of military force to enable them to carry on the ordinary functions of government'.[175] The Government of India, however, rejected the principle that lay behind the request: 'The primary function of internal security troops is to restore order when necessary; they cannot be made responsible to prevent disorder.'[176] The military authorities agreed with the central government, on this occasion at least. 'This duty of preserving order is one that should be met by the civil government and their police, and not by regular troops, who have more important functions to fulfil.' The Government of Madras were bewildered. 'They fail to understand what functions these troops are expected to perform more important than those of preserving peace and order.'

The confusion of the Madras Government was understandable, for the high command seemed to be contradicting their many previous assertions that the army did have a preventive role. The visible power and discipline of soldiers could deter unrest, and the military often claimed that the mere presence of a cantonment caused would-be rebels to think twice before defying the Raj. 'It is not wise to withdraw our troops from the actual sight of the people, or to trust them entirely to police control', remarked the Commander-in-Chief in 1880, after the Santal disturbances near Delhi.[177] The General Staff *Internal Security Instructions* of 1937 officially enshrined the belief that soldiers were more useful when visible. 'In civil disturbances the presence of troops has a steadying effect, and their early appearance frequently results in the arrest of a dangerous movement before it has time to develop.'[178] The *Instructions* went on to argue that marching troops through a potentially restless area could provide its population with a sobering and perhaps preventive reminder of government power. 'Such action gives confidence to the loyal inhabitants and acts as a deterrent to others.'[179] In the summer of 1926, for example, a column of infantry, cavalry and armoured cars passed through Calcutta 'as a show of strength to the inhabitants who were unsettled owing to communal riots'.[180] It was established government policy to preserve order by constant and visible preparation to contain unrest. Prevention was better, and cheaper, than cure.[181]

There was a regional dimension to this strategy. In areas like Bengal or Madras, where the inhabitants were thought to be unwarlike, the authorities were sometimes reluctant to deploy troops – except in grave emergency – for fear of lending spurious importance to minor threats, and thus encouraging dissidents rather than deterring them.[182]

To impart added powers of intimidation to these displays of military force, the Government of India tried to disarm the civil population. No inhabitant of British India could legally keep, sell or make firearms or ammunition except by licence issued by the magistrate of the district. Licences were given only to 'persons of approved character and loyalty' for sport, protection, display or for killing wild animals.[183] Indian soldiers of 'good character' were also allowed to bear private arms, provided these were no better than those normally issued for their military duties.[184] In 1904, 221 747 people held firearms licences, but the vast majority of licensed weapons were obsolete smoothbores of little military value. Nor were Indians allowed to wear swords, except ceremonial weapons presented for services to the government, or as part of an approved uniform.[185]

Inevitably, the authorities failed to fully contain and regulate the private possession of arms. In Rajputana and Central India, for example, practically every Rajput carried a country-made sword, and many had muzzle-loading firearms.[186] By the 1920s, more and more Sikh militants were wearing large *kirpans*, openly and with impunity.[187] Other weapons were concealed. Nor could the government do much to restrict the flow of firearms to the unadministered zone of the North West Frontier, where in 1911 there were 70 000 breech-loading and 30 000 muzzle-loading rifles in tribal hands (according to General Staff estimates).[188] Nevertheless, Indian crowds in the towns were normally armed only with bricks, staves and swords.[189] The sepoys might be outnumbered, but they were rarely outgunned.

The Use of Force

Displays of military force, the presence of cantonments, and the disarmament of the civil population all helped to deter open unrest; but even together they were not a certain guarantee against it. The army was often called out to aid the civil power – far more often, indeed, than historians have usually acknowledged. In the two decades from 1860 to 1879, for example, troops were summoned to prevent or repress internal disorder at least 46 times.[190] The figures show that the regular and village police could normally contain dissent, but they also reveal that active military intervention was a periodic recourse of the colonial state. The army was being used far more frequently by the early twentieth century. Troops were called out no less than 69 times in the three years 1899 to 1901, partly because there was no formal system for collecting the armed police and sending them where required.[191] The army was needed in some areas far more often than in others. In Malabar, for example, there were 351 separate agrarian incidents between 1836 and 1919.[192] All were quickly and easily suppressed, but the army often had to help out the police.

In general, these cases of military intervention were very minor affairs – a matter of a few dozen men or a couple of companies. But the fact that minor incidents did not usually grow into major rebellions owed much to the prompt use of force. The colonial authorities rarely had to resort to force on a large scale, partly because they were willing and able to do so on a small scale.

The Government of India was ready to use force for the sake of prestige – and without prestige to hold it together, the fabric of the British Raj would have rapidly unravelled. But the prestige of the colonial state depended largely on the power of its security forces.[193] If the Raj had failed to protect the lives and property of its subjects, its standing in their eyes would quickly have declined. These concerns underlay the delight of the colonial authorties when, in 1923, the armed forces finally finished off the Babar Akali gang, which had been operating in the Punjab countryside. 'The killing of these men has had an excellent effect in the Doaba', reported the Commander-in-Chief. 'The villages, hitherto terrorized by the gang, have seen that the Government has not entirely lost the power to strike.'[194] It was especially important to protect those who openly backed the Raj, as this encouraged others to do the same. The Government of Bengal took this line when facing a widespread campaign of terrorism in the early 1930s. 'It is essential, in order that Government should receive the support which it requires, that it should demonstrate an unflinching determination to protect its servants and supporters.'[195] By the same token, the authorities would lose prestige if their orders could be openly defied. Orientalist stereotypes informed this colonial infatuation with the 'firm line'. In the words of Lord Roberts, 'doubt and indecision assist our enemies and discourage our friends; this is peculiarly the case with Asiatics who always attribute hesitation to fear'.[196]

The use of excessive force, however, could damage the prestige of the colonial state as much as any apparent timidity. According to regulations, military violence in aid of the civil power was to avoid the dangerous extremes of vacillation and brutality. The doctrine of 'minimum necessary force' was supposed to guide the actions of an army commander when protecting the British Raj from internal unrest. In scattering a crowd, for example, an officer was to apply 'as little force, and do as little injury, as may be consistent with dispersing the assembly'.[197] Before taking violent action against civilians, a military commander was to make sure he issued a clear and effective warning to the crowd. If he decided to order his men to shoot, firing was to cease at the earliest possible moment.

But colonial practice did not always respect these guidelines. The doctrine of 'minimum necessary force' was perhaps most flagrantly breached by General Dyer in 1919, during the disturbances in the Punjab connected with the Rowlatt satyagraha. On the afternoon of 13 April, Dyer took a hundred men of the Indian Army to disperse a crowd of several thousand that had assembled, in apparent defiance of his orders, in the open space of the Jallianwala Bagh, in the city of Amritsar. Without any specific warning, Dyer ordered his troops to open fire on the unarmed and peaceful gathering. The shooting continued for ten minutes, leaving nearly four hundred dead and about a thousand wounded. Dyer made no attempt to discover the minimum force which would have dispersed the assembly, he went on firing well after the crowd had begun to scatter, and he marched his men away without making any provision for the injured.[198] The gravest feature of his action was its underlying intent. In his own words, 'it was no longer a question of merely dispersing the crowd, but one of producing a sufficient moral effect, not only on those who were present, but throughout the Punjab'.[199] A committee of enquiry condemned Dyer for using excessive force, and he was given no further military employment, despite noisy support for him in some quarters.[200]

Dyer's action was an extreme case, but one that expressed a pervasive Imperial belief that force was the only language that the Indian masses could understand. In 1915, for example, Sir Harcourt Butler feared a Frontier uprising. But he was confident that the army could deal with it. 'We ought to be able to mow them down with machine guns,' he remarked.[201] His casual disregard for Indian life was far from unique.

The Amritsar massacre did subdue the unrest in the Punjab, but only at heavy cost to the legitimacy of colonial rule in the subcontinent, as the more perceptive Imperialists themselves recognized.[202] According to Winston Churchill, speaking in the House of Commons, the massacre was 'an episode without precedent or parallel in the modern history of the British Empire. It is an event of an entirely different order from any of those tragical occurrences which take place when troops are brought into collision with the civil population. It is an extraordinary event, a monstrous event, an event which stands in singular and sinister isolation.' For rhetorical effect he played down the recurrent violence of colonial rule, but there was something to his contention that 'our reign in India has never stood on the basis of physical force alone, and it would be fatal to the Empire if we were to try to base ourselves only upon it'.[203]

Indian politicians made vociferous protest at Dyer's excessive violence, and the Government of India could not ignore this criticism if it were to retain any measure of popular support. New instructions ordered civil officers to share in the administration of martial law.[204] The provincial governments were warned against the habit of relying on soldiers for the ordinary maintenance of order. The formation of additional armed police units reduced the need to resort to troops.[205] Constraints were placed upon the manner of military intervention – army officers were to order their men to open fire only with the written request of a civil magistrate, except when their own lives were clearly in danger. These various limits upon the use of force made officers sometimes hesitate when dealing with crowds, because they were unsure whether their actions would receive subsequent support.[206]

The Government of India, however, was anxious to reassure them on this point, and promised 'full support' to soldiers who opened fire 'in the legitimate discharge of their duties'.[207] Violence was too important an instrument of colonial rule to be excessively tamed. The caution which followed the Amritsar massacre turned out to be very short-lived.[208] The army was extensively employed on internal security work during the sometimes bitter civil unrest of the early 1920s. In March 1922, Henry Rawlinson told the Legislative Assembly that troops were 'being called out almost daily to preserve peace and quell disorder'.[209] He spoke no less than the truth. Between February and May of that year, soldiers went to the aid of the civil power 62 times.[210] Nor were the nice distinctions between the duties of the police and those of the army always strictly observed. Police in a tight corner often called for the help of nearby troops before any need for firing had actually arisen. The soldiers would then get mixed up with the police, could not be disengaged, and would become involved in police work without any formal procedures being invoked.[211]

Troops were used so often and so extensively because the colonial order faced a whole variety of threats that could not be contained without military assistance. Food riots and communal violence in the towns, labour unrest in factories and mines or on the railways, disturbances connected with the nationalist movement, acts of terrorism by disaffected members of the elite, and rebellions by the desperate and dispossessed in the countryside – all of these, at one time or another, brought troops to the aid of the government.

Peasant and Tribal Uprisings

One scholar has estimated that there were 77 separate episodes of violent peasant resistance during the colonial period in India.[212] A stark tally such as this, however, disguises the problem of measuring the precise extent of rural unrest, if only because the variety of resistance to lord and state was so very broad – ranging from isolated acts of arson or murder to full-scale rebellion. It is also difficult to draw clear distinctions between resistance and crime, since most forms of crime contained a strong element of social and political protest, and most political activity was labelled criminal by the colonial power.

Dacoity is a case in point.[213] In law, a dacoity was an armed robbery by five or more persons, and as such was clearly a crime. But the British stretched the term to embrace a whole range of activities, including, for example, the guerrilla resistance which followed the annexation of Upper Burma in 1885. As General Sir George White (the OC, Upper Burma Force) acknowledged, 'the dacoit leader was in many cases the chief and defender of the people in his own immediate circle. Socially he was a hero, not an outcast.'[214]

From the point of view of colonial security, however, it was the distinction between individual and collective action that was the crucial one. Individual crime was of minor concern to the colonial state, particularly if its victims were obscure. Almost any collective crime or protest, on the other hand, was seen as a possible threat to the stability of the colonial order.[215]

During the later colonial period, sporadic collective resistance was endemic among certain Indian communities – including landless labourers in Malabar, shifting cultivators hit by forest laws which curbed their traditional rights, some formerly dominant groups shouldered aside by colonialism, and itinerant traders unable to adjust to the new economic patterns created by the railways.[216] There was no insurgency on the scale of 1857, but there were several local uprisings which only the army could suppress.

In 1879 a formidable rebellion broke out in the Gudem and Rampa hill-country of the Godivari Agency.[217] The revolt – which at its greatest extent affected 4000 square miles – was a protest against police exactions, new excise on toddy, and restrictions on shifting cultivation.[218] Further risings on a smaller scale took place in the same area in 1886 and 1922–24.[219] Burma also posed constant security problems to the Raj.[220] Five years of guerrilla resistance followed the annexation of Upper Burma in 1885, and there was a major rising in Lower Burma in 1930.[221] Malabar was another region of chronic rural insecurity, with a dozen outbreaks of violence between 1858 and 1919. The rebellion which took place in 1921–22, however, was on a much larger scale, affecting over 2000 square miles. Poor villagers made up the backbone of the rising, which drew further strength and coherence from its religious idiom, fostered by traditional Islamic intellectuals.[222]

The number of troops engaged in suppressing these rebellions gives some idea of their scale. The fighting in Upper Burma in the later 1880s was by far the most widespread. In 1886, 31 571 British and Indian soldiers served in the province. Of these, more than a thousand died, mainly from disease.[223] The other episodes, however, were far from trivial. Nearly 3000 troops were deployed in the Agency hill-tracts during the revolt of 1879–80.[224] The fighting there lasted well over a year. The normal garrison of Malabar in 1921 was a mere half a company, but by the end of the Mappila rising no less than seven Indian and two British infantry battalions had been engaged, along with detachments of sappers, artillery, cavalry and armoured cars.[225] Martial law was in force in Malabar for six months. Nor were the casualties slight. According to official figures, 2339 Mappila rebels were killed and 1652 wounded during the 1921–22 rising, although unofficial estimates put the losses as high as 10 000.[226]

In most cases, the army was summoned to deal with the insurgents because the police were clearly unable to cope on their own.[227] In 1879, the Government of Madras had hoped to rely on the police in the hill tracts, keeping troops in reserve in the plains. These plans proved inadequate, and the operations against the rebels had to be placed under military control. The army did most of the fighting, as the police were weak in numbers, unhealthy, and reluctant to serve in the hills.[228] During the Mappila rebellion, even the paramilitary Special Police – armed with Lee-Enfields and Lewis guns – could not by themselves guarantee the security of landlords and loyalists.[229] A similar situation obtained during the Rampa rising of 1922–24. The Rajahmundry and Malabar Specials proved no match for the guerrillas, whose resistance crumbled only when detachments of the Assam Rifles arrived on the scene.[230]

Most of these rebellions took place in marginal and difficult areas far from the major Indian cities and the arteries of imperial communication. This was hardly surprising. Open rebellion was more likely in wooded or mountainous regions where the sketchy Imperial administration could not contain a minor outbreak as easily as in the plains. Furthermore, the encroachments of commercial forestry provoked resistance among the shifting cultivators of the hills.[231] A rising also had more chance of success in an area whose geography hampered conventional military operations, which in turn probably encouraged acts of defiance.[232] In Malabar, for example, the closely-cultivated countryside and thick jungle offered excellent cover to the Mappila insurgents, who found it easy to stage ambushes then slip to safety.[233] Broad rivers in full flood were a major obstacle to the Imperial forces. Movement off-road was almost impossible for regular troops in full equipment, and the rebels could block most highways simply by felling trees across them. After heavy losses, the Mappilas soon abandoned open confrontation in favour of more effective guerrilla methods such as cutting telegraphs and destroying bridges.[234] Sweeps by mobile columns could rarely bring the elusive insurgents to battle. The rebels in the Rampa hills employed similar tactics in similar terrain during the disturbances of 1879–80.[235]

The shortcomings of insurgent weaponry made these elusive guerrilla methods doubly prudent, although Indian rebels could sometimes field modern firearms. In 1857, armourers in Delhi and Lucknow were able to produce all kinds of ammunition to feed the rifles, muskets and artillery pieces brought over or captured by the mutinous sepoys. Later on, some Mappilas were able to seize rifles and shotguns from isolated police posts and individual Europeans. But the British policy of disarming the Indian population usually paid off, and most rebels had to face the might of the Indian Army with only the most primitive armaments. The majority of Mappilas had to make do with swords; and the Naga tribals suppressed in 1879–80 normally carried only javelins, cane shields and long knives.[236]

Many rebels hoped, however, that sympathetic spiritual forces could neutralize the fearsome firepower of the Raj. Such beliefs were a recurrent feature of peasant and tribal risings during the colonial period – understandably enough, given the grave imbalance between insurgent and imperial weapons.[237] During a movement in Vizagapatnam Agency in 1900, for instance, the rebel leader Korra Mallaya promised his followers that their bamboos would turn by magic into guns, and that the soldiers' rifles would dissolve into water.[238] There are countless similar examples from India and elsewhere. These appeals to the supernatural were deeply ambiguous. On the one hand, they expressed the hope that the superior sanctity of the rebels could ultimately invert material, as well as social, reality. On the other, they more pessimistically recognized the futility of charging, head down, shoulders hunched, into sleets of Imperial lead.

The firepower of the Indian Army availed little against elusive rebel bands, however, unless the imperial forces had accurate intelligence of their whereabouts. Without this information, apparently impressive 'drives' through rebel territory achieved little, save 'showing the flag' and demonstrating the willpower of the Indian government.[239] Even the most active mobile columns had little chance of bringing insurgents to battle if they did not know where to find them.[240] Furthermore, in areas where Imperial columns had to rely for their transport on local coolies of doubtful enthusiasm, it proved impossible to prevent their movements from being communicated at once to the rebel forces.[241] If the locals were terrified of the guerrillas, then information became especially difficult to prise from them. In Upper Burma, for instance, the villagers were reluctant to reveal the whereabouts of the insurgents because, if they did so, 'their treachery to the older established institutions was promptly punished by death'.[242] In general, the people of a rebel area were willing to trade information in return for security, which was their main concern. Intelligence about rebel movements would be forthcoming only if the Indian Army could guarantee the safety of its informants. But this required a long and costly military presence. All too often it seemed quicker and easier to destroy entire villages from which rebels had been known to operate.

Terrorism

Accurate intelligence was of particular importance in combating individual acts of terrorism. The word 'terrorist' was a derogatory official label, but one that squared with the avowed aims of the violent activists. 'Terrorise the officials, English and Indian, and the collapse of the whole machinery of oppression is not very far', read one India House pamphlet, seized in Bombay in 1910.[243] The objects of the terrorists were to take revenge on the Imperialists, to build self-confidence, and – among educated Bengalis, at least – to lay to rest the slur that they lacked courage and could not make war. The main targets of terrorism were officials of all kinds, post offices, police stations and crown witnesses. Some dacoities were also carried out to raise money.

Terrorism often increased when mass action was checked or ran out of steam. The first phase of individual violence began with the partition of Bengal and intensified after the collapse of the Swadeshi movement.[244] Its high point was the attempt to murder the Viceroy, Lord Harding, during his official entry into New Delhi in 1912.[245] There was a resurgence from the mid-1920s, as disillusionment set in with the established Congress leaders and the apparent failure of their moderate methods.[246] The terrorist climacteric came in 1930–32, but individual violence soon declined in favour of constitutional activity.

Although the terrorists emphasized propaganda by deed, and hoped the masses might draw revolutionary inspiration from their martyrdom, in practice they won little sympathy outside educated circles. The backbone of the movement was the elite *bhadralok* youth of Bengal.[247] Of a 1918 list of 186 killed or convicted revolutionaries, 165 were from the three upper castes of Brahman, Kayastha and Vaidya.[248]

The early pinpricks of terrorism did not pose an immediate threat to the state, so the British response was at first muted and legalistic.[249] An act of 1908 allowed scheduled offences to be tried without juries, whom it was thought terrorists could intimidate. The so-called Rowlatt Acts of 1919 attempted to perpetuate wartime emergency powers, but they were repealed in 1922 after a campaign of civil disobedience. Further and more lasting legislation soon followed.

The terrorist activity of 1930–32 in Bengal, however, was on a much larger scale than that which had gone before.[250] It also coincided with widespread civil unrest, thereby raising the spectre of a full-scale insurrection. Indeed, by 1932 the writ of government had practically ceased to run in half the districts of the province.[251] The British reaction was accordingly heavy-handed. Thousands of troops were brought in to help the hard-pressed police. By November 1932, one British, one Jat, one Garhwali and four Gurkha battalions were deployed in Bengal in support of anti-terrorist operations.[252] They carried out an almost military campaign to restore government authority, including large-scale house-to-house searches, and the imposition of heavy collective fines.

The army, however, was too blunt an instrument to achieve much on its own. In the winter of 1931–32, for example, a drive by 400 armed police and 1000 troops netted only a single absconder. Without an effective intelligence network the army could not defeat terrorism, although it did hold the line while such a network was being set up. Once it had come into existence, it gained results much more quickly than blind force. Terrorist actions declined by 30 per cent in 1932–33 and by 60 per cent in 1933–34. By 1936 the number of incidents had fallen to four.

Labour Unrest

The emergence of proletarian concentrations posed problems of public order very different from those of terrorism, but arguably more dangerous to the Raj. Before the 1860s there were almost no Indian factories, and industrial growth remained slow for decades after that.[253] The long-established British presence in Bengal inhibited the growth of indigenous capitalism in that province, although a jute industry under mainly European ownership began to emerge in Calcutta. From the mid-1870s, Indian-owned textile mills appeared in Bombay and later in Ahmedabad. By 1911 the Indian proletariat numbered about 2.1 million, concentrated mainly in a few large cities, but including 800 000 on the plantations.

Industrial development brought with it industrial trouble.[254] The Factory Acts of 1881 and 1891 were seldom observed, the working day was long and conditions were harsh. There were 25 major strikes in Madras and Bombay between 1882 and 1890. Stoppages on the trams, railways and in the jute mills accompanied the beginnings of labour organization in Bengal after 1905. The first really significant wave of labour unrest took place just after the Great War. In 1921 there were 396 strikes which cost nearly seven million working days. A new upsurge in 1927 saw 20 million days lost, a total which rose to nearly 32 million the following year. After a lull during the first phase of the depression, working-class militancy revived in the mid-1930s.

Although the high points of labour unrest and nationalist upsurge did not exactly coincide, the self-assertion of the proletariat gave the colonial authorities serious pause for thought. Any concentration of lower-class Indians was seen as a potential danger to the colonial order. According to a 1911 General Staff survey, the mill-hands of Cawnpore were 'a troublesome element in its population which might repeat the dreadful deeds of the mutiny if it ever had the chance'.[255] Nevertheless, the police could normally deal unaided with strikes, even major ones such as that involving 200 000 workers in Calcutta in August 1929.[256]

The military authorities were not keen to see the army directly involved in strikebreaking because it was essentially police work, and it might be bad for discipline.[257] But the army was occasionally called upon to overawe dissident workers. Military action might merely take the form of a route march through a restless area, but more heavy-handed methods were sometimes used.[258] When the extremist leader Tilak was given six years' transportation in July 1908, the Bombay workers staged a week-long walk-out which affected 76 out of 85 textile mills. The police and the army repeatedly opened fire, killing 16 and wounding 43 – according to the cautious estimates of official sources.[259] Troops might also be used to keep open vital railway and telegraph lines in the event of a strike. It was thought 'of great political importance that the mail train should continue to run regularly'.[260] Soldiers could protect workers who did not want to strike, and could patrol the track, for which duty armoured trains were invaluable.

Communal Violence

Like labour unrest, communal violence made a relatively late appearance as a problem of public order in colonial India. There was never a 'golden age' of communal harmony, but Hindu–Muslim riots were rare before the 1880s.[261] Even then, they were mainly confined to the Punjab and the United Provinces where the Hindu and Muslim elites were evenly matched in their competition for jobs and favours. The partition of Bengal in 1905 stimulated communal feeling after the British promised that the new province of East Bengal would create more posts for Muslims.[262] There was a spate of riots in 1906–7, and tension mounted as the century wore on. The short-lived Hindu–Muslim unity in the anti-colonial protests of 1919–22 was followed by a series of violent clashes in the mid-1920s. There were 63 separate communal disturbances between January 1926 and September 1927 alone.

Most of these riots were triggered by the ostensibly religious issues of Muslims slaughtering cows or Hindus playing music near mosques. But religious conflict was often the idiom through which other social tensions were voiced.[263] In February 1929, for example, communal violence in Bombay – which left 145 dead and nearly 800 injured – began with clashes between militant Hindu mill-hands and Pathan strikebreakers.[264] Mass action slipped easily between the different but related modes of economic conflict, nationalist upsurge and communal frenzy.[265]

Congress liked to blame Hindu–Muslim violence upon British tactics of *divide et impera*, but in fact British attitudes to communal tension were more complex and ambiguous than this.[266] The colonial authorities had created separate electorates in some Punjabi towns as early as 1886, but this was as much a strategy to reduce conflict as to exploit it. Nevertheless, it may have hardened lines of division by encouraging leaders to appeal exclusively to their own religious following. It is probably fair to say that the British were not averse to a mild undercurrent of communal tension, since they feared Hindu–Muslim unity in anti-colonial action.

The British, however, were not prepared to tolerate communal violence beyond a certain point, because it posed a major problem of public order. The police on their own could not contain all Hindu–Muslim riots, particularly during the heightened tension of the later 1920s. Troops were called out 14 times to deal with communal friction from October to December 1927 alone.[267] Army chiefs were not happy to see military units split into 'penny packets' – against King's Regulations – to guard temples, mosques and shops. Despite this, it was clear that even small bodies of troops patrolling the streets could deter acts of arson and murder. During the Cawnpore riots of May 1931, which left nearly 300 dead, 'whenever and wherever the troops appeared their presence was a signal for peace', according to a joint British and Indian Commission of Enquiry.[268] The military sometimes even earned some thanks. In November 1923, a letter from 'the Hindus of Malabar' offered a silver cup to the Suffolk Regiment in gratitude for their protection during the Mappila revolt; and Muslim rural bards, recalling in their poems the 1926 Calcutta riots, portrayed the Government of India as the impartial guardian of the Muslims.[269]

In general, the provincial authorities preferred to employ British troops to deal with religious or communal disturbances since they were 'by the nature of things impartial as between the disputants'.[270] But Indian troops were often used, as European units were not always to hand.[271] During the February 1929 riots in Bombay, for example, both Hindu and Muslim troops were freely employed to patrol the streets, arrest 'bad characters' and enforce the curfew. They betrayed 'no sign of any sympathy with the rioters', however, 'nor was there any reluctance to carry out their orders'.[272]

Communal tension may normally have been considered a threat to public order, but the General Staff still thought it might prove to be the salvation of the Raj if it ever came to a major rebellion. In their plans for holding India against a rising, the exploitation of communal and ethnic difference occupied a central position, as indeed it had done in practice in 1857. If a rising were to take place in the Punjab, the first objectives would be to hold Delhi, the arsenals at Ambala, Ferozepure and Rawalpindi, and the main junctions. After that, 'if the Muhammadan population only is with us, we should use the Rawalpindi area to crush the Sikhs in the Amritsar, Jullundur, Ludhiana and Ambala districts: while if the Sikhs were with us and the Muhammadans against us we could reverse the process'. Similar strategies could be employed in other regions. In the mainly Hindu areas of Central India and Rajputana, for example, they hoped that 'the jealousies between the Native Chiefs' would prevent their combination in revolt, while further south, the tensions between the Muslims of Hyderabad, the Hindus of Mysore and the Mahrattas of the West could easily be exploited. They summarized their plans thus:

> The maintenance of our supremacy is facilitated by the large number of diverse nationalities and races, those in one area of the country having little if anything in common with those in other areas. Consequently the policy of *divide et impera*, which from the military standpoint it is desirable to follow, should not be very difficult of attainment; especially in the case of the two main religious divisions, Hindus and Muhammadans.[273]

In short, the colonial authorities had no fixed attitude to communal tension – their main concern, as ever, was the security of the colonial order.

Civil Disobedience

Arguably, the Raj was placed in greatest danger by the mass campaigns of civil disobedience carried out under the leadership of M. K. Gandhi – memorably described by Winston Churchill as 'a seditious Middle Temple lawyer, posing as a fakir'.[274] By encouraging civil disobedience, Gandhi hoped to undermine the legitimacy of the Raj, forge a new unity and self-respect among the Indian people, and shatter the psychological basis of British power.[275] He favoured peaceful methods, such as the violation of specific laws (most famously that which prohibited the private manufacture of salt), mass courting of arrest, the boycott of foreign products (especially cloth) and occasional *hartals*, marches, calls for the resignation of Indian officials and refusal to pay taxes.[276] The campaigns drew in the masses, but usually in a controlled and contained way that did not alienate Congress supporters among the better-off peasantry and commercial classes. Indeed, some businessmen gave funds to Congress, partly in the hope that it would draw the sting of those who sought a revolutionary change in the social order.[277]

The Swadeshi movement in Bengal in 1905–8 was in some respects a harbinger of Gandhi's methods, which he termed satyagraha or 'soul force'.[278] The first peasant satyagraha, in Kheda district of Gujerat during the Great War, was patchy and intermittent; but two campaigns of non-cooperation achieved more striking success in 1920–22. The civil disobedience campaign of 1930 was a major challenge to British rule, attracting as it did immense popular support, especially in the Bombay presidency.[279] A shortage of funds and a government crackdown hampered the second civil disobedience campaign of 1932–33, which never won much of a following outside the Hindu urban middle classes.[280]

Despite his support for the Raj during the 1914–18 war, Gandhi was strongly attracted to peaceful methods, believing that religion should permeate all areas of life and that political action should be at one with spiritual vision.[281] His avowed purpose was to search for fundamental religious truth, and he held that it would be sinful to use violence to impose his personal and imperfect understanding upon others.[282] Means could not be separated from ends, and Gandhi believed that only through purifyingly non-violent methods could the Indian people become worthy of *swaraj*. Many of his more pragmatic followers, however, adopted non-violence as a useful tactic rather than as a religious principle.

The British authorities accepted that Gandhi himself abhorred the use of force, but they still saw incipient violence in popular action.[283] Indeed, they never really accepted that non-violent mass protest was possible.[284] The Governor of the Punjab was not alone when he speculated in 1931 that Gandhi might 'find himself to be the

Kerensky of a movement which really wants something more drastic and dreadful'.[285] Most Congress workers were reluctant to
denounce terrorism, and paramilitary units of Congress volunteers
were prominent during the disturbances of the 1920s and 1930s.[286]
Satyagraha encouraged a climate of disrespect for the law in which
violence could erupt.[287] During the winter of 1921–22, popular protest began to go further than the Congress elite would have
wished.[288] 'The movement had got beyond the control of the leaders', noted an official report. 'The spirit of violence and contempt of
all authority, which now began to show its head, was not of the
leaders, but of the masses.'[289] In February 1922 there was a serious
disturbance at Chauri Chaura near Gorakhpur in the United Provinces. To Gandhi's great dismay, a crowd of 2000 attacked a police
station, killing all 22 of the garrison.[290] Similar outbreaks occurred
on a smaller scale during the campaign of 1930.

The Government of India grew nervous at the appearance of a
peaceful mass movement with an underlying potential for violence.
They had good reason, for Gandhi's methods seemed to have
solved many of the dilemmas involved in confronting the Raj.[291]
Satyagraha was an effective mode of direct action, but one which
avoided the pitfalls of an overt call to arms. Deliberate violence
would have been difficult to organize effectively and would have
alienated much influential Indian and foreign support. Besides, the
British could always meet force with more force – provided the
Indian Army remained reliable. 'Little further can be done in the
attainment of independence by violent means so long as the authority of Government is supported by its armed forces', noted the Chief
of Staff in 1930.[292] The Indian Army would soon have smashed such
armed resistance as Congress could muster.

Gandhi acknowledged this, and adopted a strategy that enfeebled
British firepower, while at the same time undermining the Raj and
winning some public support in Britain itself.[293] He tried to attack
the British where they were weak, not where they were strong.
Satyagraha threatened the administration in a few distinct areas and
embarrassed the Government of India, who were reluctant to court
general odium by smashing a mainly non-violent movement. Any
resort to force against a peaceful crowd made the British look brutal,
a fact which Congress propagandists were quick to exploit.[294] Henry
Rawlinson (the Commander-in-Chief) neatly summed up this growing sense of armed impotence in the face of Gandhi's call for non-
cooperation. 'If he carries this through over wide areas he may

make government impossible. If large sections of the population refuse to pay taxes and adopt passive resistance I don't see how we are going to carry on. You cannot collect taxes everywhere at the point of the bayonet.'[295]

Popular rumours about Gandhi also suggest that he was widely seen as having disarmed the Raj. It was often reported that he had been shot by the British but had later reappeared alive and well. A Calcutta Hindi newspaper cited a rumour according to which sepoys had fired a volley at Gandhi 'but the bullets, instead of piercing his body, deflected from it'. A similar story circulated among Calcutta mill-hands. According to them, British soldiers threw a bomb at Gandhi but 'it melted like snow as soon as it touched his person'.[296]

During the early 1930s the Government of India became convinced of the need for firmer measures. While they tried to conciliate those who could be won over, they also sought to make it clear that they intended to enforce the law and uphold their authority as far as possible.[297] By the end of 1931, the government was under increasing pressure to strike hard. 'We cannot possibly embark on another campaign of this kind of warfare', wrote the Bombay Police Commissioner after the first civil disobedience movement. 'Instead of fear, which is the root of all decent government, it begets contempt.'[298] Partial repression in 1930 had not been very successful and the authorities were determined not to limit their actions in future.[299] But, although more and more troops were drawn into internal security work, the civil unrest of 1930–33 was contained largely by conventional police action alone.[300]

The government blow fell in January 1932 during the second civil disobedience movement.[301] Extensive bans were placed on Congress bodies, their funds and premises were seized, and leading Congressmen were swiftly arrested. The mass arrest of the leadership deterred all but a committed minority, but did not provoke violent clashes with the population. Seeing that repression had made mass civil disobedience impossible, Gandhi responded in the summer of 1933 by urging individuals to try and infect the nation with a spirit that repression could not crush. The formula was unconvincing, and did little to halt the temporary disintegration of the movement.

Conclusion: The Sepoy and the Raj

'The Indian Empire is a despotism, and the real backbone of the despotism is the Army', remarked George Orwell, reflecting upon the nature of imperial power in the early 1930s. 'Given the Army, the officials and the business men can rub along safely enough even if they are fools. And most of them are fools. A dull, decent people, cherishing and fortifying their dullness behind a quarter of a million bayonets.'[1]

Orwell, a disenchanted former colonial policeman, was an outspoken critic of empire, and his remarks should be seen in that light. But his observations curiously echoed the views of many imperialists. 'The maintenance of tranquillity, and the safety of the British Government in India, depend ultimately on the existence of a military force', noted the Eden Commission in 1879.[2] Viceroys, generals and secretaries of state – all saw the army as the final argument of the Raj, and were inclined to believe that force was the best way of dealing with troublesome colonial subjects. In the words of Harcourt Butler, 'any demonstration of strength cows the Oriental'.[3] When faced with dissent, the rulers of British India usually favoured an early display of military might to 'nip trouble in the bud'. Clemency, they thought, would be taken as a sign of weakness. As Lord Roberts once remarked, 'Eastern natives do not understand a temporizing policy.'[4]

This study of the colonial military apparatus in India has shown that Orwell's comment was not wildly off the mark. Throughout its history, the British Raj possessed prodigious coercive power. Colonial India can be fairly described as a garrison state, with security as its main concern. The finances of empire seem to bear this out. Patterns of government spending reveal much about colonial priorities and objectives; even in peacetime the army in India absorbed 40 (sometimes, even 50) per cent of central government revenue.

This substantial military force was never intended just to protect Indian frontiers. Before the Russian war-scare of 1885, the main purpose of the army, as its deployment revealed, was to defend the internal security of the colonial order. Until the Kitchener reforms at the turn of the century, most army units were scattered across India in 'obligatory garrisons' to overawe the civil population. In the 1920s and 1930s the colonial authorities saw the most likely threats to their power within India rather than without. Normally, about a quarter or a third of the troops (rarely less than 50 000 men) were directly assigned to internal security work, and others were drawn in as required. Although these forces were tiny in relation to the size of the subcontinent and to the number of its people, they deployed overwhelming firepower compared with the civil population (which had been mostly disarmed as a matter of policy).

The formation of the Indian police in the mid-nineteenth century did not much lessen the ultimate dependence of the Raj upon military power. The police were cheaper and more numerous than the army, and remained the first line of defence for the colonial order. Army chiefs were reluctant to see military units broken up into 'penny packets' for ordinary policing duties, and preferred to hold their troops in reserve in case of a major rebellion. The police also seemed a more effective means of combating the mainly non-violent campaigns of civil disobedience.

But the poorly-armed and corrupt Indian police were always an imperfect instrument of imperial authority. They lived and worked in daily contact with the local population, which exposed them and their families to social pressure and intimidation. The police were often unreliable, and a police mutiny was a constant colonial fear. During the final years of the Raj, some forces came under the control of provincial Congress ministries and were hence less than fully at the disposal of the colonial state. In the last resort – and often in the first – the British Raj relied upon its army.

Military force had to be seen to be effective. Every sizeable Indian town therefore had its nearby cantonment as visible evidence of colonial power. For the same reason, troops were periodically marched through remote rural areas. But the army was not intended just for intimidating display – it was there to be used. The Indian Army did not stand quietly on the sidelines during periods of domestic disturbance. Summoning the army to 'aid the civil power' was a frequent recourse of the Raj, becoming an almost daily one during the political crises of the twentieth century when the legitimacy of colonial rule was under growing threat. The Amritsar massacre of 1919 – when nearly 400 peaceful demonstrators were shot dead by Gurkha and Baluchi troops – was by far the most dramatic and best-known instance of this; but there were many other, less spectacular examples. Soldiers were used to quell communal riots, to control clashes between strikers and blackleg labour, to maintain communications during periods of industrial unrest, to crush peasant and tribal rebellions, to suppress terrorism, and to help contain the civil disobedience movement.

The army on the Frontier was also a form of indirect insurance against popular rebellion. After the Kitchener reforms, a large force was concentrated in the north-west, ready to take the field against any Russian attempt to absorb Afghanistan. But colonial planners did not principally fear an unstoppable Russian invasion of Afghanistan or India – logistics alone made this most unlikely. They were more concerned that the appearance of hostile forces on the Frontier would trigger an internal rebellion on the scale of 1857. Russian strategic thinking apparently moved along the same lines. After 1917, the Soviet Union posed a smaller military threat than Tsarist Russia had done, but the Soviets were thought to be more able and willing to promote internal unrest.

Applied military violence was only part of the picture, however. The British empire also depended upon its indigenous collaborators, this being no less true in the military sphere than in other areas of colonial endeavour. Throughout the colonial period, the Raj relied more upon Indian than upon British troops. Since an all-British garrison would have been too costly, the Indian empire had to co-opt local allies to carry out its essential military tasks. Even during peacetime, the Raj had to induce around 20 000 Indians to enlist in its armed forces every year. To do this, the British had to strike political bargains with the indigenous communities who provided the recruits. The troops, however, were not drawn primarily from local collaborating elites, but from the 'subaltern' classes of Indian society – above all, from the middle peasantry of the Punjab, who provided the bulk of Indian Army sepoys from the 1880s.

The British carefully fostered the structures of military collaboration on which their power depended. Every effort was made to bind the peasant-soldier communities to the Raj by the strong ties of self-interest. Some Indian groups, such as Sikhs and Rajputs, had a strongly martial self-image, and were attracted to military service. But there were also plenty of material incentives to enlist. The army drew most of its recruits from hard-pressed cultivating communities who found it difficult to survive on agriculture alone. For the enlisted classes, military service was a useful way of supplementing their income from the soil – to save in case of dearth, to buy luxuries, or to acquire more land. Soldiers were paid well (at least from the later nineteenth century) and they had no reason to doubt the honesty of the Sirkar. The main aim of much government policy was to secure the well-being and support of the peasant communities on which colonial military power depended. British officers toured the recruiting grounds to confirm the links with the military communities, and to hear their grievances. Civil suits from soldiers were granted precedence over those from civilians. Irrigated plots in the canal colonies were set aside for former soldiers and their families, which helped satisfy a deep yearning for land among the middle peasantry of the Punjab. In short, loyalty was made lucrative.

In this sense, the Indian Army was a 'mercenary' force – as nationalists often disparagingly remarked. The Indian army relied mainly on volunteers, and the decision to enlist can be seen as a self-interested choice made by a recruit after weighing up the benefits and the drawbacks of this course of action. The relationship between the sepoy and the Raj was one of active choice on both sides. On its own, British policy can explain the exclusion of a community from the ranks, but it cannot explain its inclusion. Not only did the British choose their recruits – the recruits chose the British. In this respect, sepoys were analagous to other labour migrants, like mill-hands and miners, who also made the most of the economic opportunities created by the colonial encounter.

But military collaboration was not simply a question of weighing up material self-interest. The bonds between the sepoy and the Raj were more complex and deeper than this. Had they not been so, Indian soldiers would hardly have risked their lives to fight the wars of empire. The analogy between soldiers and other labour migrants begins to break down as soon as an army goes into action. The experience of battle tests the prime military virtues of courage and loyalty, which cannot easily be bought and sold.

The British liked to believe that it was their own charisma that held the Indian Army together. Most imperial observers saw the secret of military success in the devotion which British officers inspired. There is, however, precious little evidence to support this view – although the belief may have helped to fortify colonial self-esteem. Judging from their letters, the sepoys risked death in battle above all for *izzat* – for the honour and standing of themselves, their family, their caste and their regiment. The British were conscious of the importance of honour, and tried to take advantage of it. Honourable behaviour was well rewarded, provided it supported imperial agendas. The military authorities structured the regiments of the Indian Army to exploit, and to reinforce, a soldier's most deeply-rooted values and his sense of self. Most of the tactical units of the Indian Army were recruited from a single, highly-localized community whose honour, social status and esteem depended upon its military performance. Regimental titles, customs and details of uniform encouraged the fusion of military with other identities.

Although these strategies may appear patronizing and manipulative, they did create a remarkably effective and well-disciplined military force. They also inspired loyalty of a kind. The testimony of the ranks reveals that they were intensely devoted to the King-Emperor, who was closely associated with regimental titles and army ritual.

It is therefore unwise to posit too stark a contrast between strategies of co-option and coercion. The indigenous military forces were one of the main examples of collaboration, while the coercive apparatus was the most prominent colonial exercise in winning hearts and minds. The Raj could only coerce one section of the Indian population because it had won the active support of another. British rule depended upon a subtle and pragmatic mixture of threat and promise.

The apparent strengths of the colonial military machine, however, disguised its potential fragility. Indian soldiers were not simply the passive victims of colonial manipulation. The sepoys had their own objectives, pursued their own strategies and made their own choices. Like any collaborative structure, the relationship between the sepoy and the Raj could have broken down if either party had grown disenchanted. But a collapse of military collaboration would have been disastrous for the Raj. If the military communities had ceased to furnish recruits, then British India would have been left defenceless against its enemies without and within. As Lord Roberts privately remarked in 1884:

> Let us suppose that a native army could not any longer be levied. In a moment the impossibility of holding India would become apparent to us. There is only one body of persons of which we can positively affirm that without its support the Government could not stand; this is the army.[5]

Worse still, the soldiers could have mutinied and turned their weapons against the British. The main bulwark of the Raj was also a major potential threat to colonial rule. The events of 1857 made this quite clear, and the rulers of British India never forgot the lesson. In the third quarter of the nineteenth century, before the rise of the Russian threat, an army mutiny was the most vivid and recurrent colonial nightmare.

Recruiting strategy after the Mutiny reflected this fear. The British were reluctant to depend upon a single military community, because to do so would leave them vulnerable to local disaffection. The reconstruction of the Indian Army after 1857 was largely pragmatic and reactive – the British enlisted those who would fight for them, and excluded those who had recently rebelled. But the results were still consistent with a policy of divide and rule, and were later justified on these grounds. The Indian Army of the 1860s and 1870s had four separate regional components – the Punjab Frontier Force and the Armies of Bombay, Madras and Bengal. As in 1857, a mutiny in one part of the army could be crushed by troops from the others. Only from the 1880s did this cautious policy of balance give way to the search for the 'martial races', when the British tried to enlist the reputedly most warlike people of India so that the army could better withstand a possible Russian invasion.

After 1857, the sepoys remained the central pillar of the Raj, but the British never fully trusted them again. The presence of a sizeable British garrison in India was one measure of this mistrust. The duties of the Indian Army included supporting the police, but also containing them in case they showed signs of dissent. After 1858, British troops performed a similar function in relation to the sepoys. Before the mutiny, the Indian troops in the garrison had outnumbered the British by five or six to one. After 1857, it became official policy to have one British soldier to every two or three sepoys. This prescribed ratio, abandoned in theory in the 1920s, was maintained in practice until the end of the colonial period.

As it turned out, these precautions were hardly needed. After 1858, there was no major mutiny in the Indian Army. This imperial success partly reflected the efforts of the government to secure the loyalty of its military allies. The Government of India always pursued a generous policy towards the communities that provided the recruits, making some major concessions rather than risking dissent in the recruiting grounds. Army chiefs always paid careful attention to the grievances of the ranks and treated their religious feelings with scrupulous – and fearful – respect.

Nevertheless, the sepoys sometimes threatened to flex their muscles. There were 14 minor mutinies in the Indian Army between 1886 and 1930, none of them involving more than one battalion. Few of these outbreaks resembled, even in miniature, the events of 1857. Instead, they were usually trade disputes more akin to the strikes of other migrant labourers. Soldiers mutinied mainly over their terms and conditions of service – for more generous pay and allowances, or in protest against brutal or partial officers. The sepoys normally conducted their protest in an orderly fashion, and often appealed to colonial authority rather than rejecting it. Above all, mutinies were rarely violent. The British therefore reacted moderately to most military indiscipline, and tried to play down its significance. The authorities avoided collective reprisals, preferring instead to make an example of a few non-commissioned ringleaders while treating the majority of the rank-and-file to a warning.

Military dissent assumed a rather different and sometimes more threatening character during the Great War. Four divisions of Indian troops were sent to France to help stem the German invasion in 1914. After a few months of hard fighting and heavy losses, most of these men succumbed to intense depression. The rate of malingering and the number of self-inflicted wounds reached alarming proportions. The Indian infantry had to be moved to Mesopotamia at the end of 1915, where the fighting was less fierce and the conditions of service perhaps less arduous. By 1917, however, the soldiers who remained in France seemed less war-weary than they had done two years before. The troops apparently grew accustomed to the fact of battle on the Western Front, and accepted their lot with increasing resignation.

The entry of Turkey into the war led to some indiscipline among Muslim troops, particularly Pathans. The British eventually had to abandon their efforts to induce Pathans to fight the Turks in Mesopotamia. There were numerous desertions, and three Muslim regiments mutinied (one of them violently) rather than march against their co-religionists near the Holy Places of Islam. There were also some protests in the recruiting grounds. The demand for men went far beyond anything that had been seen before, and the traditional sources of recruits began to run dry. In the Punjab, more and more pressure was brought to bear to induce men to enlist, sometimes with explosive results. But these instances of military and war-related protest were scattered and isolated. In the end, the Indian Army came through the Great War rather more robustly than many European forces.

During and after the war, Indian nationalists made some half-hearted attempts to subvert the army, without much success. Even in the 1930s, the sepoys remained fairly well-insulated from the main currents of Indian elite political life. The troops lived in clearly-defined military spaces or cantonments, quite separate from the civilian areas of a town. As far as possible, all subversive influences were banished from the sepoy lines. Soldiers still went home on leave, but leave was not normally granted to an area currently troubled by civil unrest. Anyway, nationalism was unlikely to appeal to troops who were selected from isolated rural communities untouched by Western education and political ideas. Nationalism had no detectable influence on the ranks before the outbreak of the Second World War.

Unable to subvert the army, the nationalists confined themselves to criticizing many of the fundamentals of the colonial military structure. In particular they objected to the divisive 'martial races' policy, according to which most Indians – especially the educated classes of the east and south – were deemed effete and unwarlike. Particular hostility was reserved for the Nepalese Gurkhas, who were castigated as the foreign mercenaries of an unpopular colonial autocracy. These sentiments were also tinged with the contempt felt by the urban elite for a poorly-educated hill-people. (The repulsion was mutual, of course, which was one reason why Gurkhas were enlisted in the first place.) Indian politicians like Gokhale wanted the Indian Army to become a short-service conscript force that was much more national in character. Gokhale drew confidence from the Japanese victory over Imperial Russia in 1904–5, which seemed to prove that Asian conscripts could fight with ferocity and success.

The nationalist critique changed its emphasis after the Great War. The reforms of 1919 set up the system of 'dyarchy' which gave indigenous politicians a scent of real power. The Legislative Assembly allowed Indian moderates the chance to air their views, and to influence military policy. The nationalists continued to denounce the swollen military budget, and demanded that more money be spent on socially useful projects. They resented the costly and demeaning presence of large numbers of British troops. Nationalists still objected to the 'mercenary' character and colonial structure of the Indian Army. But, by the 1920s they had become more concerned to gain control of the army than to change its nature. Nationalists demanded, above all, that the officer corps of the army be opened to Indians – especially those, like themselves, with a Western education. In seeking this, they sought control over the army, and ultimately over the political destinies of India itself.

The demand for Indianization challenged many of the cherished legitimizing myths of the colonial enterprise; and British reactions exposed many of their assumptions about the nature of colonial power and about the people that they governed. It was an axiom of British military policy that educated nationalists – especially from Bengal – were inherently unwarlike. Many of the British elite found it almost unthinkable that educated Indians could make good officers. To accept this would have been to accept their own super-fluity and the imminent end of the Raj. The British also argued that Indian officers could not settle communal or caste disputes among the ranks with a convincing appearance of impartial aloofness. These stereotypes do much to explain the extreme fear and hostility with which Indianization was received in some imperial circles. The British liked to believe that the martial races shared their views, although the evidence is inconclusive. The British respect and admiration for their favourite martial races, however, often thinly disguised an element of contempt for their poor education and apparent backwardness. Within colonial military doctrine, the 'martial races' were seen as able to fight but unable to lead. Only the British – according to themselves – possessed the right combination of courage and intelligence that was needed to win the respect of the martial races and to lead them to victory.

British concessions to the nationalists over Indianization were very grudging. The British elite were aware that the army was one of the main levers of colonial power, and were therefore most unwilling to relinquish their grip upon it. Military policy was an area of administration reserved to the Government of India, and excluded from the direct interference of elected assemblies. It was therefore constitutionally possible to resist the most vociferous nationalist military demands. Over Indianization, the British tried to give just enough to 'rally the moderates' to an apparently reform-ing Raj, without surrendering real power. Eight units of the Indian Army were opened to Indian officers in 1923, and a further four in 1931. Although an Indian Sandhurst was set up in 1932 to train Indian youths for a military career, progress was very slow. By the outbreak of war, only a few hundred Indians had received commis-sions. Despite major concessions in the political sphere, the military structures of colonial power remained very much intact until the Second World War.

The resilience and reliability of the colonial military apparatus did much to shape the nature of the Congress challenge to the Raj. The chilling example of peasant and tribal insurgencies – which were always crushed by overwhelming force – showed that effective armed revolt was out of the question. Indian nationalists could not have directly confronted the military power of the Raj with any hope of success. Gandhi's tactic of satyagraha avoided a head-on collision with the military, and struck instead at the legitimacy of British rule. This policy may have accorded with his peaceful temperament, but the firm discipline of the Indian Army ensured that he could not have struck effectively at anything else, even had he tried. Civil disobedience had some success – as the British soon realized, they could not collect taxes everywhere at the point of the bayonet. But civil disobedience did not fundamentally threaten the essential structures of the Raj, even if it did weaken them. It was too difficult to prevent a mass movement from becoming violent, and thereby forfeiting its claim to superior legitimacy. And when the security forces did strike back in earnest, they were able to contain Congress – even during the widespread disturbances associated with the Quit India movement of 1942.

Why then did this finely-balanced and effective structure of co-option and coercion fail to prevent the disintegration of the Raj? Arguably, the extensive use of force was becoming politically impossible in the Indian conditions of 1946–47 – precisely when the erosion of Imperial legitimacy and the rise of popular anti-colonial unrest was making the Raj all the more dependent upon its coercive apparatus. In 1942, a heavyhanded response to the Quit India movement had been possible – it was wartime, the Indian Army had been vastly expanded, and India was clearly under threat from the Japanese. By 1946, however, a military solution to the political problems of the Raj was neither possible nor desirable. The Labour government assumed office in 1945 determined to honour the promise, made during the Cripps mission of 1942, that India would get some form of self-government after the war. This alone made military repression a very unattractive option. Furthermore, it was one that the British people would have been most reluctant to tolerate. As Clement Attlee remarked, early in 1947, 'if you proposed to govern by main force, you would be driven into shootings and the like for which you would find very little support in this country'.[6] British public opinion was also less than willing to accept loss of life to white conscripts in apparently pointless colonial wars, as the

Zionist insurgency in Palestine was making clear. UN and American anti-colonial opinion was a further constraint upon British policy-makers, who were reluctant to court the international condemnation that repression would certainly have invited.

Moreover, there were also fears that the discipline of the Indian Army itself might be affected in any attempt to prop up the Raj by force. There was increasing evidence that the Indian Army would no longer serve as a pliant instrument of colonial authority. The fall of the Far Eastern empire to the Japanese in 1941–42 had damaged British prestige in Asia beyond repair, and the previous isolation of the army from nationalist sentiment had begun to break down. One-third of all Indian Army prisoners had joined the Japanese-sponsored Indian National Army, and there had also been more than 360 000 wartime desertions from ranks.[7] All regiments of the Indian Army had been opened to Indian officers from 1940, as a result of pressing military need. Many of the 15 000 Indians who had obtained commissions during the war had become sympathetic to the cause of independence. As Sir Claude Auchinleck, the Commander-in-Chief, remarked in February 1946, 'every Indian officer worth his salt is today a nationalist'.[8]

More paralyzing still was the fear that the army might fall prey to the growing communal conflict. As late as 1946, military discipline seemed to be holding firm, despite mounting Hindu–Muslim strife, but there was no willingness to put it to the test. British rule could not survive a collapse in military discipline, and any involvement of the army in communal riots would have visibly ruined the image of a peaceful and orderly transfer of power which the British were so anxious to cultivate. For many decades, as a matter of policy, the British had fostered the various communal identities of the troops as a means of promoting *esprit de corps* and discouraging mutinous combinations. By 1946, there was a grave danger that this strategy might backfire, particularly as most of the troops came from the Punjab, where communal tensions were running especially high. By then, moreover, the nationalists had lost interest in subverting the colonial army they were about to inherit – professional ethos, 'martial races', Gurkhas and all. As Sardar Patel remarked – shortly after the Feburary 1946 mutinies in the Royal Indian Navy had shown that the armed forces might not always remain aloof from popular protest – 'discipline in the Army cannot be tampered with... we will want the Army even in free India'.[9]

Biographical Notes

Ambedkar, Bhimrao Ramji (1893–1956). Born Mhow, of Mahar Untouchable military family; awarded scholarship by Gaekwar of Baroda; educated at universities in United States, Britain and Germany; contested Gandhi's claim to speak for Untouchables; founded several journals on their behalf; Law Minister, India, 1947–51; took leading part in framing Indian constitution, which outlawed discrimination against Untouchables; converted to Buddhism, with 200 000 fellow Untouchables, in mass ceremony at Nagpur, 1956.

Auchinleck, Field Marshal Sir Claude John Eyre 'The Auk' (1884–1981). Educated Wellington; Egypt, 1914–15; Mesopotamia, 1916–19; IDC, 1927; Instructor, Staff College, Quetta, 1930–33; OC Peshawar Brigade, 1933–36; DCGS India, 1936–38; C-in-C India, 1941 and 1943–47; C-in-C Middle East, 1941–42; Supreme Commander in India and Pakistan, 1947.

Balfour, Arthur James (1848–1930). Educated Eton and Cambridge; Unionist Prime Minister, 1902–5; First Lord of the Admiralty, 1915–16; Foreign Secretary, 1916–19; Lord President of the Council, 1919–22 and 1925–29.

Birdwood, William Riddell (first Baron Birdwood) (1865–1951). Born in India; educated Clifton; commissioned Royal Scots Fusiliers, 1883; served in India, 1885–99; served in South Africa, 1899–1902; military secretary to Lord Kitchener, 1905–9; OC Kohat Independent Brigade, 1909–12; Secretary to Army Department, 1912–14; C-in-C ANZAC, 1914–17; C-in-C Fifth Army, 1918; OC Northern Army, India, 1920–24; C-in-C India, 1925–30; Master of Peterhouse, Cambridge, 1930–38.

Birkenhead, Earl (Smith, Frederick Edwin) (1872–1930). Educated Wadham College, Oxford; President of the Union, 1893; called to the Bar, 1899; Conservative MP, 1906–18; Lord Chancellor, 1919–22; Secretary of State for India, 1924–28.

Butler, Sir (Spencer) Harcourt (1869–1938). Educated Harrow and Balliol College, Oxford; ICS; Deputy Commissioner, Lucknow District, 1906–8; Secretary, Foreign Department, GI, 1907–10; Lt-Governor of Burma, 1915–18; Lt-Governor, UP, 1918–21; Governor, 1921–23; Governor of Burma, 1923–27; Chairman, Indian States Committee, 1927–29; Chairman of the Governors, School of Oriental and African Studies, University of London, 1931.

Chatfield, Admiral of the Fleet Alfred Ernle Montacute (1873–1967). Entered Royal Navy, 1886; Flag Captain to Beatty, 1914–18; DCNS, 1920–22; Third Sea Lord, 1925–28; C-in-C Atlantic Fleet, 1929–30; C-in-C Mediterranean, 1930–32; First Sea Lord and CNS, 1933–38; Minister for the Coordination of Defence, 1939–49.

Chelmsford, first Viscount (Thesiger, Frederic John Napier) (1868–1933). Educated Winchester and Magdalen College, Oxford; first-class honours; called to the Bar, 1893; Governor of Queensland, 1905–9; Governor of New South Wales, 1909–13; Viceroy of India, 1916–21; helped draft *Report on Indian Constitutional Reforms*, 1918; First Lord of the Admiralty, 1924; Warden of All Souls, Oxford, 1932–33.

Chetwode, Philip Walhouse (1869–1950). Educated Eton; Burma, 1892–93; South Africa; OC 5 Cavalry Brigade, 1914–15; 2 Cavalry Division, 1915–16; Desert Corps, Egypt, 1916–17; OC XX Corps, Palestine and Syria, 1917–18; Military Secretary, WO, 1919–20; DCIGS, 1920–22; AG, 1922-23; C-in-C Aldershot, 1923–27; CGSI, 1928–30; C-in-C India, 1930–35.

Churchill, Sir Winston Spencer (1874–1965). Educated Harrow and Sandhurst; First Lord of the Admiralty, 1911–15 and 1939–40; Chancellor of the Duchy of Lancaster, 1915; commanded a battalion in France, 1915–16; Minister of Munitions, 1917–19; Secretary of State for War and Air, 1919–21; Colonial Secretary, 1921–22; Conservative MP, 1924–64; Chancellor of the Exchequer, 1924–29; Prime Minister, 1940–45 and 1951–55.

Clerk, Sir George (1800–89). Educated Haileybury; Political Agent, Ambala, 1831; British Envoy at Lahore; Governor of Bombay, 1846–48 and 1860–62; Permanent Under-Secretary to India board, 1856; Secretary, 1857; Permanent Under-Secretary of State for India, 1858; Member of Indian Council, 1863.

Creagh, Sir Garrett O'Moore (1843–1923). Joined army, 1886; awarded VC during Afghan War, 1879–80; Political Resident, Aden; GOC BEF, China, 1901; C-in-C India, 1909–14.

Cromer, first Earl of (Evelyn Baring) (1841–1917). Educated Woolich; commissioned, 1858; Private Secretary to Lord Northbrook, Viceroy of India, 1872; Financial Member of Viceroy's Council, 1880–83; British Agent and Consul-General, Egypt, 1883–1907; President of the Dardanelles Commission, 1916.

Curzon, George Nathanial (Marquess Curzon of Kedleston) (1859–1925). Educated Eton and Balliol College, Oxford; President of the Union; MP, 1886–92; Parliamentary Under-Secretary for Foreign Affairs, 1895–98; Viceroy of India, 1899–1905; Chancellor of Oxford University, 1907; Lord Privy Seal, 1915–16; President of Air Board, 1916; Foreign Secretary, 1919–24; Lord President, 1924–25.

Deverell, Field-Marshal Sir Cyril John 'Butcher' (1874–1947). Educated Bedford School; commissioned West Yorkshire Regiment, 1895; OC 20 Brigade, 1915–16; OC 3 Division, 1916–19; OC UP, 1921–25; QMG India, 1927–30; CGSI, 1930–31; GOC-in-C Western Command, 1931–33; GOC-in-C Eastern Command, 1933–36; CIGS, 1936–37.

Dyer, Reginald Edward Harry (1864–1927). Born in India; educated Sandhurst; commissioned Queen's Royal Regiment, 1885; transferred to Indian Army; on active service, 1886–1908; commanded operations, SE Persia, 1916; commanded training brigade, Jullundur, India, 1916; commanded troops at Amritsar, 1919; responsible for the Jallianwala Bagh massacre; resignation demanded by C-in-C India, 1920.

Elphinstone, John (thirteenth Baron Elphinstone) (1807–1860). Commissioned in Royal Horse Guards, 1826; Lord in Waiting to William IV, 1835–7; Governor of Madras, 1837–42; Lord in Waiting to the Queen, 1847–53; Governor of Bombay, 1853–59.

Gandhi, Mohandas Karamchand 'Mahatma' (1869–1948). Leader of Indian nationalist movement against British rule and devoted believer in non-violent means of political action. Began law studies in England, 1888; campaigned against racial discrimination in South Africa, 1893–1914; imprisoned; entered Indian politics, 1919; led salt satyagraha, 1930; imprisoned during much of the Second World War; negotiated with British for independent India, 1946–47; assassinated by Hindu fanatic.

Gokhale, Gopal Krishna (1866–1915). Social reformer and moderate Indian nationalist. Born Ratnagiri District; resigned as professor of history and political economy at Fergusson College, Poona, 1902; entered politics; became an influential Congress moderate; social concerns led him to found Servants of India Society, 1905; took vows of service to the underprivileged; opposed ill-treatment of Untouchables.

Haines, Sir Frederick (1819–1909). Educated Brussels and Dresden; commissioned 4th (King's Own) Regiment, 1839; served in India; dangerously wounded, First Sikh War; Military Secretary to Lord Gough, 1846–49; fought in the Crimea; Assistant ADC, Aldershot, 1855–56; Military Secretary to the C-in-C Madras, 1856–60; OC Mysore Division, 1865–70; C-in-C Madras, 1871–75; C-in-C India, 1876–81; dissented from findings of Eden Commission, 1879.

Jacob, Field-Marshal Sir Claud William (1863–1948). Born in Bombay; educated Sherbourne and Sandhurst; commissioned Worcester Regiment, 1882; transferred to Indian Army, 1884; served on North West Frontier, 1890–1911; OC 106 Hazara Pioneers, 1904–11; GSO1 Meerut Division, 1912; OC Dehra Dun Brigade, France, 1915; wounded, 1916; OC II Corps, 1916–19; CGSI, 1920–24; C-in-C Northern Command, 1924–25; temporary C-in-C India, 1925; Secretary, Military Department, India Office, 1926–30.

Jinnah, Mohammed Ali, 'Qaid-e-Azam' (1876–1948). Muslim political leader and founder of Pakistan. Born in Karachi; educated Sind Madrassah High School, Mission High School; called to the Bar, 1895; married daughter of a Parsi millionaire; Member of Legislative Council, 1910; joined Muslim League, 1913; left the League and Congress, 1920; delegate at Round Table Conferences, London, 1930–32; remained in London, 1930–35; demanded Muslim state in Lahore Declaration, 1940; Governor-General of Pakistan, 1947–48.

Kitchener, Horatio Herbert (first Earl Kitchener of Khartoum and Broome) (1850–1916). Born in Ireland; educated France and Woolich; served in Army of the Loire, 1870; commissioned RE, 1871; attached Palestine Exploration Fund, 1874; surveyed Cyprus, 1878–82; served Egypt, 1882; delimited territory of Sultan of Zanzibar, 1885–86; Governor-General, Eastern Sudan, 1886–88; appointed *sirdar* of Egyptian Army, 1892; conquered the Sudan, 1896–98; victorious at Omdurman, 1898; Baron, Governor-General of the

Sudan, 1899; Chief of Staff to Lord Roberts, South Africa, 1899–1902; C-in-C India, 1902–9; reformed Indian Army; British Agent and Consul-General, Egypt, 1911–14; Secretary of State for War, 1914–16.

Lawrence, Sir Henry Montgomery (1806–57). Born Matura, Ceylon; educated Addiscombe; commissioned Bengal Artillery, 1822; Assistant Revenue Surveyor, North Western Provinces, 1933–35; Surveyor, 1835; served Kabul expedition, 1842; Resident, Nepal, 1843–46; Resident, Lahore, 1846; President, Board of Administration, Punjab Affairs, 1849–53; Agent to Governor-General in Rajputana, 1853; Chief Commissioner, Oudh, 1856; OC troops in Oudh, 1857; killed at Lucknow.

Lawrence, Sir John Laird Mair (first Baron Lawrence) (1811–72). Educated Haileybury; Assistant Magistrate and Collector at Delhi, 1830–34; Administrator, Jullundur Doab, 1846–48; member of Board of Administration, Punjab, 1848–52; Chief Commissioner, Punjab, 1853–57; captured Delhi, 1857; India Office, 1859–62; Viceroy of India, 1863–69.

Lloyd George, David (1863–1945). Liberal MP, 1890–1945; Chancellor of the Exchequer, 1908–15; Minister of Munitions, 1915–16; Secretary for War, 1916; Prime Minister, 1916–22; Leader of the Liberal Party, 1926–31.

Lytton, Edward Robert Bulwer (first Earl of Lytton) (1831–91). Educated Harrow and Bonn; diplomat in Europe, 1862–72; popular poet; Viceroy of India, 1876–80; responsible for Afghan War, 1879; Ambassador at Paris, 1887–91.

MacMunn, Lt-Gen. Sir George Fletcher (1869–1952). Commentator on Indian military affairs; educated Kensington School; commissioned RA, 1888; served Upper Burma, 1892; North West Frontier, 1897–98; South Africa with artillery and staff, 1899–1902; European War, Dardanelles, Mesopotamia, 1914–19; C-in-C Mesopotamia, 1919–20; QMG India, 1920–24.

Minto, fourth Earl of (Elliot, Gilbert John Murray Kynynmond) (1845–1914). Educated Eton and Trinity College, Cambridge; entered army, 1867; served widely, 1870–82; Military Secretary to Governor-General of Canada, 1883–85; Governor-General of Canada, 1898–1904, Viceroy of India, 1905–10.

Montagu, Edwin Samuel (1879–1924). Educated City of London and Trinity College, Cambridge; President of the Union, 1902; Liberal MP, 1906–22; Private Secretary to Herbert Asquith, 1906–10; Parliamentary Under-Secretary, India, 1910–14; Financial Secretary to Treasury, 1914–16; Chancellor of the Duchy of Lancaster, 1915; Minister of Munitions, 1916; Secretary of State for India, 1917–22; helped draft *Report on Indian Constitutional Reforms*, 1918.

Nehru, Motilal (1861–1931). Born in Delhi of prosperous Kashmiri Brahmin family; admitted to Allahabad High Court, 1896; entered politics, 1907;

joined Non-Cooperation movement, 1919; arrested and jailed for six months, 1921; co-founder of Swaraj Party, 1923; wrote Nehru Report, a constitution based on grant of Dominion status, 1928; took part in civil disobedience movement and jailed, 1930.

O'Dwyer, Sir Michael Francis (1864–1940). Born in Ireland; ICS, Punjab, 1885; Revenue Commissioner, NWFP, 1901–8; Lt-Governor, Punjab, 1913–19; assassinated by an Indian at meeting of Royal Central Asian Society.

Pownall, Lt-General Sir Henry Royds (1887–1961). Educated Rugby and Woolich; Assistant Secretary and Deputy Secretary, CID, 1933–36; DMOI, 1938–39; CGS BEF, France, 1939–40; VCIGS, 1941; C-in-C Far East, 1941–42; Chief of Staff to Supreme Allied Commander, SE Asia, 1943–44.

Rawlinson, General Henry Seymour 'Rawly' (Baron Rawlinson of Trent) (1864–1925). Educated Eton and Sandhurst; commissioned King's Royal Rifles, 1884; ADC to Sir Frederick Roberts, Burma, 1886; transferred to Coldstream Guards, 1892; passed into Staff College, Camberley, 1893; Brigade Major at Aldershot, 1895; served on Kitchener's staff at Omdurman, 1898; mentioned in despatches; served in South Africa, 1899–1902; mentioned in despatches five times; commandant, Staff College, 1903–6; OC, Third Division, 1910–14; OC Fourth Division, France, 1914; OC IV Corps, France, 1914–15; OC Fourth Army, 1916–19; C-in-C India, 1920–25.

Ripon, first Marquis (Robinson, George Frederick Samuel) (1827–1909). Born at 10 Downing Street; influenced by Christian Socialist movement as a young man; helped inaugurate the Volunteer movement; a Yorkshire Liberal MP, 1853–59; Under-Secretary of State of War, 1859–63; Secretary of War, 1863–66; Secretary of State for India, 1866–68; Lord of the Council, 1868; converted to Catholicism, 1874; Governor-General of India, 1880–84; First Lord of the Admiralty, 1886; Colonial Secretary, 1892 and 1894–95.

Roberts, Frederick Sleigh, 'Bobs' (First Earl Roberts of Kandahar, Praetoria and Waterford) (1832–1914). Born Cawnpore; educated Eton and Sandhurst; commissioned Bengal Artillery, 1852; served on North West Frontier, during Mutiny and in Abyssinia; C-in-C Punjab Frontier Force, 1878–80; C-in-C Madras Army, 1880–85; C-in-C India, 1885–93; C-in-C Ireland, 1859–99; C-in-C South Africa, 1899–1901; C-in-C British Army, 1901–4; President, National Service League, 1905–14.

Simon, Sir John Allesbrook (first Earl Simon) (1873–1954). Educated Bath Grammar School, Fettes and Wadham College, Oxford; first-class honours and President of the Union, 1896; called to the Bar, 1899; Liberal MP, 1906–18 and 1922–40; Solicitor-General, 1910; Attorney-General, 1913–15; Home Secretary, 1915–16 and 1935–37; Chairman, Indian Statutory Commission, 1927–30; Foreign Secretary, 1931–35; Chancellor of the Exchequer, 1935–40; Lord Chancellor, 1940–45.

Skeen, General Sir Andrew (1873–1935). North West Frontier, 1897–98; China, 1900; East Africa, 1902–4; Third Afghan War, 1919; OC Peshawar District, 1922–23; GOC-in-C Southern Command, 1923–24; CGSI, 1924–28.

Wavell, Field-Marshal Archibald Percival (first Earl Wavell) (1883-1950). Educated Winchester and Sandhurst; commissioned Black Watch, 1901; served South Africa; India, 1903–11; France, 1914–16; Military Attaché, Russian Army, Caucasus, 1916–17; Egyptian Expeditionary Force, 1917–29; OC Second Division, Aldershot, 1935–37; OC Palestine and Transjordan, 1937–38; GOC-in-C Southern Command, 1938–39; GOC-in-C Middle East, 1939–41; C-in-C India, 1941-43; Viceroy of India, 1943–46.

Notes

Preface

1. Brown, *Modern India*.
2. Sarkar, *Modern India*, especially pp. xxi–xxii and 16–17.
3. Mason, *A Matter of Honour*.
4. Cohen, *Indian Army*.
5. Heathcote, *Indian Army*.
6. We also have some very solid (but unpublished) theses by David Brief, Mark Jacobsen and A. H. Shibly; and a few articles by Clive Dewey. The Cambridge University theses by Namrata Narain and Tan Tai Yong were unfortunately not yet available while I was conducting my own research. Tim Moreman's London PhD, about the North West Frontier, is still in progress.
7. Guha, *Subaltern Studies*, Vols I–VI. A seventh volume, under different editorship, is currently in the press.
8. Arnold, *Police Power and Colonial Rule*; and articles.
9. Anderson and Killingray, *Policing the Empire* and *Policing and Decolonisation*.

1 Recruiting Strategy

1. Roberts to Dillon, 16 June 1882, Roberts Papers, 7101/33/97.
2. Havildar Ramji Lal, 107 Pioneers, Barton to Chandra Singh, Jaipur, August 1915 L/MIL/5/825/Pt. 5.
3. On ethnicity in European armies during the same period, see for example Deak, *Beyond Nationalism*.
4. Cohen, *Indian Army*, pp. 6–8.
5. Shibly, PhD thesis, pp. 7–15.
6. Report of Eden Commission, 15 November 1879, L/MIL/7/5445.
7. Peers, 'Contours of the Garrison State', pp. 15–16.
8. Report of Peel Commission, Appendix 64, Evidence of Lord Harris, 14 August 1858. The Government of Madras officially sanctioned the practice of maintaining a rough balance between Tamils from the Carnatic and Ceded Districts, Telingas from the Northern Circars, Muslims from various parts of the presidency, and low caste, Christian or untouchable recruits. Shibly, PhD thesis, pp. 316–17. Report of Peel Commission, Appendix 22.
9. Report of Peel Commission, paras 2871 and 2872, and Appendix 67, Evidence of Lord Elphinstone.
10. Report of Peel Commission, Appendix 58, Evidence of Lord Clyde. Kolff, *Naukar, Rajput and Sepoy*, passim.
11. Mukherjee, *Awadh in Revolt*, pp. 77–8. Alavi, D.Phil thesis, p. 37.
12. Report of Peel Commission, Appendix 71, Evidence of Lt-Col Durand. Alavi, D.Phil thesis, p. 36.

13. Report of Peel Commission, Appendix 62, Evidence of Maj.-Gen. Mansfield. Alavi, D.Phil thesis, p. 38.
14. Report of Peel Commission, paras 763–6.
15. Peers, 'Contours of the Garrison State', p. 15.
16. Report of Peel Commission, Appendix 61, Evidence of Maj.-Gen. Birch, and Appendix 71, Evidence of Lt-Col Durand. Shibly, PhD thesis, p. 315.
17. Cohen, *Indian Army*, pp. 34–5.
18. Most of the following paragraph is based on Brief, MPhil thesis, pp. 4–9.
19. Heathcote, *Indian Army*, p. 27.
20. Report of Peel Commission, Appendix 58, Evidence of Lord Clyde, and Appendix 61, Evidence of Maj.-Gen. Birch.
21. Alavi, D.Phil thesis, p. 220.
22. Palmer, *The Mutiny Outbreak at Meerut*. On pollution rumours see Guha, *Elementary Aspects of Peasant Insurgency in Colonial India*, Ch. 6.
23. Mukherjee, *Awadh in Revolt*, pp. 184–6.
24. Bayly, *Indian Society and the Making of the British Empire*, pp. 179–84.
25. Peers, 'Contours of the Garrison State', pp. 4–5. Stokes, *The Peasant Armed*.
26. Shibly, PhD thesis, p. 319.
27. Brief, MPhil thesis, pp. 11–12. MacMunn, *Armies of India*, pp. 84–5.
28. Bayly, *Indian Society and the Making of the British Empire*, pp. 183–4.
29. Kapur, *Sikh Separatism*, p. 10.
30. Brief, MPhil thesis, pp. 13–14.
31. Report of Peel Commission, Appendix 55, Memo by Canning, and Appendix 70, Evidence of Lt-Col Durand.
32. Report of Peel Commission, pp. 5–7.
33. Report of Peel Commission, para. 1192.
34. Report of Peel Commission, Appendix 70, Evidence of Lt-Col Durand.
35. Brief, MPhil thesis, p. 19.
36. Report of Peel Commission, p. 14.
37. MacMunn, *Armies of India*, pp. 107–9. *Indian Army and Civil List, 1862*.
38. Ripon to Hartington, 28 Feb. 1881, L/MIL/7/5445.
39. Report of Peel Commission, Appendix 67, Evidence of Lord Elphinstone.
40. Morris, *Gurkhas*, pp. 48, 51. Roberts to Kitchener, 28 Dec. 1904, Kitchener Papers, PRO 30/57/28.
41. Barstow, Sikhs, pp. 15–16; Christie, Jats, Gujars and Ahirs, 52. Shibly, PhD thesis, p. 313.
42. Report of Peel Commission, Appendix 62, Evidence of Maj.-Gen. Mansfield.
43. Report of Eden Commissions, 15 Nov. 1879, L/MIL/7/5445.
44. Memo by Newmarch, 30 April 1890, L/MIL/7/2203.
45. Shibly, PhD thesis, p. 364; Brief, MPhil thesis, p. 19.
46. Sarkar, *Modern India*, p. 15.
47. Memo by Newmarch, 30 April 1890, L/MIL/7/2203.
48. Memo by Newmarch, 30 April 1890, L/MIL/7/2203.
49. GI Advance Despatch, 27 Aug. 1920, L/MIL/7/5483.

50. Roberts to Dillon, 16 June 1882, to Stephen, 14 June 1884, to Churchill, 20 June 1884, to Cambridge, 21 June 1884; all in Roberts Papers, 7101/23/97. Memo by Roberts, 1 April 1893, L/MIL/7/7056. White to Adjutant-General, 1 July 1890. L/MIL/7/7270.
51. Report of the Eden Commission, 15 Nov. 1879, L/MIL/7/5445.
52. Roberts to Cambridge, 9 July 1884, Roberts Papers, 7101/23/97.
53. Arbuthnot to Adjutant-General, 26 July 1889, L/MIL/7/7270. Masters, *Bugles and a Tiger*, p. 137.
54. Heathcote, *Indian Army*, p. 88.
55. Brief, MPhil thesis, pp. 20–25.
56. Barstow, *Sikhs*, p. 22.
57. Christie, *Jats, Gujars and Ahirs*, p. 52.
58. GI Advance Despatch, 27 Aug. 1920, Annexure II, L/MIL/7/5483.
59. Brief, MPhil thesis, p. 31.
60. Northbrooke to Cardwell, 2 Dec. 1872 and 2 March 1873, Cardwell Papers, PRO 30/48/21. See also Chapman to Baring, 30 Dec. 1872, Cromer Papers, FO 633/1.
61. Inspection Reports, Madras, 1887–1892, L/MIL/7/17007.
62. White to GI, 22 Feb. 1889, L/MIL/7/7270.
63. Report by Baker, 3 Dec. 1885, L/MIL/7/7268. Extract from Letter of Madras Army Officer in Roberts to Brownlow, 28 Dec. 1885, Roberts Papers, 7101/33/100.
64. Report by Eyre on Rebellion in N. Yaw, undated, c. Feb. 1889, L/MIL/7/7270.
65. Reports on Operations in Yaw, Upper Burma, Dec. 1888–Jan. 1889; White to Adjutant-General, 1 July 1890; both in L/MIL/7/7270.
66. Roberts to Napier, 10 Oct. 1884, Roberts Papers, 7101/23/97.
67. Minute by Arbuthnot, 12 April 1880, L/MIL/7/5445.
68. Ripon to Hartington, 28 Feb. 1881, L/MIL/7/5445.
69. Brief, MPhil thesis, p. 26.
70. AG to MD, 3 April 1875, Cmd. 1698 (1877). Ripon to Hartington, 28 Feb. 1881, L/MIL/7/5445. White to AG, 1 July 1889, L/MIL/7/7270.
71. The resemblance to contemporary academia is striking.
72. Shibly, PhD thesis, pp. 244, 247–8, 308–9.
73. Report of the Eden Commission, 15 Nov. 1879, L/MIL/7/5445.
74. Roberts to Cambridge, 29 May 1884, Roberts Papers, 7101/23/97.
75. Brief, MPhil thesis, pp. 45–6.
76. Caste Returns, 1 Jan. 1893, L/MIL/7/17081.
77. Minute by Haines, 22 March 1880, L/MIL/7/5445.
78. Memo by Newmarch, 30 April 1890, L/MIL/7/2203.
79. Report of Nicholson Committee, 24 Dec. 1901, L/MIL/7/5459.
80. Minto to Morley, 28 March 1907, L/MIL/7/7147.
81. MacMunn, *Armies of India*, pp. 123, 169–70.
82. For the Mappila background, see Panikkar, *Against Lord and State*; Holland-Pryor, *Mappillas or Moplahs*; Arnold, 'Islam, the Mappilas and Peasant Revolt in Malabar'; and Dhanagare, 'Agrarian Conflict, Religion and Politics'.
83. Military Department Minute, 14 May 1907, L/MIL/7/7147.
84. Minto to Morley, 28 March 1907, L/MIL/7/7147.

85. Military Department to SSI, 25 July 1901, L/MIL/7/7108.
86. Srinivas, *Religion and Society among the Coorgs of South India*.
87. Commissioner of Coorg to Secretary to Chief Commissioner of Coorg, 23 June 1900, L/MIL/7/7108.
88. Adjutant-General to Military Department, 17 Oct. 1900, L/MIL/7/7108.
89. Viceroy to India Office, 11 Aug. 1904, L/MIL/7/7108. Memo by Mullaby, 30 June 1904, CID 64-D, CAB 6/2, Mouat, *Madras Classes*, pp. 70–3.
90. Kitchener to Roberts, 27 April 1904, Kitchener Papers, PRO 30/57/29.
91. Kitchener to Roberts, 10 May 1903, and 16 June 1904, Kitchener Papers, PRO 30/57/29.
92. MacMunn, *Armies of India*, p. 170.
93. Memo by Roberts, 23 June 1903, CID 27-D, CAB 6/1.
94. Class Composition, 1 Jan. 1904, L/MIL/7/17084. The figures understate the numbers from the Punjab, since they list Punjabi Muslims from districts East of the Sutlej with those from Hindustan.
95. GI Advanced Despatch, 27 Aug. 1920, Appendix D to Annexure I, L/MIL/7/5483.
96. GI Advanced Despatch, 27 Aug. 1920, Annexure II, L/MIL/7/5483.
97. Memo by Roberts, 23 June 1903, CAB 6/1, CID 27-D.
98. Report of Peel Commission, Appendix 61, Evidence of Maj.-Gen. Birch, and Appendix 65, Evidence of Sir Patrick Grant. Cole, *Rajputana Classes*, Ch. 15.
99. Holland-Pryor, *Mappillas or Moplahs*, p. 58.
100. Christie, *Jats, Gujars and Ahirs*, pp. 26–7, 45.
101. Christie, *Jats, Gujars and Ahirs*, pp. 88–90, Morris, *Gurkhas*, pp. 128–30.
102. GI Advance Despatch, 27 Aug. 1920, Annexure II, L/MIL/7/5483.
103. Barstow, Sikhs, p. 178.
104. GI Advance Despatch, 27 Aug. 1920, Annexure II, L/MIL/7/5483. Brief, MPhil thesis, p. 132.
105. See Indian Constitutional Reforms (The Montagu-Chelmsford Report) 22 April 1918, CAB 6/4 CID 112-D for a later example.
106. Bayly, *Imperial Meridian*, pp. 147–55.
107. Peers, 'Contours of the Garrison State', pp. 20–1.
108. Report of Peel Commission, para. 1213. Prebble, Mutiny, passim.
109. MacMunn, *Armies of India*, 129.
110. Arnold, '"Criminal Tribes" and "Martial Races"', p. 7; 'Recruitment in the Madras Constabulary', p. 18.
111. Kapur, *Sikh Separatism*, pp. 2–5, 9–10; MacMunn, *Armies of India*, pp. 133–4; Barstow, *Sikhs*, Ch. 5.
112. Sayid Mohanban Hussain to Mahomed Idris Khan, 34 Poona Horse, 29 May 1917, L/MIL/5/827 Pt.3.
113. Arnold, "Criminal Tribes" and "Martial Races", p. 7.
114. Bayly, *Indian Society and the Making of the British Empire*, p. 100; Betham, *Marathas and Dekhani Musalmans*, p. 15; Morris, *Gurkhas*, pp. 24–5; Evatt, *Garhwalis*, Ch. 2.
115. Brief, MPhil thesis, pp. 35–6. Arnold, 'Recruitment in the Madras Constabulary, 7; Srinivas, *Religion and Society Among the Coorgs of South India*, pp. 28–9.

116. Memo by Kirkpatrick (CGSI), 6 May 1916, WO 106/5443.
117. Cole, *Rajputana Classes*, pp. 28–9.
118. Dafadar, 34 Poona Horse, to Panch Singh, Ajmer, Rajputana, 9 June 1917, L/MIL/5/827 Pt 3.
119. Cole, *Rajputana Classes*, pp. 5–6.
120. Ridgway, *Pathans*, pp. 14–15.
121. Cunningham, *Dogras*, pp. 89–90.
122. Wikeley, *Punjabi Mussalmans*, pp. 67, 69; Betham, *Marathas and Dekhani Musalmans*, p. 74; Evatt, *Garhwalis*, p. 43; Barstow, *Sikhs*, p. 151.
123. Sheo Ram, Allahabad to Dharam Singh, 2 Lancers, 20 April 1917, L/MIL/5/827 Pt 3.
124. Masters, *Bugles and a Tiger*, p. 201.
125. Wikeley, *Punjabi Musalmans*, p. 8; Christie, *Jats, Gujars and Ahirs*, pp. 30, 37.
126. Masters, *Bugles and a Tiger*, p. 88.
127. MacMunn, *Armies of India*, p. 139.
128. Christie, *Jats, Gujars and Ahirs*, p. 10.
129. Cohen, *Indian Army*, p. 51.
130. This argument draws on Belich, *The New Zeland Wars*, passim.
131. Jacobsen, PhD thesis, pp. 221–2. A similar view informed the *ad hoc* structures of the Spanish Infantry in the sixteenth century: Parker, *The Army of Flanders and the Spanish Road*, pp. 15–16.
132. Masters, *Bugles and a Tiger*, p. 95.
133. Cunningham, *Dogras*, p. 89.
134. Holland-Pryor, *Mappillas or Moplahs*, p. 47.
135. *Census of India, 1901, Part I, Report*. Sarkar, *Modern India*, p. 66.
136. *Census of India, 1891, General Tables, Vol. 1.*
137. Bourne, *Hindustani Musalmans and Musalmans of the Eastern Punjab*, p. 25.
138. OC 10 Jats to DAAG, Allahabad Bgd., 15 July 1907, L/MIL/7/7156.
139. Morris, *Gurkhas*, pp. 3–6.
140. Cole, *Rajputana Classes*, Ch. 1.
141. Evatt, *Garhwalis*, Ch. 6; Latham, *Kumaonis*, p. 39.
142. Roberts to Cambridge, 21 March 1883, Roberts papers, 7101/23/97.
143. Cole, *Rajputana Classes*, Ch. 13; Cunningham, *Dogras*, p. 96; Bourne, *Hindustani Musalmans and Musalmans of the Eastern Punjab*, p. 47.
144. Betham, *Marathas and Dekhani Musalmans*, p. 167.
145. Arnold, '"Criminal Tribes" and 'Martial Races'", p. 9.
146. Barstow, *Sikhs*, p. 2.
147. Christie, *Jats, Gujars and Ahirs*, pp. 10, 50.
148. Cole, *Rajputana Classes*, Ch. 5.
149. Rosselli, 'The Self-Image of Effeteness'.
150. Brief, MPhil thesis, pp. 40–1.
151. Jacobsen, PhD thesis, p. 216.
152. MacMunn, *Armies of India*, pp. 132, 147; Heathcote, *Indian Army*, pp. 92–3.
153. Classes who have withstood Afghan campaign, 1881, L/MIL/7/7018.
154. Brief, MPhil thesis, p. 25.
155. Bayly, *Imperial Meridian*, p. 150.

156. Said, *Orientalism*, pp. 36, 39.
157. Yate to Montagu, 30 Nov. 1918, L/MIL/7/7280.
158. There are parallels with colonial medical discourse. See Vaughan, *Curing their Ills*, p. 25.
159. Christie, *Jats, Gujars and Ahirs*, pp. 19–20, 42; Wikeley, *Punjabi Musalmans*, pp. 82, 101; Morris, *Gurkhas*, p. 30; Betham, *Marathas and Dekhani Musalmans*, pp. 42, 62–3; Cunningham, *Dogras*, pp. 11–12.
160. Roberts to Kitchener, 28 Dec. 1904, *Kitchener Papers*, PRO 30/57/28.
161. Holland-Pryor, *Mappillas or Moplahs*, p. 56. Report of Peel Commission, Appendix 71, Evidence of Lt-Col Durand.
162. Ridgeway, *Pathans*, pp. 48, 87–94, 167, 189.
163. Morris, *Gurkhas*, pp. 69–72, 77–83.
164. Holland-Pryor, *Mappillas or Moplahs*, p. 56; Christie, *Jats, Gujars and Ahirs*, pp. 45–6; Morris, *Gurkhas*, p. 123; Ridgeway, *Pathans*, pp. 47–8.
165. Morris, *Gurkhas*, p. 145.
166. Betham, *Marathas and Dekhani Musalmans*, p. 96.
167. Pant, 'The Cognitive Status of Caste in Colonial Ethnography', p. 161.
168. Caplan, '"The Gurkha" in British Military Writings', p. 572.
169. Arnold, '"Criminal Tribes" and "Martial Races"', pp. 2–3.
170. Cunningham, *Dogras*, p. 57.
171. Barstow, *Sikhs*, p. 152; Cohen, *Indian Army*, p. 51.
172. Barstow, *Sikhs*, p. 122.
173. Mouat, *Madras Classes*.
174. Christie, *Jats, Gujars and Ahirs*, p. 20; Evatt, *Garhwalis*, pp. 20–1; Cole, *Rajputana Classes*, p. 34; Holland-Pryor, *Mappillas or Moplahs*, p. 47.
175. Mouat, *Madras Classes*, p. 40.
176. Cunningham, *Dogras*, pp. 34–5, 45.
177. Mouat, *Madras Classes*, pp. 26, 32.
178. Pant, 'The Cognitive Status of Caste in Colonial Ethnography', pp. 145–7, pp. 150–1.
179. Arnold, '"Criminal Tribes" and "Martial Races"', pp. 1–4.
180. Christie, *Jats, Gujars and Ahirs*, pp. 1–6, Cunningham, *Dogras*, pp. 1–2.
181. MacMunn, *Armies of India*, pp. 129–30; Evatt, *Garhwalis*, pp. 16–19.
182. Barstow, *Sikhs*, Appendix 5; Wikeley, *Punjabi Musalmans*, pp. 2–3; Cunningham, *Dogras*, pp. 2–3.
183. Bingley, *Brahmins*, p. 50; Holland-Pryor, *Mappillas or Moplahs*, p. 47.
184. I am grateful to Chandrika Kaul and Amrit Singh for this point.
185. Heathcote, *Indian Army*, p. 93.
186. Arnold, '"Criminal Tribes" and "Martial Races"', pp. 6–7.
187. Betham, *Marathas and Dekhani Musalmans*, pp. 8, 10.
188. Inden, 'Orientalist Constructions of India', pp. 416, 425.
189. Morris, *Gurkhas*, p. 37.
190. Brief, MPhil thesis, p. 36; Cole, *Rajputana Classes*, pp. 28–9; Mason, *Matter of Honour*, pp. 356–8.
191. Cunningham, *Dogras*, p. 89.
192. Christie, *Jats, Gujars and Ahirs*, pp. 75–6.
193. Mason, *Matter of Honour*, pp. 352–4.
194. Wikeley, *Punjabi Musalmans*, pp. 93–7.

195. Evatt, *Garhwalis*, pp. 45, 48.
196. Radhakrishna, 'The Criminal Tribes Act in the Madras Presidency', pp. 269–82.
197. Minto to Morley, 28 March 1907, L/MIL/7/7147. Arnold, 'Recruitment in the Madras Constabulary', pp. 13–14.
198. Cole, *Rajputana Classes*, pp. 42, 66.
199. Wikeley, *Punjabi Musalmans*, pp. 63–4; Mouat, *Madras Classes*, p. 36.
200. Punjab Government Memo, 2 June 1951, CAB 16/38/2.
201. Roberts to Cranbrook, 30 June 1882. And see Roberts to Cambridge, 29 June 1883, to Cowell, 6 Feb. 1884, and to Lytton, 23 March 1884. All in Roberts Papers, 7101/23/97.
202. Minute by Dalyell, 18 Feb. 1882, L/MIL/7/5445.
203. GI Advance Despatch, 27 Aug. 1920, Annexure II, L/MIL/7/5483. Cohen, *Indian Army*, p. 70.
204. Brief, MPhil thesis, p. 48.
205. Kapur, *Sikh Separatism*, p. 57.
206. GS Strategical Survey of India and Burma, 1911, WO 106/154.
207. Cohen, *Indian Army*, pp. 66–7.
208. Zelliot, 'Learning the Use of Political Means', pp. 29–34; Cohen, *Indian Army*, pp. 59–61.
209. Sarkar, *Modern India*, p. 56.
210. Srinivas, *Religion and Society Among the Coorgs of South India*, pp. 25–31.
211. Sarkar, *Modern India*, p. 55; Pant, 'The Cognitive Status of Caste in Colonial Ehtnography', p. 159.
212. Petition by Merat-Kathats, 24 May 1905, L/MIL/7/7139.
213. Zelliot, 'Learning the Use of Political Means', p. 35.
214. Sarkar, *Modern India*, p. 243.
215. Brief, MPhil thesis, p. 52.
216. Barstow, *Sikhs*, p. 179.
217. Greenhut, 'Imperial Reserve'.
218. O'Dwyer, *India As I Knew It*, p. 221.
219. Morris, *Gurkhas*, pp. 37–8; Barstow, *Sikhs*, pp. 67, 71.
220. Mouat, *Madras Classes*, pp. 68, 72.
221. Cunningham, *Dogras*, pp. 69, 62–3.
222. Mouat, *Madras Classes*, p. 8.
223. Mahomed Nawaz Khan to Mir Baz Khan, 18 Lancers, 5 Sept. 1917, L/MIL/5/827 Pt.5.
224. Brief, Mphil thesis, pp. 123–4.
225. O'Dwyer, *India As I Knew It*, p. 215.
226. Barstow, *Sikhs*, p. 5; Cohen, *Indian Army*, pp. 69–70.
227. Morris, *Gurkhas*, p. 175.
228. Mason, *Matter of Honour*, p. 439.
229. Cohen, *Indian Army*, pp. 72–3.
230. Shooting Affray in 49 Bengalis, L/MIL/7/7279.
231. IMR.16, CAB 16/38/2.
232. Kitchener to Crewe, 1 April 1915, PRO 30/57/69.
233. Cohen, *Indian Army*, p. 76.
234. GI Advanced Despatch, 27 Aug. 1920, L/MIL/7/5483.
235. IMR, Report, June 1922, CID 125-D, CAB 6/4.

236. 7th IMR, 11 Jan. 1972, and 8th IMR, 12 Jan. 1922, CAB 16/38/1.
237. Indian Army List, January 1923.
238. AD to SSI, 24 June 1926, CID 154-D, CAB 6/5.
239. Mouat, *Madras Classes*.
240. Mason, *Matter of Honour*, pp. 343, 348–9.
241. The British Element in Internal Security Troops, Appendix E to Annexure 2, CID 198-D, CAB 6/6.
242. Brief, MPhil thesis, pp. 29–30.
243. Memo by Kitchener, 9 Sept. 1908, L/MIL/17/5/1746
244. GS Strategical Survey of India and Burma, 1911, WO 106/154.
245. Jacobsen, PhD thesis, pp. 201–2. Roberts Papers, 7101/23/97.
246. MD to SSI, 30 March 1921, CID 122-D, CAB 6/4.
247. Legislative Assembly Debates, 14 March 1939, L/MIL/7/19156.
248. Legislative Assembly Debates, 14 March 1939, L/MIL/7/19156. Italics mine.

2   Enlisting Strategies

1. C-in-C to Military Department, 14 Aug. 1875, Cmd. 1698 (1877) LXII. And see minute by Gibbs, 25 June 1875, in the same collection.
2. MacMunn, *Armies of India*, p. 211.
3. Peers, 'Contours of the Garrison State', p. 16.
4. Barstow, *Sikhs*, p. 156.
5. Ali, 'Malign Growth', pp. 118–19.
6. Brief, MPhil thesis, pp. 53–4.
7. Barstow, *Sikhs*, pp. 177, 187.
8. Kapur, *Sikh Separatism*, p. 64.
9. In Russia during the Great War, peasant communes tended to send in men from the larger families, since they would be less hard-hit than the smaller families by losing the labour of a fit adult male. Figes, 'The Red Army and Mass Mobilization'.
10. Brief, MPhil thesis, p. 66.
11. Barstow, *Sikhs*.
12. Wikeley, *Punjabi Musalmans*, pp. 101–2.
13. Latham, *Kumaonis*, p. 22.
14. Dewey, 'Some Consequences of Military Expenditure', pp. 95–8.
15. Brief, MPhil thesis, p. 55.
16. Barstow, *Sikhs*, p. 121.
17. Dewey, 'Some Consequences of Military Expenditure', p. 117.
18. Christie, *Jats, Gujars and Ahirs*, p. 55.
19. Cole, *Rajputana Classes*, Ch.5; Christie, *Jats, Gujars and Ahirs*, pp. 29–30.
20. Memo by Roberts, 23 June 1903, CID 27-D, CAB 6/1.
21. Memo by Wigram, 7 April 1931, WO 106/5443.
22. Holland-Pryor, *Mappillas or Moplahs*, p. 59.
23. Memo by Martindale, 28 Oct. 1904, L/MIL/7/7139.
24. Brief, MPhil thesis, pp. 59–63.

25. In the Russian Civil War, for example, few Red Army conscripts joined their units during the summer. At the same time, the weekly desertion rate in the central agricultural region rose to crippling heights as troops slipped away to help with the harvest. Figes, 'The Red Army and Mass Mobilization', pp. 177, 182, 201.

26. Bourne, *Hindustani Musalmans and Musalmans of the Eastern Punjab*, p. 30.

27. Ridgeway, *Pathans*, p. 47.

28. Roberts to Cambridge, 14 April 1886, Roberts Papers, 7101/33/100.

29. Betham, *Marathas and Dekhani Musalmans*, p. 97.

30. O'Dwyer, *India As I Knew It*, pp. 226–7.

31. Cunningham, *Dogras*, pp. 62–3.

32. Christie, *Jats, Gujars and Ahirs*, p. 34.

33. Lumsden to MD, 30 June 1875, Appendix E, Cmd. 1698 (1877) LXII. Christie, *Jats, Gujars and Ahirs*, p. 27; Wikeley, *Punjabi Musalmans*, pp. 67–8, 52.

34. Barstow, *Sikhs*, p. 187.

35. Most detail in this paragraph comes from Brief, MPhil thesis, pp. 2–3, 71–88; and Dewey, 'Some Consequences of Military Expenditure', pp. 149–55.

36. Cunningham, *Dogras*, p. 39.

37. Christie, *Jats, Gujars and Ahirs*, p. 11.

38. For the next two paragraphs see Brief, MPhil thesis, pp. 77, 84.

39. GI Advanced Despatch, 27 Aug. 1920, L/MIL/7/5483.

40. Esher Committee Report, 1921, Pt.5, L/MIL/7/5522.

41. Report of Peel Commission, Appendix B to Appendix 54.

42. Lumsden to MD, 30 June 1875, Appendix B, Cmd. 1698 (1877) LXII.

43. Dufferin to Churchill, 14 Aug. 1885, L/MIL/7/7025.

44. Cohen, *Indian Army*, p. 70.

45. Betham, *Marathas and Dekhani Musalmans*, p. 156. Minto to Morley, 28 March 1907, L/MIL/7/7147.

46. Sarkar, *Modern India*, p. 41; Betham, *Marathas and Dekhani Musalmans*, p. 74.

47. Betham, *Marathas and Dekhani Musalmans*, p. 97.

48. Esher Committee Report, Pt.5, L/MIL/7/5523. Barstow, *Sikhs*, pp. 154, 185.

49. Morris, *Gurkhas*, pp. 137–8.

50. Morris, *Gurkhas*, p. 141.

51. Morris, *Gurkhas*, p. 144.

52. Barstow, *Sikhs*, p. 180.

53. Peers, 'Contours of the Garrison State', pp. 8–9. The crippling financial burdens of warfare did not hamper Indian states alone. Early modern polities faced similar problems almost everywhere. From the 1530s, European armies began a period of sustained and competitive growth in numbers. Neither France nor Spain fielded more than 30 000 effectives during the Italian Wars of 1494 to 1529; but a century later Philip IV of Spain had perhaps ten times as many under his command. Finding the money to feed, clothe, equip and – above all – to pay these hordes tested some early modern financial machinery

beyond its limits. Mutinies for arrears of pay often disrupted vital campaigns, most notably during the Spanish attempts to reconquer the rebellious Dutch provinces in the later sixteenth and early seventeenth centuries. See Parker, *The Army of Flanders and the Spanish Road*, esp. Introduction and Ch.8.

54. Alavi, DPhil thesis, p. 33.
55. Bayly, *Indian Society and the Making of the British Empire*, p. 85.
56. Sultan Khan, 36 Jacob's Horse, to Mahomed Khan, Shahpur District, 10 Jan. 1917, L/MIL/5/827 Pt.1.
57. Khahil-ur-Rahman to Abdul Rahman, NWFP, 2 Jan. 1917, L/MIL/5/827 Pt.1.
58. Sattar Khan, 38 CIH, to Rustan Pawari, 3 Nov. 1916, L/MIL/5/826 Pt.9.
59. Sher Ali Khan, 18 Lancers, to Mahomed Khan, Depot 18 Lancers, Sialkot, 6 March 1917, L/MIL/5/827 Pt.2.
60. Jemadar Shamsher Ali, 34 Poona Horse, to Raja Rustan Ali Khan, Gujranwala, 20 April 1917, L/MIL/5/827 Pt.2.
61. Major, Cavalry, Kashmir, to two Sepoys, 41 Dogras, May 1915, L/MIL/5/825 Pt.3.
62. Umrao Singh, Moradabad District, to Umrao Singh, 29 Lancers, 16 Dec. 1916, L/MIL/5/827 Pt.1.
63. Gian Singh, 38 CIH, to his mother, Ferozepur District, 25 Sept. 1917.
64. Sabir Ali, 6 Cavalry, to his father, Sultanpur, 22 July 1917, L/MIL/5/827 Pt.4.
65. Brief, MPhil thesis, pp. 166–7.
66. Dewey, 'Some Consequences of Military Expenditure', pp. 151–2.
67. GI Advance Despatch, 27 Aug. 1920, Annexure II, L/MIL/7/5483.
68. O'Dwyer, *India As I Knew It*, p. 214.
69. See for example, Dost Muhammad Khan to Karachi, 29 March 1915, L/MIL/5/825 Pt.1.
70. Amir Khan, France, to Bavar Khan, 127 Infantry, Karachi, 20 May 1915, L/MIL/5/825 Pt.3.
71. Punjabi Muslim, 58 Rifles, France, to his brother, India, L/MIL/5/825 Pt.1. Memo by Howell, 24 April 1915, L/MIL/7/17347.
72. Barstow, *Sikhs*, p. 180. And see Morris, *Gurkhas*, pp. 170–2.
73. Aziz Ahmad Khan, 4 Cavalry, to Lawab Ali Khan, 4 Cavalry, France, 1 July 1915, L/MIL/5/825 Pt.4.
74. Beauchamp Duff to Kitchener, 18 Feb. 1916, Kitchener Papers, PRO 30/57/70.
75. Montagu–Chelmsford Report, 22 April 1918, CID 112-D, CAB 6/4. Indian Military Requirements Committee, Report, 1921, CAB 16/38/2.
76. O'Dwyer, *India As I Knew It*, pp. 222–3. Brief, MPhil thesis, pp. 163–4.
77. Esher Committe Report, Pt.5, L/MIL/7/5523.
78. O'Dwyer, *India As I Knew It*, pp. 218–20.
79. Kapur, *Sikh Separatism*, pp. 61–6. Amar Singh, 2 Lancers, to Kam Singh, Ludhiana District, 18 Sept. 1917, L/MIL/5/827 Pt.4.
80. Military Events, India, April to June 1923, WO 33/1036 Pt.2. Viceroy to SSI, 18 Feb 1921, L/MIL/7/5523.

81. Esher Committee, Report, Pt.5, L/MIL/7/5523.
82. Viceroy, AD to SSI, 19 March 1920, CID 119-D, CAB 6/4.
83. House of Lords, Debates, 24 Feb. 1921, L/MIL/7/5523.
84. Yate to Montagu, 5 April 1921, L/MIL/7/5523.
85. Report on Army in India, June 1931, CID 138-D, CAB 6/6.
86. Brief, MPhil thesis, pp. 94–7.
87. Ganaishi Lall to Ganga Ram, Indian General Base Depot, France, 7 April 1917, L/MIL/5/827 Pt.3.
88. Khalas Khan, France, to Abeda Khan, Mianwali, 27 Feb. 1916; Makhand Ali Khan, France to Pay Dafadar Mahomed Ishaq Khan, Depot 3 Cavalry, 6 March 1916; Mahomed Rahni Khan, France to Wazir Khan, Depot 6 Cavalry, 6 March 1916; L/MIL/5/826 Pt.3.
89. Cunningham, *Dogras*, p. 102.
90. Most of this paragraph comes from Dewey, 'Some Consequences of Military Expenditure', pp. 93, 96, 99, 117–140.
91. Caplan, '"The Gurkha" in British Military Writings', p. 573.
92. Most of this paragraph comes from Dewey, 'Some Consequences of Military Expenditure', pp. 112–15, 148–51.
93. Barstow, *Sikhs*, p. 106.
94. Viceroy, AD to SSI, 19 March 1920, CID 119-D, CAB 6/4.
95. *Army Regulations, India, II, 1923*, pp. 171–2.
96. Cunningham, *Dogras*, pp. 79–80, 83.
97. Betham, *Marathas and Dekhani Musalmans*, pp. 122–3.
98. GI AD Despatch 76, 22 Sept. 1916, L/MIL/7/17517.
99. Report of Peel Commission, Appendix 80.
100. Lumsden to MD, 30 June 1875, Appendix E, Cmd. 1698 (1877) LXII.
101. Evatt, *Garhwalis*, pp. 47–8; Cunningham, *Dogras*, p. 40.
102. Dewey, 'Some Consequences of Military Expenditure', pp. 101–4.
103. Arnold, 'Cholera and Colonialism in British India'.
104. Heathcote, *Indian Army*, pp. 158–61.
105. Arnold, 'Cholera and Colonialism in British India'.
106. Report on Army in India, June 1931, CID 138-D, CAB 6/6.
107. Heathcote, *Indian Army*, pp. 63–4.
108. Mason, *Matter of Honour*, pp. 423–4.
109. Eden Commission Report, 15 Nov. 1879, L/MIL/7/5445.
110. Saif Ali, France, to Kazim Din, 19 Punjabis, Persia, 17 Aug. 1915, L/MIL/5/825 Pt.5.
111. Brief, MPhil thesis, pp. 26–7.
112. Peel Commission Report, para. 2411.
113. Memo by Dalyell, 18 Feb. 1882, L/MIL/7/5445.
114. MacMunn, *Armies of India*, p. 101.
115. Heathcote, *Indian Army* pp. 112–13.
116. AGI to GI MD, 21 Oct. 1890, L/MIL/7/7054.
117. Viceroy to SSI, 2 May 1921, L/MIL/7/5523.
118. MD minute, 17 Aug. 1921, L/MIL/7/5523.
119. Steedman (ed.), *The Radical Soldier's Tale*, p. 39.
120. Report by Howell, 24 April, 1915, L/MIL/5/825 Pt.2.
121. Mangal Singh to friend in India, 23 March 1915; M. N. Pandit to friend in Sholapur, 23 March 1915, L/MIL/5/825 Pt.1.

122. British medical subordinate to wife in India, 4 Feb. 1915, L/MIL/5/825 Pt.1.
123. Maratha soldier, France, to ward orderly, Ambala, April 1915, L/MIL/5/825 Pt.2.
124. Report by Howell, 21 Aug. 1915, L/MIL/5/825 Pt.4.
125. Report by Howell, 24 April 1915, L/MIL/5/825 Pt.2.
126. Report by Censor, 19 June 1915, L/MIL/5/825 Pt.3.
127. Two sepoys, 57 Rifles, to two sepoys, S. Waziristan Militia, 24 April 1915, L/MIL/5/825 Pt.2.
128. Sepoy, 47 Sikhs, to sepoy Depot, 12 May 1915, L/MIL/5/825 Pt.2.
129. Zeri Shah, Indian Military Depot, Milford-on-Sea, to Sher Alam, 58 Rifles, France, 2 Sept. 1915.
130. Jewan Singh, 2 Lancers, France, to his wife, Gurdaspur District, 20 Jan. 1917.
131. Abdul Alim Khan, 6 Cavalry, France, to Hafiz Abdul Karim, 30 May 1917, L/MIL/5/827 Pt.3.
132. Abdul Ali, 6 Cavalry, France, to Fazand Ali Khan, 6 Cavalry, Sialkot, 28 Feb. 1917, L/MIL/5/827 Pt.2.
133. Mahomed Khan, 6 Cavalry, to Ghans Mahomed Khan, Rohtak, 5 June 1917, L/MIL/5/827 Pt.3.
134. Mahomed Khan, 6 Cavalry, to Ahmad Khan, 11 Rajput Infantry, Calcutta, 15 June 1917, L/MIL/5/827 Pt.3.
135. Father, Rawalpindi, to Mehta Deoki Nandan, Supply and Transport Agent, Marseilles, 18 June 1917, L/MIL/5/827 Pt.4.
136. Inyat Ali Khan, Depot, 6 Cavalry, Sialkot, to Abdul Jabbar Khan, 6 Cavalry, France, 2 Feb. 1917, L/MIL/5/827 Pt.2.
137. Heathcote, *Indian Army*, p. 112. Peel Commission Report, para. 2353.
138. Lumsden to Military Department, 30 June 1875, Cmd. 1698 (1877) LXII.
139. Dufferin to Churchill, 14 Aug. 1885, L/MIL/7/7025.
140. Eden Commission Report, 15 Nov. 1879, L/MIL/7/5445.
141. Heathcote, *Indian Army*, p. 110.
142. Betham, *Marathas and Dekhani Musalmans*, p. 94.
143. Dufferin to Churchill, 14 Aug. 1885, L/MIL/7/7025.
144. Peel Commission Report, Appendix 58 and Appendix 61.
145. Enclosures 1 and 2 in Despatch to Salisbury (SSI), 3 March 1876, Cmd. 1698 (1877) LXII.
146. Lumsden to Burne, 16 Nov. 1874, Cmd. 1698 (1877) LXII.
147. Peel Commission Report, para. 2358.
148. C-in-C to Military Department, 14 Aug. 1875; and Salisbury to Governor-General, 10 Aug. 1876; Cmd. 1698 (1877) LXII.
149. Eden Commission Report, 15 Nov. 1879, L/MIL/7/5445.
150. Heathcote, *Indian Army*, pp. 111–12.
151. Esher Committee Report, Pt.5; House of Lords, Debates, 24 Feb. 1921; L/MIL/7/5523.
152. Morris, *Gurkhas*, pp. 146–7.
153. Military Events, India, July–Sept. 1923, WO 33/1036 Pt.3.
154. Morris, *Gurkhas*, pp. 147–50.
155. Brief, MPhil thesis, p. 99.

156. Kitchener to Roberts, 24 March 1904, Kitchener Papers, PRO 30/57/29.
157. Diary, 1 Jan. 1903, Rawlinson Papers, 5201/33/11.
158. Brief, MPhil thesis, pp. 165–6. Smith to Kitchener, 27 Oct. 1914, Kitchener Papers, PRO 30/57/31.
159. Sarkar, *Modern India*, p. 36.
160. Ali, 'Malign Growth', p. 114.
161. Whitcombe, 'Irrigation', pp. 700–30.
162. Montagu–Chelmsford Report, 22 April 1918, CID 112-D, CAB 6/4.
163. Military Events, India, April to June 1923, WO 33/1036 Pt.2.
164. Brief, MPhil thesis, pp. 99–100.
165. Ali, 'Malign Growth', pp. 129–30.
166. Brief, MPhil thesis, pp. 101–2.
167. O'Dwyer, *India As I Knew It*, p. 216.
168. Esher Committee Report, 1919–29, Pt.5, L/MIL/7/5523.
169. Dewey, 'Some Consequences of Military Expenditure', p. 98.
170. Brief, MPhil thesis, p.103. Barstow, *Sikhs*.
171. Mason, *Matter of Honour*, p. 388.
172. Ali, 'Malign Growth', p. 112.
173. Brief, MPhil thesis, p. 105.
174. Ali, 'Malign Growth', p. 125.
175. Report by Pressey, 28 Feb. 1910, L/MIL/7/7156.
176. Lumsden to Military Department, 30 June 1875, Appendix F, Cmd. 1698 (1877) LXII.
177. Military Events, India, Oct. to Dec. 1923, WO 33/1036 Pt.4.
178. Memo by Deverell (CIGS) 26 May 1930, WO 106/5443.
179. Peel Commission Report, paras 654–5, 1291.
180. Peel Commission Report, paras 1623–6.
181. Peel Commission Report, paras 653, 1389, Appendix 6, Memo by Merewether, 25 Aug. 1858, and Appendix 72.
182. Monro to Montagu, 28 Dec 1917, L/MIL/7/15130.
183. OC 3 Horse to Meerut Cavalry Bgd, 29 Oct. 1915, L/MIL/7/15129.
184. Minute, 11 March 1918, L/MIL/7/15130.
185. Report on Silladar System, 31 Oct. 1915, L/MIL/7/15129.
186. Monro to Montagu, 28 Dec. 1917; OC 39 KGO CIH to HQ Jhansi Bgd., 27 Jan. 1919; L/MIL/7/15130.
187. Heathcote, *Indian Army*, pp. 39–40.
188. Memo by Remington, OC Indian Cavalry Corps, Nov. 1915, L/MIL/7/15129.
189. Peel Commission Report, Appendix 6, Memo by Merewether, 25 Aug. 1858.
190. Heathcote, *Indian Army*, pp. 39–40.
191. Younghusband to Cox, 16 Dec. 1918, L/MIL/7/15130.
192. Silladar Cavalry Committee Report, July 1920, L/MIL/7/15130.
193. Note by Jacob, OC Meerut Division, 1 Nov. 1915, L/MIL/7/15129. Younghusband to Cox, 16 Dec. 1918, L/MIL/7/15130.
194. OC 6 Cavalry to Sialkot Cavalry Bgd, 29 Oct. 1915; OC 20 Horse to Secunderabad Cavalry Bgd., 30 Oct. 1915; L/MIL/7/15129.
195. Parsons to HQ Indian Cavalry Corps, 28 Oct. 1915, L/MIL/7/15129.

196. OC 3 Horse to Meerut Cavalry Bgd, 29 Oct. 1915, L/MIL/7/15129. Monro to Montagu, 28 Dec. 1917, L/MIL/7/15130.
197. Ricketts to Lahore Division, 3 Nov. 1915, L/MIL/7/15129.
198. Montagu to Governor-General, 17 May 1918, L/MIL/7/15130.
199. SSI to Viceroy, 3 Nov. and 9 Nov. 1920, L/MIL/7/15130.
200. Viceroy to SSI, 6 March 1920, L/MIL/7/15130.

3 Fighting Spirit

1. L/MIL/5/827 Pt.3.
2. Eden Commission, Report, 15 Nov. 1879, L/MIL/7/5445.
3. Barstow, *Sikhs*, p. 155.
4. Brief, MPhil thesis, pp. 79–80.
5. Barstow, *Sikhs*, p. 106.
6. Naik Gaekwar, 107 Pioneers, Brighton, to Poona District, nd., L/MIL/5/825 Pt.4.
7. MacMunn, *Armies of India*, p. 142.
8. Brief, MPhil thesis, p. 120.
9. Dewey, 'Some Consequences of Military Expenditure in British India', p. 107.
10. Betham, *Marathas and Dekhani Musalmans*, p. 98.
11. Latham, *Kumaonis*, p. 40.
12. See also Figes, 'The Red Army and Mass Mobilisation', pp. 186–7.
13. Kartar Singh, 38 CIH, France to Jhaman Singh, Lyallpur District, 8 June 1917, L/MIL/5/827 Pt.3.
14. Bariam Singh, 47 Sikhs, to friend in India, 31 March 1915, L/MIL/5/825 Pt.1.
15. Gajan Singh, 18 Lancers, to Sirdar Harbans Singh, Ludhiana District, 25 July 1916, L/MIL/5/826 Pt.6.
16. Kala Singh, 16 Cavalry, Baluchistan Agency, to Sheo Deo Singh, 22 Cavalry, Rouen, 6 Oct. 1916, L/MIL/5/826 Pt.9.
17. Wali Mahomed Khan, 18 Lancers, France to Sadiq Mahomed Khan, Shahpur, 3 April 1917; and Habib Khan, 29 Lancers, France to Habib Khan, Rohtak, 4 April 1917; L/MIL/5/827 Pt.2.
18. *Oxford English Dictionary*, Second Edn, VIII, 158.
19. Dost Mahomed Khan, 18 Lancers, France to Malik Mohamed Umar Hayat Khan, Shahpur, 1 Feb. 1917, L/MIL/5/827 Pt.1.
20. Khan Alam Khan, 37 Lancers, Jullunder to Mir Alam Khan, attached 18 Lancers, France, 12 April 1917, L/MIL/5/827 Pt.3.
21. Mohammad Ali Bey, Deccan Horse, France to trooper in Depot, India, nd., c. May 1915, L/MIL/5/825 Pt.3.
22. Maha Singh, Sialkot Cavalry Bgd, France to his wife, Patiala, 25 Feb. 1916, L/MIL/5/826 Pt.3.
23. Nasarulla Khan, Nowshera, NWFP to Saubat Khan, 36 Jacob's Horse, France, 10 Aug. 1917, L/MIL/5/827 Pt.4.
24. Mother, Dera Ismail Khan to Mahomed Sadiq Khan, 36 Jacob's Horse, France, 19 April 1917, L/MIL/5/827 Pt.3.

25. Heathcote, *Indian Army*, pp. 112–13.
26. French to WO, 22 June 1915, L/MIL/7/17347.
27. *Army Regulations, India, II, 1923*, p. 122.
28. Indianization of the Army, 1938, L/MIL/7/19154.
29. *Army Regulations, India, II, 1923*, pp. 125–6.
30. Abdul Walub Khan, France to Atta Khan, Pertabagh, UP, 9 Jan. 1917, L/MIL/5/827 Pt.1.
31. Nazir Ahmad Mar Khan Bahadur, 18 Lancers to Malik Sekandar Khan, Shahpur, 20 Feb. 1917, L/MIL/5/827 Pt.2.
32. Jai Singh, 6 Cavalry, France to Abdul Karim, Bhatinda, India, 3 Jan. 1917, L/MIL/5/827 Pt.1.
33. Sham Singh, 6 Cavalry, France to Kehar Singh, Ludhiana District, 30 July 1916, L/MIL/5/826 Pt.6.
34. Azim-ud-Din Khan, 20 Deccan Horse, Depot to Abdul Aziz Khan, 20 Deccan Horse, 13 Feb. 1916, L/MIL/5/826 Pt.3. Sheikh Azimuddin, 27 Light Cavalry, Lucknow to Mahomed Hussein, attached 20 Deccan Horse, France, 8 Dec. 1916, L/MIL/5/827 Pt.1.
35. Mir Dost, attached 57 Rifles, Brighton to Subedar at Kohat, 12 July 1915, L/MIL/5/825 Pt.4.
36. Sepoy in hospital, England to Sepoy, 57 Rifles, France, 20 July 1915, L/MIL/5/825 Pt.4.
37. Behari Lal, 6 Lucknow Cavalry Bgd, France to friend in Punjab, 28 March 1915, L/MIL/5/825 Pt.2.
38. Sikh Sowar, 18 Lancers, 28 Oct. 1916, L/MIL/5/826 Pt.9.
39. Gurbaks Singh, 19 Lancers, France to Hoshiarpur, 22 Jan. 1917, L/MIL/5/827 Pt.1.
40. Kartar Singh, 38 CIH, France to Jhaman Singh, Lyallpur District, 8 June 1917, L/MIL/5/827 Pt.3.
41. Gulah Singh, 29 Lancers, France to Mathwar Zemindar, Delhi, 17 Sept. 1917, L/MIL/5/827 Pt.4.
42. Mashuz Ali Khan, Rohtak to Nur Mahomed Khan, 38 CIH, 14 Dec. 1916, L/MIL/5/827 Pt.1.
43. Extracts from Reports of Censor, Indian Mails, France, 15 Jan. 1915, L/MIL/7/17347. Sheikh Mohiuddin, 20 Deccan Horse, France to Pensioned Risaldar-Major, Hyderabad, 27 July, 1916, L/MIL/5/826 Pt.6. Proceedings of Court of Enquiry, 28 April to 7 May 1930, L/MIL/7/7282.
44. Sultan Khan, 36 Jacob's Horse, France to Yar Mahomed Khan, 36 Jacob's Horse, Amballa, Punjab, 10 Jan. 1917, L/MIL/5/827, Pt.1. Mastan Singh, 38 CIH, France to Daya Singh, Ludhiana District, 28 Feb. 1917, L/MIL/5/827 Pt.2.
45. Tak Chand, 6 Cavalry, France to Hariwant Singh, Rohtak, 1 Nov. 1916, L/MIL/5/826 Pt.9.
46. Sios Ram, Depot 6 Jats, Jhansi, UP to Dahri Singh, 2 Lancers, France, 4 Feb. 1917, L/MIL/5/827 Pt.2.
47. Sultan Khan, 18 Lancers, France to Malik Fateh Mahomed Khan Tiwana, Shahpur, 5 June 1917, L/MIL/5/827.
48. See for example, Mir Zada Khan, 127 Baluchis, England to Azim-ud-Din Khan, Karachi, 12 July 1915, L/MIL/5/825 Pt.4.

49. Sultan Khan, 36 Jacob's Horse to his father, Mahomed Khan, Shahpur District, 10 Jan. 1917, L/MIL/5/827 Pt.1.
50. Major in Cavalry, Kashmir to two friends, 41 Dogras, May 1915, L/MIL/5/825 Pt.3.
51. Hehal Singh, 2 Lancers, France to his mother, Rohtak District, 28 Feb. 1917, L/MIL/5/827 Pt.2.
52. Man Singh, 6 Cavalry, France to Sirdar Gurdatt Singh, 6 Cavalry Depot, Sialkot, 9 June 1917, L/MIL/5/827 Pt.3.
53. Proceedings of Court of Enquiry, Dec. 1878, L/MIL/7/7266.
54. Arsalla Khan, Sujliana, Rajputana to Abdul Khan, Sirdar Bahadur, 34 Poona Horse, 11 Oct. 1916, L/MIL/5/826 Pt.9.
55. From his mother, Jhelum, Punjab to Ahmed Khan, 34 Poona Horse, 10 Nov. 1916, L/MIL/5/827 Pt.1.
56. Maj.-Gen. F. M. Richardson, *Fighting Spirit*, quoted in Chibber, 'Regimental System and Esprit de Corps'.
57. Niyam Mir Khan, 129 Infantry to Nur Shah, 127 Infantry, Karachi, 4 April 1915, L/MIL/5/825 Pt.2.
58. Ganga Singh, 34 Poona Horse, France to Gainda Ram, Rohtak District, 11 May 1917, L/MIL/5/827 Pt.3.
59. Havildar, 26 Punjabis to Subedar, 57 Rifles, 11 June 1915, L/MIL/5/825 Pt.4.
60. Mehta Ishar Das, 2 Lancers, France to Mehta Amer Das, Campbellpur, 20 June 1917, L/MIL/5/827 Pt.3.
61. C-in-C India to WO, 25 May 1918, L/MIL/7/18848.
62. GI Defence Dept. to MD IO, 21 Dec. 1938, L/MIL/7/7284.
63. Quoted in Chibber, 'Regimental System and Esprit de Corps'.
64. Masters, *Bugles and a Tiger*, p. 130.
65. 'Stiff' in this context refers to the regimental colours, on which battle honours were sewn. Such embroidery would stiffen the flag of a much-honoured regiment.
66. Masters, *Bugles and a Tiger*, p. 98.
67. James, *Mutiny*, p. 28.
68. Cohen, *Indian Army*, p. 50.
69. Military Events, India, March to June 1921, WO 106/157.
70. Physical Efficiency, Memo by Rawlinson, Nov. 1921, Rawlinson Papers, 5201/33/23.
71. Mason, *Matter of Honour*, pp. 384–5.
72. Barstow, *Sikhs*, p. 185.
73. Memo by Wigram, 15 Dec. 1931, WO 106/5443.
74. Cross to Governor-General, 4 Aug. 1892, L/MIL/7/7052.
75. Report of Eden Commission, 15 Nov. 1879, L/MIL/7/5543.
76. Report of Peel Commission, Appendix 71, Evidence of Lt-Col Durand.
77. Report of Peel Commission, Appendix 61, Evidence of Maj.-Gen. Birch.
78. Report of Peel Commission, Appendix 71, Evidence of Lt-Col Durand.
79. MDM, 7 June 1892, L/MIL/7/7052.
80. Report of Peel Commission, Appendix 71, Evidence of Lt-Col Durand.
81. Lansdown to Cross, 7 June 1892, L/MIL/7/7052.

82. MacMunn, *Armies of India*, p. 141.
83. Cross to Governor-General, 4 Aug. 1892, L/MIL/7/7023.
84. MD to USS, 14 Jan. 1918, L/MIL/7/18327.
85. Shibly, PhD thesis, pp. 359, 391. Memo by Roberts, 23 June 1903, CID 27-D, CAB 6/1.
86. Insubordination of Hindu coys. of 25 Native Infantry, Shwebo, Oct. 1894, L/MIL/7/7273.
87. Eden Commission, Report, 15 Nov. 1879, L/MIL/7/5445.
88. C-in-C to MD, 14 Aug. 1875, Cmd. 1698 (1877).
89. Yate to Montagu, 20 Nov. 1918, L/MIL/7/7280. Eden Commission, Report, 15 Nov. 1879, L/MIL/7/5445.
90. Lansdown to Cross, 7 June 1892, L/MIL/7/7052. And see Barrow to AG, 15 March 1910, L/MIL/7/7156.
91. Shibly, PhD thesis, pp. 361–3, 367, 392.
92. Lansdown to Cross, 7 June 1892, L/MIL/7/7052. GI Advance Despatch, 27 Aug. 1920, L/MIL/7/5483.
93. *Indian Army List, July 1914.*
94. Report by Pressey, 28 Feb. 1910, L/MIL/7/7156. Note by Harris, 17 Feb. 1915.
95. Cross to Governor-General, 4 Aug. 1892, L/MIL/7/7052.
96. Note by Col. Nawab Sir Umar Hayat Khan, Jan. 1932, L/MIL/7/19112.
97. Ridgeway, *Pathans*, p. 44. Morris, *Gurkhas*, p. 143.
98. GI Advance Despatch, 27 Aug. 1920, L/MIL/7/5483.
99. Tirkha Dam, 20 Deccan Horse, Neemuch to Ganga Bishan, 20 Deccan Horse, 8 Dec. 1916; Diwan Chand, 2 Lancers, France to Hakim Dati Dyal, Jhelum, 10 Jan. 1917; Amolak Ram, 2 Lancers, France to Sita Ram, Rawalpindi, 17 Jan. 1917; all in L/MIL/5/827 Pt.1.
100. Heathcote, *Indian Army*, pp. 104–5.
101. Khalil Ullah, 2 Lancers, France to Salim Ullah, UP, 21 April 1917, L/MIL/5/827 Pt.2.
102. Man Chand, 2 Lancers, France to Jemadar, Rohtak, 27 Dec. 1916, L/MIL/5/827 Pt.1.
103. GI to MD, IO, 1 June 1939, L/MIL/7/7284.
104. MDM, 21 Jan. 1932, L/MIL/19112.
105. Kingston to Assistant AG, Allahabad District, 25 Jan. 1897, L/MIL/7/7052.
106. *Indian Army List, July 1914.*
107. Lumsden to Burne, 16 Nov. 1878, Cmd. 1698 (1877).
108. Roberts to Kitchener, 17 April 1903, Kitchener Papers, PRO 30/57/28.
109. Kitchener to Roberts, 28 Oct. and 5 Nov. 1903, Kitchener Papers, PRO 30/57/29.
110. Report by Howell, 1 May 1915, L/MIL/5/825 Pt.2.
111. IO to WO, 28 July 1915, L/MIL/7/17347.
112. Said Badshah, 57 Rifles, France to Hayat Khan, Boulogne Depot, Aug. 1915, L/MIL/5/825 Pt.5.
113. Brief, MPhil thesis, p. 123.
114. Stavely, C-in-C Bombay to Bombay MD, 26 April 1875, Enclosures A and B, Cmd. 1698 (1877). Eden Commission, Report, 15 Nov. 1879, L/MIL/7/5445.

115. C-in-C to MD, 14 Aug. 1875, Cmd. 1698 (1877).
116. Ripon to Hartington, 29 Oct. 1881, L/MIL/7/5445.
117. Dufferin to Cross, 17 Oct. 1885, L/MIL/7/7025.
118. Roberts to Kitchener, 28 Dec. 1904, Kitchener Papers, PRO 30/57/28.
119. Mason, *Matter of Honour*, pp. 341–2. Heathcote, *Indian Army*, p. 76.
120. Military Events, India, Oct. 1921 to Jan. 1922, WO 106/157.
121. GI Advance Despatch, 27 Aug. 1920; SSI to AD, GI 23 Dec. 1921; L/MIL/7/5483. Military Events, India, July to Sept. 1921, WO 106/157.
122. Heathcote, *Indian Army*, p. 77.
123. GI Advance Despatch, 27 Aug. 1920, L/MIL/7/5483.
124. GI Advance Despatch, 27 Aug. 1920, L/MIL/7/5483.
125. Kitchener to Roberts, 10 May 1904, Kitchener Papers, PRO 30/57/29.
126. Memo by Churchill, 22 April 1920, CP.1152, CAB 24/104.
127. Mollo, *Indian Army*, pp. 66, 93, 101, 128.
128. Report of Peel Commission, paras 2414 ff., 3074 and 3248, and Appendix 68, Evidence of Lord Elphinstone.
129. Report of Peel Commission, Appendix 71, Evidence of Lt-Col Durand.
130. Heathcote, *Indian Army*, p. 56.
131. Report of Peel Commission, para. 3073.
132. Mason argues that this tradition grew from a friendship formed between 2 Gurkhas and the British 60 Rifles during the siege of Delhi in 1857; Mason, *Matter of Honour*, pp. 380–1. See also Roberts to Kitchener, 28 Dec. 1904, Kitchener Papers, PRO 30/57/28.
133. Roberts to Cambridge, 10 April 1882, Roberts Papers, 7101/23/97. Roberts to Kitchener, 4 June 1903 and 10 June 1904, PRO 30/57/28. Rawlinson to Clive (Climo?), 25 Nov. 1920, Rawlinson Papers, 5201/33/22. Military Events, India, Jan. to March 1923, WO 33/1036.
134. Minute by Barrow, L/MIL/7/5483.
135. Bingley, *Brahmans*, pp. 41–2.
136. This paragraph and the next draw heavily on the early chapters of Kapur, *Sikh Separatism*.
137. Kapur, *Sikh Separatism*, pp. 12–13.
138. Barstow, *Sikhs*, p. 94.
139. Kapur, *Sikh Separatism*, pp. 26–8.
140. Sarkar, *Modern India*, pp. 74–5. Barstow, *Sikhs*, p. 23.
141. Brief, MPhil thesis, p. 8.
142. Kapur, *Sikh Separatism*, p. 11.
143. Heathcote, *Indian Army*, p. 103.
144. Harnam Singh, 6 Cavalry, France to Gurdial Singh, Ludhiana District, 21 July 1916, L/MIL/5/826 Pt.6.
145. Barstow, *Sikhs*, Appendix 2.
146. Kapur, *Sikh Separatism*, pp. 24–5.
147. Kapur, *Sikh Separatism*, pp. 24, 37–8, 51–2.
148. Barstow, *Sikhs*, pp. 19–20.
149. Barstow, *Sikhs*, pp. 20, 136, 154.
150. MacMunn, *Armies of India*, pp. 134–5.
151. Kapur, *Sikh Separatism*, p. 25. Cunningham, *Dogras*, p. 59
152. Kapur, *Sikh Separatism*, pp. 173–88.

153. Kapur, *Sikh Separatism*, p. 186.
154. For this paragraph see Kapur, *Sikh Separatism*, pp. 68–88.
155. Indian Constitutional Reforms (The Montagu–Chelmsford Report), 22 April 1918, CID 112-D, CAB 6/4.
156. Sarkar, *Modern India*, pp. 140–1.
157. Dewey, 'Some Consequences of Military Expenditure', pp. 108–11, 153.
158. For the Mer background see Memo by Bramley, 19 May 1904, L/MIL/7/7139.
159. Cole, *Rajputana Classes*, Ch.9.
160. Memo by Bramley, 19 May 1904, L/MIL/7/7139.
161. Curzon to SSI, 12 Oct. 1905, L/MIL/7/7139.
162. James, *Mutiny*, p. 210.
163. Principles of Army Administration in India, Memo by Roberts, 1 April 1893, L/MIL/7/7056.
164. SSI to Governor-General, 13 Dec. 1883, L/MIL/7/5445.
165. Holland-Pryor, *Mappillas or Moplahs*, pp. 61–2. Barstow, *Sikhs*, p. 182.
166. Bourne, *Hindustani Musalmans and Musalmans of the Eastern Punjab*.
167. Masters, *Bugles and a Tiger*, pp. 75–6.
168. Wikeley, *Punjabi Musalmans*, Chs. 3 and 4. Holland-Pryor, *Mappillas or Moplahs*, Ch. 3.
169. Cohen, *Indian Army*, p. 53.
170. Cohen, *Indian Army*, p. 53.
171. Memo by Deverell, 26 May 1930, WO 106/5443.
172. Masters, *Bugles and a Tiger*, pp. 173–84. Morris, *Gurkhas*, pp. 45–6.
173. Morris, *Gurkhas*, p. 41. Masters, *Bugles and a Tiger*, pp. 259–60.
174. Memo by Kirkpatrick, 13 July 1916, WO 106/5443.
175. Waryam Singh, attached 1/1 Gurkhas to Phula Singh, Punjab, 29 July 1915, L/MIL/5/825 Pt.4.
176. Report by Howell, 9 Aug. 1915, L/MIL/5/825 Pt.4.
177. Hewett to Strachey, 27 Aug. 1915, L/MIL/5/828 Pt.1.
178. Ghufran Khan, 129 Baluchis, Brighton to Zamen Khan, Karachi, 4 Aug. 1915, L/MIL/5/825 Pt.4.
179. Abdul Karim Khan, 6 Cavalry, France to Fazl Ali Khan, 33 Cavalry, Multan, 22 July 1917, L/MIL/5/827 Pt.4. And see Faiz Alim Khan, attached 20 Deccan Horse, France to *Fauji Akbar*, Simla, 5 Aug. 1917, L/MIL/5/827 Pt.4.
180. Balwant Sikh, Brighton to Ishar Singh, 21 Punjabis, Peshawar, 11 Aug. 1915, L/MIL/5/825 Pt.5.
181. Sikh Dafadar, 18 (?) Lancers to his son, Mohinder Singh, 30 Oct. 1916, L/MIL/5/826 Pt.9.
182. Tawan Singh, 38 CIH, Base Depot, France to Amar Singh, 38 CIH, France, 10 Nov. 1916, L/MIL/5/826 Pt.9.
183. Budh Singh, Sirdar Bahadur, Batala to Amar Singh, CIH, France, 23 Feb. 1917, L/MIL/5/827 Pt.2.
184. Report by Howell, 31 July 1915, L/MIL/5/825 Pt.4. Holderness to Howell, 26 Aug. 1915, L/MIL/7/17347.
185. Holderness to WO, 19 Dec. 1914, L/MIL/7/17347.
186. *Army Regulations, India*, 1923, II, pp. 46, 93.

187. Memo by Wigram, 15 Dec. 1931, WO 106/5443.
188. Memo by Deverell, 26 May 1930, WO 106/5443.
189. Redistribution of Army in India, 1904, CID 58-D, CAB 6/2.
190. Heathcote, *India Army*, p. 111.
191. Dewey, 'Some Consequences of Military Expenditure', p. 128.
192. Proceedings of Court of Enquiry, 28 April to 7 May 1930, L/MIL/7/ 7282.
193. Shambhi Nath, Brighton to friend in Simla, Aug. 1915, L/MIL/5/825 Pt.5.
194. Aitchison to MD, 9 Nov. 1872; C-in-C to MD, 14 Aug. 1875; Cmd. 1698 (1877).
195. Report of Peel Commission, Appendix 69, Evidence of Lt.-Gen. Somerset.
196. Report of Peel Commission, Appendix 65, Evidence of Sir Patrick Grant.
197. MacMunn, *Armies of India*, pp. 211–14.
198. Roberts to Kitchener, 28 Dec. 1904, Kitchener Papers, PRO 30/57/28.
199. C.12(22) Appendix I, 9 Feb. 1922, CAB 23/29.
200 Cohen, *Indian Army*, pp. 50, 114.
201. Mason, *Matter of Honour*, pp. 328, 338, 386, 390–1.
202. Heathcote, *Indian Army*, p. 154. And see James, *Mutiny*, pp. 29–30.
203. Palit, 'Indianisation of the Army's Officer Cadre', p. 56.
204. Greenhut, 'Imperial Reserve', pp. 60–1.
205. There is an interesting discussion of this point in Heathcote, *Indian Army*, pp. 116–24, 128–9, 140–1
206. Roberts to Kitchener, 23 Dec. 1904, Kitchener Papers, PRO 30/57/28.
207. *Army Regulations, India, 1904, II*, pp. 122, 146–7, *1923, II*, p. 19.
208. Masters, *Bugles and a Tiger*, pp. 125, 128. Palit, 'Indianization: A Personal Experience', p. 60.
209. Shibly, PhD thesis, pp. 35–8, 194–5.
210. Report of Peel Commission, Appendix 66, Evidence of Sir Patrick Grant.
211. Stavely to Bombay MD, 26 April 1975; C-in-C to MD, 14 Aug. 1875; Cmd. 1698 (1877). Shibly, PhD thesis, pp. 248–9, 258–9.
212. Minute by Gibbs, 25 June 1875, Cmd. 1698 (1877).
213. Ripon to Hartington, 29 Oct. 1881, L/MIL/7/5445.
214. But the antagonism was mutual. 'If the War Office generals call themselves first rate, then we must be permitted to hold our sides with laughter', remarked General Townshend. (Pride comes before a fall – two years later, at Kut in Mesopotamia, he and his entire force were captured by the Turks.)
215. Kitchener to Roberts, 12 Feb. 1903, Kitchener Papers, PRO 30/57/29.
216. Mason, *Matter of Honour*, p. 413. Greenhut, 'Imperial Reserve', p. 55.
217. Heathcote, *Indian Army*, pp. 141–5.
218. Army in India (Esher) Committee, Report, 1919, L/MIL/7/5523.
219. Foreign and Political Department to SSI, 22 Dec. 1919, CP.362, CAB 24/95.
220. Physical Efficiency, Memo by Rawlinson, Nov. 1921, Rawlinson Papers, 5201/33/23.

221. Masters, *Bugles and a Tiger.*
222. Report by Howell, 4 Sept. 1915, L/MIL/5/825 Pt.5.
223. Abdul Razak, 25 Cavalry, NWFP to Ayab Khan, attached 6 Cavalry, France, 22 June 1917; Chattan Singh to Harman Singh, Gurdaspur, 17 Aug. 1917; L/MIL/5/827 Pt.4.
224. Baghail Singh, attached 2 Lancers, France to Sher Singh, 26 Light Cavalry, Baluchistan, 20 Feb. 1917, L/MIL/5/827 Pt.2.
225. Behari Lal, Supply and Transport Corps, France to Pundit Mathura Pershad, Quetta, 24 July 1917, L/MIL/5/827 Pt.4.
226. Army in India Committee, Report, 3 Nov. 1919, CP. 1109, CAB 24/104.
227. Roberts to Kitchener, 17 June 1909, Kitchener Papers, PRO 30/57/28.
228. Jacobsen, PhD thesis, pp. 306–7.
229. Ali Gaukar Khan, 17 Cavalry, Allahabad to Gul Nawaz Khan, 18 Lancers, France, 21 June 1916, L/MIL/5/826 Pt.6.
230. Saiyid Mahomed Sharaf, 10 Lancers, Loralai to Nur Khan, attached 9 Lancers, France, 15 June 1916; Mahomed Ayab, 11 Lancers, Peshawar to Nadin Ali Khan, attached 9 Hodson's Horse, France, 14 June 1916; Ganda Singh, 18 Lancers, Sialkot to Gul Nawaz Khan, 18 Lancers, France, 18 June 1916; L/MIL/5/826 Pt.6.
231. Taja Singh, 2 Lancers, France to Maj. A. N. Scott, 2 Lancers, India, 21 July 1916, L/MIL/5/826 Pt.6.
232. *Indian Army List, July 1914.*
233. Rawlinson Diary, 19 Feb. 1922, Rawlinson Papers, 5201/33/23.
234. Military Events, India, July to Sept. 1921, WO 106/157.
235. Rawlinson Diary, 23 Feb. 1922, Rawlinson Papers, 5201/33/23.
236. Nuckolls, 'Durbar Incident', passim.
237. Trevithick, 'British Imperial Assemblages at Delhi', pp. 561–70.
238. Rawlinson Diary, 29 Dec. 1902 to 9 Jan. 1903, Rawlinson Papers, 5201/33/11.
239. Prince of Wales to Kitchener, 18 March 1906, Kitchener Papers, PRO 30/57/31.
240. Indian Officer, 6 Cavalry to Regimental Clerk, 28 March 1915, L/MIL/5/825 Pt.2.
241. Hassan Shah, 9 Hodson's Horse, France to Bicha Mal, Jhelum, 13 Feb. 1917, L/MIL/5/827 Pt.2.
242. Iman Khan to Wali Mohamad Khan, 18 Lancers, France, L/MIL/5/827 Pt.3. Chattan Singh, 19 Lancers or 6 Cavalry, France, to Harman Singh, Gurdaspur, 17 Aug. 1917, L/MIL/5/827 Pt.4.
243. Abd-ush-Shukur Beg, 4 Cavalry, France to Editor *Fauji Akhbar*, Simla, 23 March 1915, L/MIL/5/825 Pt.1. Tek Chand, 6 Cavalry, France to Girja Singh, Rohtak, 23 July 1917, L/MIL/5/827 Pt.4.
244. Extracts from Reports of Censor, Indian Mails, France, L/MIL/7/17347.
245. Santa Singh, attached 20 Deccan Horse, France to Indar Singh, Ludhiana District, 22 Dec. 1916, L/MIL/5/827 Pt.1. Taj Mahomed, Bulandshahr to Murtaza Khan, 6 Cavalry, France, 14 Aug. 1917, L/MIL/5/827 Pt.4.
246. Balwant Singh, 19 Lancers, France to Sundar Singh, Amritsar District, 21 Jan. 1917, L/MIL/5/827 Pt.1.

247. Dost Mahomed Khan, 36 Jacob's Horse, France to Sher Khan, Punjab, 18 Feb. 1917, L/MIL/5/827 Pt.2.
248. Alam Khan, 36 Jacob's Horse, France to Abbu Samand Khan, Punjab, 17 Jan. 1917, L/MIL/5/827 Pt.1.
249. Pritam Das, 2 Lancers, France to Bashi Thakar Das, Rawalpindi District, 24 Jan. 1917, L/MIL/5/827 Pt.1.
250. Hashim Khan, NWFP to Sawar Khan, 19 Lancers, France 29 Jan. 1917, L/MIL/5/827 Pt.1.
251. Khizan Singh, 36 Jacob's Horse to his wife, Nabha, India, 6 Feb. 1917, L/MIL/5/827 Pt.1.
252. Fuller, *Troop Morale and Popular Culture*, passim.
253. Sikh sowar, 18 Lancers, France, 28 Oct. 1916, L/MIL/5/826 Pt.9.
254. Censor's Quarterly Report, to end June 1917, L/MIL/5/827 Pt.4.
255. Behari Lal, Supply and Transport Agent, Secunderabad Bgd, France to Daya Shankar, Ajmer, 5 June 1917, L/MIL/5/827 Pt.3.
256. Sant Singh, 2 Lancers, France to Madho Singh, UP, 14 June 1917, L/MIL/5/827 Pt.3.

4 Dissent

1. *Structural Anthropology*, I, p. 13.
2. Sobha Ram, 2 Lancers, France to Kalu Ram, Hissar, 24 Jan. 1917, L/MIL/5/827 Pt.1.
3. C-in-C to MD, 14 Aug. 1875, Cmd. 1698 (1877).
4. IMR, 7th Meeting, 11 Jan. 1922, CAB 16/38/1.
5. Peel Commission, Report, Appendix 62, Evidence of Maj.-Gen. Mansfield.
6. A glance at the methods of discipline confirms this picture of relatively quiescent sepoys. The degrading physical punishments and brutal floggings that were so prominent a feature of the mid-Victorian British Army were much less common in the regiments of India. Peers, 'A Science Without Professors'.
7. Greenhut, 'Imperial Reserve', p. 56.
8. Willcocks to Kitchener, 13 Jan. 1915, Kitchener Papers PRO 30/57/52.
9. Note by Censor, 23 Jan. 1915, L/MIL/7/17347.
10. Memo by Roberts, 28 Jan. 1907, Kitchener Papers, PRO 30/57/28. Military Requirements of Empire (India) Subcommittee, Report, CID 98-D, CAB 6/2.
11. Sher Singh, 20 Deccan Horse to Zemindar Dungar Singh, Delhi, 26 Feb. 1917, L/MIL/5/827 Pt.2.
12. Punjabi Muslim, France to his brother, India, L/MIL/7/17347.
13. Nur Khan, 36 Jacob's Horse, France to his mother, 21 July 1917, L/MIL/5/827.
14. Feroz Khan, Rawalpindi to Mir Khan, 129 Baluchis, L/MIL/5/825 Pt.2.
15. Syed Amir Khan, 6 Cavalry, Mesopotamia to Dafadar Siadan Shah, 9 Hodson's Horse, France, 10 Dec. 1916, L/MIL/5/827 Pt.1.
16. Tamil woman, India to her husband, France, 21 Feb. 1915, L/MIL/7/17347.

17. Report by Howell, 3 July 1915, L/MIL/5/825 Pt.3.
18. Insan Khan, NWFP to Ghandal Khan, attached 19 Lancers, France, 20 June 1917, L/MIL/5/827 Pt.4.
19. Buta Singh, Brighton to Harnam Singh, 23 Pioneers, Aden, 5 Aug. 1915, L/MIL/5/825 Pt.4. Fahir Mohammed, Peshawar to his son, 38 CIH, 14 July 1916, L/MIL/5/826 Pt.6. Atta Mohamed, Patiala State to Abdul Majid Khan, 34 Poona Horse, France, 23 May 1917, L/MIL/5/827 Pt.4.
20. Feroz Khan, 6 Cavalry to his father, Hissar, 23 Sept. 1917, L/MIL/5/827 Pt.5.
21. IMR Subcommittee, 2nd Meeting, 24 Nov. 1921, CAB 16/38/1. Note by FPD, 6 Oct. 1919, CID 116-D, Appendix, CAB 6/4.
22. Vet Daya Ram, 2 Lancers, France to a schoolmaster, Amballa, 7 April 1917, L/MIL/5/827 Pt.2.
23. Greenhut, 'Imperial Reserve', p. 63.
24. Greenhut, 'Imperial Reserve', p. 67.
25. Note by Townshend, nd., L/MIL/7/18848.
26. Greenhut, 'Imperial Reserve', passim.
27. Sikh in hospital to brother, Amritsar, 21 Jan. 1915, L/MIL/7/17347.
28. Nanak Singh, 6 Cavalry, France to Gaur Singh, Jhelum District, 6 March 1917, L/MIL/5/827 Pt.2.
29. Wounded Sikh to friend, India, 29 Jan. 1915, L/MIL/7/17347.
30. Wounded Gurkha to friend, India, 22 Jan. 1915, L/MIL/7/17347.
31. South Indian Muslim, hospital ship to friend, India, 9 Feb. 1915, L/MIL/7/17347.
32. Wounded Rajput to relative, India, 24 Jan. 1915, L/MIL/7/17347.
33. Wounded Sikh to his brother, India, 10 Feb. 1915; wounded Garhwali to parents, India, 17 Feb. 1915, L/MIL/7/17347.
34. Sikh, France to his father, India, 17 March 1915, L/MIL/7/825 Pt.1.
35. Report by Howell, 16 Feb. 1915, L/MIL/5/825 Pt.1.
36. Mason, *Matter of Honour*, p. 424.
37. Report on Indian Troops at Marseille, nd., c. June 1915, L/MIL/7/17347.
38. Wounded Punjabi Muslim to his mother, nd., c. Jan. 1915, L/MIL/7/17347.
39. Greenhut, 'Imperial Reserve', passim.
40. Lumsden to Burne, 16 Nov. 1874, Cmd. 1698 (1877).
41. Despatch to Salisbury (SSI) 3 March 1876, Enclosures 1 and 2, Cmd. 1698 (1877).
42. Ludar Singh, 41 Dogras, Brockenhurst to friend, 56 Regt, Egypt, May 1915, L/MIL/5/825 Pt.3.
43. Sadar Singh, Brockenhurst to friend, Punjab, May 1915, L/MIL/5/825 Pt.3.
44. Pathan sepoy, India to brother, France, 1 Jan. 1915, L/MIL/7/17347. Naik Main Ram, Brighton to Dani Ram, 102 Grenadiers, Muscat, 9 June 1915, L/MIL/5/825 Pt.3.
45. Haq Nawaz, 18 Lancers, France to Rab Nawaz, Shahpur, 4 June 1917, L/MIL/5/827 Pt.3.
46. Greenhut, 'Imperial Reserve', passim.

47. Mangul Singh, Brighton to Bhur Singh, India, 20 July 1915, L/MIL/5/825 Pt.4.
48. HQ 6 Division to OC Bgds, 29 Dec. 1915, L/MIL/7/18848.
49. Sepoy, 107 Pioneers to retired Indian Officer, 128 Pioneers, India, 23 March 1915, L/MIL/5/825 Pt.1.
50. Niamat Ullah, 9 Hodson's Horse, France to Ali Mohamed Khan, 10 Lancers, Baluchistan, 9 July 1916.
51. Sepoy, 37 Dogras, Brighton to sepoy, Marseille, 17 July 1915, L/MIL/5/825 Pt.4.
52. Muslim, UP to sowar, 30 Lancers, 6 June 1915, L/MIL/5/825.
53. Figes, 'The Red Army and Mass Mobilization', p. 202.
54. Greenhut, 'Imperial Reserve', passim.
55. Report by Howell, 27 March 1915, L/MIL/5/825 Pt.1. Isa Khan, 40 Pathans, France to Ali Baz Khan, 46 Punjabis, India, 22 April 1915; Mir Asghar, 58 Rifles to Manza Khan, 55 Rifles, India, 21 April 1915; L/MIL/5/825 Pt.2. Report on Twelve Months' Working of the Indian Mail Censorship, 7 Nov. 1915, L/MIL/7/17347.
56. Viceroy to Kitchener, 29 Jan. 1915, Kitchener Papers, PRO 30/57/69.
57. Havildar Lal Khan, 129 Baluchis, Karachi to Havildar of 129 Regt, 22 April 1915, L/MIL/5/825 Pt.2.
58. CIGS to GOC Mesopotamia, 7 Dec. 1917, L/MIL/7/18848.
59. Havildar 26 Punjabis, Bannu to Subedar, 57 Regt, France, 11 June 1915, L/MIL/5/825 Pt.4.
60. Mason, *Matter of Honour*, p. 425.
61. Note by Viceroy, 15 Feb. 1916; GOC Egypt to WO, July 1918; L/MIL/7/18848.
62. Order No. 1208, 20 Oct. 1918, L/MIL/7/18848.
63. Townshend to GHQ, 14 March 1916, L/MIL/7/18848.
64. Note by Townshend, nd., L/MIL/7/18848.
65. Lakha Singh, 9 Hodson's Horse, France to Sujjan Singh, 4 Bullock Corps, Poona, 17 May 1917, L/MIL/5/827 Pt.3.
66. Abdul Rahim Khan, 36 Jacob's Horse, France to Mir Hassan Khan, Hyderabad, 7 Feb. 1917, L/MIL/5/827 Pt.1.
67. Bhagail Singh, 38 CIH, France to Cham Singh, Lahore District, 22 Jan. 1917, L/MIL/5/827 Pt.1.
68. Natha Singh, Secunderabad Cavalry Bgd. to his mother, Ludhiana District, 11 July 1916, L/MIL/5/826 Pt.6.
69. Sowar, 6 Cavalry, France to Sirdar Ram Rakha Singh, Jalandar, 6 Nov. 1916, L/MIL/5/826 Pt.9. Inayat Ali, Lucknow Stationary Clearing Hospital, France to Bandu Ali, Gurgaon, 10 March 1917; Chief Censor Indian Mails to Military Secretary IO, 18 March 1917; L/MIL/5/827 Pt.2. Hira Singh, 1 Jodhpur Lancers to Sarup Narain Singh, Jodhpur State, 18 June 1917, L/MIL/5/827 Pt.3.
70. Chief Censor Indian Mails to GHQ, 10 May 1917, L/MIL/5/827 Pt.3.
71. Chief Censor Indian Mails to Military Secretary, IO, 6 July 1917, L/MIL/5/827 Pt.3.
72. Jai Singh, 6 Cavalry, France to Shiv Singh, Hoshiarpur District, 14 May 1917, L/MIL/5/827 Pt.3.

73. Wounded Sikh to his brother, Punjab, 18 Jan. 1915; Mahratta Brahman, England to female friend, India, 21 Jan. 1915; Punjabi Muslim, Boulogne to friend, Rawalpindi, 2 Feb. 1915; L/MIL/7/17347.
74. Shah Nawaz, Marseille to sepoy, Allahabad, 1 Sept. 1915, L/MIL/5/825 Pt.5.
75. Jit Singh, 6 Cavalry, France to Sirdar Harwant Singh, Punjab, 10 Aug. 1915, L/MIL/5/825 Pt.5.
76. Pal Singh, 38 CIH, France to Sher Singh, Amritsar, 9 Jan. 1917, L/MIL/5/827 Pt.1.
77. Sher Singh, 20 Deccan Horse to Sirdar Risaldar Prem Singh, Hyderabad, 12 Feb. 1917, L/MIL/5/827 Pt.1. Muliyim Ali Khan, 29 Lancers, France to Wazir Ali Khan, Panipat, 6 March 1917, L/MIL/5/827 Pt.2. Chief Censor Indian Mails to GHQ, 10 May 1917, L/MIL/5/827 Pt.3.
78. Chattar Singh, 38 CIH, France to Sirdar Hira Singh, Jullundur District, 31 Jan. 1917, L/MIL/5/827 Pt.1.
79. Shamsher Ali, 34 Poona Horse, France to Raja Rustam Ali Khan, Gujranwala, 20 April 1917, L/MIL/5/827 Pt.2.
80. Bishan Singh, 6 Cavalry, France to Choudhuri Debi Dyal, Jalandar, 28 Aug. 1917, L/MIL/5/827 Pt.4.
81. Jemadar Abdul Khan, 18 Lancers to Hazrat Sahib Khauka Mujidali, Delhi, 20 Feb. 1917, L/MIL/5/827 Pt.2.
82. Fateh Mohamed Khan, 19 Lancers, France to Pandit Ramsaran Das, Rohtak, 25 Sept. 1917, L/MIL/5/827 Pt.5.
83. Azad Khan, 19 Lancers, France to Zaidullah Khan, 19 Lancers, Sialkot, 14 June 1917, L/MIL/5/827 Pt.3.
84. Sarkar, *Modern India*, pp. 168–9.
85. Brief, MPhil thesis, pp. 107–16.
86. Brief, MPhil thesis, p. 119.
87. Kapur, *Sikh Separatism*, pp. 61–2.
88. For this paragraph see Brief, MPhil thesis, pp. 125–62.
89. Brief, MPhil thesis, pp. 169–76.
90. Brief, MPhil thesis, p. 178.
91. Brief, MPhil thesis, p. 187.
92. Brief, MPhil thesis, p. 180.
93. Memo by Punjab Government, 2 June 1921, IMR 16, CAB 16/38/2. Military Events, India, April to June 1923, WO 33/1036.
94. Beauchamp Duff to Kitchener, 18 Feb. 1916, Kitchener Papers, PRO 30/57/70.
95. Shehab Khan, Meerut Division Signal Coy, France to Abdulla Khan, 112 Infantry, NWFP, 15 March, 1915, L/MIL/7/825 Pt.1. Chief Censor Indian Mails to IO, 17 Jan. 1917, L/MIL/5/827 Pt.1.
96. For example in Rohtak, Hissar and Gurgaon: Christie, *Jats, Gujars and Ahirs*, p. 87.
97. Military Events, India, July to Sept. 1921, WO 106/157.
98. Military Events, India, July to Sept. 1929, WO 33/1194.
99. Military Events, India, Oct. 1921 to Jan. 1922, WO 106/157.
100. Memo by Wigram, 15 Dec. 1931, WO 106/5443.

101. For which see Kapur, *Sikh Separatism*, pp. 49–50.
102. Kapur, *Sikh Separatism*, pp. 49–50.
103. Kitchener to Roberts, 4 July 1907, Kitchener Papers, PRO 30/57/29.
104. Sarkar, *Modern India*, pp. 128–9.
105. Kitchener to Roberts, 3 Oct. 1907, Kitchener Papers, PRO 30/57/29.
106. Brief, MPhil thesis, p. 105.
107. Kapur, *Sikh Separatism*, p. 155.
108. Military Events, India, Jan. to March 1923; and Military Events, India, April to June 1923; WO 33/1036. Barstow, *Sikhs*, pp. 44, 47. Kapur, *Sikh Separatism*, p. 137.
109. Military Events, India, July to Sept. 1923, WO 33/1036.
110. Rawlinson Diary, 12 and 14 Feb. 1922, Rawlinson Papers, 5201/33/23.
111. Kapur, *Sikh Separatism*, p. 92. Military Events, India, Feb. to May 1922; and Oct. to Dec. 1922; WO 106/157.
112. Military Events, India, April to June 1923, WO 33/1036.
113. Barstow, *Sikhs*, passim.
114. Military Events, India, Oct. to Dec. 1922, WO 106/157.
115. Military Events, India, April to June 1923, WO 33/1036.
116. Memo by Deverell, 26 May 1930, WO 106/5443.
117. Lumsden to Secretary to GI, 2 Jan. 1879, L/MIL/7/7266.
118. Roberts to Colley, 10 Dec. 1878, Roberts Papers, 7101/33/101.
119. Roberts to AHQ, 24 Dec. 1878, L/MIL/7/7266. Roberts to AGI, 24 Dec. 1878, Roberts Papers, 7101/33/101. Roberts to Kitchener, 28 Dec. 1904, Kitchener Papers, PRO 30/57/28.
120. James, *Mutiny*, p. 216.
121. Sarkar, *Modern India*, pp. 78–9, 143, 147.
122. Memo by Montagu, 18 Dec. 1919, CP.326, CAB 24/95. Panikkar, *Against Lord and State*, p. 122.
123. GI Telegram, 18 May 1919, CP.437, CAB 24/96.
124. Viceroy, FPD, 9 June 1919, GT.7450, CAB 24/81.
125. Military Events, India, Jan. to March 1923, WO 33/1036 Pt.1.
126. MacMunn, *Armies of India*, p. 216.
127. Jacobsen, PhD thesis, pp. 84–8.
128. Note by Montagu, 30 April 1920, CID 116-D, CAB 6/4.
129. MD to SSI, 7 July 1898, L/MIL/7/7121.
130. Redistribution of the Army in India, 1904, CID 58-D, CAB 2/6.
131. Military Events, India, Oct. 1921 to Jan. 1922, WO 106/157.
132. AD to SSI, 11 June 1919, GT.7461, CAB 24/81.
133. Note by Viceroy, 28 May 1919, GT.7375, CAB 24/80.
134. Note by Montagu, 30 April 1920, CID 119-D, CAB 6/4.
135. FPD to SSI, 22 Dec. 1919, CAB 24/95. AD to SSI, 4 March 1920, CP.800, CAB 24/90.
136. AD to SSI, 20 June 1919, GT.7542, CAB 24/82. Note by Viceroy, 20 July 1919, GT.7854, CAB 24/85.
137. AD to SSI, 9 July 1919, GT.7669, CAB 24/83.
138. AD to SSI, 16 July 1919, GT.7733; CAB 24/84.
139. AD to SSI, 1 July 1919, GT.7608; Note by FPD, 1 July 1919, GT. 7694; CAB 24/83.
140. Note by FD, 6 July 1919, GT.7647, CAB 24/83.

141. Note by FD, 22 June 1919, GT.7553, CAB 24/82. Note by FD, 11 July 1919, GT.7695, CAB 24/83.
142. Note by FD, 26 May 1919, GT.7356, CAB 24/80.
143. FPD to SSI, 24 March 1920, Appendix, CID 116-D, CAB 6/4.
144. Memo on Indian Defence, 28 Jan. 1907, Kitchener Papers, PRO 30/57/78.
145. Viceroy to Kitchener, 16 Feb. 1915, Kitchener Papers, PRO 30/57/69.
146. Memo by CGSI, 5 May 1915, WO 106/5443.
147. Note by Viceroy, 20 May 1919, GT.7302, CAB 24/80. AD to SSI, 1 Oct. 1919, GT.8265, CAB 24/89. Memo by Wigram, 7 April 1931, WO 106/5443.
148. IMR, 8th Meeting, 12 Jan. 1922, CAB 16/38/1. Rawlinson to Clive (?), 17 Jan. 1921, Rawlinson Papers, 5201/33/22. AD to SSI, 27 Sept. 1921; IO to WO, 7 Oct. 1921, IMR.19; CAB 16/38/2. Rawlinson to SSI, 26 Nov. 1921, Rawlinson Papers, 5201/33/23. Report on Indian Military Requirements, June 1922, CID 125-D, CAB 6/4.
149. Jacobsen, PhD thesis, pp. 364–5.
150. Peel Commission Report, para. 858.
151. Peel Commission Report, pp. 9, 13. Mason, *Matter of Honour*, pp. 318–19.
152. Porter, *Lion's Share*, pp. 238–9. Mason, *Matter of Honour*, 411.
153. Viceroy to Kitchener, 16 Feb. 1915, Kitchener Papers, PRO 30/57/69. Brief, MPhil thesis, p. 115.
154. Viceroy to Kitchener, 5 March 1915, PRO 30/57/69.
155. Rawlinson Diary, 10 July 1921, Rawlinson Papers 5201/33/23.
156. Report on Indian Military Requirements, 22 June 1922, CID 125-D, CAB 6/4.
157. The British Element in Internal Security Troops, Appendix E to Annex 2, CID 198-D, CAB 6/6.
158. Bond, *British Military Policy*, p. 111.
159. Jacobsen, PhD thesis, p. 130.
160. James, *Mutiny*, Ch.1.
161. Mutinous Behaviour of 14 Bombay Infantry, Bareilly, Sept. 1897, L/MIL/7/7294.
162. Insubordination of 17 Bombay Infantry, Bhuj, Nov. 1897, L/MIL/7/7275.
163. Birdwood to Seton, 10 June 1930, L/MIL/7/7280.
164. Guha, *Elementary Aspects of Peasant Insurgency in Colonial India*, Ch.6.
165. Insubordination of 17 Bombay Infantry, Bhuj, Nov. 1897, L/MIL/7/7275.
166. Memo by Lake, 6 Sept. 1915, WO 106/5443.
167. Kapur, *Sikh Separatism*, pp. 53–68.
168. Barstow, *Sikhs*, pp. 29–32.
169. James, *Mutiny*, pp. 218–19.
170. GOC Mhow Division to AG, 27 Oct. 1887, L/MIL/7/7269.
171. Peel Commission Report, Appendix 58, Evidence of Lord Clyde, and Appendix 65, Evidence of Sir Patrick Grant.
172. *Army Regulations, India, II, 1904*, p. 73.
173. AD to SSI, 28 July 1910, L/MIL/7/7156.
174. Cowans to AG, 2 Feb. 1910, L/MIL/7/7156.

175. Insubordination of Hindu Companies of 25 Madras Infantry, Oct. 1894, L/MIL/7/7273.
176. Insubordination of 3 Gurkha Regiment, Almorah, April 1886, L/MIL/7/7267. Insubordination of Rangur Sepoys of 17 Bengal Infantry, 1894, L/MIL/7/7271. Insubordination of Hindu Companies of 25 Madras Infantry, Shwebo, Oct. 1894, L/MIL/7/7273. Mutinous Behaviour of 14 Bombay Infantry, Bareilly, Sept. 1897, L/MIL/7/7274. Insubordination of 27 Madras Infantry, Sept. 1897, L/MIL/7/7276. Insubordination of 17 Bombay Infantry, Bhuj, Nov. 1897, L/MIL/7/7275. Conduct of 3 Brahmans in Mesopotamia, L/MIL/7/7277.
177. Mason, *Matter of Honour*, p. 313.
178. Ridgway, Pathans, p. 272.
179. Iman Khan, Sargodha, Punjab to Sirdar Wali Mahomed Khan, 18 Lancers, France, 16 Jan. 1917, L/MIL/5/827 Pt.1. Fatteh Mohamed Khan, 9 Hodson's Horse, France to Hayat Mahomed Khan, Depot, 15 Lancers, Sialkot, 8 May 1917, L/MIL/5/827 Pt.3. Viceroy to Kitchener, 5 March 1915, Kitchener Papers, PRO 30/57/69.
180. Pathan, France to friend in India, 17 Feb. 1915; Pathan, Hong Kong, to sepoy, 57 Rifles, France; L/MIL/5/825 Pt.1.
181. Report by Howell, 3 April 1915, L/MIL/5/825 Pt.1.
182. AD to SSI, 6 March 1920, CP.596, CAB 24/97.
183. Morris, *Gurkhas*, pp. 163–4.
184. 18 Infantry in China, L/MIL/7/7278.
185. Court of Enquiry, 28 April to 7 May 1930, L/MIL/7/7282. Cohen, *Indian Army*, 96–8. Brown, *Gandhi and Civil Disobedience*, p. 110.
186. Question by Brockway, 30 June 1930; Hon. Sec. Catholic Crusade to SSFA, 13 Aug. 1930; L/MIL/7/7280. Amalgamated Society of Woodworkers to Hoare, 12 July 1934; ILA Question, 19 July 1934; L/MIL/7/7282.
187. Sinha repeats this error: 'The Indian Army', p. 179.
188. Court of Enquiry, 28 April to 7 May 1930, L/MIL/7/7282.
189. Mason, *Matter of Honour*, pp. 451–3.
190. Guha and Gadgil, 'State Forestry and Social Conflict in British India' and Guha, *Unquiet Woods*.
191. Court of Enquiry, 28 April to 7 May 1930, L/MIL/7/7282.
192. Insubordination of Hindu Companies of 25 Madras Infantry, Shwebo, Oct. 1894, L/MIL/7/7273.
193. Viceroy to Kitchener, 29 Jan. 1915, Kitchener Papers, PRO 30/57/69.
194. Notes from War Diary, D Force, L/MIL/7/18327.
195. Memo by Kirkpatrick, 6 May 1916, WO 106/5543.
196. Roberts to Cambridge, 29 June 1883, Roberts Papers, 7101/23/97.
197. Insubordination of 3 Gurkha Regiment, Almorah, April 1886, L/MIL/7/7267.
198. Insubordination of 17 Bombay Infantry, Bhuj, Nov. 1897, L/MIL/7/7275.
199. Insubordination of Rangur Sepoys of 17 Bengal Infantry, 1894, L/MIL/7/7271. Insubordination of Hill Brahmans attached to Depot of 38 Dogras, L/MIL/7/7280.
200. Conduct of 3 Brahman Regiment in Mesopotamia, L/MIL/7/7277.

201. Mutinous Behaviour of 14 Bombay Infantry, Bareilly, Sept. 1897, L/MIL/7/7294.
202. Insubordination of 3 Gurkha Regiment, Almorah, April 1886, L/MIL/7/7267. Italics mine.
203. Memo by Lake, 6 Sept. 1915, WO 106/5443.
204. Insubordination of 3 Gurkha Regiment, Almorah, April 1886, L/MIL/7/7267.
205. Notes from War Diary, D Force, L/MIL/7/18327.
206. Insubordination of 17 Bombay Infantry, Bhuj, Nov. 1897, L/MIL/7/7275.
207. Insubordination of 17 Bombay Infantry, Bhuj, Nov. 1897, L/MIL/7/7275.
208. Insubordination of Rangur Sepoys of 17 Bengal Infantry, 1894, L/MIL/7/7271.
209. Mutinous Behaviour of 14 Bombay Infantry, Bareilly, Sept. 1897, L/MIL/7/7294. Insubordination of 3 Gurkha Regiment, Almorah, April 1886, L/MIL/7/7267.
210. Insubordination of 3 Gurkha Regiment, Almorah, April 1886, L/MIL/7/7263.
211. Insubordination of Hindu Companies of 25 Madras Infantry, Shwebo, Oct. 1894, L/MIL/7/7273.
212. Insubordination of Rangur Sepoys of 17 Bengal Infantry, 1894, L/MIL/7/7271.
213. Insubordination of 3 Gurkha Regiment, Almorah, April 1886, L/MIL/7/7267.
214. Insubordination of Hindu Companies of 25 Madras Infantry, Shwebo, L/MIL/7/7273.
215. Insubordination of 3 Gurkha Regiment, Almorah, April 1886, L/MIL/7/7267.
216. Insubordination of 17 Bombay Infantry, Bhuj, Nov. 1897, L/MIL/7/7275.
217. Insubordination of 3 Gurkha Regiment, Almorah, April 1886, L/MIL/7/7267.
218. Memo by Kirkpatrick, 6 May 1916, WO 106/5443.
219. AD to IO, 24 Feb. 1916, L/MIL/7/18327.
220. Memo by SSI, 29 April 1930, CP.133 (30), CAB 24/211.
221. Insubordination of Hill Brahmans attached to Depot of 38 Dogras, L/MIL/7/7280.
222. They were soldiers of the 130 Baluchis, executed after their mutiny at Rangoon in 1915: Viceroy to Kitchener, 29 Jan. 1915, Kitchener Papers, PRO 30/57/69.
223. AD to SSI, 1 March 1916, L/MIL/7/18327. Telegram from Viceroy, 17 June 1930, L/MIL/7/7282.
224. Conduct of 3 Brahmans in Mesopotamia, L/MIL/7/7277.
225. Mutinous Behaviour of 14 Bombay Infantry, Bareilly, Sept. 1897.
226. Fateh Ullah, Lyallpur to Fateh Ahmed, No.5 Base Supply Depot, France, 30 June 1916, L/MIL/5/826 Pt.6.
227. SSI to AD, 28 Feb. 1917, L/MIL/7/18327.
228. AD to SSI, 16 May 1917, L/MIL/7/18327.
229. King George V to SSI, 19 May 1917, L/MIL/7/18327.

230. Safdar Ali Khan, 15 Lancers attached 27 Lancers, Sangor, UP to Jalib Hussain Khan, 18 Lancers, France, 17 July 1917, L/MIL/5/827 Pt.4.
231. Roberts to Cambridge, 11 June 1886, Roberts Papers, 7101/33/100.
232. Insubordination of 3 Gurkha Regiment, Almorah, April 1886, L/MIL/7/7267. Insubordination of Hindu Companies of 25 Madras Infantry, Shwebo, Oct. 1894, L/MIL/7/7273.
233. Insubordination of 27 Madras Infantry, Sept. 1897, L/MIL/7/7276.
234. 18 Infantry in China, L/MIL/7/7278. Mutinous Behaviour of 14 Bombay Infantry, Bareilly, Sept. 1897, L/MIL/7/7294.
235. Shooting Affray in 49 Bengalis, L/MIL/7/7279.
236. Court of Enquiry, 24 Nov. 1938, Evidence of Subedar Mirza Khan.
237. Coleridge to AG, 12 Dec. 1938, L/MIL/7/7284.
238. Court of Enquiry, 24 Nov. 1938, Evidence of Maj. Walsh, L/MIL/7/7284.
239. CGS to SSI, 22 Dec. 1938, L/MIL/7/7284. See *Army Regulations, India, 1923, II*, 47 for official guidance on correct action in such circumstances.
240. GI to MD, IO, 21 Dec. 1938, L/MIL/7/7284.
241. Mason, *Matter of Honour*, pp. 426–7.
242. Mutiny of 5 Light Infantry, Singapore, L/MIL/17/19/48.
243. James, *Mutiny*, pp. 223–7.
244. Mutiny of 5 Light Infantry, Singapore, pp. 197–210, L/MIL/17/19/48.
245. Mutiny of 5 Light Infantry, Singapore, pp. 7–8, L/MIL/17/19/48.
246. Mutiny of 5 Light Infantry, Singapore, pp. 8–10, L/MIL/17/19/48.
247. Mutiny of 5 Light Infantry, Singapore, pp. 145, L/MIL/17/19/48.
248. Mutiny of 5 Light Infantry, Singapore, pp. 29, L/MIL/17/19/48.
249. Mutiny of 5 Light Infantry, Singapore, pp. 367–9, 367, L/MIL/17/19/48.
250. Mutiny of 5 Light Infantry, Singapore, pp. 220, L/MIL/17/19/48.

5   Indian Officers and Indianization

1. Jacobsen, PhD thesis, p. 223.
2. Shibly, PhD thesis, p. 268.
3. Rawlinson Diary, 31 July 1921, Rawlinson Papers, 5201/33/23.
4. For a recent discussion of this argument, see the debate between the author and Anna-Maria Misra in *Contemporary Record*.
5. C-in-C to MD, 14 Aug. 1875, Cmd. 1698 (1877) LXII.
6. Army Regulations, India, II (1904), 73.
7. For a failure of this 'safety-valve' function, during the Ghadr conspiracy, see Memo by Lake (CGSI), 6 Sept. 1915, WO 106/5443.
8. Peel Commission, Report, Cmd. 2515 (1859), paras 1280 ff.
9. Peel Commission, Report, Cmd. 2515 (1859), Appendix 65.
10. Peel Commission, Report, Cmd. 2515 (1859), para. 493.
11. Peel Commission, Report, Cmd. 2515 (1859), paras 985–6.
12. This dilemma of imperial policy is neatly summed up in Indian Constitutional Reforms (Montagu–Chelmsford Report), 22 April 1918, CID 112-D, CAB 6/4.

13. Peers, 'Contours of the Garrison State', p. 16.
14. Cohen, *Indian Army*, p. 8.
15. Cohen, *Indian Army*, pp. 42–3.
16. Cohen, *Indian Army*, pp. 62–3.
17. Peel Commission, Report, Cmd. 2515 (1858), Appendix 2.
18. Cohen, *Indian Army*, p. 63.
19. Peel Commission, Report, Cmd. 2515 (1858), paras 702–3.
20. Peel Commission, Report, Cmd. 2515 (1859), paras 240–9.
21. Peel Commission, Report, Cmd. 2515 (1859), paras 416–30, 516, 595–604.
22. Peel Commission, Report, Cmd. 2515 (1859), para. 989.
23. Peel Commission, Report, Cmd. 2515 (1859), para. 1054.
24. Peel Commission, Report, Cmd. 2515 (1859), paras 1838 ff.
25. Peel Commission, Report, Cmd. 2515 (1859), para. 997.
26. Peel Commission, Report, Cmd. 2515 (1859), para. 686.
27. Peel Commission, Report, Cmd. 2515 (1859), Appendix 58.
28. Heathcote, *Indian Army*, p. 38.
29. Shibly, PhD thesis, p. 120. Mason, *Matter of Honour*, pp. 320–5.
30. Shibly, PhD thesis, pp. 117–18.
31. Peel Commission, Report, Cmd. 2515 (1859), Evidence of Capt. G.F.S. Browne and Appendix 71, Evidence of Lt-Col H.M. Durand.
32. Peel Commission, Report, Cmd. 2515 (1859), Evidence of Sir G. Clerk and of Maj.-Gen. Low.
33. Peel Commission, Report, Cmd. 2515 (1859), Appendix 6, Memo by Maj. W. L. Merewether on Constitution of Scinde Horse, 25 Aug. 1858. C-in-C to MD, 14 Aug. 1875, Cmd.1698 (1877) LXII.
34. Peel Commission, Report, Cmd. 2515 (1859), paras 2372 ff., and Evidence of Maj. Merewether.
35. Shibly, PhD thesis, pp. 121–7.
36. Peel Commission, Report, Cmd. 2515 (1859), paras 469, 721–37 and 1451.
37. Peel Commission, Report, Cmd. 2515 (1859), Evidence of J. F. Thomas.
38. Peel Commission, Report, Cmd. 2515 (1859), Evidence of Col. Belcher.
39. Peel Commission, Report, Cmd. 2515 (1859), Evidence of Lt-Col Harington and paras 1430–1.
40. Peel Commission, Report, Cmd. 2515 (1859) Evidence of Capt. G. F. S. Browne.
41. Mason, *Matter of Honour*, pp. 326–8.
42. Shibly, PhD thesis, pp. 138–45.
43. Shibly, PhD thesis, pp. 159–60.
44. Shibly, PhD thesis, pp. 149, 171, 176.
45. Shibly, PhD thesis, pp. 228–9.
46. Shibly, PhD thesis, pp. 179, 183, 187.
47. C-in-C to MD, 14 Aug. 1875; Salisbury to GG, 10 Aug. 1876; Cmd. 1698 (1877) LXII. Eden Commission, Report, 15 Nov. 1879, L/MIL/7/5445. Mason, *Matter of Honour*, pp. 38–9, 377–9.
48. Eden Commission, Report, 15 Nov. 1879, L/MIL/7/5445.
49. Aitchison to MD, 9 Nov. 1872, Cmd. 1698 (1877) LXII.
50. Salisbury to GG, 10 Aug. 1876, Cmd. 1698 (1877) LXII.

51. C-in-C to MD, 14 Aug. 1875, Cmd. 1698 (1877) LXII.
52. AG Madras to MD, 3 April 1875, Cmd. 1698 (1877) LXII.
53. Eden Commission, Report, 15 Nov. 1879, L/MIL/7/5445.
54. Despatch to Salisbury, Enclosures 1 and 2, 3 March 1876, Cmd. 1698 (1877) LXII.
55. Shibly, PhD thesis, p. 176.
56. Eden Commission, Report, 15 Nov. 1879, L/MIL/7/5445.
57. Heathcote, *Indian Army*, pp. 52–5.
58. SSI to GI MD, 2 Feb 1882, L/MIL/7/5445. Shibly, PhD thesis, p. 188.
59. Sarkar, *Modern India*, p. 90.
60. Sarkar, *Modern India*, pp. 19–20.
61. Shibly, PhD thesis, pp. 381–2.
62. Roberts to Churchill, 26 June 1885, Roberts Papers, 7101/23/97. For Roberts' own views see Memo by Kitchener, 9 Sept. 1908, L/MIL/17/5/1746 and Mason, *Matter of Honour*, pp. 347–8.
63. Memo by Brownlow, 24 May 1885, L/MIL/17/5/1719.
64. Cohen, *Indian Army*, pp. 63–4.
65. Rawlinson Diary, 1 Jan. 1903, Rawlinson Papers, 5201/33/11.
66. Memo by Kitchener, 9 Sept. 1908, L/MIL/17/5/1746.
67. Memo by Kitchener, 9 Sept. 1908, L/MIL/17/5/1746.
68. Roberts to Cambridge, 4 Jan. 1886, Roberts Papers, 7101/33/100.
69. Defence of India, July 1903, CAB 6/1, CID 27-D.
70. *Indian Army List, July 1914*. Heathcote, *Indian Army*, pp. 52–5.
71. Mason, *Matter of Honour*, pp. 343–4.
72. Greenhut, 'Imperial Reserve', p. 66.
73. French to WO, 22 June 1915, L/MIL/7/17347.
74. Greenhut, 'Imperial Reserve', pp. 66–7.
75. Sarkar, *Modern India*, pp. 150–2.
76. Cohen, *Indian Army*, pp. 91–3.
77. Indian Constitutional Reforms (Montagu–Chelmsford Report), 22 April 1918, CID 112-D, CAB 6/4.
78. Cohen, *Indian Army*, pp. 73–5.
79. Heathcote, *Indian Army*, pp. 146–7.
80. Jacobsen, PhD thesis, p. 225.
81. Indian Constitutional Reforms (Montagu–Chelmsford Report), 22 April 1918, CID 112-D, CAB 6/4.
82. Memo by Montagu, 29 May 1918, CID 112-D, CAB 6/4.
83. Sarkar, *Modern India*, pp. 165–8.
84. Brown, *Gandhi and Civil Disobedience*, p. 2.
85. Jacobsen, PhD thesis, pp. 193–6.
86. Jacobsen, PhD thesis, pp. 190–207.
87. Report on Indian Constitutional Reforms (Montagu–Chelmsford Report), 22 April 1918, CID 112-D, CAB 6/4.
88. AD to SSI, 30 March 1921, CID 122-D, CAB 6/4.
89. Report on Indian Constitutional Reforms (Montagu–Chelmsford Report), 22 April 1918, CID 112-D, CAB 6/4.
90. Report on Indian Military Requirements, 22 June 1922, CID 125-D, CAB 6/4. 158th CID, 5 July 1922, CAB 2/3.

91. Heathcote, *Indian Army*, p. 78.
92. Rawlinson to WO, 7 July 1922, CID 127-D, CAB 6/4.
93. Report on Indian Military Requirements, 22 June 1922, CID 125-D, CAB 6/4.
94. 13th IMR, 19 June 1922, CAB 16/38/1.
95. 160th CID, 21 July 1922, CAB 2/3.
96. Telegram from Viceroy, 28 June 1922, CID 126-D, CAB 6/4. Memo by Birkenhead, May 1927, CID 154-D, CAB 6/5.
97. 158th CID, 5 July 1922, CAB 2/3.
98. Report of the Auxiliary and Territorial Forces Committee, 1925, Appendix 1(a), CID 154-D, CAB 6/5.
99. Memo by Birkenhead, May 1927, CID 154-D, CAB 6/5.
100. AD to SSI, 24 June 1926, CID 154-D, CAB 6/5.
101. Indian Territorial Force, Sept. 1929, CID 173-D, CAB 6/5.
102. Indian Territorial Force, Sept. 1929, CID 173-D, CAB 6/5.
103. Military Events, India, Oct. 1920 to Feb. 1921, WO 106/157.
104. AD to SSI, 30 March 1921, CID 122-D, CAB 6/4.
105. Cohen, *Indian Army*, pp. 78–9.
106. Jacobsen, PhD thesis, pp. 226–7.
107. Cohen, *Indian Army*, p. 80.
108. Wikeley, *Punjabi Musalmans*, p. 8. Arnold, '"Criminal Tribes"and "Martial Races"', p. 10.
109. Jacobsen, PhD thesis, pp. 240–2.
110. Heathcote, *Indian Army*, pp. 145–6.
111. 8th IMR, 12 Jan. 1922, CAB 16/38/1. MacMunn, *Armies of India*, p. 130.
112. Rawlinson Diary, 31 July 1921, Rawlinson Papers, 5201/33/23. Mason, *Matter of Honour*, p. 454.
113. MacMunn, *Armies of India*, pp. 148, 153.
114. India: An Appreciation, 21 July 1921, Rawlinson Papers, 5201/33/22.
115. Military Events, India, Jan. to March 1926, WO 33/1121 Pt.1.
116. Jacobsen, PhD thesis, pp. 240–3.
117. Minute by Cobb, 14 Sept. 1921, IMR.17, CAB 16/38/2.
118. Report on Indian Military Requirements, June 1922, CID 125-D, CAB 6/4.
119. Cohen, *Indian Army*, pp. 82–3.
120. Rawlinson Diary, 28 May 1921, Rawlinson Papers, 5201/33/23. Rawlinson to Willie, 8 June 1921; India: An Appreciation, 21 July 1921; both in Rawlinson Papers, 5201/33/22.
121. AD to SSI, 6 Feb. 1922, IMR.62, CAB 16/38/2.
122. Rawlinson Diary, 9 June 1921 and 10 March 1922, Rawlinson Papers, 5201/33/23.
123. India: An Appreciation, 21 July 1921, Rawlinson Papers, 5201/33/22.
124. Jacobsen, PhD thesis, pp. 227–9.
125. Rawlinson Diary, 2 July 1921, Rawlinson Papers, 5201/33/23.
126. Memo by Cobb, 14 Sept. 1921, IMR.17, CAB 16/38/2.
127. Memo by Cobb, 14 Sept. 1921, IMR.17, CAB 16/38/2. Cohen, *Indian Army*, pp. 83–4.
128. Report on Indian Military Requirements, June 1922, CID 125-D, CAB 6/4.

129. Report of Committee appointed by C-in-C India, 6 Jan. 1922, CAB 16/38/2.
130. Viceroy to SSI, 24 Jan. 1922, IMR.59, CAB 16/38/2.
131. Viceroy to SSI, 11 Jan. 1922, IMR.42, CAB 16/38/2.
132. Report of Committee appointed by C-in-C India, 6 Jan. 1922, IMR.80, CAB 16/38/2.
133. Viceroy to SSI, 24 Jan. 1922, IMR.59, CAB 16/38/2.
134. Jacobsen, PhD thesis, p. 229.
135. Conference of Ministers, 9 Feb. 1922, Appendix 1, C.12(22), CAB 23/29.
136. 9th IMR, 10 Feb. 1922, CAB 16/38/1.
137. Viceroy to SSI, 18 Feb. 1922, IMR.73, CAB 16/32/2.
138. Conference of Ministers, 10 Feb. 1922, Appendix 3, C.12(22), CAB 23/29.
139. SSI to Viceroy, 14 Feb. 1922, IMR.71, CAB 16/38/2.
140. 9th IMR, 10 Feb. 1922, CAB 16/38/1.
141. Conference of Ministers, 9 Feb. 1922, Appendix 1, C.12(22), CAB 23/29.
142. SSI to Viceroy, 22 Feb. 1922, IMR.75, CAB 16/38/2.
143. SSI to Viceroy, 13 Jan. 1922, IMR.48 and 14 Feb. 1922, IMR.72, CAB 16/38/2.
144. Conference of Ministers, 9 Feb. 1922, C.12(22), CAB 23/29.
145. Report on Indian Military Requirements, June 1922, CID 125-D, CAB 6/4. Jacobsen, PhD thesis, pp. 229–30.
146. Conference of Ministers, 9 Feb. 1922, Appendix 1, C.12(22), CAB 23/29.
147. Conference of Ministers, 9 Feb. 1922, Appendix 1, C.12(22), CAB 23/29.
148. 10th IMR, 21 Feb. 1922, CAB 16/38/1.
149. Report on Indian Military Requirements, 22 June 1922, CID 125-D, CAB 6/4.
150. Rawlinson Diary, 28 July 1922, Rawlinson Paper, 5201/33/23.
151. Viceroy to SSI, 18 Feb. 1922, IMR.73, CAB 16/38/2.
152. C.3(23)5, 26 Jan. 1923, CAB 23/45. Mason, *Matter of Honour*, pp. 454–6.
153. The units were 7 and 16 Light Cavalry, 2/1 Punjab Regt, 5/5 Mahratta LI, 1/7 Rajput Regt, 1/14 Punjab Regt, 4/19 Hyderabad Regt, and 2/1 Madras Pioneers.
154. Jacobsen, PhD thesis, pp. 230–2.
155. Lecture delivered to Imperial Defence College, 15 Oct. 1931, L/MIL/5/857.
156. Report on Indian Military Requirements, Amended, Jan. 1923, CID 130-D, CAB 6/4. Indian Sandhurst Committee, Report, Nov. 1926, CID 155-D, CAB 6/5.
157. Rawlinson Diary, 18 Feb. 1923, Rawlinson Papers, 5201/33/23.
158. Rawlinson Diary, 12 March 1923, Rawlinson Papers, 5201/33/23.
159. Military Events, India, Jan. to March 1923, WO 33/1036 Pt.1.
160. Heathcote, *Indian Army*, p. 145.
161. *Daily Telegraph,* cutting from May 1923, L/MIL/7/19057.

162. AD to SSI, 7 July 1923, L/MIL/7/19057.
163. 8th IMR, 12 Jan. 1922, CAB 16/38/1. Report on Indian Military Requirements, 22 June 1922, CID 125-D, CAB 6/4.
164. Rawlinson Diary, 11 May 1922, Rawlinson Papers, 5201/33/23.
165. Memo by Cobb, 14 Sept. 1921, IMR.17, CAB 16/38/2.
166. Cohen, *Indian Army*, p. 84.
167. Indian Sandhurst Committee Report, Nov. 1926, CID 155-D, CAB 6/5. Mason, *Matter of Honour*, pp. 462–3.
168. *Prince of Wales' Royal Indian Military College, Dehra Dun.*
169. *Prince of Wales' Royal Indian Military College, Magazine,* Feb. 1933.
170. GS to Brown, 17 Dec. 1927, Brown Papers, L/MIL/5/847.
171. Askew to Brown, 2 May 1928, L/MIL/5/847.
172. Scott to Brown, 25 Aug. 1927, L/MIL/5/847.
173. Askew to AD, 26 May 1928, L/MIL/5/847.
174. Jacobsen, PhD thesis, pp. 234–5.
175. Indian Sandhurst Committee, Report, Nov. 1926, CID 155-D, CAB 6/5.
176. Mason to MD, 16 Aug. 1934, L/MIL/7/19145.
177. Confidential Reports, 1923–28, L/MIL/9/319.
178. Cohen, *Indian Army*, p. 119.
179. GI to MD, 23 Dec. 1927, Enclosure, L/MIL/7/19088.
180. For details of which see Heathcote, *Indian Army*, p. 146.
181. Indian Constitutional Reforms (Montagu–Chelmsford Report), 22 April 1918, CID 112-D, CAB 6/4.
182. Cohen, *Indian Army*, pp. 121–2.
183. Palit, 'Indianisation: A Personal Experience', pp. 55, 60.
184. AD to SSI, 16 May 1925, CID 150-D, Appendix B, CAB 6/5.
185. Indian Sandhurst Committee, Report, Nov. 1926, CID 155-D, CAB 6/5.
186. Indian Sandhurst Committee, Report, Nov. 1926, CID 155-D, CAB 6/5.
187. Cohen, *Indian Army*, pp. 107–8.
188. Report of CID Subcommittee on Indianisation, Dec. 1927, CID 159-D, CAB 6/5.
189. AD to SSI, 18 July 1927, CID 159-D, Appendix C, CAB 6/5.
190. Jacobsen, PhD thesis, pp. 237–8.
191. AD to SSI, 13 Oct. 1927, CID 159-D, CAB 6/5.
192. C.57(27).14, CAB 23/55. Jacobsen, PhD thesis, pp. 238–9.
193. Subcomittee on Indianisation, 1st Mtg. 28 Nov. 1927, CAB 16/78.
194. Report of Subcommittee on Indianisation, Dec. 1927, CID 159-D, CAB 6/5.
195. Jacobsen, PhD thesis, pp. 238–9.
196. Report of Subcommittee on Indianisation, Dec. 1927, CID 159-D, CAB 6/5.
197. Indian Sandhurst Committee, Report, Nov. 1926, Appendix III, CID 155-D, CAB 6/5.
198. Diary, 31 July 1921, Rawlinson Papers, 5201/33/23.
199. Subcommittee on Indianisation, 1st Mtg. 28 Nov. 1927, CAB 16/78. Jacobsen, PhD thesis, p. 242.

200. Report of Subcommittee on Indianisation, Dec. 1927, CID 159-D, CAB 6/5.
201. Indianisation of the Indian Army, 22 Dec. 1927, CID 160-D, CAB 6/5.
202. Lecture Delivered to IDC, 15 Oct. 1931, Brown Papers, L/MIL/5/857.
203. Note by Birkenhead, 24 Jan. 1928, CID 161-D, CAB 6/5. 232nd CID, 26 Jan. 1928, and 234th CID, 29 March 1928; CAB 2/5.
204. Lecture Delivered at IDC, 15 Oct. 1931, Brown Papers, L/MIL/5/857.
205. MD Memo, 21 Jan. 1932, L/MIL/7/19112.
206. Extract from GI Despatch on Proposals for Constitutional Reform, 20 Sept. 1931, CID 178-D, Appendix 1, CAB 6/5. Indianisation of the Army, 1938, L/MIL/7/19154. Jacobsen, PhD thesis, pp. 233–4.
207. Review of Indianisation, Pt.I, nd., L/MIL/7/19156.
208. Review of Indianisation, Pt.II, nd., L/MIL/7/19156. Palit, 'Indianisation: A Personal Experience'. Heathcote, *Indian Army*, p. 147. He misdates the change.
209. Lecture Delivered to IDC, 15 Oct. 1931, Brown Papers, L/MIL/5/857.
210. Palit, 'Indianisation of the Army's Officer Cadre', p. 57.
211. Progress to 31 Dec. 1934, L/MIL/7/19154.
212. Jacobsen, PhD thesis, pp. 244–8.
213. Jacobsen, PhD thesis, pp. 249–52.
214. C.6(31).1, 14 Jan. 1931, CAB 23/66.
215. Review of Indianisation, Pt.I, nd., L/MIL/7/19156.
216. Indian Round Table Conference, Report of Subcommittee VII (Defence), Feb. 1931, CID 177-D, CAB 6/5.
217. Indianisation, June 1931, CID 178-D, CAB 6/5.
218. GI to SSI, April 1931, CID 178-D, CAB 6/5.
219. Note by Hankey, 17 Nov. 1931, CID 179-D, CAB 6/5.
220. Review of Indianisation, Pt.I, nd., L/MIL/7/19156.
221. Indianisation, June 1931, CID 178-D, CAB 6/5.
222. IA Order, 26 March 1932, L/MIL/7/19112.
223. MD Memo, 30 Dec. 1931, L/MIL/7/19112. The units selected were 3 Light Cavalry, 5/2 Punjab Regt, 5/6 Rajputana Rifles, 5/8 Punjab Regt, 5/10 Baluch Regt, 5/11 Sikh Regt, 4/12 Frontier Force Regt and 6/13 Frontier Force Rifles. Memo by AG, 15 April 1932, L/MIL/7/19113.
224. Note by Chair of Defence of India Subcommittee, 22 Dec. 1931, CID 180-D, CAB 6/5.
225. Memo on Indianisation, nd., Brown Papers, L/MIL/5/844.
226. Lecture Delivered at IDC, 15 Oct. 1931, Brown Papers, L/MIL/5/827.
227. Indianisation, June 1931, CID 178-D, CAB 6/5.
228. Mason, *Matter of Honour*, pp. 463–4.
229. Cohen, *Indian Army*, p. 108.
230. Quality of Cadets at IMA, 19 March 1934, L/MIL/7/19145.
231. Council of State, Debates, 4 March 1937, L/MIL/7/19145.
232. Indianisation: A Summary of Progress to Date, 31 Dec. 1934, L/MIL/7/19154.
233. Macdonald to Brown, 1 March 1934, L/MIL/7/19145.
234. Minute from PD, 7 Sept. 1934, L/MIL/7/19145.
235. Heathcote, *Indian Army*, pp. 79–80.

236. Mason to MD IO, 18 Feb. 1936, L/MIL/7/19145.
237. Mason to MD IO, 16 Aug 1934, L/MIL/7/19145.
238. Macdonald to Brown, 1 March 1934, L/MIL/7/19145.
239. Mason to MD, 16 Aug. 1934, L/MIL/7/19145.
240. Jacob, PhD thesis, p. 259.
241. Palit, 'Indianisation: A Personal Experience', pp. 59–60.
242. Legislative Assembly Debates, 1 Dec. 1938, L/MIL/7/19156.
243. MD Memo, 20 Oct. 1938, L/MIL/7/19156.
244. Legislative Assembly Debates, 2 Sept. 1938, L/MIL/7/19156.
245. Legislative Assembly Debates, 14 March 1939, L/MIL/7/19156.
246. Memo by Turnbull, 13 Nov. 1940, L/MIL/7/19156.
247. Memo by Akbar, nd., c. Oct. 1940, L/MIL/7/19156.
248. Legislative Assembly Debates, 8 Sept. 1939, L/MIL/7/19156.
249. Cohen, *Indian Army*, pp. 135–6.
250. Auchinleck to Amery, 12 Oct. 1940, L/MIL/7/19156.

6 Military Power and Colonial Rule

1. Kitchener Papers, PRO 30/57/28.
2. L/MIL/7/7280.
3. Memo by SSI, 24 Dec. 1920, CID 118-D, CAB 6/4. AD to SSI, 6 Feb. 1922, IMR.63, CAB 16/38/2. Sarkar, *Modern India*, p. 16.
4. Memo by Hailey, 12 July 1921, IMR.14, CAB 16/38/2.
5. Dewey, 'Some Consequences of Military Expenditure in Colonial India', p. 139.
6. Cohen, *Indian Army*, pp. 23–31. Memo on Constitutional Position of Defence Forces in India, CID 198-D, CAB 6/6.
7. Jacobsen, PhD thesis, pp. 196–7.
8. Bond, *British Military Policy*, pp. 111–12.
9. Indian Military Expenditure, 7 Dec. 1920, CID 117-D, CAB 6/4.
10. Note by Hoare, 21 Oct. 1932, CID 183-D, CAB 6/6. GI to IO, 9 Feb. 1938, CID 198-D, CAB 6/6.
11. Rawlinson Diary, 8 Jan. 1922, Rawlinson Papers 5201/33/23. Note by FD, IO, 11 April 1922, IMR.88, CAB 16/38/2.
12. Jacobsen, PhD thesis, pp. 164ff.
13. Peers, 'Contours of the Garrison State', pp. 23–4.
14. Roberts to Cambridge, 13 July 1882, Roberts Papers 7101/23/97. Note by MD, IO, Jan. 1922, IMR.53, CAB 16/38/2.
15. IMR 2nd Mtg., 24 Nov. 1921, CAB 16/38/1.
16. Rawlinson Diary, 2 July 1921, Rawlinson Papers 5201/33/23.
17. Rawlinson to Wilson, 16 Nov. 1920, Rawlinson Papers 5201/33/22.
18. Arnold, *Police Power and Colonial Rule*, p. 13.
19. Eden Commission, Report, 15 Nov. 1879, L/MIL/7/5445.
20. Redistribution of Army in India, 1904, CID 58-D, CAB 6/2.
21. Arnold, *Police Power and Colonial Rule*, p. vii.
22. Arnold, *Police Power and Colonial Rule*, pp. 15, 101.
23. Viceroy to SSI, 10 Feb. 1922, IMR.77, CAB 16/38/2.
24. Indian Military Requirements, Report, June 1922, CID 125-D, CAB 6/4.

25. GS Internal Security Instructions, India, 1933, WO 33/1493.
26. Arnold, *Police Power and Colonial Rule*, pp. 50–61.
27. Arnold, 'Recruitment in the Madras Constabulary', p. 32.
28. Arnold, 'Recruitment in the Madras Constabulary', pp. 14–15.
29. Memo by O'Donnell, 24 Nov. 1921, L/MIL/7/5496.
30. AD to SSI, 27 Nov. 1921, IMR.26, CAB 16/38/2.
31. The British Element in Internal Security Troops, Appendix E to Annex 2, nd., c. early 1938, CID 198-D, CAB 6/6.
32. Arnold, 'Recruitment in the Madras Constabulary', pp. 8–9.
33. Arnold, *Police Power and Colonial Rule*, pp. 25–7.
34. Redistribution of Army in India, 1904, CID 58-D, CAB 6/2.
35. IMR.14, 1921, CAB 16/38/2.
36. Indian Military Requirements Committee, 7th Mtg., 11 Jan. 1922, CAB 16/38/1.
37. Indian Military Requirements, Report, 22 June 1922, CID 125-D, CAB 6/4.
38. Redistribution of Army in India, 1904, CID 58-D, CAB 6/2.
39. Arnold, *Police Power and Colonial Rule*, p. 72.
40. Minute by Ellis, 10 April 1875, Cmd. 1698 (1877) LXII.
41. Arnold, 'The Armed Police', p. 123.
42. Arnold, *Police Power and Colonial Rule*, p. 62; 'Recruitment in the Madras Constabulary', pp. 34–6.
43. Kitchener to Roberts, 24 March 1903, Kitchener Papers, PRO 30/57/29.
44. Redistribution of Army in India, 1904, CID 58-D, CAB 6/2.
45. *Daily Telegraph*, 21 April 1928, Liddell Hart Papers, 10/1928/45.
46. Jacobsen, PhD thesis, pp. 54–5.
47. Jacobsen, PhD thesis, p. 58.
48. Indian Military Requirements, 7th Mtg., 11 Jan. 1922, CAB 16/38/1.
49. The British Element in Internal Security Troops, Appendix E to Annex 2, nd., c. early 1938, CID 198-D, CAB 6/6.
50. GI MD to Government of Madras, 29 March 1904, CID 58-D, CAB 6/2.
51. See for just two examples, Curzon to SSI, 2 Nov. 1899, L/MIL/7/12029 and Note by Hoare, 21 Oct. 1932, CID 183-D, CAB 6/6.
52. Peers, 'Contours of the Garrison State', pp. 2–3, 21.
53. Governor of Bombay to GI MD, 29 June 1875, Cmd. 1698 (1877) LXII.
54. Cohen, *Indian Army*, p. 94.
55. GS Internal Security Instructions, India, 1937, WO 33/1493.
56. Minute by Risley, 19 April 1910, L/MIL/7/7174.
57. Note by Roberts, 8 June 1891, CID 7-D, CAB 6/1.
58. GI MD to SSI 24 June 1881, L/MIL/7/5445.
59. Mason, *Matter of Honour*, pp. 327, 375–7.
60. Eden Commission, Report, 15 Nov. 1879, L/MIL/7/5445.
61. Minute by Johnson, 4 March 1880, L/MIL/7/5445.
62. Sarkar, *Modern India*, p. 30.
63. Hurd, 'Railways', p. 737.
64. Redistribution of the Army in India, 1904, CID 58-D, CAB 6/2.
65. Eden Commission, Report, 15 Nov. 1879, L/MIL/7/5445.
66. GS Strategical Study of India and Burma, 1911, WO 106/154.

67. Report on Indian Military Requirements, June 1922, CID 125-D, CAB 6/4.
68. GS Internal Security Instructions, India, 1937, WO 33/1493.
69. Report of Committee on Military Defence of India, 24 Dec. 1901, CAB 6/1.
70. Heathcote, *Indian Army*, p. 74.
71. GS Internal Security Instructions, India, 1937, WO 33/1493.
72. Redistribution of Army in India, 1904, CID 58-D, CAB 6/2.
73. For this paragraph see Heathcote, *Indian Army*, pp. 70–4.
74. Eden Commission, Report, 15 Nov. 1879, L/MIL/7/5445.
75. Principles of Army Administration in India, Memo by Roberts, 1 April 1893, L/MIL/7/7056.
76. Heathcote, *Indian Army*, p. 75.
77. Auxiliary and Territorial Forces Committee, Report, 1925, CID 150-D, CAB 6/5.
78. 158th CID, 5 July 1922, CAB 2/3.
79. IMR 7th Mtg., 11 Jan. 1922, CAB 16/38/1. Indian Military Requirements, Report, 22 June 1922, CID 125-D, CAB 6/4.
80. Military Events, India, Jan. to March 1927, WO 33/1121 Pt.5.
81. GS Strategical Study of India and Burma, 1911, WO 106/154.
82. GS Strategical Study of India and Burma, 1911, WO 106/154.
83. Roberts to Seely, 2 April 1884, Roberts Papers 7101/23/97. Note by Roberts, 8 June 1891, CID 7-D, CAB 6/1.
84. IO Memo on Defence of India, 10 March 1903, CID 6-D, CAB 6/1.
85. Possibility of an Invasion of India by Russia, Note by Roberts, 16 May 1904, CID 51-D, CAB 6/2.
86. Roberts to Kitchener, 21 May 1903, PRO 30/57/28.
87. IMR 7th Mtg., 11 Jan. 1922, CAB 16/38/1. Peers, 'Contours of the Garrison State', p. 9.
88. Nicholson Committee on Defence of India, Second Report, 30 Dec. 1902, CAB 6/1.
89. Peers, 'Contours of the Garrison State', p. 10.
90. Nicholson Committee, Report, 24 Dec. 1901, L/MIL/7/5459.
91. GS Internal Security Instructions, India, 1937, WO 33/1493.
92. Defence of India, 23 May 1903, CID 18-D and 13 June 1903, CID 22-D; both in CAB 6/1. Defence of India, Memo by Mullaly, 30 June 1904, CID 64-D, CAB 6/2. Animal Transport in Afghanistan, 18 Feb. 1907, CID 97-D, CAB 6/3.
93. Note by CID Secretary, 20 May 1906, CID 93-D, CAB 6/3.
94. Memo on Defence of India, 10 March 1903, CID 6-D, CAB 6/1.
95. Note on Threatened Invasions of India, 3 April 1905, CID 100-D, CAB 6/3.
96. General Kouropatkin's Scheme for a Russian Advance Upon India, c. June 1886, CID 7-D, CAB 6/1.
97. Note by Roberts, 22 May 1885, CID 7-D, CAB 6/1.
98. Roberts to Cambridge, 9 March 1882, Roberts Papers, 7101/23/97. Note by Roberts, 8 June 1891, CID 7-D, CAB 6/1.
99. Report of Subcommittee on Military Requirements of Empire (India), May 1907, CID 98-D, CAB 6/3.

100. Indian Defence, Memo by Roberts, 28 Jan. 1907, Kitchener Papers, PRO 30/57/28.
101. Note by JMG, 28 June 1906, CID 93-D, CAB 6/3.
102. Indian Defence, Memo by Roberts, 28 Jan. 1907, Kitchener Papers, PRO 30/57/28.
103. Roberts to Marvin, 6 June 1885, Roberts Papers, 7101/23/97. Note by Roberts, 8 June 1891, CID 7-D, CAB 6/1. Principles of Army Administration in India, Memo by Roberts, 1 April 1893, L/MIL/7/7056. GS Memo, 20 July 1905, CID 82-D, CAB 6/3.
104. Indian Defence, Memo by Roberts, Kitchener Papers, 28 Jan. 1907, PRO 30/57/28.
105. GI MD to Government of Madras, 29 March 1904, CID 58-D, CAB 6/2.
106. Ripon to Hartington, 28 Feb. 1881, L/MIL/7/5445.
107. Ripon to Hartington, 29 Oct. 1881, L/MIL/7/5445. Note by Roberts, 8 June 1891, CID 7-D, CAB 6/1. Principles of Army Administration in India, Memo by Roberts, 1 April 1893, L/MIL/7/7056.
108. Memo by Nicholson, 19 Nov. 1906, Kitchener Papers, PRO 30/57/30.
109. For a survey of organizational reform in general see IMR.4, Annexure 1, 3 Feb. 1921, CAB 16/38/2.
110. Kitchener to Roberts, 12 Jan. 1903, Kitchener Papers, PRO 30/57/29.
111. Redistribution of Army in India, 1904, CID 58-D, CAB 6/2.
112. Committee on Defence of India, Report, 24 Dec. 1901, CAB 6/1.
113. GI MD to Government of Madras, 29 March 1904, CID 58-D, CAB 6/2.
114. Kitchener to Roberts, 26 Nov. 1903, Kitchener Papers, PRO 30/57/29. Memo by Mullaly, 30 June 1904, CID 64-D, CAB 6/2.
115. Birdwood to Derby, 21 July 1916, Kitchener Papers, PRO 30/57/71. Heathcote, *Indian Army,* pp. 30–1.
116. Kitchener to Roberts, 27 July 1903, Kitchener Papers, PRO 30/57/29. GI MD to Government of Madras, 29 March 1904, CID 58-D, CAB 6/2.
117. GI MD to Government of Bombay, 29 March 1904, CID 58-D, CAB 6/2.
118. GI FD to GG Rajputana, 29 March 1904, CID 58-D, CAB 6/2.
119. Establishment of the Army in India, 10 March 1905, CID 90-D, CAB 6/3.
120. Redistribution of Army in India, 1904, CID 58-D, CAB 6/2.
121. GI MD to Government of Bombay, 29 March 1904, CID 58-D, CAB 6/2.
122. 85th CID, 9 March 1906, and 111th CID, 26 May 1911; both in CAB 2/2.
123. 215th CID, 22 July 1926, CAB 2/4. Subcommittee on Defence of India, Report, 19 Dec. 1927, CID 158-D, CAB 6/5.
124. Humphreys to SSFA, 21 Feb. 1927, CID 152-D, CAB 6/5. Jacobsen, PhD thesis, pp. 155–6.
125. Jacobsen, PhD thesis, pp. 326–333.
126. Bond, *British Military Policy,* pp. 107–11.
127. Indian Military Requirements, Report, 22 June 1922, CID 125-D, CAB 6/4. Army in India, Report, June 1931, CID 138-D, CAB 6/6. Note by

Hoare, 21 Oct. 1932, CID 183-D, CAB 6/6. GS Internal Security Instructions, India, 1937, WO 33/1493.

128. Bond, *British Military Policy*, p. 111.
129. Jacobsen, PhD thesis, pp. 145–7.
130. HM Minister Kabul to SSFA, 21 Feb. 1927, CID 152-D, CAB 6/5.
131. Army in India, Report, June 1931, CID 138-D, CAB 6/6. Jacobsen, PhD thesis, p. 161.
132. Note by MD, Jan. 1922, IMR.53, CAB 16/38/2. The British Element in Internal Security Troops, nd., c. early 1938, CID 198-D, CAB 6/6.
133. 147th CID, 21 Oct. 1921, CAB 2/3. Conference of Ministers, Appendix 1, 9 Feb. 1922, C.12(22), CAB 23/29. IMR 9th Mtg., 10 Feb. 1922, CAB 16/38/1.
134. Army in India, Report, June 1931, CID 138-D, CAB 6/6. GS Internal Security Instructions, India, 1937, WO 33/1493.
135. IMR.14, 1921, CAB 16/38/2.
136. GS Internal Security Instructions, India, 1937, WO 33/1493.
137. Heathcote, *Indian Army*, pp. 32–3.
138. Jacobsen, PhD thesis, pp. 49–60.
139. Bond, *British Military Policy*, p. 105.
140. Memo by Jacob, 10 May 1921, CAB 16/38/2.
141. Indian Military Requirements, Report, 22 June 1922, CID 125-D, CAB 6/4.
142. Army in India, Report, June 1931, CID 138-D, CAB 6/6.
143. Jacobsen, PhD thesis, pp. 52, 57.
144. IMR 7th Mtg., 11 Jan. 1922, CAB 16/38/1.
145. Military Events, India, Oct. 1920 to Feb. 1921, WO 106/157. Holland-Pryor, *Mappillas or Moplahs*, pp. 11, 14.
146. IMR.14, 1921, CAB 16/38/2.
147. Memo by Roberts on Indian Defence, 28 Jan. 1907, Kitchener Papers, PRO 30/57/28.
148. Pownall Subcommittee on Defence of India, Report, 12 May 1938, CID 198-D, CAB 6/6.
149. The British Element in Internal Security Troops, Appendix E to Annex 2, nd., c. early 1938, CID 198-D, CAB 6/6.
150. GI to IO, 9 Feb. 1938, CID 198-D, CAB 6/6.
151. Bond, *British Military Policy*, p. 125.
152. Military Events, India, Oct. 1920 to Feb. 1921, WO 106/157. IMR.14, 1921, CAB 16/38/2.
153. Rawlinson Diary, 10 July 1921, Rawlinson Papers, 5201/33/23.
154. Jacobsen, PhD thesis, p. 43.
155. IMR.14, 1921, CAB 16/38/2.
156. Army in India, 24 Nov. 1932, CID 183-D, CAB 6/6.
157. Viceroy to SSI, 4 Aug. 1921, IMR.15 and SSI to Viceroy, 14 Feb. 1922, IMR.72; both in CAB 16/38/2. Indian Military Requirements, Report, 22 June 1922, CID 125-D, CAB 6/4. 258th CID, 6 April 1933, CAB 2/5.
158. Rawlinson Diary, 21 Dec. 1920, Rawlinson Papers, 5201/33/23.
159. GS Strategical Study of India and Burma, 1911, WO 106/154.

160. Indian Military Requirements, Report, 22 June 1922, CID 125-D, CAB 6/4.
161. Redistribution of Army in India, 1904, CID 58-D, CAB 6/2.
162. Government of Madras to GI AD, 18 Jan. and 3 July 1922, L/MIL/7/5496.
163. IMR 7th Mtg., 11 Jan. 1922, CAB 16/38/1.
164. IMR.16, II, 1921, CAB 16/38/2.
165. Note by SSI, 25 Nov. 1921, IMR.20, CAB 16/38/2. Rawlinson to GI AD, 6 Oct. 1922, L/MIL/17/12/33.
166. Barrow to AG, 15 March 1910, L/MIL/7/7156.
167. IMR 7th Mtg., 11 Jan. 1922, CAB 16/38/1. Indian Army, Report, 1931, CID 138-D, CAB 6/6.
168. Jacobsen, PhD thesis, p. 52. Cohen, *Indian Army*, p. 129.
169. See, for example, Ram Kishan Thapa, Brighton to Naik Kishan Sing Kanwar, 1/4 Gurkha Rifles, July 1915, L/MIL/5/825/Pt.4.
170. Roberts to Kitchener, 13 April and 14 July 1904, Kitchener Papers, 30/57/28. Rawlinson to SSI, 26 Nov. 1921, Rawlinson Papers, 5201/33/23. AD to SSI, 27 Nov. 1921, IMR.26, CAB 16/38/2.
171. Court of Enquiry, Proceedings, 28 April to 7 May 1930, L/MIL/7/7282.
172. IMR 8th Mtg., 12 June 1922, CAB 16/38/1. Legislative Assembly Debates, 14 March 1939, L/MIL/7/19156.
173. Jacobsen, PhD thesis, p. 209.
174. Arnold, *Police Power and Colonial Rule*, pp. 119–20.
175. Government of Madras to GI AD, 10 March 1922, L/MIL/7/5496.
176. GI AD to Government of Madras, 9 June 1922, L/MIL/7/5496.
177. Minute by Hames, 22 March 1880, L/MIL/7/5445.
178. GS Internal Security Instructions, India, 1937, WO 33/1493. And see IMR 7th Mtg., 11 Jan. 1922, CAB 16/38/1.
179. GS Internal Security Instructions, India, 1937, WO 33/1493. And see Government of Madras to GI AD, 20 Dec. 1920 and GI AD to Government of Madras, 21 Nov. 1921; both in L/MIL/7/5496.
180. Military Events, India, July to Sept. 1926, WO 33/1121 Pt.3.
181. Government of Madras to GI AD, 3 July 1922, L/MIL/7/5496.
182. Minute by Risley, 19 April 1910, L/MIL/7/7174.
183. Redistribution of Army in India, 1904, CID 58-D, CAB 6/2.
184. *Army Regulations, India, 1904*, II, p. 76.
185. Kapur, *Sikh Separatism*, p. 145; Holland-Pryor, *Mappillas or Moplahs*, pp. 13–14.
186. GS Strategical Survey of India and Burma, 1911, WO 106/154.
187. Kapur, *Sikh Separatism*, pp. 76, 87–8, 92–3, 140–6.
188. GS Strategical Survey of India and Burma, 1911, WO 106/154.
189. IMR 7th Mtg., 11 Jan. 1922, CAB 16/38/1.
190. Eden Commission, Report, 15 Nov. 1879, L/MIL/7/5445.
191. Redistribution of Army in India, 1904, CID 58-D, CAB 6/2.
192. Panikkar, *Against Lord and State*, pp. 85–6.
193. GS Strategical Study of India and Burma, 1911, WO 106/154.
194. Military Events, India, July to Sept. 1923, WO 33/1036 Pt.3.
195. Government of Bengal to GI MD, 16 Jan. 1930, CP.100(30), CAB 24/210.

196. Roberts to Goschen, 7 June 1884 and to Lytton, 27 June 1884, Roberts Papers, 7101/23/97.
197. *Army Regulations, India, 1904*, II, p. 76.
198. Townshend, *Britain's Civil Wars*, pp. 134–7.
199. Indian Disorders Committee, Conclusions, CP.1240, CAB 24/105.
200. C.39(20)1, 7 July 1920, CAB 23/22.
201. Harcourt Butler to Kitchener, 20 Oct. 1915, Kitchener Papers, PRO 30/57/70.
202. Mason, *Matter of Honour*, p. 448; Townshend, *Britain's Civil Wars*, pp. 138–9.
203. Gilbert, *Churchill*, IV, pp. 401–9.
204. Indian Disorders Committee, Conclusions, 6 May 1919, CP.1240, CAB 24/105. Arnold, 'The Armed Police', pp. 105–6.
205. Arnold, *Police Power and Colonial Rule*, pp. 191–2.
206. Court of Enquiry, Proceedings, 28 April to 7 May 1930, L/MIL/7/7280.
207. HD to all Local Governments, 24 Nov. 1921, L/MIL/7/5496. GS Internal Security Instructions, India, 1937, WO 33/1493.
208. Arnold, 'The Armed Police', pp. 106–7; *Police Power and Colonial Rule*, p. 173.
209. AD to SSI, 13 March 1922, Rawlinson Papers, 5201/33/23.
210. Military Events, India, Feb. to May 1922, WO 106/157.
211. Court of Enquiry, Proceedings, 28 April to 7 May 1930, L/MIL/7/7282. The same was also true for the imposition of martial law: see GS Internal Security Instructions, India, 1937, WO 33/1493.
212. Kathleen Gough, cited in Sarkar, *Modern India*, p. 44.
213. Arnold, 'Dacoity and Rural Crime', pp. 140–52.
214. White to AG, 6 July 1889, L/MIL/7/9182.
215. Freitag, 'Crime in Colonial North India', pp. 229–33.
216. Guha and Gadgil, 'State Forestry and Social Conflict in British India'; Arnold, 'Dacoity and Rural Crime'; Sarkar, *Modern India*, pp. 49–50, 154–5.
217. QMG to MD, 16 Aug. 1880, L/MIL/7/14687.
218. Sarkar, *Modern India*, pp. 45–6.
219. Sarkar, *Modern India*, p. 240.
220. Memo by IO, 25 June 1935, CID 191-D, CAB 6/6.
221. Sarkar, *Modern India*, p. 15.
222. Panikkar, *Against Lord and State*; Arnold, *Police Power and Colonial Rule*, pp. 105–7.
223. Parliamentary Debates, 17 Feb. 1887, L/MIL/7/9181.
224. For the units engaged see QMG to MD, 19 Aug. 1880, L/MIL/7/14687.
225. Military Events, India, July to Sept. 1921, WO 106/157. Note by SSI, IMR.20, 25 Nov. 1921, CAB 16/38/2.
226. Rawlinson to GI AD, 6 Oct. 1922, L/MIL/17/12/33.
227. Arnold, *Police Power and Colonial Rule*, pp. 98–9.
228. QMG to MD, 19 Aug. 1880, L/MIL/7/14687.
229. Panikkar, *Against Lord and State*, pp. 96, 139–41; Arnold, 'The Armed Police', pp. 109–13.

230. Arnold, 'The Armed Police', pp. 113–14.
231. Guha and Gadgil, 'State Forestry and Social Conflict', pp. 151–5.
232. See, for example, some of the opening remarks in Naga Hills Expedition, 1879–80, L/MIL/7/13464.
233. Military Events, India, July to Sept. 1921 and Oct. to Jan. 1922, WO 106/157. Rawlinson to GI AD, 6 Oct. 1922, L/MIL/17/12/33.
234. Military Events, India, July to Sept. 1921, WO 106/157.
235. QMG to MD, 19 Aug. 1880, L/MIL/7/14687.
236. Naga Hills Expedition, 1879–80, L/MIL/7/13464. Rawlinson to GI AD, 6 Oct. 1922, L/MIL/17/12/33.
237. Sarkar, 'The Conditions and Nature of Subaltern Militancy', pp. 311–12.
238. Sarkar, *Modern India*, p. 45.
239. Townshend, *Britain's Civil Wars*, p. 144.
240. QMG to MD, 19 Aug. 1880, L/MIL/7/14687.
241. Nation to AGI, 6 May 1880, L/MIL/7/13464.
242. White to AGI, 6 July 1889, L/MIL/7/9187.
243. Terrorism in India, WO 106/5445.
244. Townshend, *Britain's Civil Wars*, pp. 130–1. Sarkar, *Modern India*, pp. 124–5.
245. Sarkar, *Modern India*, p. 144.
246. Sarkar, *Modern India*, pp. 251–3.
247. Sarkar, 'Conditions and Nature of Subaltern Militancy', pp. 271–2.
248. Sarkar, *Modern India*, p. 125.
249. Townshend, *Britain's Civil Wars*, pp. 132–3.
250. Most of the next two paragraphs comes from Townshend, *Britain's Civil Wars*, pp. 148–9.
251. Jacobsen, PhD thesis, p. 48.
252. Terrorism in India, WO 106/5445.
253. Sarkar, *Modern India*, pp. 28, 39–40.
254. For this paragraph see Sarkar, *Modern India*, pp. 61–3, 118–19, 171–5, 199.
255. GS Strategical Study of India and Burma, 1911, WO 106/154.
256. Military Events, India, July to Sept. 1929, WO 33/1194 Pt.3.
257. Government of Madras to GI AD, 20 Dec. 1920, L/MIL/7/5496.
258. Sarkar, *Modern India*, p. 218.
259. Sarkar, *Modern India*, p. 134.
260. GS Internal Security Instructions, India, 1937, WO 33/1493.
261. Sarkar, *Modern India*, pp. 59–60, 80, 121.
262. Das, *Communal Riots in Bengal*.
263. See, for example, District Magistrate, Benares to Commissioner, Benares Division, 23 Feb. 1931, L/P&J/7/75. Hashmi, 'The Communalisation of Class Struggle', p. 195.
264. Military Events, India, Jan. to March 1929, WO 33/1194 Pt.1. And see Military Events, India, April to June 1929, WO 33/1194 Pt.2.
265. See, for example, Military Events, India, June to Sept. 1927, WO 33/1121; and Report on Communal Outbreak at Cawnpore, May 1931, L/P&J/7/75.
266. Sarkar, *Modern India*, pp. 20–1.
267. Military Events, India, Oct. to Dec. 1927, WO 33/1121, Pt.8.
268. Commission of Enquiry into Communal Outbreak at Cawnpore, Report, May 1931, L/P&J/7/75.

269. Military Events, India, Oct. to Dec. 1923, WO 33/1036 Pt.4.
270. Memo by IO, 25 June 1935, CID 191-D, CAB 6/6.
271. See, for example, Military Events, India, April to June 1927, WO 33/1121 Pt.6; and District Magistrate, Benares to Commissioner, Benares Division, 23 Feb. 1931, L/P&J/7/75.
272. Military Events, India, Jan. to March 1929, WO 33/1194 Pt.1.
273. GS Strategical Study of India and Burma, 1911, WO 106/154.
274. Owen, 'More than a Transfer of Power', p. 437.
275. Brown, *Gandhi and Civil Disobedience*, p. 18.
276. Gopalankutty, 'Mobilization Against the State', pp. 468–70; Brown, *Gandhi and Civil Disobedience*, pp. 90–113; Sarkar, *Modern India*, pp. 178–9, 196–200, 205, 207.
277. Brown, *Gandhi and Civil Disobedience*, p. 148.
278. Sarkar, *Modern India*, pp. 111–25.
279. Brown, *Gandhi and Civil Disobedience*, pp. 123–32.
280. Brown, *Gandhi and Civil Disobedience*, pp. 289–93, 360–1, 380, 387.
281. For this paragraph see Brown, *Gandhi and Civil Disobedience*, pp. 14–17, 80–3, 88–9, 116–17.
282. Sarkar, *Modern India*, pp. 197–80.
283. GI HD to SSI, 10 Jan. 1930, CP.18(30), CAB 24/209.
284. Arnold, *Police Power and Colonial Rule*, p. 193.
285. Brown, *Gandhi and Civil Disobedience*, p. 152.
286. O'Donnell to all local Governments, 24 Nov. 1921, L/MIL/7/5496. Military Events, India, to May 1922, WO 106/157.
287. Townshend, *Britain's Civil Wars*, pp. 130, 141.
288. Sarkar, *Modern India*, p. 220.
289. Sarkar, 'Conditions and Nature of Subaltern Militancy', p. 271.
290. Military Events, India, Feb. to May 1922, WO 106/157. Sarkar, *Modern India*, pp. 224–6.
291. Brown, *Gandhi and Civil Disobedience*, pp. 386–8.
292. Memo by Deverell, 26 May 1930, WO 106/5443.
293. Brown, *Gandhi and Civil Disobedience*, p. 88.
294. Brown, *Gandhi and Civil Disobedience*, pp. 113–14.
295. Rawlinson Diary, 28 Dec. 1921, Rawlinson Papers, 5201/33/23.
296. Sarkar, 'Conditions and Nature of Subaltern Militancy', pp. 310–11. And see Amin's excellent essay, 'Gandhi as Mahatma'.
297. GI HD to SSI, 10 Jan. 1930, CP.18(30), CAB 24/209.
298. Brown, *Gandhi and Civil Disobedience*, p. 272.
299. Brown, *Gandhi and Civil Disobedience*, pp. 215–16.
300. Army in India, Report, 1931, CID 138-D, CAB 6/6. Arnold, 'The Armed Police', p. 116.
301. Brown, *Gandhi and Civil Disobedience*, pp. 282, 345–7.

Conclusion: The Sepoy and the Raj

1. Orwell, *Burmese Days*, pp. 68–9.
2. Eden Commission, Report, 15 Nov. 1879.

3. Harcourt Butler to Kitchener, 18 Feb. 1916, Kitchener Papers, PRO 30/57/70.
4. Roberts to Cambridge, 13 July 1882, Roberts Papers, 7101/23/97.
5. Roberts to Seely, 2 April 1884, Roberts Papers, 7101/23/97.
6. Attlee to Bevin, 2 Jan. 1947, *Transfer of Power*, IX, Doc. 243.
7. Narain, 'A Non-Cooperative Army'.
8. Singh, 'Decolonization in India', p. 196.
9. Sarkar, *Modern India*, pp. 423–5.

Bibliography

A   PRIMARY SOURCES, UNPUBLISHED

(i) Official Documents

(a) India Office Library and Records
Military Department Papers

L/MIL/5 Compilations and Miscellaneous. Includes useful reports on the state of Indian Army morale in the Great War.

L/MIL/7 Military Collections. A huge class of over 19 000 files, made up of material withdrawn from the correspondence classes and gathered in collections, each on a single topic. One of the main sources for the present book. I have found the following collections especially useful:
    120 Reorganization, 1861–1936 (Pieces 5441–5509)
    120 Army in India Committee, 1919–39 (Pieces 5501–5544)
    156 Reorganization, 1883–1938 (Pieces 7015–7235)
    159 Insubordination in Native Regiments (Pieces 7266–7284)
    405 Confidential Reports on Regiments (Pieces 17007–17037)
    430 Indianization (Pieces 19006–19158)

L/MIL/9 Entry into the Service. Includes confidential reports on Indians at Sandhurst, 1922–28.

L/MIL/17 Military Department Library. A large and haphazardly organized collection of official publications, including the very useful series of *Handbooks on the Indian Army*.

Political and Judicial Department Papers

L/P&J/7 Public and Judicial Department. Includes reports on communal disturbances in a number of Indian towns between the two world wars.

(b) Public Record Office, Kew, London
Cabinet Office Papers

CAB 2 Committee of Imperial Defence: Minutes of Meetings, 1902–1939 (microfilm, 9 pieces). Useful for tracing the broad outlines of policy debate in the twentieth century.

CAB 6 CID Memoranda: Defence of India or D-Papers, 1901–1939 (microfilm, six pieces). These contain material on the major policy decisions concerning the defence of India in the twentieth century. They have been especially useful for Chapter 6.

CAB 16 Cabinet Subcommittees. This class contains reports, proceding and memoranda of various committees dealing with Indian defence matters after 1919.

CAB 23 Cabinet Minutes, Known as Conclusions (microfilm and photocopies). These minutes date only from the Great War. They are normally very brief, but helpful for dating key decisions.

CAB 24 Cabinet Memoranda (Microfilm). Contains a vast assortment of material on the Indian military policy since the Great War. I have drawn on this class mainly for events on the Frontier in 1919–20.

CAB 27 Cabinet Committees.

Foreign Office Papers

FO 2 General Correspondence, Africa. Some material on the use of Indian troops in East Africa in the 1890s.

War Office Papers

WO 33 General Correspondence. Includes quarterly reviews of military events in India from 1923.

WO 106 Director of Military Operations and Intelligence. Includes a few files on selected internal security matters.

(ii) Private Papers

India Office Library and Records
Brown Papers (L/MIL/5/842–857). The papers of Stuart Kelson Brown, 1920–1931. These contain a small amount of material on Indianization.

Liddell Hart Centre for Military Archives, King's College, London
Liddell Hart Papers. The papers of Captain Sir Basil Liddell Hart. A large collection of over 1000 boxes, although with little Indian material. I have consulted clippings from his period as military correspondent for the *Daily Telegraph* and *The Times* in the late 1920s and 1930s.

National Army Museum
Rawlinson Papers (7212–6 and 5201–33). The papers of Field Marshal Sir Henry Rawlinson. Mainly personal letters written during his service in India with the 60 Rifles, 1884–88; papers concerning his visit to India, 1902–3; and diaries and letters written while C-in-C India, 1920–25.

Roberts Papers (7101–23). The papers of Field-Marshal Lord Roberts of Kandahar. A large and very informative collection, including microfilms and published collections of letters written by Roberts while C-in-C Afghanistan, 1878–80, C-in-C Madras, 1880–85, and C-in-C India, 1885–95.

Public Records Office
Cardwell Papers (PRO 30/48). Correspondence with the Viceroy, Lord Northbrook, 1872–73.

Cromer Papers (FO 633/1). The papers of Evelyn Baring, Lord Cromer. Correspondence as Chief Secretary to Lord Northbrook, Viceroy of India, 1872–73.

Kitchener Papers (PRO 30/57 and WO 159). The papers of Field Marshal Lord Kitchener of Khartoum. A substantial collection, including a very useful run of correspondence with Lord Roberts, covering most Indian Army matters in the early twentieth century, besides other material on the Indian Army in the Great War.

B PRIMARY SOURCES, PUBLISHED

(i) Parliamentary Command Papers

Cmd. 2516 (1859 Sess. 1). Report of the Commission under Lord Peel on the organization of the Indian Army.

Cmd. 2516 (1859 Sess. 1). Report of Maj.-General Hancock on the Organization of the Indian Army.

Cmd. 1698 (1877). Correspondence on the Indian Army.

Cmd. 9109 (1918). Report on Indian Constitutional Reforms (The Montagu–Chelmsford Report).

Cmd. 943 (1920). Report of the Committee on the Organization of the Army in India (the Esher Committee).

(ii) Other Contemporary Publications

Barstow, A. E., *Handbooks for the Indian Army: Sikhs* (Calcutta: Government of India, 1928).

Betham, R. M., *Handbooks for the Indian Army: Marathas and Dekhani Musalmans* (Calcutta: Government of India, 1908).

Bingley, A. M., *Caste Handbooks for the Indian Army: Brahmans* (Calcutta: Government of India, 1918).

Bourne, W. F. G., *Handbooks for the Indian Army: Hindustani Musalmans and Musalmans of the Eastern Punjab* (Calcutta: Government of India, 1914).

Census of India, 1891 (London: Eyre and Spottiswoode, 1892).

Christie, R. C., *Handbooks for the Indian Army: Jats, Gujars and Ahirs* (Delhi: Government of India, 1937).

Cole, B. L., *Handbooks for the Indian Army: Rajputana Classes* (Simla: Government of India, 1924).

Cunningham, W. B., *Handbooks for the Indian Army: Dogras* (Calcutta: Government of India, 1932).

Evatt, J., *Handbooks for the Indian Army: Garhwalis* (Calcutta: Government of India, 1924).

General Staff, India, *A Strategical Study of the Conditions in India and Burma with Special Reference to Internal Defence* (Simla: Government of India, 1911).

—— *Internal Security Instructions, India, 1937* (New Delhi: Government of India, 1937).

Gwynn, C., *Imperial Policing* (Macmillan, 1934).

Holland-Pryor, P., *Handbooks on the Indian Army: Mappillas or Moplahs* (Calcutta: Government of India, 1904).
Indian Army List (Government of India, 1891–1939).
Indian Sandhurst Committee, Report (London: HMSO, 1927).
Indianisation of the Army and Formation of the Indian Air Force (New Delhi: Government of India, 1938).
Latham, A., *Handbooks for the Indian Army: Kumaonis* (Delhi: Government of India, 1933).
Leigh, M. S., *The Punjab and the War* (Lahore: Government of India, 1922).
MacMunn, G., *The Martial Races of India* (London: Sampson Low, 1933).
Marx, K., and Engels, F., *The First Indian War of Independence, 1857–59* (Moscow: Progress Publishers, 1959).
Military Requirements Committee, 1921, Report (Simla: Government of India, 1921)
Morris, C. J., *Handbooks for the Indian Army: Gurkhas* (Delhi: Government of India, 1933).
Mouat, G. E. D., *Handbooks for the Indian Army: Madras Classes* (New Delhi: Government of India, 1938).
Mutiny of 5th Light Infantry at Singapore, 1915 (Simla: Government of India, 1915).
Non-Regular Military Forces in India: Report of the Auxiliary and Territorial Forces Committee (Calcutta: Government of India, 1925).
Orwell, G., *Burmese Days* (New York: Harper, 1934).
Prince of Wales' Royal Indian Military College, Dehra Dun (Calcutta: Government of India, n.d.)
Prince of Wales' Royal Indian Military College, Magazine.
Ridgeway, R. T., *Handbooks for the Indian Army: Pathans* (Calcutta: Government of India, 1910).
Wikeley, J. M., *Handbooks for the Indian Army: Punjabi Musalmans* (Calcutta: Government of India, 1915).
Yule, H., and A. C. Burnell, *Hobson-Jobson: A Glossay of Colloquial Anglo-Indian Words and Phrases, and of Kindred Terms, Etymological, Historical, Geographical and Discursive* (London: John Murray, 1903; first edn. 1886).

(iii) Published Diaries, Letters and Memoirs

Birdwood, Lord, *Khaki and Gown* (London: Ward Lock, 1941).
Churchill, W. S., *The Story of the Malakand Field Force: An Episode of Frontier War* (London: Longmans, 1898).
—— *My Early Life: A Roving Commission* (London: Thornton Butterworth, 1930).
Communist Party, *British Soldier in India: The Letters of Clive Branson* (London, 1944).
Jeffery, K. (ed.), *The Wilson Letters: The Military Correspondence of Field Marshal Sir Henry Wilson, 1918–1922* (Army Records Society, 1985).
Masters, J., *Bugles and a Tiger: A Personal Adventure* (London: Michael Joseph, 1957).
O'Dwyer, M., *India as I Knew it, 1885–1925* (London: Constable, 1925).
Palit, D. K., 'Indianisation: A Personal Experience', *Indo-British Review*, 16 (1989).

Roberts, F., *Correspondence with England while Commander-in-Chief in Madras, 1881–85* (Simla: Government of India, 1890).

—— *Correspondence with England while Commander-in-Chief in India* (Calcutta: Government of India, 1890).

—— *Correspondence with Indian and England while Commanding Troops in Afghanistan, 1878–80* (Simla: Government of India, 1891).

Robson, B. (ed.), *Roberts in India: The Military Papers of Field Marshal Lord Roberts, 1876–1893* (Army Records Society, 1993).

Steedman, C. (ed.), *The Radical Soldiers' Tale: John Pearman, 1819–1908* (London: Routledge, 1988).

Yeats-Brown, F., *Bengal Lancer* (London: Anthony Mott, 1984; orig. edn. 1930).

C   SECONDARY SOURCES

(i) Articles and Chapters

Ahmed, A. S., 'The Colonial Encounter on the North-West Frontier', *Asian Affairs*, 9 (1978).

Ali, I., 'Malign Growth? Agricultural Colonization and the Roots of Backwardness in the Punjab', *Past and Present*, 114 (1987).

Amin, S., 'Gandhi as Mahatma: Gorakhpur District, Eastern UP, 1921–2', in Guha (ed.), *Subaltern Studies III*.

Arnold, D., 'The Armed Police and Colonial Rule in South India, 1914–47', *Modern Asian Studies*, 9 (1977).

—— 'Looting, Grain Riots and Government Policy in South India, 1918', *Past and Present*, 84 (1979).

—— 'Dacoity and Rural Crime in Madras, 1860–1940', *Journal of Peasant Studies*, 6 (1979).

—— 'Islam, the Mappilas and Peasant Revolt in Malabar', *Journal of Peasant Studies*, 9 (1982).

—— 'Rebellious Hillmen: The Gudem Rampa Risings, 1839–1922', in Guha (ed.), *Subaltern Studies I*.

—— 'Famine in Peasant Consciousness and Peasant Action: Madras, 1876–8', in Guha (ed.), *Subaltern Studies III*.

—— 'Bureaucratic Recruitment and Subordination in Colonial India: The Madras Constabulary, 1859–1947', in Guha (ed.), *Subaltern Studies IV*.

—— 'Cholera and Colonialism in British India', *Past and Present*, 113 (1986).

—— 'Police Power and the Demise of British Rule in India, 1930–1947', in Anderson and Killingray, *Policing and Decolonisation*.

Belich, J., 'The Victorian Interpretation of Racial Conflict and the New Zealand Wars: An Approach to the Problem of One-Sided Evidence', *Journal of Imperial and Commonwealth History*, 15 (1987).

Burroughs, P., 'Imperial Defence and the Victorian Army', *Journal of Imperial and Commonwealth History*, 15 (1986).

Caplan, L., '"Bravest of the Brave": Representations of "The Gurkha" in British Military Writings', *Modern Asian Studies*, 25 (1991).

Chibber, M. L., 'Regimental System and Esprit-de-Corps in the Indian Army', *Indo-British Review,* 16 (1989).

Cohn, B. S., 'Representing Authority in Victorian India', in Hobsbawm and Ranger (eds), *The Invention of Tradition.*

—— 'The Command of Language and the Language of Command', in Guha (ed.), *Subaltern Studies IV.*

Crawford, E. R., 'The Sikh Wars', in Bond (ed.), *Victorian Military Campaigns.*

Deshpande, A., 'Sailors and the Crowd: Popular Protest in Karachi, 1946', *Indian Economic and Social History Review,* 26 (1989).

Dewey, C., 'Some Consequences of Military Expenditure in British India: The Case of the Upper Sind Sagar Doab, 1849–1947', in Dewey (ed.), *Arrested Development in India.*

Dhanagare, D. N., 'Agrarian Conflict, Religion and Politics: The Moplah Rebellions in Malabar in the Nineteenth and Early Twentieth Centuries', *Past and Present,* 74 (1977).

Figes, O., 'The Red Army and Mass Mobilization During the Russian Civil War, 1918–1920', *Past and Present,* 129 (1990).

Furedi, F., 'Britain's Colonial Wars: Playing the Ethnic Card', *Journal of Commonwealth and Comparative Politics,* 28 (1990).

Freitag, S. B., 'Crime in the Social Order of Colonial North India', *Modern Asian Studies,* 25 (1991).

Frykenberg, R., 'India's Past Seen "From Below"', *Journal of Imperial and Commonwealth History,* 17 (1989).

Goldthorpe, J., 'The Uses of History in Sociology: Reflections on Some Recent Tendencies', *British Journal of Sociology,* 42 (1991).

Gopalankutty, K., 'Mobilisation Against the State and not against the Landlords: the Civil Disobedience Movement in Malabar', *Indian Economic and Social History Review* 26 (1989).

Greenhut, J., 'The Imperial Reserve: The Indian Corps on the Western Front, 1914–15', *Journal of Imperial and Commonwealth History,* 12 (1983).

Grove, R. H., 'Colonial Conservation, Ecological Hegemony and Popular Resistance: Towards a Global Synthesis', in MacKenzie (ed.), *Imperialism and the Natural World.*

Guha, Ramachandra., 'Forestry and Social Protest in British Kumaun, c. 1893–1921', in Guha (ed.), *Subaltern Studies IV.*

—— and Gadgil, M., 'State Forestry and Social Conflict in British India', *Past and Present,* 123 (1989).

Hardiman, D., 'From Custom to Crime: The Politics of Drinking in Colonial South Gujerat' in Guha (ed.), *Subaltern Studies IV.*

Hashmi, T.-I., 'The Communalisation of Class Struggle: East Bengal Peasantry, 1923–29', *Indian Economic and Social History Review,* 25 (1988).

Haycock, R., 'British Arms in India' in Jordan (ed.), *British Military History.*

Hobsbawn, E., 'Introduction: Inventing Traditions', in Hobsbawm and Ranger (eds), *The Invention of Tradition.*

Inden, R., 'Orientalist Constructions of India', *Modern Asian Studies,* 20 (1986).

Jeffery, K., 'Sir Henry Wilson and the Defence of the British Empire, 1918–1922', *Journal of Imperial and Commonwealth History,* 5 (1977).

—— 'The Eastern Arc of Empire: A Strategic View, 1850–1950', *Journal of Strategic Studies,* 5 (1982).

Kennedy, P., 'The Costs and Benefits of British Imperialism, 1846–1914', *Past and Present*, 125 (1989).

Killingray, D., 'The Mutiny of the West African Regiment in the Gold Coast, 1901', *International Journal of African Historical Studies*, 16 (1983).

Kumar, D., 'The Evolution of Colonial Science in India: Natural History and the East India Company', in MacKenzie (ed.), *Imperialism and the Natural World*.

Kirk-Greene, A. H., '"Damnosa Hereditas": Ethnic Ranking and the Martial Races Imperative in Africa', *Ethnic and Racial Studies*, 3 (1980).

Krishnamurty, S., 'Real Wages of Agricultural Labourers in the Bombay Deccan, 1874–1922', *Indian Economic and Social History Review*, 24 (1987).

Leach, E., 'Tribal Ethnography: past, present, future', in Tonkin *et al.* (eds), *History and Ethnicity*.

MacKenzie, J. M., 'Introduction', in MacKenzie (ed.), *Imperialism and the Natural World*.

Mukherjee, R., 'The Kanpur Massacres in India in the Revolt of 1857', *Past and Present*, 128 (1990).

Nuckolls, C. W., 'The Durbar Incident', *Modern Asian Studies*, 24 (1990).

Omissi, D. E., 'Britain, the Assyrians and the Iraq Levies, 1919–32', *Journal of Imperial and Commonwealth History*, 17 (1989).

—— 'Technology and Repression: Air Control in Palestine, 1922–1936', *Journal of Strategic Studies*, 13 (1990).

—— 'Co-option and Coercion in India, 1857–1947: The Indian Army', *Contemporary Record*, 6 (1992).

—— 'The Mediterranean and Middle East in British Global Strategy, 1935–39', in Cohen and Kolinsky (eds), *Britain and the Middle East in the 1930s*.

—— 'The Hendon Pageant, 1920–37', in MacKenzie (ed), *Popular Imperialism and the Military*.

——'The Balance of Firepower in Colonial India' (forthcoming).

Owen, N., 'The Attlee Governments and the End of Empire', *Contemporary Record*, 3 (1990).

—— '"More than a Transfer of Power": Independence Day Ceremonies in India, 15 August 1947', *Contemporary Record*, 6 (1992).

Palit, D. K., 'Indianisation of the Army's Officer Cadre, 1920–1947', *Indo-British Review*, 16 (1989).

Pant, R., 'The Cognitive Status of Caste in Colonial Ethnography: a Review of some Literature on the North-Western Provinces and Oudh', *Indian Economic and Social History Review*, 24 (1987).

Peers, D. M., 'Between Mars and Mammon: The East India Company and Efforts to Reform its Army, 1796–1832', *Historical Journal*, 33 (1990).

—— 'The Habitual Nobility of Being: British Officers and the Social Construction of the Bengal Army in the Early Nineteenth Century', *Modern Asian Studies*, 25 (1991).

Radhakrishna, M., 'The Criminal Tribes Act in Madras Presidency: Implications for Itinerant Trading Communities', *Indian Economic and Social History Review*, 26 (1989).

Rosselli, J., 'The Self-Image of Effeteness: Physical Education and Nationalism in Nineteenth-Century Bengal', *Past and Present*, 86 (1980).

Sarkar, S., 'The Conditions and Nature of Subaltern Militancy: Bengal from Swadeshi to Non-Co-operation, c. 1905–22', in Ranajit Guha (ed), *Subaltern Studies III*.

Sinha, S. K., 'The Indian Army: Before and After Independence', *Indo-British Review*, 16 (1989).

Stokes, E., 'Traditional Resistance Movements and Afro-Asian Nationalism: The Context of the 1857 Mutiny Rebellion in India', *Past and Present*, 48 (1970).

Storch, R. D., '"The Plague of the Blue Locusts": Police Reform and Popular Resistance in Northern England, 1840–57', *International Review of Social History*, 20 (1975).

—— 'The Policeman as Domestic Missionary: Urban Discipline and Popular Culture in Northern England, 1850–1880', *Journal of Social History*, 9 (1976).

Talbot, I. A., 'Deserted Collaborators: The Political Background to the Rise and Fall of the Punjab Unionist Party, 1923–1947', *Journal of Imperial and Commonwealth History*, 11 (1982).

Trevithick, A., 'Some Structural and Segmented Aspects of the British Imperial Assembleges at Delhi, 1877–1911', *Modern Asian Studies*, 24 (1990).

Trevor-Roper, H., 'The Invention of Tradition: The Highland Tradition of Scotland', in Hobsbawn and Ranger (eds) *The Invention of Tradition*.

Wood, C., 'The First Moplah Rebellion Against British Rule in Malabar', *Modern Asian Studies*, 10 (1976).

Zelliot, E., 'Learning the Use of Political Means: The Mahars of Maharashtra', in Kothari, *Caste in Indian Politics*.

(ii) Books

Al Rasheed, M., *Politics in an Arabian Oasis: The Rashidi Tribal Dynasty* (London: Tauris, 1991).

Anderson, D. M. and D. Killingray (eds), *Policing and Decolonisation: Nationalism, Politics and the Police, 1917–65* (Manchester: Manchester University Press, 1992).

—— *Policing the Empire: Government, Authority and Control, 1830–1940* (Manchester: Manchester University Press, 1991).

Arnold, D., *Police Power and Colonial Rule: Madras 1858–1947* (Delhi: Oxford University Press, 1986).

Ballhatchet, K., *Race, Sex and Class under the Raj* (London: Weidenfeld and Nicholson 1980).

Bayly, C. A., *Indian Society and the Making of the British Empire: The New Cambridge History of India, II, 1* (Cambridge: Cambridge University Press, 1988).

—— *Imperial Meridian: The British Empire and the World, 1780–1830* (London: Longman, 1989).

Belich, J., *The New Zealand Wars and the Victorian Interpretation of Racial Conflict* (Harmondsworth: Penguin, 1988; orig. edn. 1986).

Bond, B. J., (ed.) *Victorian Military Campaigns* (London, 1967).

—— *British Military Policy Between the Two World Wars* (Oxford: Clarendon Press, 1980).

Bougle, C., *Essays on the Caste System* (Cambridge: Cambridge University Press, 1971).

Braudel, F., *The Mediterranean and the Mediterranean World in the Age of Philip II* (London: Collins, 1972).

Braun, P., *Die Verteidigung Indiens, 1800–1907: Das Problem Der Vorwärtsstrategie* (Köln: Boehmer Verlag, 1966).

Brown, J. M., *Gandhi and Civil Disobedience: The Mahatma in Indian Politics, 1928–34* (Cambridge: Cambridge University Press, 1977).

——*Modern India: The Origins of an Asian Democracy* (Oxford: Oxford University Press, 1985).

Busch, B. C., *Britain, India and the Arabs, 1914–1921* (Berkeley: University of California Press, 1971).

Cobb, R., *Death in Paris, 1795–1801* (Oxford: Oxford University Press, 1978).

Cohen, M. J. and Kolinsky, M., (eds), *Britain and the Middle East in the 1930s: Security Problems, 1935–39* (London: Macmillan, 1992).

Cohen, S. P., *The Indian Army: Its Contribution to the Development of the Indian Nation* (Berkeley: University of California Press, 1971).

Deak, I., *Beyond Nationalism: A Social and Political History of the Hapsburg Officer Corps, 1848–1918* (New York and Oxford: Oxford University Press, 1990)

Dewey, C., (ed.), *Arrested Development in India: The Historical Dimension* (Riverdale, Md: Riverdale, 1988).

Dixon, C., and Heffernan, M., (eds), *Colonialism and Development in the Contemporary World* (London: Mansell, 1991).

Duffy, C., *The Army of Frederick the Great* (London: PBS, 1974).

Echenberg, M., *Colonial Conscripts: The Tirailleurs Senegalais in French West Africa, 1857–1960* (London: James Currey, 1991).

Enloe, C., *Ethnic Soldiers: State Security in Divided Societies* (Harmondsworth: Penguin, 1980).

Farrington, A., *Guide to the Records of the India Office Military Department* (London: India Office Library, 1982).

Farwell, B., *The Armies of the Raj: from the Great Indian Mutiny to Independence, 1858–1947* (London: Viking, 1989).

Featherstone, D., *At Them with the Bayonet: The First Sikh War* (London, 1968).

Femia, J. V., *Gramsci's Political Thought: Hegemony, Consciousness and the Revolutionary Process* (Oxford: Clarendon Press, 1987).

Finer, S. E., *The Man on Horseback* (London: Pall Mall, 1962).

Forrest, A., *Conscripts and Deserters: The Army and French Society During the Revolution and Empire* (Oxford and New York: Oxford University Press, 1989)

Foucault, M., *Discipline and Punish: The Birth of the Prison* (London: Penguin, 1979).

Fuller, J. G., *Troop Morale and Popular Culture in the British and Dominion Armies 1914–1918* (Oxford: Clarendon Press, 1991).

Fussell, P., *The Great War and Modern Memory* (New York: Oxford University Press, 1975).

Ginzburg, C., *The Cheese and the Worms: the Cosmos of a Sixteenth-Century Miller* (London: Routledge and Kegan Paul, 1980; orig. ed., 1976).

Gooch, J., *Army, State and Society in Italy, 1870–1915* (London: Macmillan, 1989).

Gowers, E., *The Complete Plain Words* (HMSO, 1986).

Gray, W. S. and B. E. Leary, *What Makes a Book Readable* (Chicago, 1935).

Grewal, J. S., *The Sikhs of the Punjab: The New Cambridge History of India, II, 3* (Cambridge: Cambridge University Press, 1990).

Guha, Ramachandra, *The Unquiet Woods: Ecological Change and Peasant Resistance in the Himalaya* (Delhi: Oxford University Press, 1989).

Guha, Ranajit., *Elementary Aspects of Peasant Insurgency in Colonial India* (Delhi: Oxford University Press, 1983).

—— (ed.), *Subaltern Studies: Writings on South Asian History and Society I–VI* (Delhi: Oxford University Press, 1982–9).

—— and Spivak, G. C. (eds), *Selected Subaltern Studies* (Oxford: Oxford University Press, 1988).

Gunning, R., *The Technique of Clear Writing* (New York: McGraw-Hill, 1952).

Hardiman, D., *The Coming of the Devi: Adivasi Assertion in Western India* (Delhi: Oxford University Press, 1987).

Headrick, D. R., *The Tools of Empire: Technology and European Imperialism in the Nineteenth Century* (New York: Oxford University Press, 1981)

—— *The Tentacles of Progress: Technology Transfer in the Age of Imperialism, 1850–1940* (NY: Oxford University Press, 1988).

Heathcote, T. A., *The Indian Army: The Garrison of British Imperial India, 1822–1922* (London: David and Charles 1974).

Hobsbawn, E. and Ranger, T. (eds), *The Invention of Tradition* (Cambridge: Cambridge University Press, 1983)

Howard, M., *The Franco-Prussian War* (London: Methuen, 1981; orig. edn. 1961).

—— *The Lessons of History* (Oxford: Clarendon Press, 1991).

Huntington, S. P., *The Soldier and the State* (Cambridge: Harvard University Press, 1960).

James, L., *Mutiny: In the British and Commonwealth Forces, 1797–1956* (London: Buchan and Enright, 1987).

Jeffery, K., *The British Army and the Crisis of Empire, 1918–22* (Manchester: Manchester University Press).

Jordan, G. (ed.), *British Military History: A Supplement to Robin Higham's Guide to the Sources* (New York and London, Garland, 1988).

Kapur, R., *Sikh Separatism: The Politics of Faith* (Delhi, 1986).

Kiernan, V., *The Lords of Human Kind: Black Man, Yellow Man and White Man in an Age of Empire* (London: Cresset, 1988; orig. ed., 1969).

—— *European Empires from Conquest to Collapse, 1815–1960* (London: Fontana, 1982).

Kolf, D. H. A., *Naukar, Rajput and Sepoy: The Ethnohistory of the Military Labour Market in Hindustan, 1450–1850* (Cambridge: Cambridge University Press, 1990).

Kothari, R. (ed.), *Caste in Indian Politics* (Delhi, 1971).

Kumar, D., (ed.), *The Cambridge Economic History of India, 2, c. 1757–c.1970* (Cambridge: Cambridge University Press, 1983).

Levi-Strauss, C., *Structural Anthropology I* (Harmondsworth, Penguin, 1968).

Lynn, J. A., *The Bayonets of the Republic: Motivation and Tactics in the Army of Revolutionary France, 1791–1794* (Urbana: Illinois University Press, 1984).

MacKenzie, J. M., *The Empire of Nature: Hunting, Conservation and British Imperialism* (Manchester: Manchester University Press, 1988).

—— (ed.), *Imperialism and the Natural World* (Manchester: Manchester University Press, 1990).

—— (ed.), *Popular Imperialism and the Military, 1850–1950* (Manchester: Manchester University Press, 1992).

Mangan, J. A. (ed.), *Making Imperial Mentalities: Socialisation and British Imperialism* (Manchester: Manchester University Press, 1990).

Mason, P., *A Matter of Honour: An Account of the Indian Army, its Officers and Men* (Jonathan Cape, 1974).

Metcalf, T. R., *Land, Landlords and the British Raj: Northern India in the Nineteenth Century* (California, 1974).

Moir, M., *A Guide to the India Office Records* (London: British Library, 1988).

Mukherjee, R., *Awadh in Revolt, 1857–1858: A Study of Popular Resistance* (Delhi: Oxford University Press, 1984).

Offer, A., *The First World War: An Agrarian Interpretation* (Oxford: Clarendon Press, 1989).

Ogot, B. A., *War and Society in Africa* (London: Frank Cass, 1972).

Omissi, D. E., *Air Power and Colonial Control: The Royal Air Force, 1919–1939* (Manchester: Manchester University Press, 1990).

Palmer, J. A. B., *The Mutiny Outbreak at Meerut in 1857* (Cambridge: Cambridge University Press, 1966).

Panikkar, K. M., *Against Lord and State: Religion and Peasant Uprisings in Malabar, 1836–1921* (Delhi: Oxford University Press, 1989).

Paret, P., *Yorck and the Era of Prussian Reform, 1807–1815* (Princeton: Princeton University Press, 1966).

Parker, G., *The Army of Flanders and the Spanish Road, 1567–1659: The Logistics of Spanish Victory and Defeat in the Low Countries' Wars* (Cambridge: Cambridge University Press, 1972).

Porter, B., *The Lion's Share: A Short History of British Imperialism, 1850–1983* (London and New York: Longman, 1984).

Prebble, J., *Mutiny: Highland Regiments in Revolt, 1743–1804* (London: Penguin, 1977; orig. edn, 1975).

Roger, N. A. M., *The Wooden World: An Anatomy of the Georgian Navy* (London: Fontana, 1988; orig. edn, 1986).

Said, E., *Orientalism: Western Conceptions of the Orient* (London: Routledge and Kegan Paul, 1978).

Sarkar, S., *Modern India, 1885–1947* (London: Macmillan, 1983 and 1989).

Sen, S. N., *Eighteen Fifty Seven* (Delhi, 1958).

Singh, A. I., *The Origins of the Partition of India, 1936–1947* (Delhi: Oxford University Press, 1987).

Spiers, E. M., *Radical General: Sir George de Lacy Evans, 1787–1870* (Manchester: Manchester University Press, 1983).

Srinivas, M. N., *Religion and Society Among the Coorgs of South India* (Oxford: Clarendon Press, 1952).

—— *The Dominant Caste and Other Essays* (Oxford: Oxford University Press, 1987).

Stepan, N., *The Idea of Race in Science: Great Britain, 1800–1960* (London: Macmillan, 1982).

Stocking, G., *Victorian Anthropology* (London: Collier Macmillan, 1987).
Stokes, E., *The Peasant and the Raj: Studies in Agrarian Society and Peasant Rebellion in Colonial India* (Cambridge: Cambridge University Press, 1978).
—— *The Peasant Armed: The Indian Revolt of 1857* (Oxford: Clarendon Press, 1986).
Talbot, I., *Punjab and the Raj, 1849–1947* (Delhi: Manohar, 1988)
Tarbush, M. A., *The Role of the Military in Politics: A Case Study of Iraq to 1941* (London: KPI, 1982).
Tonkin, E., M. McDonald and M. Chapman (eds), *History and Ethnicity* (Routledge, 1989).
Townshend, C., *Britain's Civil Wars: Counterinsurgency in the Twentieth Century* (Faber, 1986).
Vaughan, M., *Curing their Ills: Colonial Power and African Illness* (Cambridge: Polity, 1991).

(iii) Unpublished Theses and Papers

Alavi, S., 'North Indian Military Culture in Transition, c. 1770–1830'. University of Cambridge DPhil Thesis (1991).
Arnold, D., ' "Criminal Tribes" and "Martial Races": Crime and Social Control in Colonial India'. Paper presented to Institute of Commonwealth Studies, University of London (1984).
Brief, D., 'The Punjab and Recruitment to the Indian Army, 1846–1918'. University of Oxford M.Litt Thesis (1979).
Jacobsen, M. H., 'The Modernization of the Indian Army, 1925–1939'. University of California PhD Thesis (1979).
Layte, R., 'Towards a Grounded Theory of Rational Choice'. University of Oxford MPhil Paper (1992).
Moreman, T., 'The Indian Army and Hill Warfare'. Paper presented to the Military History Seminar, Institute of Historical Research, University of London (1991).
Omissi, D. E., 'Indian Mutinies, 1886–1939'. Paper presented to Commonwealth History Seminar, University of Oxford (1991).
—— 'Peasants in Uniform: Sepoy Motivation in the Indian Army, 1859–1939'. Paper presented to Imperial History Seminar, Institute of Historical Research, University of London (1991) and to South Asian History Seminar, University of Oxford (1992).
—— 'Honour, Identity and Loyalty in the Indian Army, 1880–1920'. Paper presented to the South Asian History Seminar, School of Oriental and African Studies, University of London (1992) and to Military History Seminar, Institute of Historical Research, University of London (1992).
—— 'Military Power and Colonial Rule: India, 1860–1940'. Paper presented to the South Asian Studies Seminar, University of Hull (1993).
Owen, N., 'Labour and the Quit India Movement'. Paper presented to Commonwealth History Seminar, University of Oxford (1989).
Peers, D. M., 'Contours of the Garrison State: The Army and the Historiography of Early Nineteenth Century India'. University of Calgary Research Paper (1990).

—— 'A Science Without Professors Must Inevitably Fall into Disgrace: Discipline and the Discourse of Military Law in Early Nineteenth Century India'. University of Calgary Research Paper (1991).

Rawson, J. O., 'The Role of India in Imperial Defence Beyond Indian Frontiers and Home Waters, 1919–1939'. University of Oxford D.Phil Thesis (1976).

Shibly, A. H., 'The Reorganisation of the Indian Armies, 1858–79'. University of London PhD Thesis (1969).

Index

Afghanistan, 11–12, 129–31; Russian threat to, 203–6, 234; Second Afghan War (1878–80), 12, 14, 21–2, 29, 91, 206; Third Afghan War (1919), 129–31; *see also* Frontier militias, North West Frontier Province, Pathans

Akali movement, 41, 127–9

Ambedkar, B. R. (1893–1956), 37–8

Amritsar massacre, 218–19, 233

Anderson, David, xx

Anglo-Indians, 201

Arnold, David, xix, xx

Arya Samaj, 95, 137

Aryans, 32–4; *see also* Martial races theory, Social Darwinism

Auxiliary Force (India), 202

Awadh, 4–6, 9; *see also* Brahmins

Balance, policy of, 10–12; introduced, 10; abandoned by Roberts, 12, 44; *compare* Martial races theory; *see also* Divide and rule

Batta, 5, 54, 140; *see also* Incentives, Motives for enlistment, Pay, Pensions

Barracks, 63, 103, 197; *see also* Cantonments

Bengal Army, 3–7, 87–9; ethnic composition of, 6–7, 9; influence, 13; recruiting, 3, 4–6, 43; regimental organization, 87–9; *compare* Bombay Army, Madras Army

Bengal, 223–5, 226; communal violence in, 226; financial importance of, 56; labour unrest in, 225; strategic environment in, 202; Swadeshi movement in, 229; terrorism in, 217, 223–5

Bengalis, stereotypes of, 29, 40, 181, 223–4; *compare* Martial races theory

Bihar, 4, 11

Birdwood, Lord (1865–1951), 107, 135

Bombay, 225, 226; communal violence in, 227, 228

Bombay Army, 21, 22; as counterweight to Bengal Army, 10; in mutiny of 1857, 5; numbers, 11, 21; recruiting policy of, 3, 21, 22; unaffected by changes after 1857, 9; *compare* Bengal Army

Brahmins, eating habits of, 62, 94; and mutiny, 141; number of in Indian Army, 7, 20; recruitment of by Bengal Army, 4; and sanskritization, 94; *see also* Awadh, Bihar

British Army, 104, 105, 132–4, 209–12, 234, 237; and communal disturbances, 210; cost of, 193, 234; and internal security, 209–12; ratio of British to Indian troops, 8, 132–4, 209–12, 237; nationalist resentment of, 193, 239

British officers, 103–6; and communal disturbances, 168, 190; heavy drinking by, 105, 186; and Indian religion, 99–100, 139–40; and Indianization, 168, 169, 170–1, 174, 177–8, 180, 183; mess life of, 186; murder of, 84, 147–8; and mutiny, 142–3; pay of, 54; and propaganda, 128–9; quality of, 14–15, 44, 104–5; self-image of, 27, 103–4, 153, 167, 235–6; sepoy attitudes to, 105–6, 112; *compare* Commander-in-Chief, Indian officers, King-Emperor

Burma, 220, 221, 223; strategic environment, 202–3; Third Burma War (1885–9), 12, 14

Calcutta, 4, 166, 202, 231; defence of, 203; labour unrest in, 225

Canal Colonies, 35, 48, 69–70, 126; *see also* Irrigation

Cantonments, 102–3; colour bar at, 177–8; isolation of, 102–3; and local economy, 60; and politics, 102; *see also* Barracks

Casualties, sepoy attitudes to, 117–18; *see also* Depression, Desertion, Malingering, Self-inflicted wounds

Ceremonies, 61, 108, 144; *see also* Durbars

Chenab Colonies Bill (1906) 126–7

Cholera, 62–3

Civil disobedience, 71, 132, 224, 228–31, 241

Civil unrest, 208–9, 210, 214–31, 241; after the Great War, 59, 123, 129–30, 173, 208–9; attempts to deter, 214–16; and the Indian Army, 125–9, 132, 139, 173, 212; and mutiny, 139; in Peshawar, 41, 139; in Punjab, 35, 41,